VICTORIA PARADE
FITZROY SQUARE
WELLINGTON
SPRING STREET
GARDENS
EVYLYN ST.
SITE APPLIED FOR NATIONAL SCHOOL
ST PETER'S CHURCH
RESERVE FOR LEGISLATIVE ASSEMBLY
ALBERT STREET
GREY ST Wt
GIPPS ST Wt
FITZROY ST Wt
GEORGE ST Wt
GISBOURNE
LANSDOWNE STREET
GREY ST Et
GIPPS ST
FITZROY ST
GEORGE ST
"EAST"
CLARENDON STREET
NICHOLSON
PALMER ST.
PRINCES ST.
FLEET ST.
HANOVER
WILLIAM
FITZROY
BRUNSWICK
GERTRUDE
YOUNG STREET
ATHERTON ST.
NAPIER STREET
GEORGE
GORE STREET
SMITH
CHARLES
CHARLOTTE
WEBB
CONDELL STREET
DAVID STREET
LITTLE OXFORD
OXFORD
CAMBRIDGE STREET
DERBY
STANLEY ST.
NAPOLEON ST.
OTTER
CROMWELL
PERRY ST.
WELLINGTON
GLASGOW ST
NORTHUMBERLAND ST
NORTHUMBERLAND
RYDE TERRACE OR HODGSONS ROAD
ROKEBY
RUPERT
ISLINGTON
HODDLE
DIGBY
CAMPBELL
PALMER
HARWOOD
VERE
LANE
SIMPSON'S
JAMES ST
ELIZABETH
LITTLE ELIZABETH
SMITH
YORK
Govt Reserve

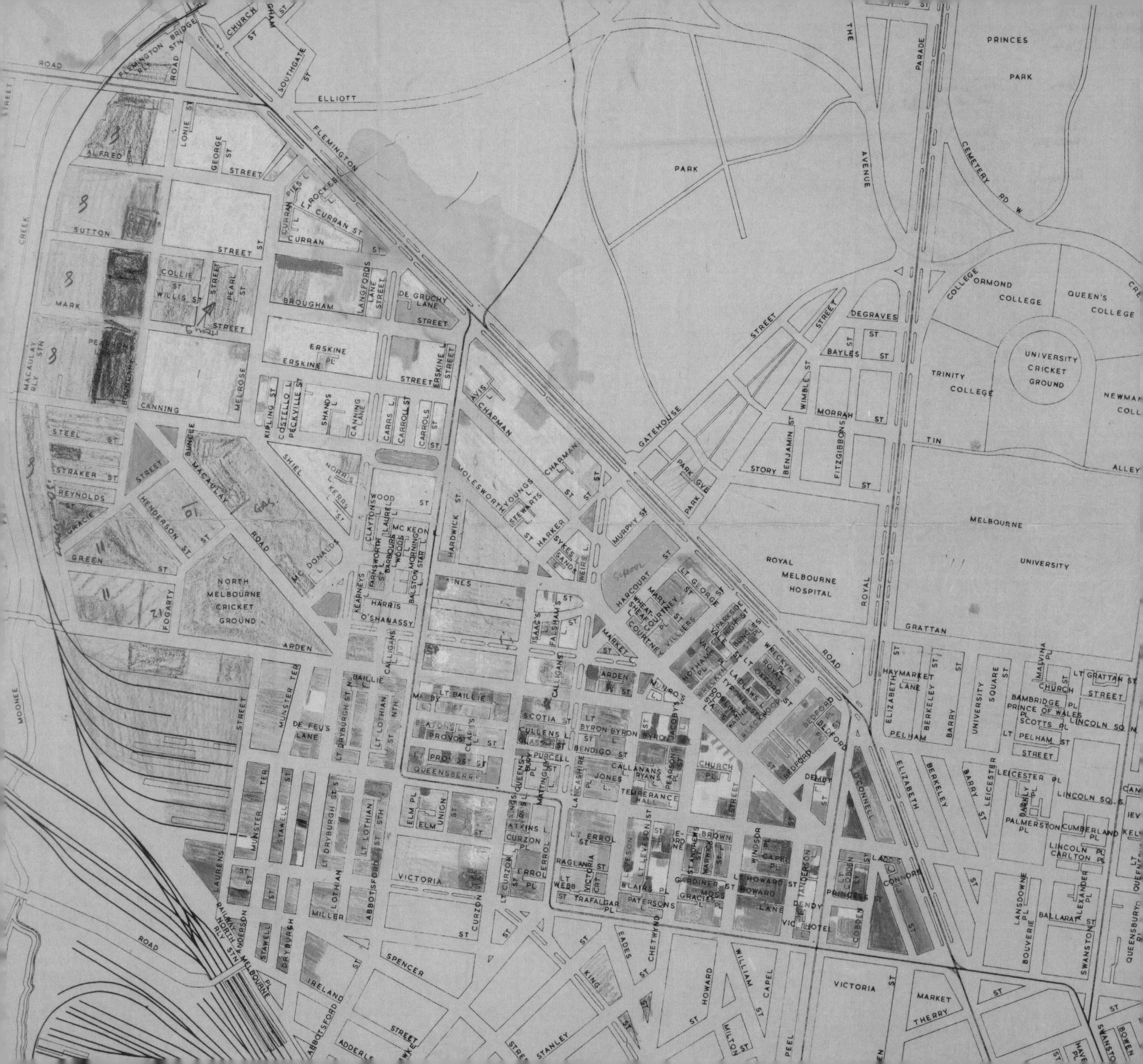

PRINCES PARK
PARK
THE AVENUE
PARADE
ELLIOTT
FLEMINGTON
FLEMINGTON BRIDGE RLY STN
SOUTHGATE ST
CHURCH ST
ALFRED
GEORGE ST
STREET
LONIE ST
SUTTON
MARK
COLLIE ST
WILLIS ST
PEARL ST
BROUGHAM
LANGFORDS LANE STREET
DE GRUCHY LANE STREET
CURRAN
CURRAN ST
ERSKINE
ERSKINE PL
STREET
CANNING
MELROSE
MACAULAY RLY STN
STEEL ST
STRAKER ST
REYNOLDS
GRACIE ST
GREEN
HENDERSON ST
MACAULAY ROAD
BUNCLE
SHIEL
NORTH MELBOURNE CRICKET GROUND
FOGARTY
MC DONALDS L
HARRIS
O'SHANASSY
ARDEN
CHAPMAN
MOLESWORTH
HARDWICK ST
GATEHOUSE STREET
CHARMAN
MURPHY ST
HARCOURT ST
DEGRAVES
BAYLES ST
MORRAH ST
WIMBLE ST
BENJAMIN ST
FITZGIBBONS
STORY
PARK ST
TIN ALLEY
COLLEGE CEMETERY RD W
ORMOND COLLEGE
QUEEN'S COLLEGE
UNIVERSITY CRICKET GROUND
TRINITY COLLEGE
MELBOURNE UNIVERSITY
ROYAL MELBOURNE HOSPITAL
ROYAL
GRATTAN
ROYAL PARADE
MOONEE CREEK
ROAD
MUNSTER TER
DE FEU'S LANE
BAILLIE
QUEENSBERRY
ELM
UNION
VICTORIA
ABBOTSFORD
CURZON
ERROL
ELIZABETH
BERKELEY
BARRY
LEICESTER
PELHAM
LINCOLN SQ. N
LINCOLN SQ. S
SWANSTON
LANSDOWNE
BOUVERIE
CONNORS
O'CONNELL
CHURCH ST
VICTORIA ST
SPENCER
STANLEY
KING
CHETWYND
EADES
HOWARD
WILLIAM ST
CAPEL
PEEL
MILTON
MARKET
THERRY
IRELAND
ADDERLEY
NORTH MELBOURNE RLY STN

OLD VINTAGE MELBOURNE

Chris Macheras is a Melbourne-born lawyer and artist. His Greek Australian upbringing instilled an appreciation for the hardships his migrant grandparents endured in pursuit of a better life. His combined love of Melbourne, history, and photography led him to establish *Old Vintage Melbourne*, using social media as the platform to reach tens of thousands of others with shared interests.

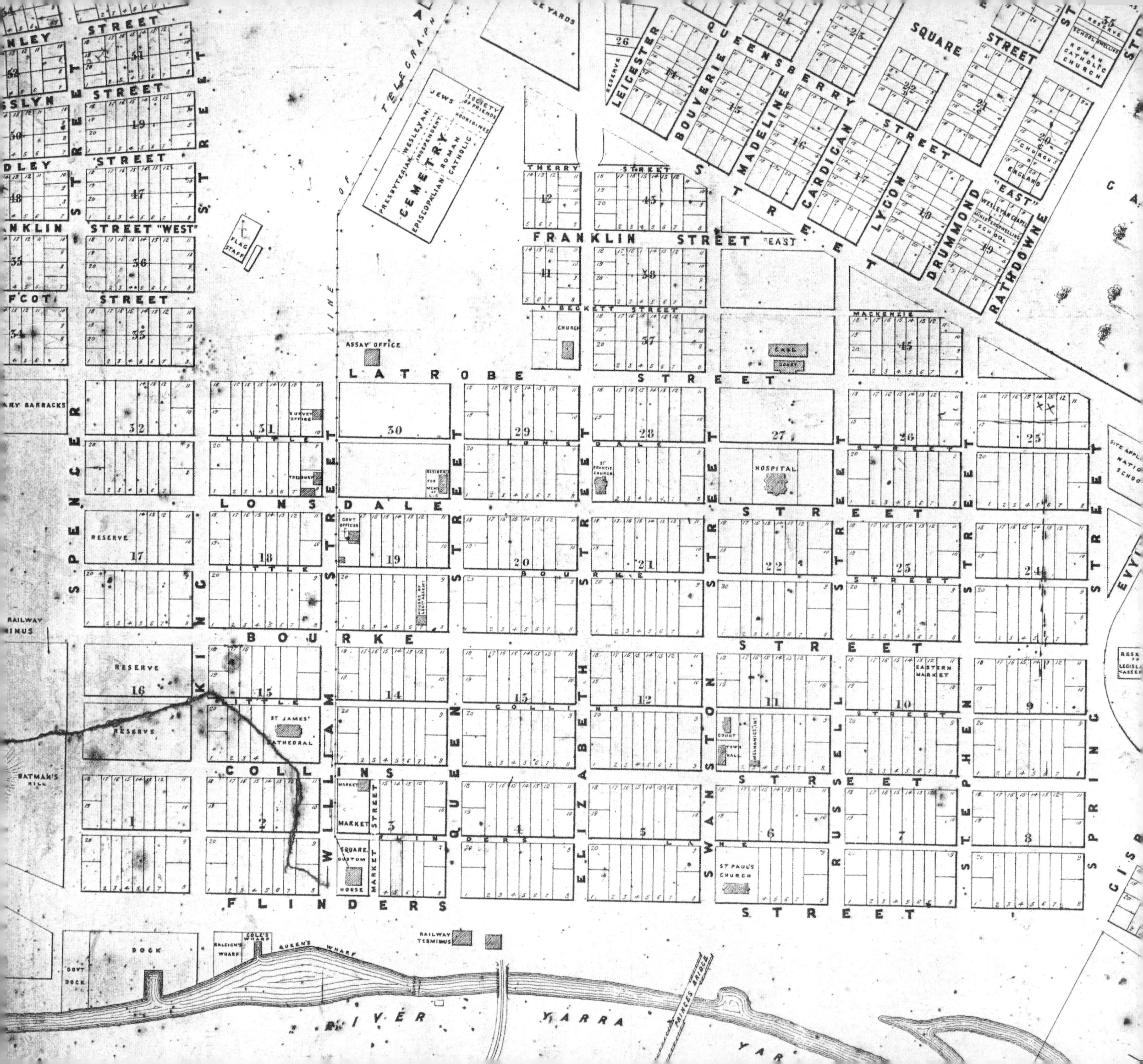

LATROBE STREET
LONSDALE STREET
BOURKE STREET
COLLINS STREET
FLINDERS STREET
FRANKLIN STREET "EAST"
FRANKLIN STREET "WEST"
SPENCER STREET
KING STREET
WILLIAM STREET
QUEEN STREET
ELIZABETH STREET
SWANSTON STREET
RUSSELL STREET
STEPHEN STREET
SPRING STREET
LITTLE LONSDALE
LITTLE BOURKE
LITTLE COLLINS
FLINDERS LANE
MARKET STREET
A'BECKETT STREET
THERRY STREET
MACKENZIE
QUEENSBERRY STREET
LEICESTER
BOUVERIE
MADELINE
CARDIGAN
LYGON
DRUMMOND
RATHDOWNE
SQUARE STREET
CEMETERY
PRESBYTERIAN
WESLEYAN
INDEPENDENT
JEWS
SOCIETY OF FRIENDS
ABORIGINES
EPISCOPALIAN
ROMAN CATHOLIC
LINE OF TELEGRAPH
FLAG STAFF
ASSAY OFFICE
SURVEY OFFICE
TREASURY
GOVT OFFICES
RESIDENCE FOR MEMBERS
ST FRANCIS CHURCH
HOSPITAL
GAOL
COURT
CHURCH
RESERVE
ST JAMES' CATHEDRAL
MARKET
MARKET SQUARE
CUSTOM HOUSE
TOWN HALL
MECHANICS' INST
ST PAUL'S CHURCH
EASTERN MARKET
WESLEYAN CHAPEL
SCHOOL
CHURCH OF ENGLAND
ROMAN CATHOLIC CHURCH
BATMAN'S HILL
RAILWAY TERMINUS
DOCK
GOVT DOCK
RALEIGH'S WHARF
COLE'S WHARF
QUEEN'S WHARF
PRINCES BRIDGE
RIVER YARRA

OLD VINTAGE
Melbourne

CHRIS MACHERAS

SCRIBE
Melbourne • London

Scribe Publications
18–20 Edward St, Brunswick, Victoria 3056, Australia
2 John St, Clerkenwell, London, WC1N 2ES, United Kingdom
3754 Pleasant Ave, Suite 100, Minneapolis, Minnesota 55409, USA

Published by Scribe 2021
Reprinted 2021

Typeset in Tiempos by the publishers

Printed and bound in China by 1010 Printing Co. Ltd

Scribe is committed to the sustainable use of natural resources and the use of paper products made responsibly from those resources.

Scribe acknowledges Australia's First Nations peoples as the traditional owners and custodians of this country. We recognise that sovereignty was never ceded, and we pay our respects to their elders, past and present.

978 1 922310 94 1 (Australian edition)
978 1 914484 63 6 (UK edition)

Catalogue records for this book are available from the National Library of Australia.

scribepublications.com.au
scribepublications.co.uk
scribepublications.com

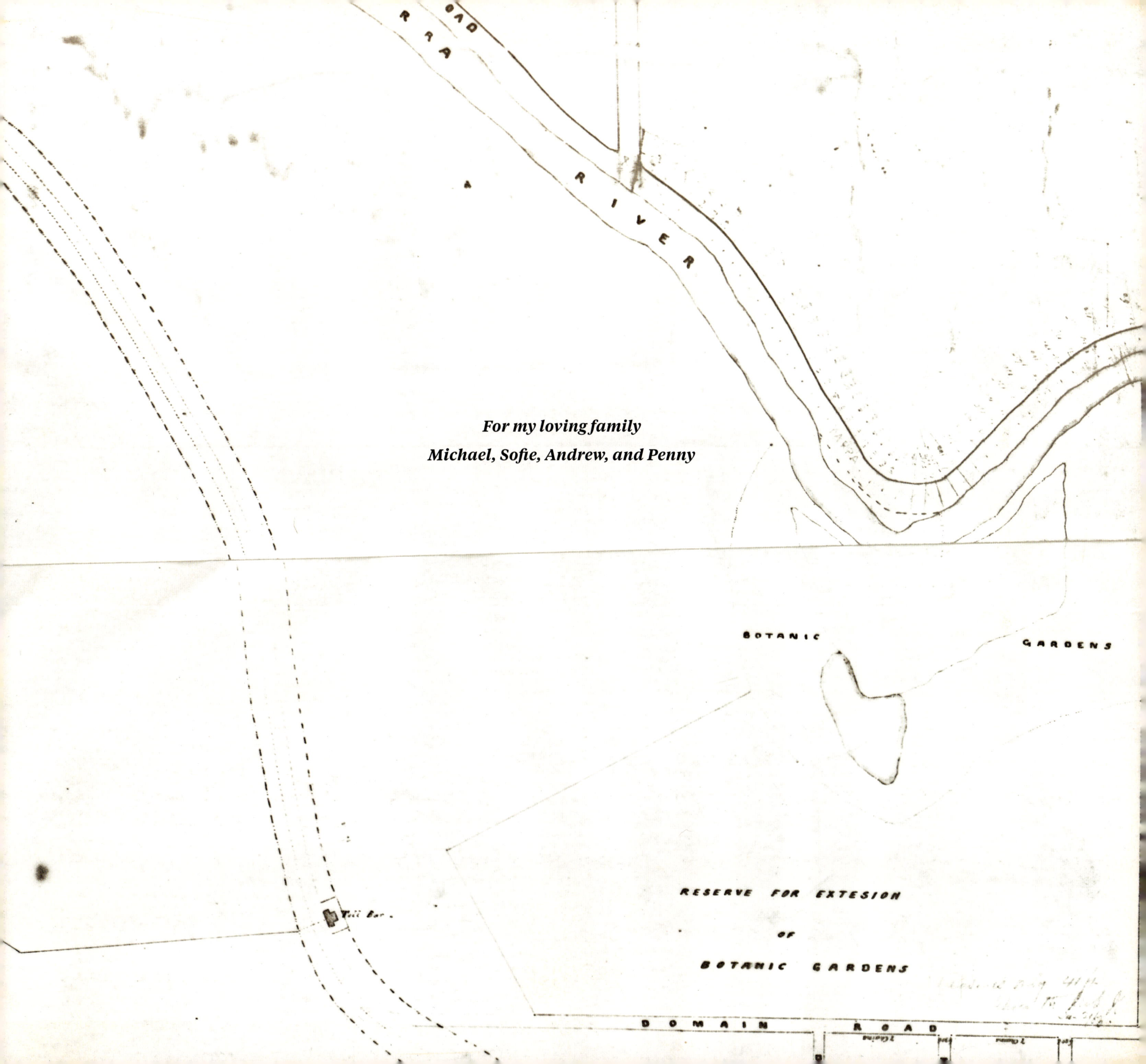

For my loving family

Michael, Sofie, Andrew, and Penny

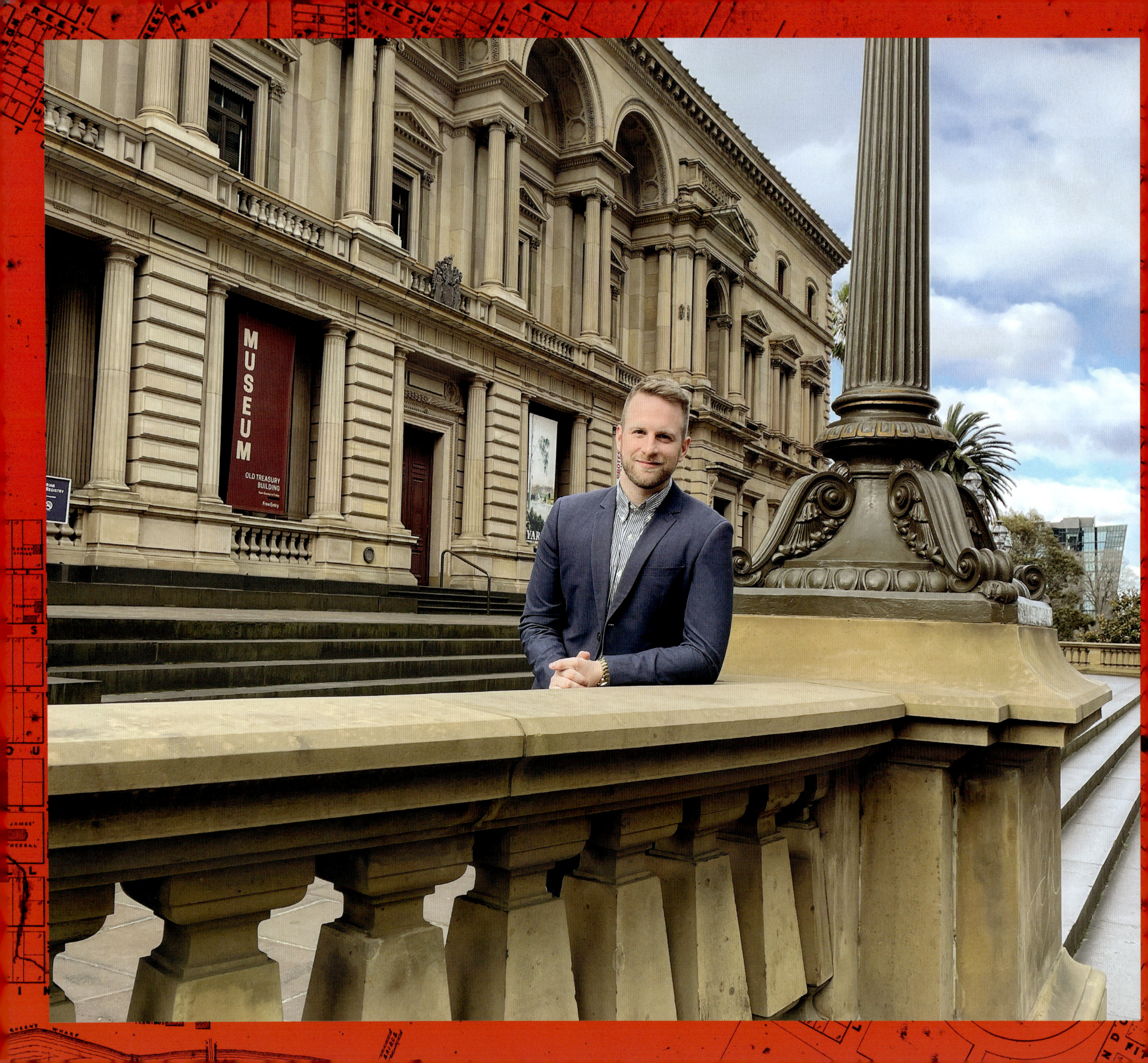
MUSEUM
OLD TREASURY BUILDING
Free Entry

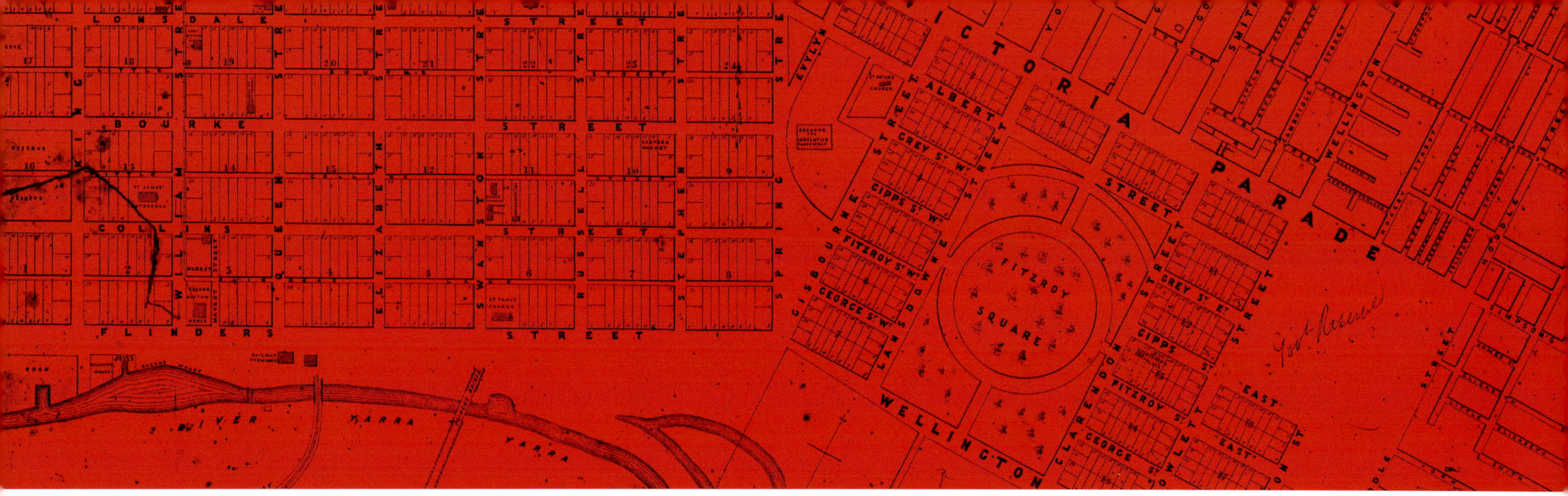

OLD VINTAGE MELBOURNE was a project inspired by nostalgia and a fascination with the past. The very circumstances that allowed for it to be born, however, were highly relevant and contemporary.

June 2020 was a tough month for Melburnians. We were dealing with unprecedented times, like the rest of the world, amidst a pandemic. We were suddenly thrust into a lockdown. I was working from home, overeating and failing to exercise. But despite the adversity, the cancelled overseas trips, and the adjustment to a new lifestyle, I found myself engaging more with my own city. I stumbled upon Trove and the myriad of digitised archival materials on the State Library VIctoria website.

After an hour of downloading a high-quality image of Flinders Street Station in 1910, I waved my Photoshop wand and removed much of the damage that the photograph had endured. My light bulb 'A-ha' moment came shortly after when I realised that Instagram was the perfect platform to share this image and the thousands of others I could get my hands on. On that day I created *Old Vintage Melbourne* — an Instagram account through which I shared fascinating images depicting a past Melbourne, often presenting then-and-now images as a reminder of how much our city has changed and continues to do so. Adding fun facts to the posts gave context and boosted engagement.

Before long, the Instagram account was getting attention from all over, with followers growing rapidly by the hour, from 1,000 to 10,000 to 20,000, and more. It's since been followed by many renowned people and organisations, from the National Gallery of Australia and local politicians, to athletes and, how can I not mention, Kylie and Dannii!

The popularity of the account led to me being interviewed on television and radio, and by the press. I couldn't be more proud of how this passion project has turned out. I continue to receive messages of gratitude every day from followers who admit that the account was a saviour during the lockdown. I want to thank all of the incredible followers, for their contributions and opinions. They have taught me so much about our spectacular city, both its iconic landmarks and its lesser-known sites. We are often rushing off to our next destination so single-mindedly we forget about the incredible history that surrounds us.

And, on that note, I give you *Old Vintage Melbourne* in print.

Chris Macheras, founder and author,
Old Vintage Melbourne

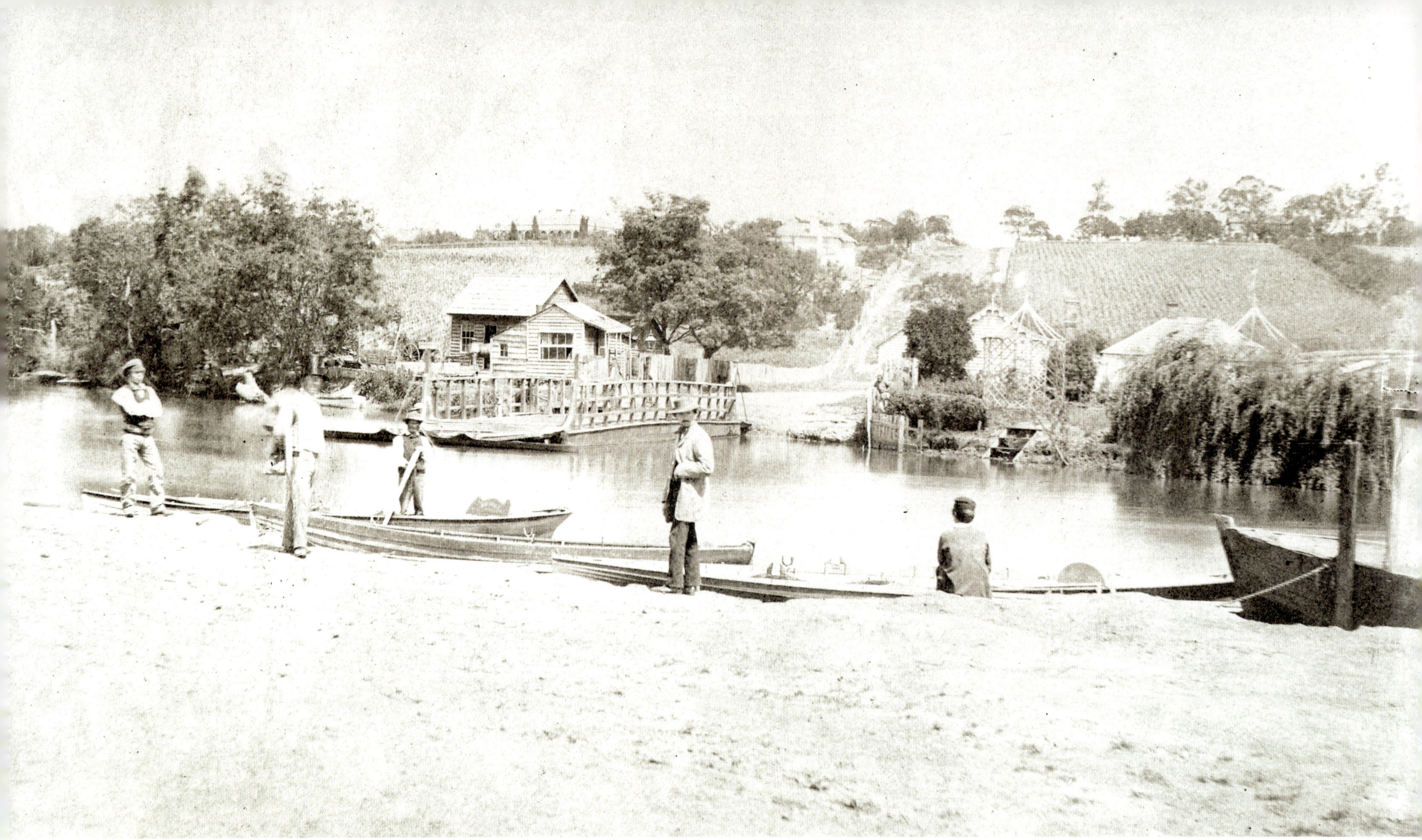

PUNT ROAD, RICHMOND

c.1856

PHOTOGRAPHER: UNKNOWN

This photo is taken from the Richmond side, and beyond the Yarra River you can see Punt Road. Inhabitants continuing up Punt Road would reach what is now Domain Road in South Yarra.

The Yarra River was narrower at that time than it is now, and possibly slightly displaced from its present channel.

Punts were used to cross the river before the Punt Road bridge was built. A punt is a flat-bottomed boat with a square-cut bow, designed for use on small rivers. One of them — the wooden structure that looks like a jetty — is visible on the other side of the riverbank. You can see how Punt Road got its name.

Across the river on the right is a vineyard owned by Mr David Ogilvie. Ogilvie was the first president of The Law Institute of Victoria and, coincidentally, a passenger on the very first train that ran in Victoria.

BOURKE STREET

c. 1858

PHOTOGRAPHER: ANTOINE FAUCHERY & RICHARD DAINTREE

Where it all began!

I was unsuccessful in finding the store that sells those delicious raspberry drops because, well, this isn't Sovereign Hill.

It's the top of Bourke Street, looking west from Spring Street. This is also considered to be one of the earliest photographs depicting Melbourne.

Around the time this photo was taken, the first recorded game of Australian Rules football was played between Melbourne Grammar School and Scotch College. At the same time, Fitzroy became a municipality in its own right, and the construction of St Patrick's Cathedral had just begun.

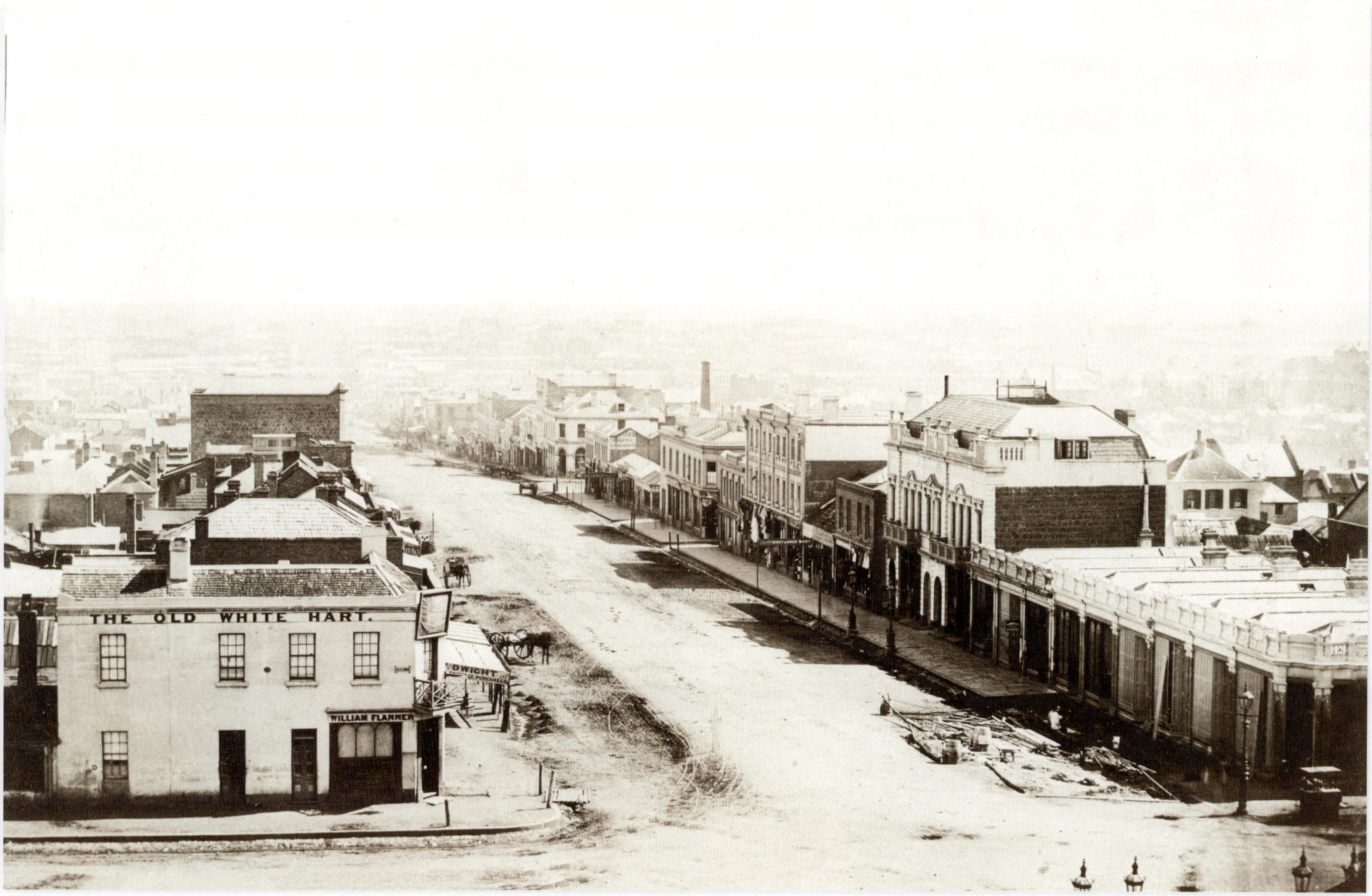

SWANSTON STREET

c.1858

PHOTOGRAPHER: ANTOINE FAUCHERY & RICHARD DAINTREE

This is one of the earliest known photos of Melbourne. The view is of Swanston Street, looking north from Collins Street. There's not a 7/11 or Maccas in sight!

The bluestone building on the right was the original town hall, demolished to make way for the current Melbourne Town Hall.

The foundation stone for the new town hall was laid on 20 November 1867 by the visiting Prince Alfred, Duke of Edinburgh.

The City of Melbourne as we know it had only been named twenty years earlier.

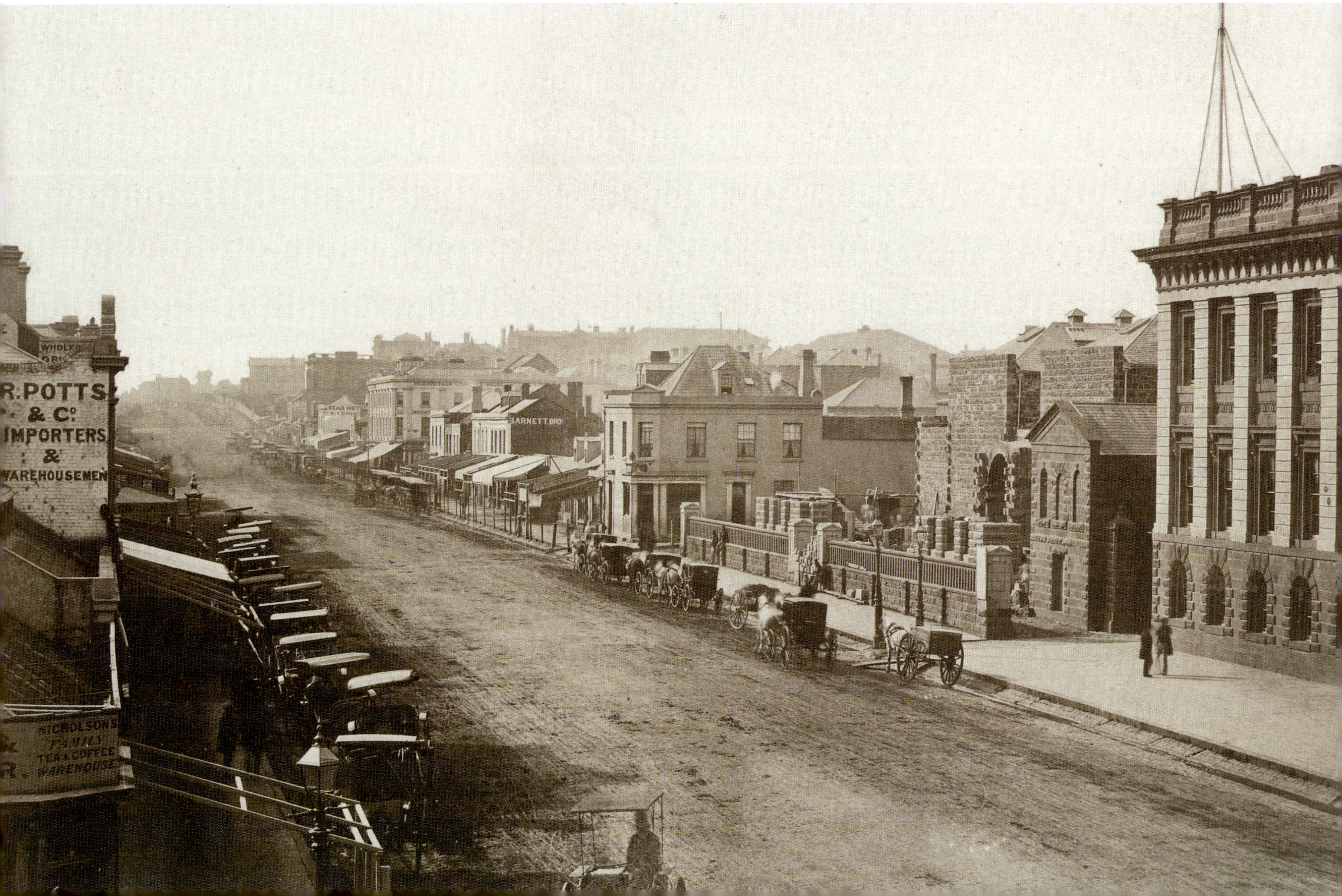

OLD TREASURY BUILDING CONSTRUCTION

c.1858

PHOTOGRAPHER: BARNETT JOHNSTONE

Presiding over the top of Collins Street in the 'Paris end', the Old Treasury Building has stood for 160 years.

This overwhelmingly lavish piece of architecture is yet another reminder of Melbourne's boom era in the mid-to-late nineteenth century. This building represents wealth even in a literal sense, having housed all the gold bullion acquired during the Victorian gold rush.

This Melbourne icon was constructed using bluestone mined from Footscray for its foundations, and Bacchus Marsh sandstone for its exterior. The floor above the barrel-vaulted basement is a metre thick.

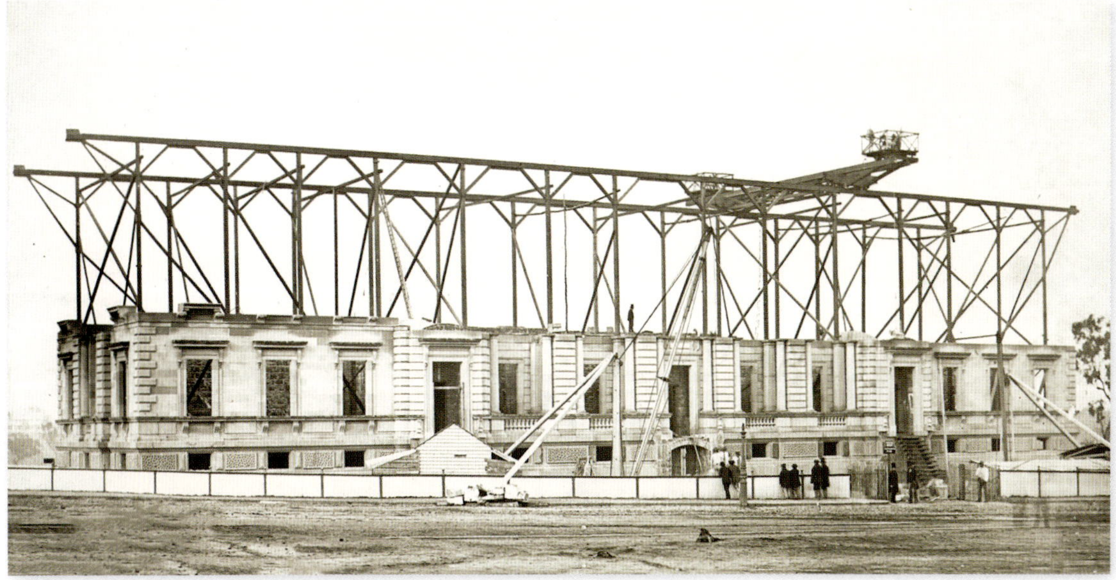

OLD TREASURY BUILDING

c.1900

PHOTOGRAPHER: CLIFFORD WILLIAMS (RIGHT IMAGE);
CHRIS MACHERAS (BOTTOM RIGHT IMAGE)

THEN AND NOW: Forty-odd years after its completion, here is the stunning Old Treasury Building with a comparison to today's, unaltered and commanding as ever over Spring and Collins streets.

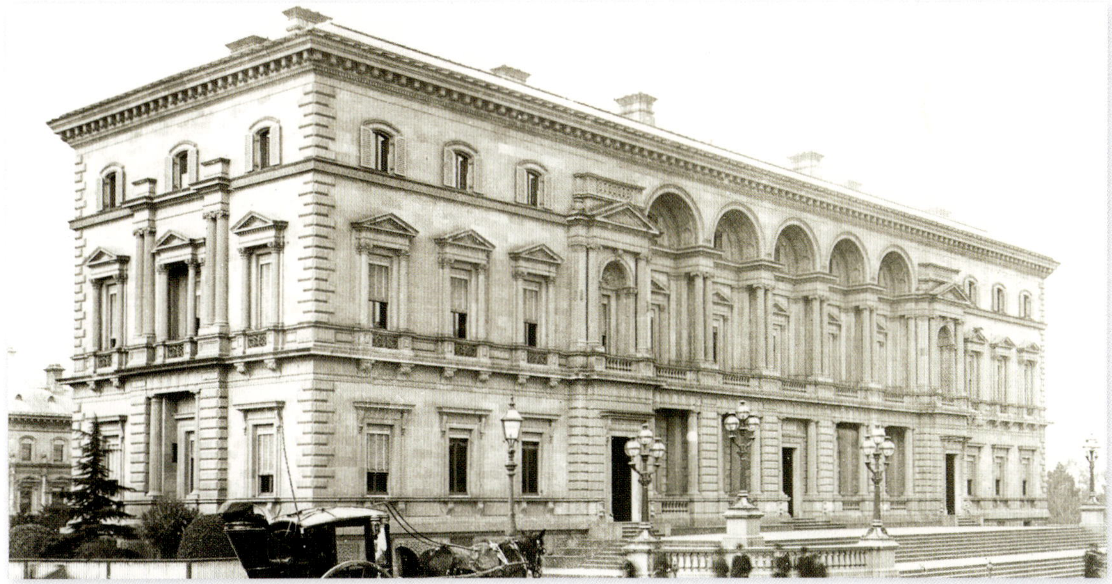

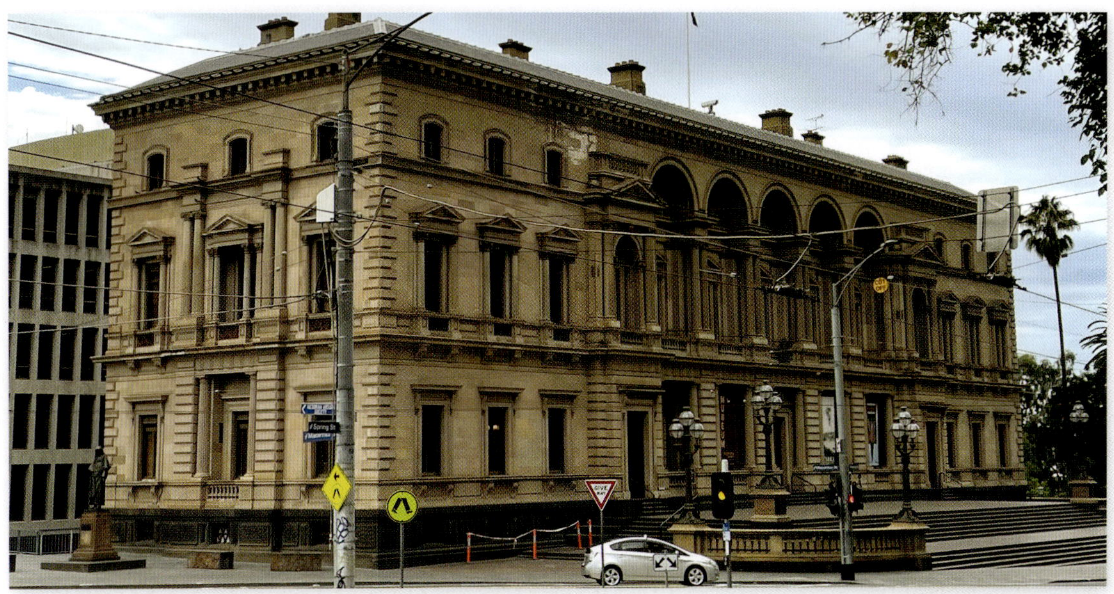

BOURKE STREET

c.1861

PHOTOGRAPHER: CHARLES NETTLETON

Looking down Bourke Street from the steps of Parliament House.

Note the verandas only on one side and the ghosts walking the streets! What I mean by ghosts are the faint human figures in the frame, visible if you look closely.

The cameras of the time were not yet able to capture moving images. As a result, you will often find photos like this, from the 1800s, that make it appear as though the streets are deserted. In fact, it is likely that these streets were bustling with people.

A major difference you will find today throughout the city is the abundance of trees lining the streets, offering much-needed shade on hot and sunny days.

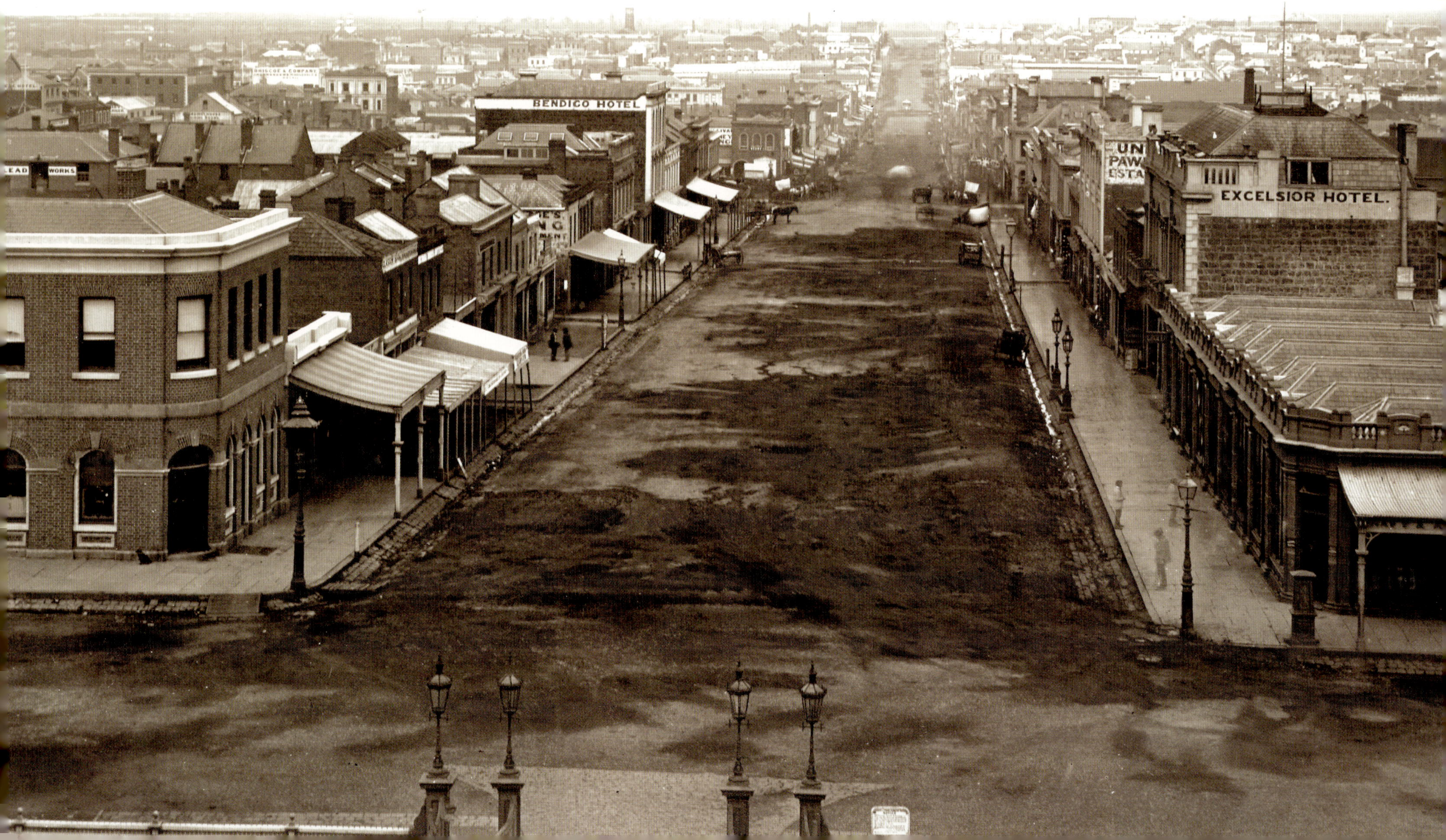

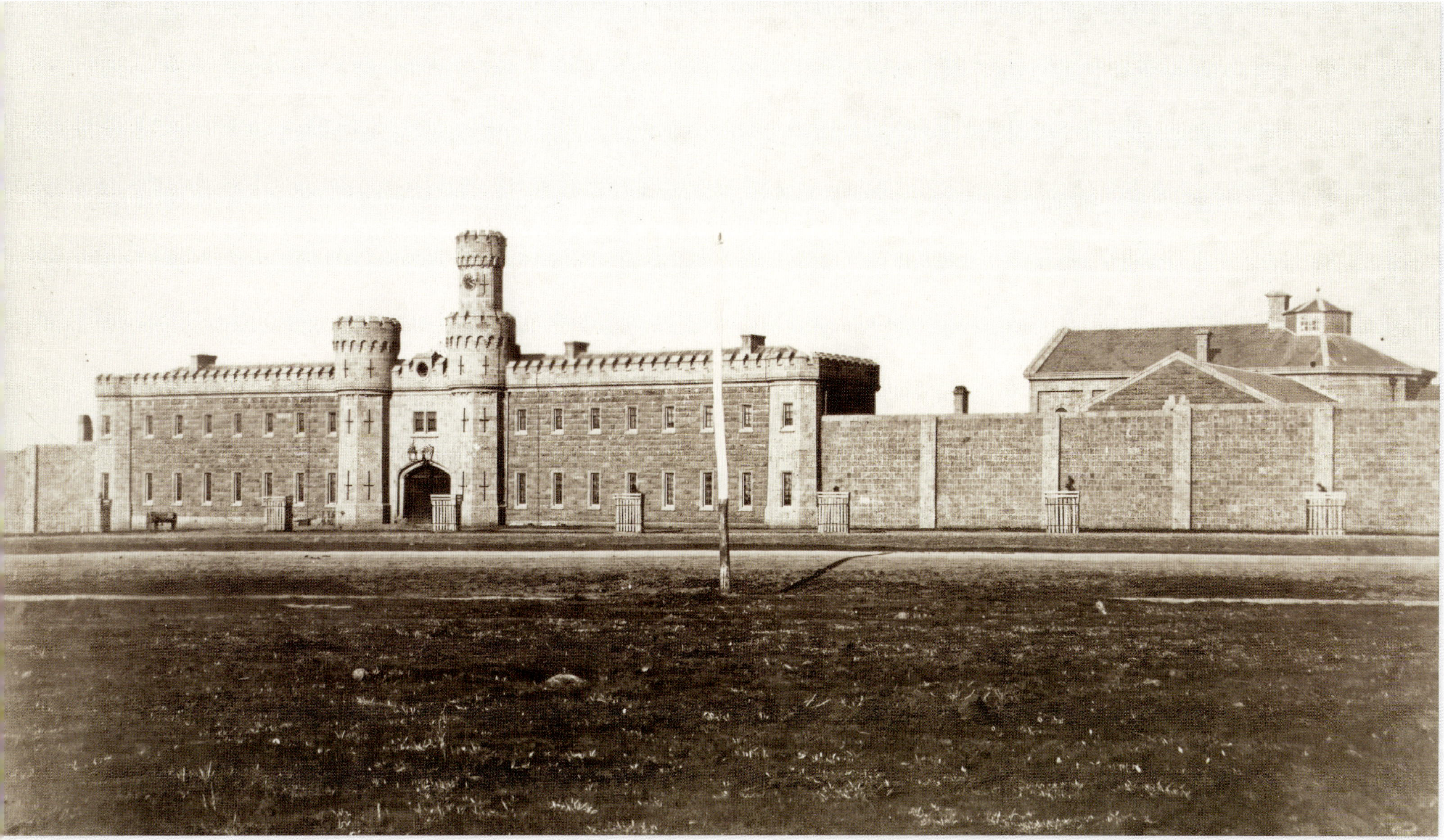

H.M. PENTRIDGE PRISON, COBURG

c.1861

PHOTOGRAPHER: JEAN-BAPTISTE CHARLIER

In 1851, Pentridge opened its secure doors to prisoners, and closed them in 1997. The suburb of Coburg was originally called Pentridge.

The area was specifically chosen for the prison as it was relatively close to central Melbourne but sufficiently isolated and distant from residential areas. The village reserve that it was built on was also the only unsold Crown land in Melbourne.

Its first prisoners were transferred from an overcrowded Melbourne Gaol, and its initial purpose was to provide labour for the construction of Sydney Road.

Prison conditions at the time were substantially different from today, with prisoners working, sleeping, and eating in chains. It has been recorded that passers-by would often talk to the prisoners and offer them tobacco.

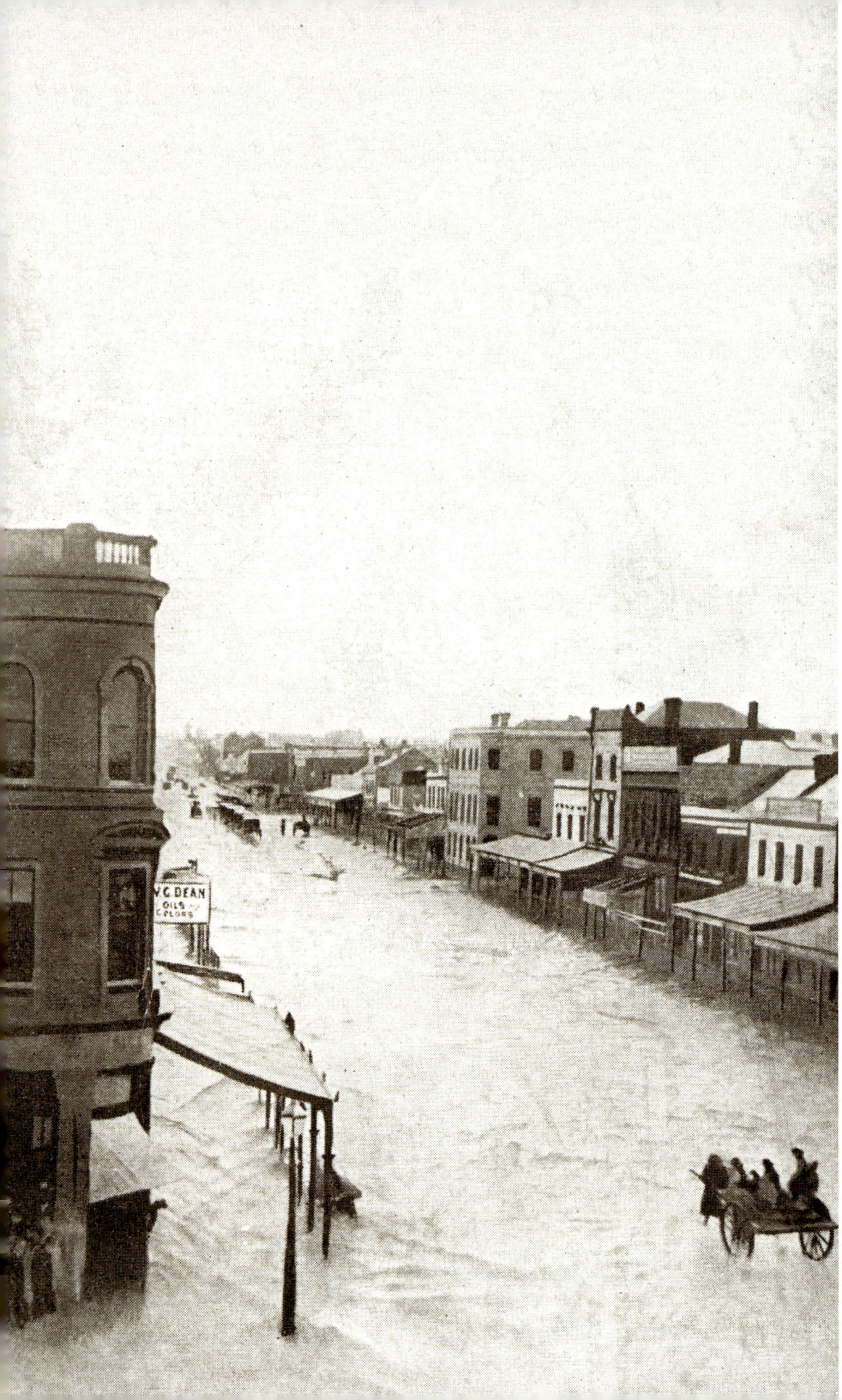

ELIZABETH STREET IN FLOOD

1862

PHOTOGRAPHER: UNKNOWN

Flash flooding has hit Melbourne many times over the years, as in this image taken at 6.00 pm on 8 December 1862, on Elizabeth Street. When the city was founded, there was a creek where Elizabeth Street is today. Better drainage management over time has helped ensure that flooding to this extent will not occur again.

In 1880 and 1882, Elizabeth Street flooded to an even greater extent. The great flood of 1880 caused the Yarra River to swell to 305 metres in width. This amounted to the most significant flood in Melbourne's recorded history, forcing thousands of locals to vacate their homes, and at least one person died in the disaster.

More recently, in February 1972, 75mm of rain fell on Melbourne over a short period, sending waves of water down the street. You may recall that this was famously captured in an award-winning photo in *The Age*.

MELBOURNE CEMETERY

c. 1864

PHOTOGRAPHER: CHARLES NETTLETON

A group of men pose with a large block of granite at Melbourne Cemetery. As the image indicates, the granite was excavated and used for the Burke and Wills Monument, which at the time of writing is in storage due to the Metro Tunnel project.

The 2,000-mile Burke and Wills Expedition set off from Melbourne in 1860, led by Robert O'Hara Burke and William John Wills.

On 2 November 1861, news of the death of Burke and Wills reached Melbourne, and within days grief swept the city; more than 40,000 people are said to have paid their last respects.

The bronze statue was mounted on this piece of granite and was unveiled in 1865.

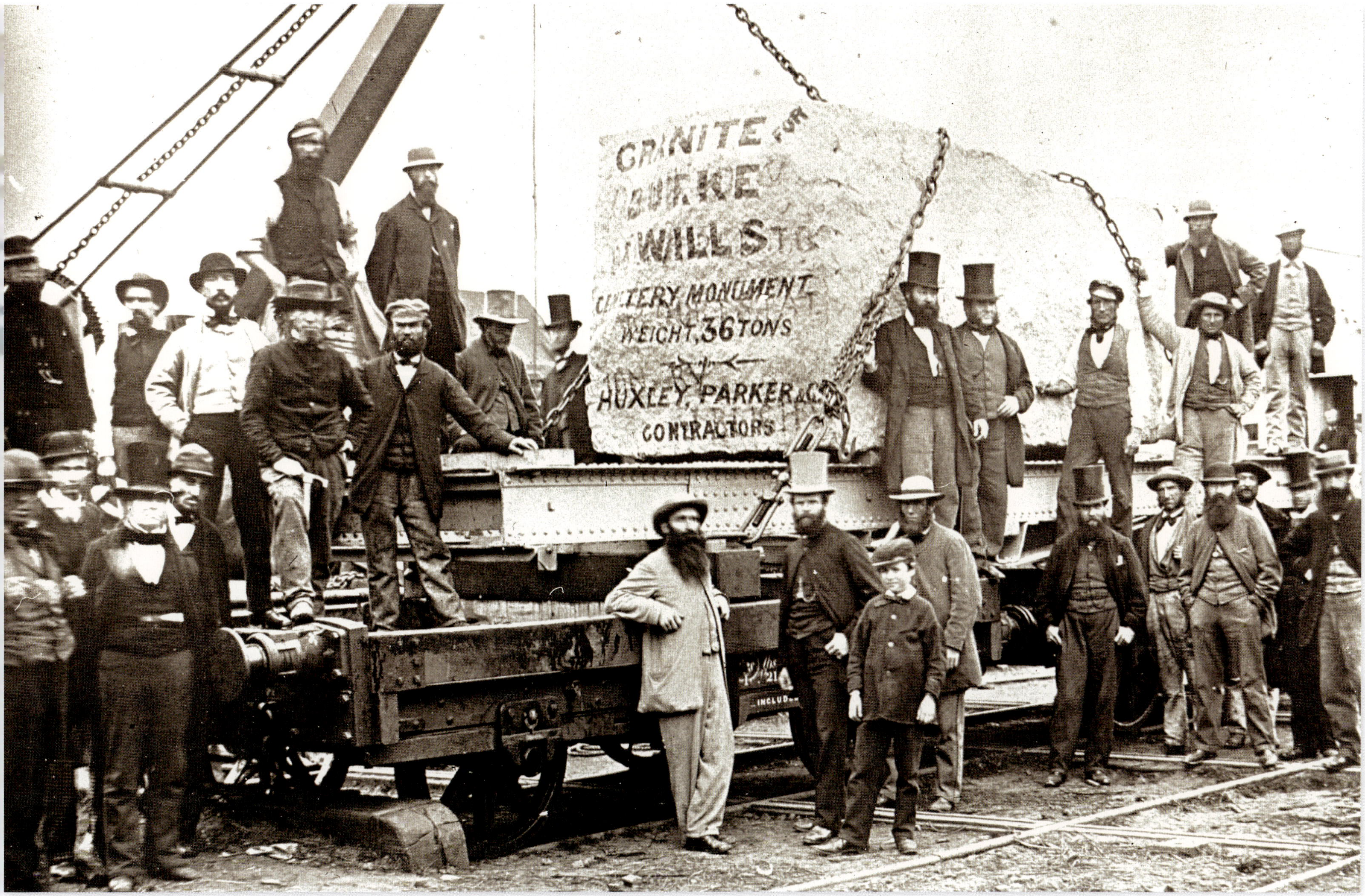

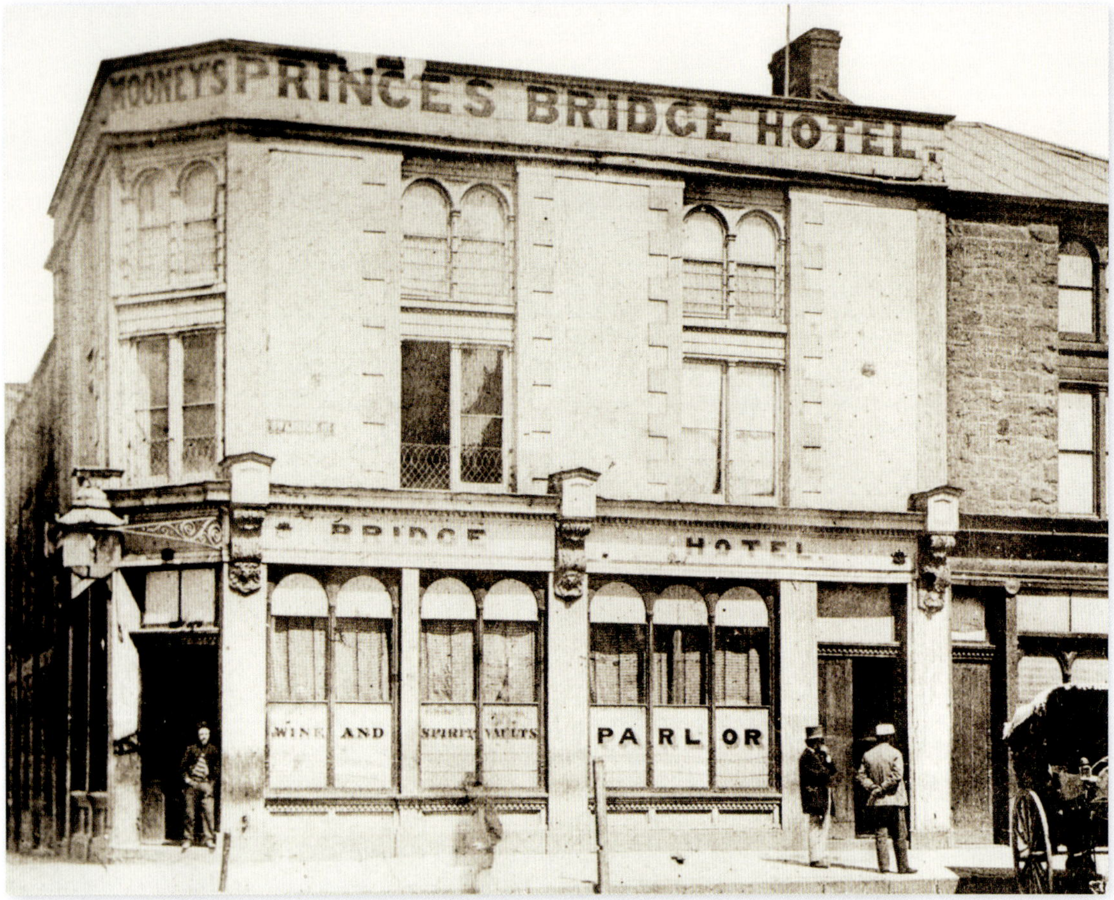

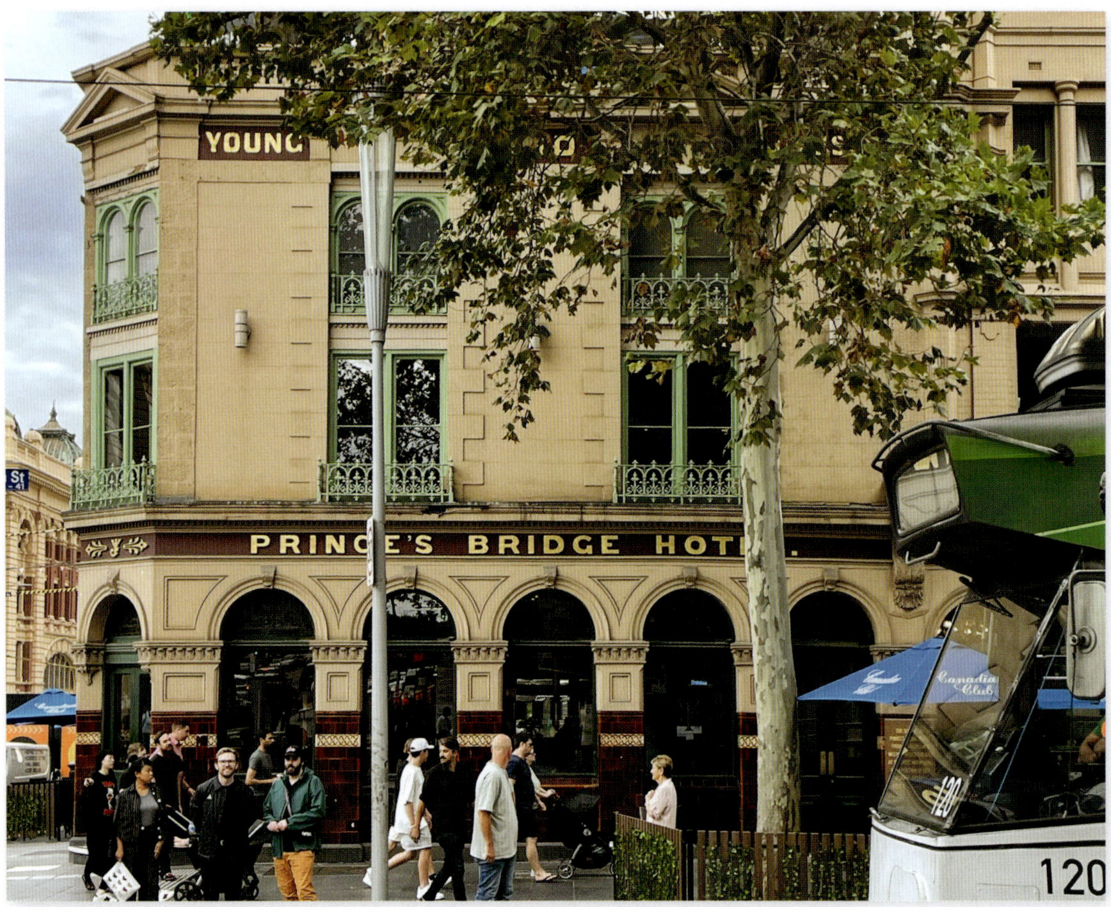

PRINCES BRIDGE HOTEL

c.1864

PHOTOGRAPHER: UNKNOWN (TOP IMAGE);
CHRIS MACHERAS (BOTTOM IMAGE)

THEN AND NOW: The Princes Bridge Hotel was only three years old here, having opened in 1861. Today you may recognise it as the iconic Young and Jackson Hotel on the corner of Flinders and Swanston streets.

You may not be aware that John Batman himself, one of the city's founders, originally purchased this site in 1837. He had a home built there for his children, which became a schoolhouse two years later. After the schoolhouse was demolished, warehouses were erected on the site in 1853. In 1861, Mr John Toohey, along with his brother, converted the space into the Princes Bridge Hotel. They later moved to Sydney and went on to found Tooheys Brewery, a brand of beer still around today.

CHAPEL STREET, PRAHRAN

c. 1864

PHOTOGRAPHER: JOHN YEOMAN & CO.

Can anyone identify this lovely rural town? It's actually Chapel Street, Prahran.

You can see the intersection with Malvern Road, as well as a horse and cart doing some of the first recorded 'chap laps' (the colloquialism referring to modified cars driving up and down Chapel Street without any real destination — other than to be seen!).

This happens to be one of the earliest photos ever taken of Prahran, and the view is looking north from the town hall.

The photo was taken the same year that Banjo Patterson was born, which was also the year that the Carlton Football Club was founded.

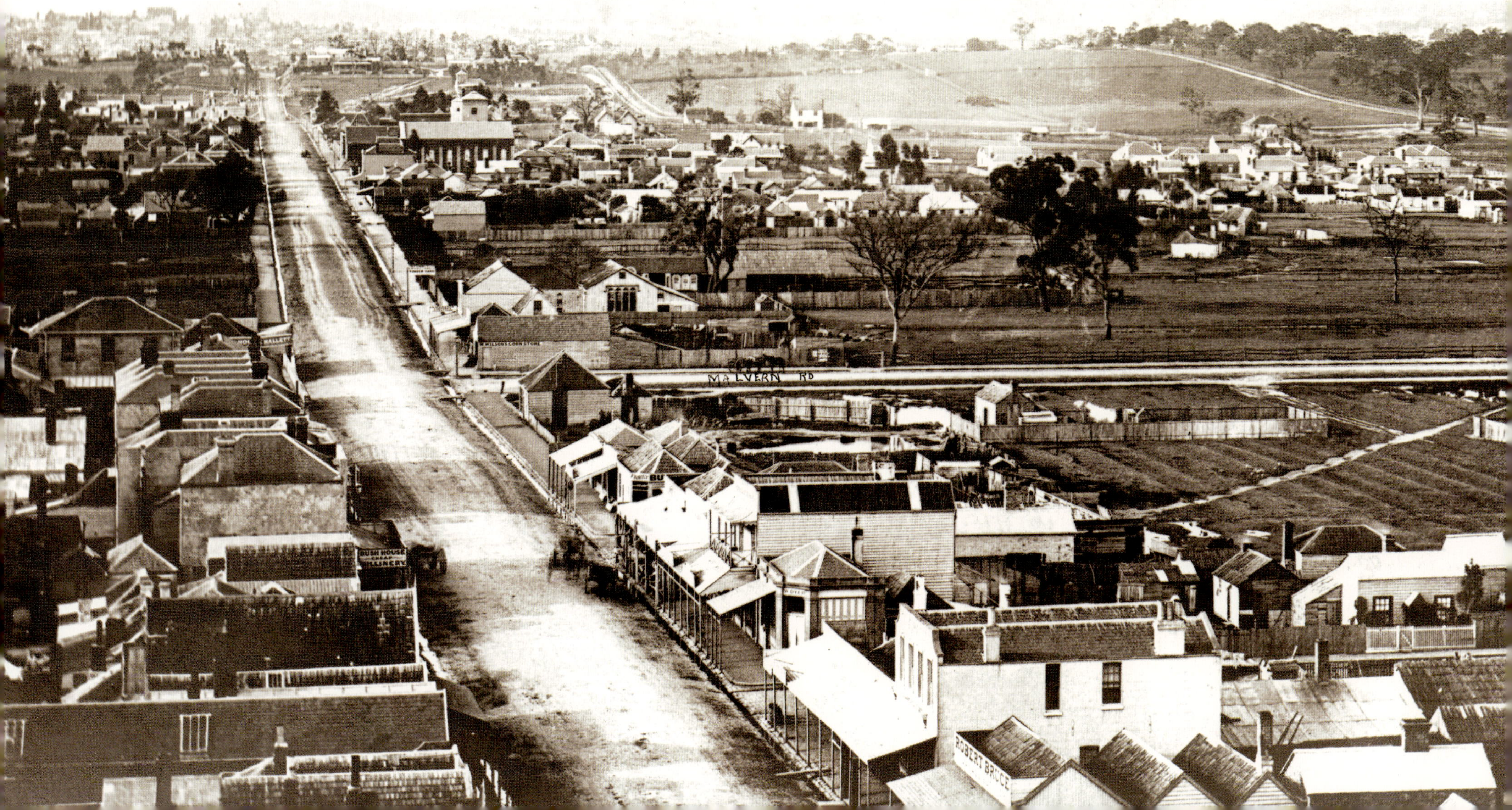

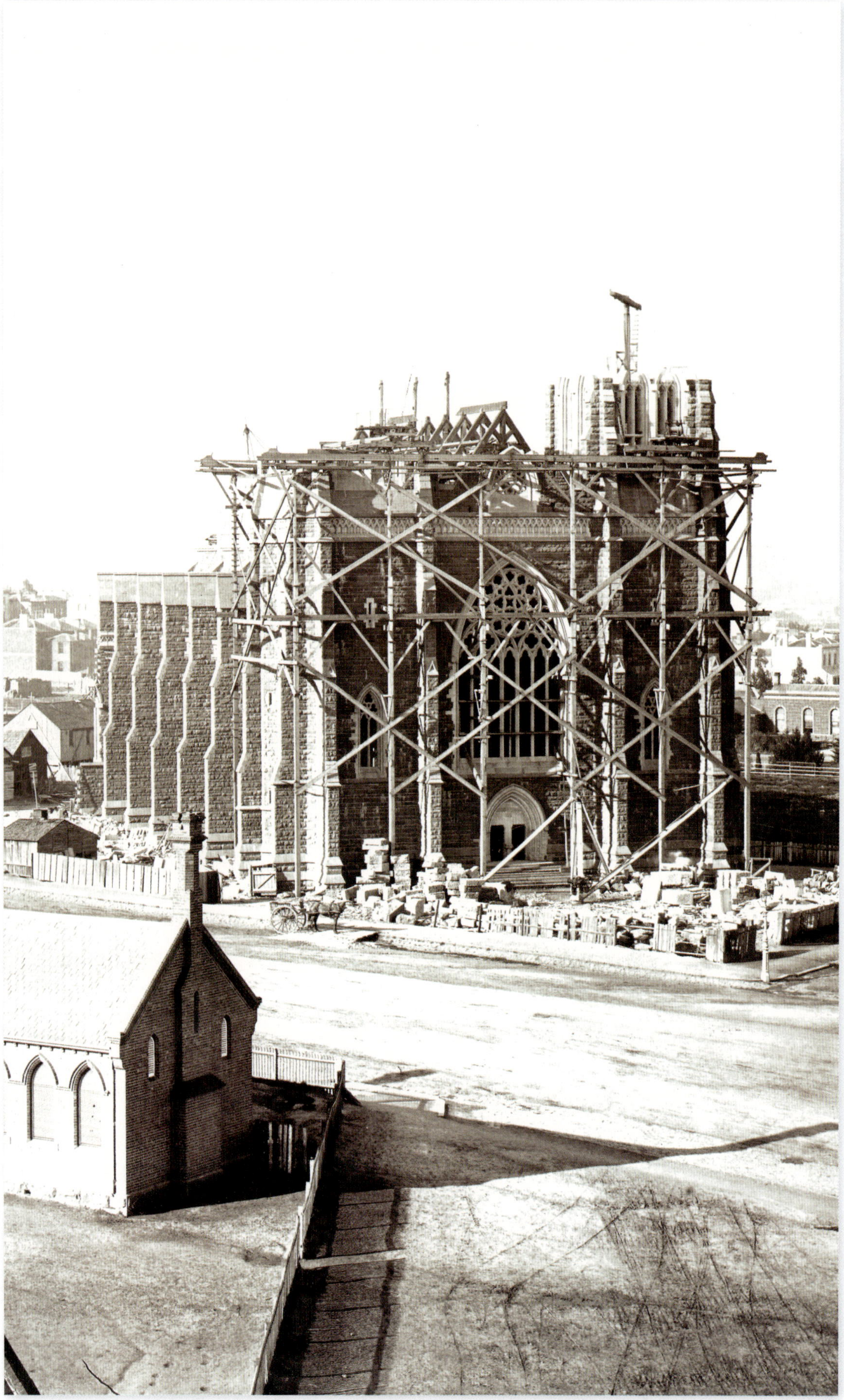

ST PATRICK'S CATHEDRAL

c.1866

PHOTOGRAPHER: CHARLES NETTLETON

You are looking at St Patrick's Cathedral in East Melbourne, still covered in scaffolding. The renowned cathedral-to-be is eight years into its construction.

There is a great controversy surrounding its construction, which involved Archbishop Gould being shot in Brighton by Peter Andrew Charles O'Farrell, his former solicitor.

Archbishop Gould was the founding Roman Catholic bishop and archbishop of Melbourne, whose later life was devoted to raising funds for the cathedral.

O'Farrell had taken to drink after losing his fortune during the Depression. He was unable to obtain funds willed to the construction of the cathedral by his father, even though he had demanded it from the archbishop.

Archbishop Gould lost the top of one of his fingers when O'Farrell furiously fired a gun at him. O'Farrell was subsequently charged with attempted murder, but was convicted of a lesser charge. Ultimately, he died a penniless alcoholic.

Side note: O'Farrell's brother was the first person to attempt a political assassination in Australia. He was convicted and hanged for shooting and wounding the Duke of Edinburgh during his visit to Sydney.

Construction of the cathedral proceeded slowly, and was further delayed by the severe depression that hit Melbourne in 1891. The building was officially completed in 1939.

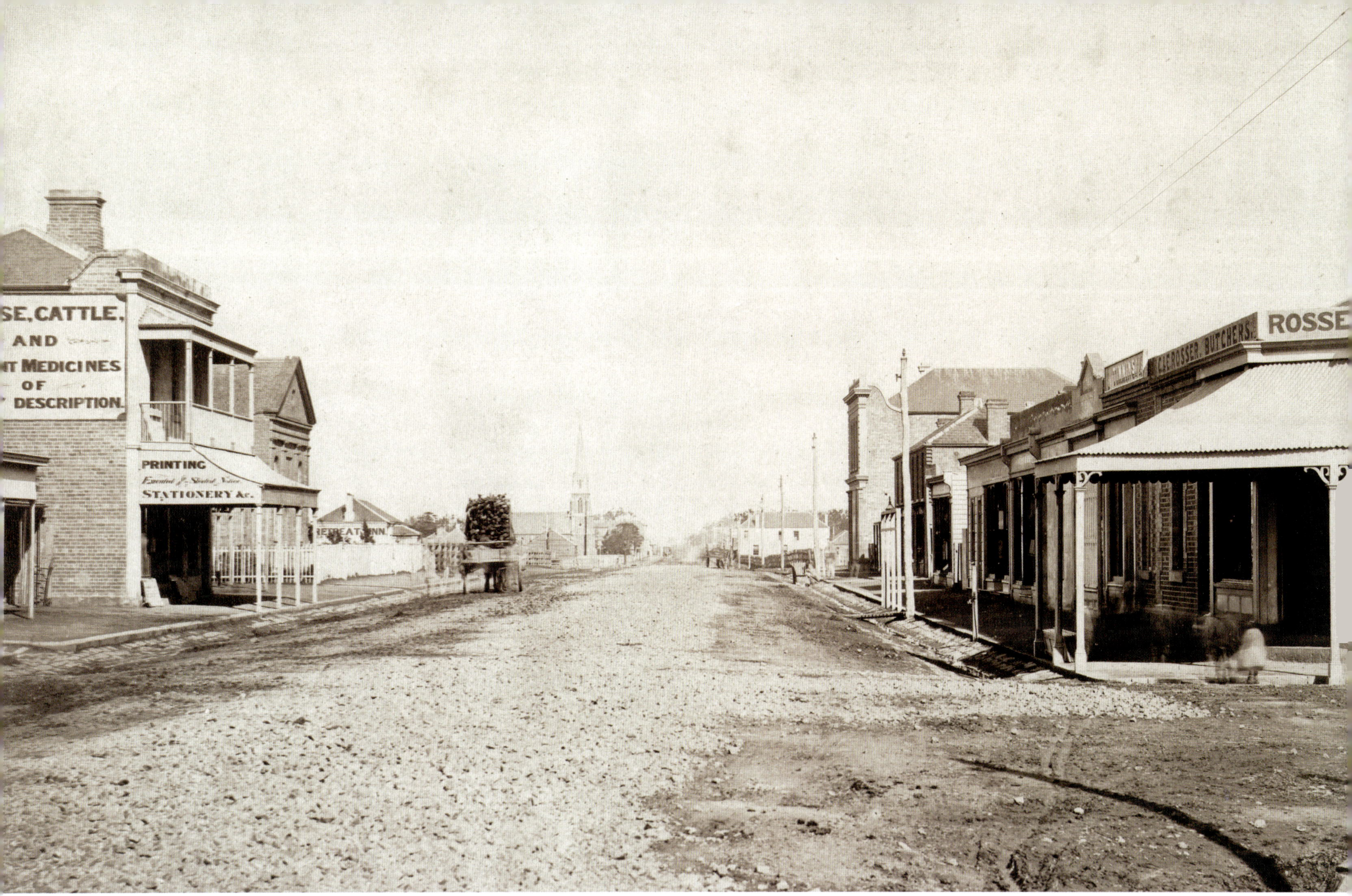

SYDNEY ROAD, BRUNSWICK

c. 1866

PHOTOGRAPHER: UNKNOWN

It's hard to believe that this is the corner of Sydney Road and Albert Street, Brunswick, in 1866. You can see the old Brunswick Presbyterian Church (now the Uniting Church), built in 1865, in the distance on the left.

The first land sales in Brunswick were held in 1839, with most of the land bought by investors who never lived there. One of the first purchasers in the area was a man named Daniel Campbell. In 1840, his land portions were sold on to Edward Stone Parker and Thomas Wilkinson. They named their property 'Brunswick' after the royal wedding that had occurred 'back home' in England — Brunswick being the name of the royal house of the bride, Princess Caroline. Mr Wilkinson was quite active in the area's local affairs, and came to be known as the 'Father of Brunswick'.

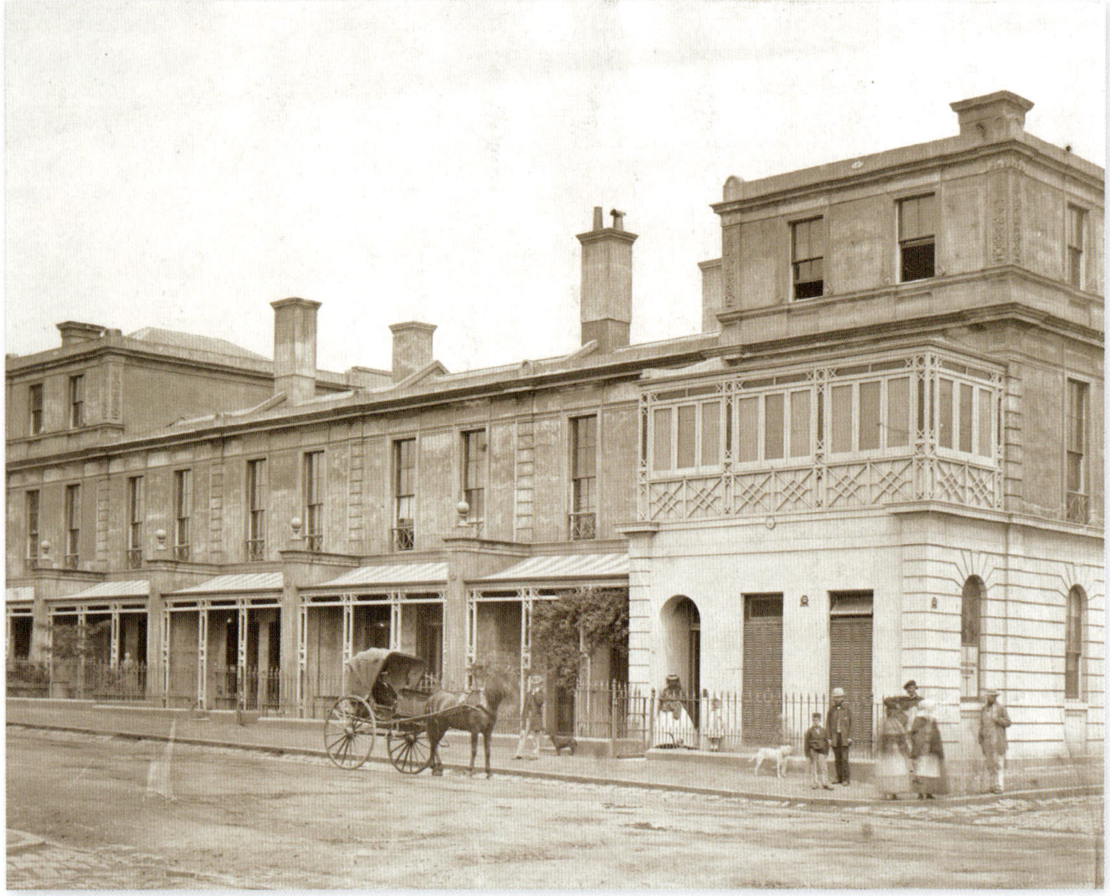

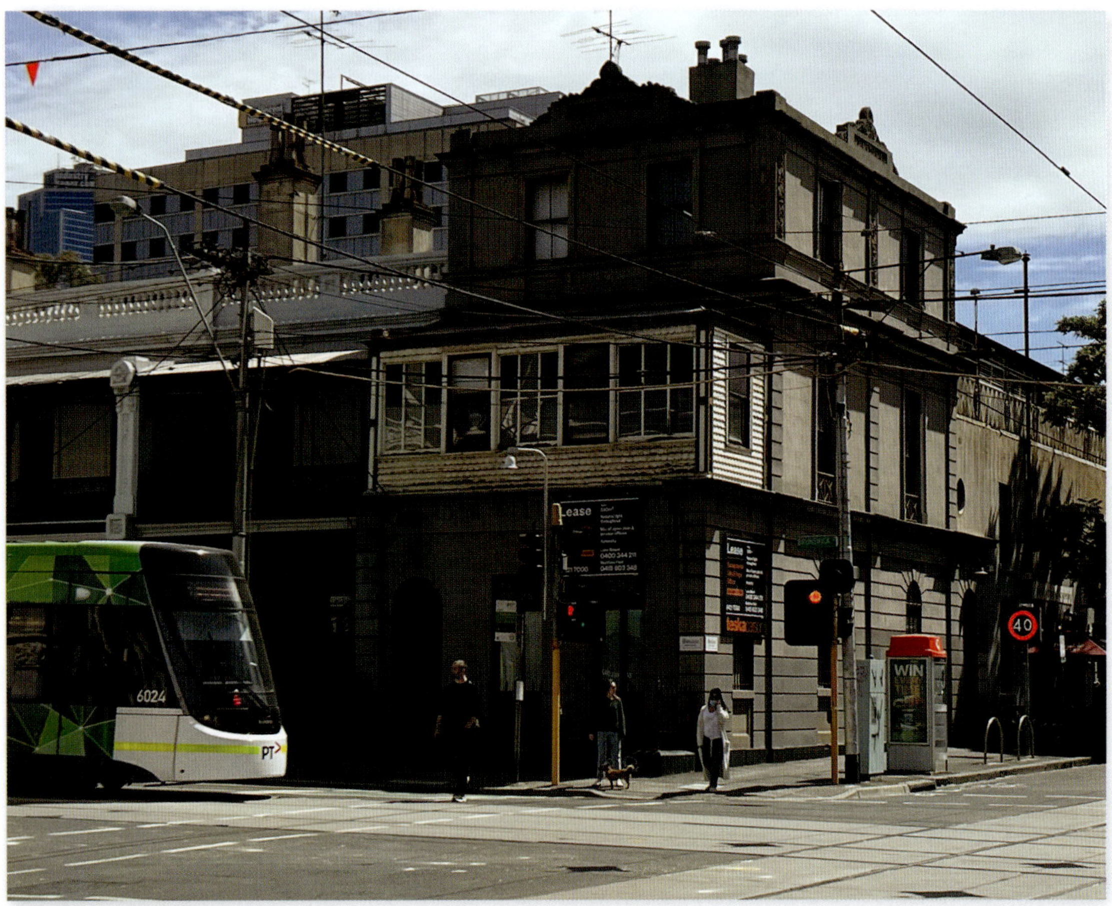

BRUNSWICK & GERTRUDE STREETS, FITZROY

c.1866

PHOTOGRAPHER: DAVIES & CO. (TOP IMAGE); CHRIS MACHERAS (BOTTOM IMAGE)

THEN AND NOW: The building on the corner remains after 162 years! Located at 49 Brunswick Street, it was Dr William Crooke's Surgery.

Brunswick Street owes its origins to a man named Benjamin Baxter, who owned a lot of land along Victoria Parade. Baxter owned Lot 49, which was adjacent to Lot 48 on the north-west corner of Victoria Parade and Nicholson Street. In 1839, he subdivided his lot into quarters, creating roads between the subdivisions. These roads became Brunswick Street and Gertrude Street. Initially, Brunswick Street only ran as far as what is now Hanover Street.

DICKSON'S PRINCE OF WALES HOTEL, ST KILDA

c.1867

PHOTOGRAPHER: PATERSON

When Fitzroy Street was a dirt road.

That's the Prince of Wales Hotel, which opened in 1862 on the corner of Fitzroy and Acland streets. It was originally built as a guesthouse, later becoming a rather casual, unpretentious drinking pub.

Its reputation as one of Melbourne's most distinguished hotels did not come about until it was demolished and rebuilt in 1936 in the sleek Art Deco style we associate it with today.

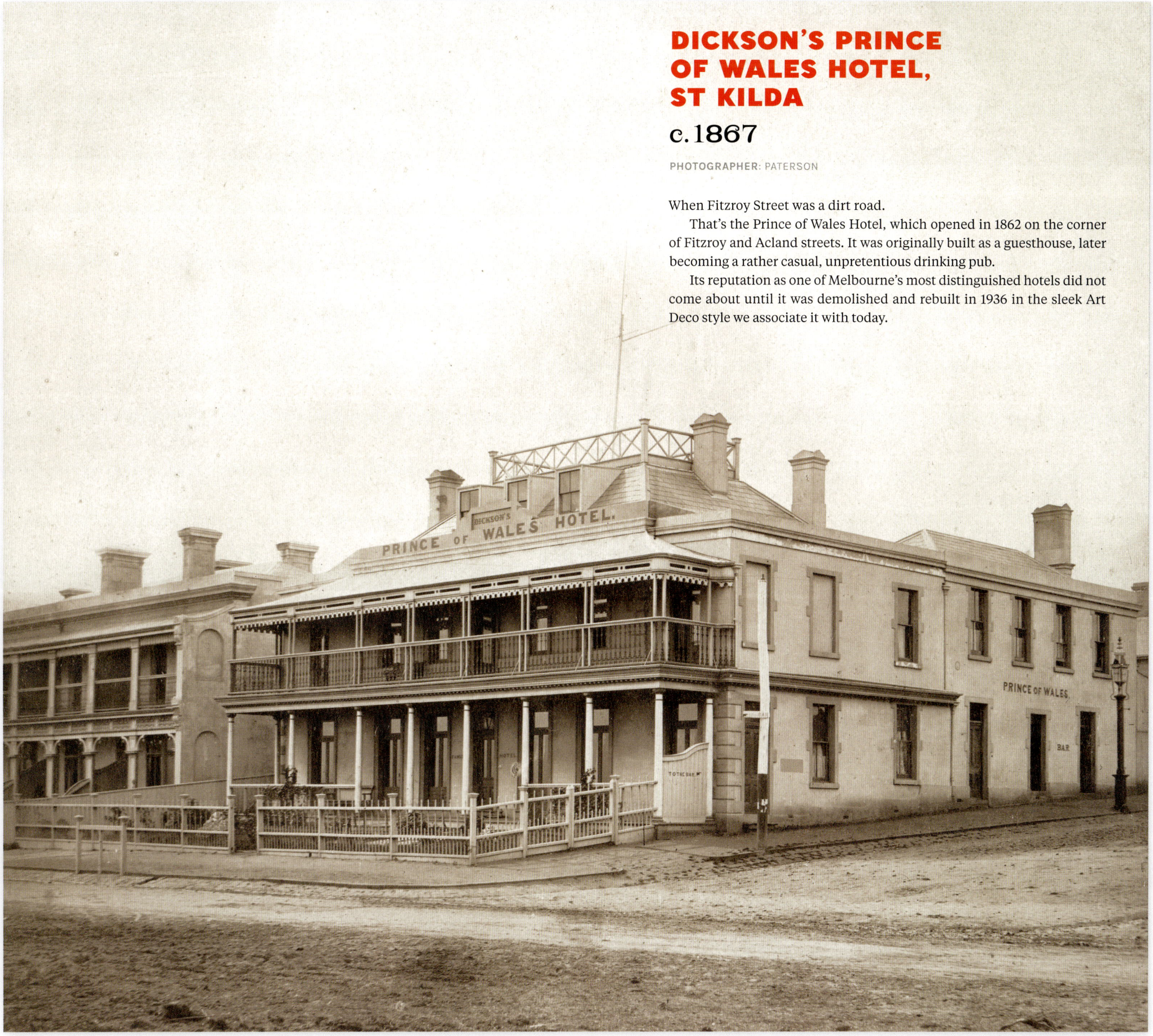

LONSDALE STREET

c. 1869

PHOTOGRAPHER: JOHN NOONE

This image shows Lonsdale Street looking west from William Street, taken from the tower of Dr Fitzgerald's residence, 'Rostella'.

Sandridge and Hobson's Bay, the area we know today as Port Melbourne, are in the distance.

The bluestone church in the foreground was demolished in 1935 and re-erected as St Andrews in Box Hill, using the same bluestone bricks. Today, that corner is occupied by the County Court in Melbourne's legal district.

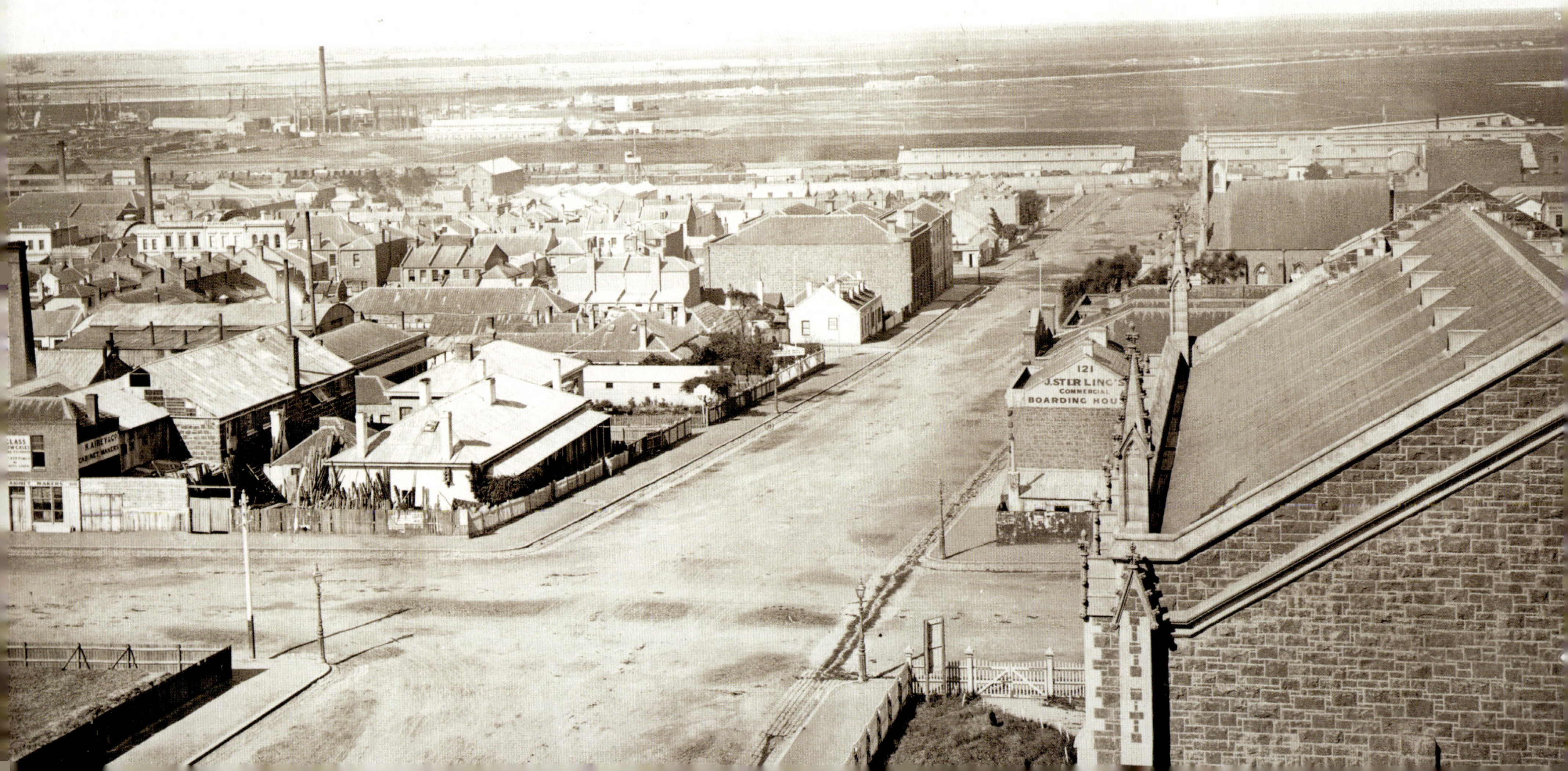

SWANSTON & FLINDERS STREETS

c.1870

PHOTOGRAPHER: AMERICAN & AUSTRALASIAN PHOTOGRAPHIC COMPANY (TOP IMAGE); CHRIS MACHERAS (BOTTOM IMAGE)
SOURCE: MITCHELL LIBRARY, STATE LIBRARY OF NEW SOUTH WALES

THEN AND NOW: If you have ever wondered what the corner of Swanston and Flinders streets looked like before St Paul's Cathedral was built, here it is.

This is where the first public Christian service in Melbourne was conducted in 1835. The block was then a government reserve far from the centre of town to the west, and was used as a corn market. By 1848 the first Princes Bridge across the Yarra had been built directly adjacent to it, and the now-prominent site was granted to the Anglican Church. The bluestone Church of St Paul the Apostle was consecrated in 1852. Nearly thirty years later, with the rapid growth of the city, and Swanston Street having become a major thoroughfare, the diocese decided to build the grand cathedral we know as St Paul's Cathedral. These photographs were taken exactly 150 years apart.

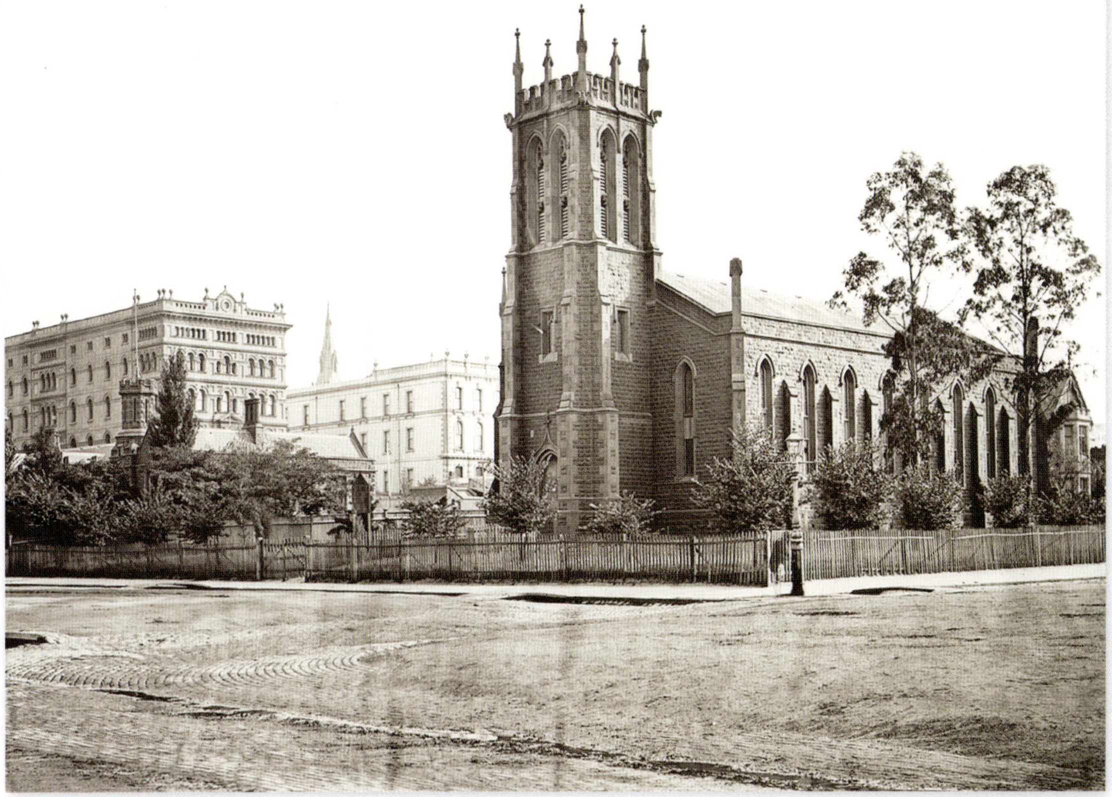

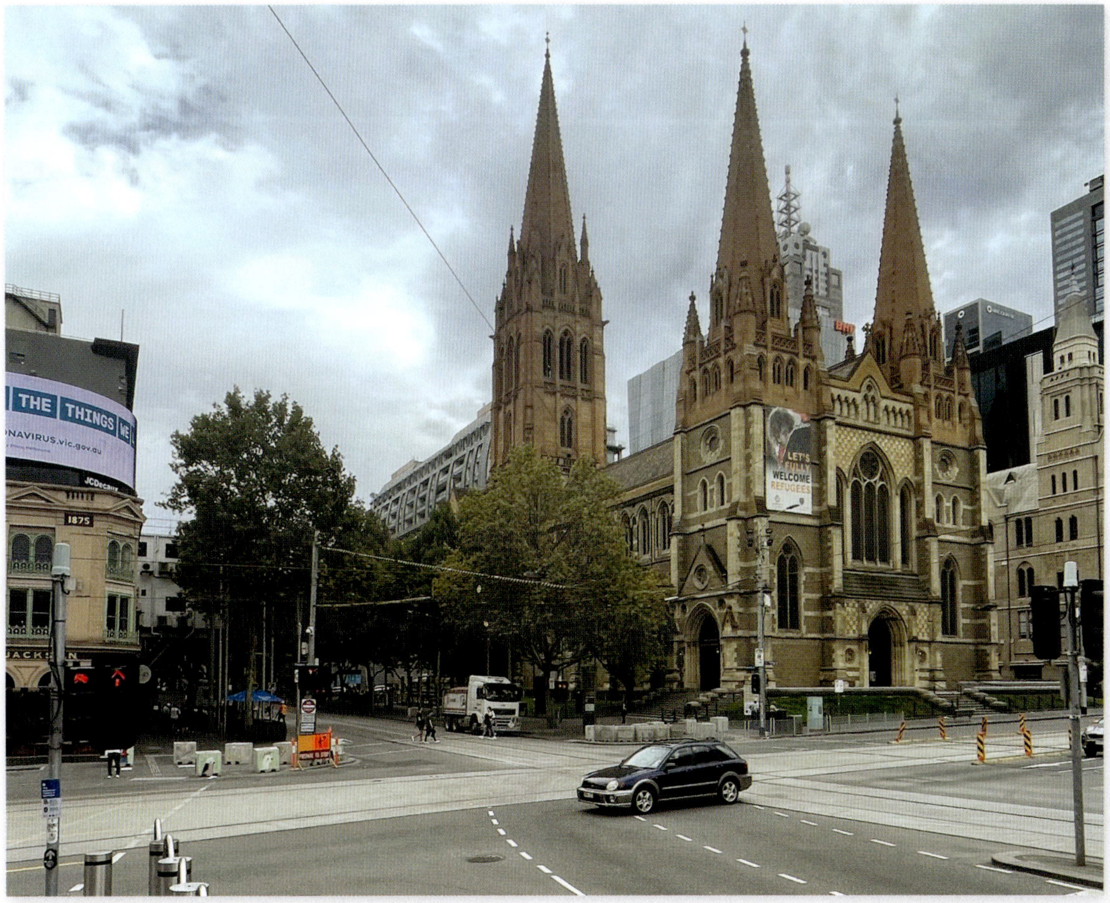

BAY STREET, PORT MELBOURNE

c.1870

PHOTOGRAPHER: AMERICAN & AUSTRALASIAN PHOTOGRAPHIC COMPANY
SOURCE: MITCHELL LIBRARY, STATE LIBRARY OF NEW SOUTH WALES

The area known today as Port Melbourne was originally named Sandridge. It represented the area between Hobson's Bay and the Yarra.

In 1839, the man who surveyed the area, William Darke, noted the ridge of sand dunes along the beach. He got quite creative, and called the area Sandridge.

Darke and his family reportedly camped on the beach in a carpeted wooden caravan. Darke cut the first track to the beach through the seaside tea trees — there he hoisted a barrel on a tall pole that pointed locals towards the settlement of central Melbourne.

It looks like an abandoned trailer or wagon has been captured in this photograph of Bay Street. But if you look closely, there is a ghost-like figure beside it.

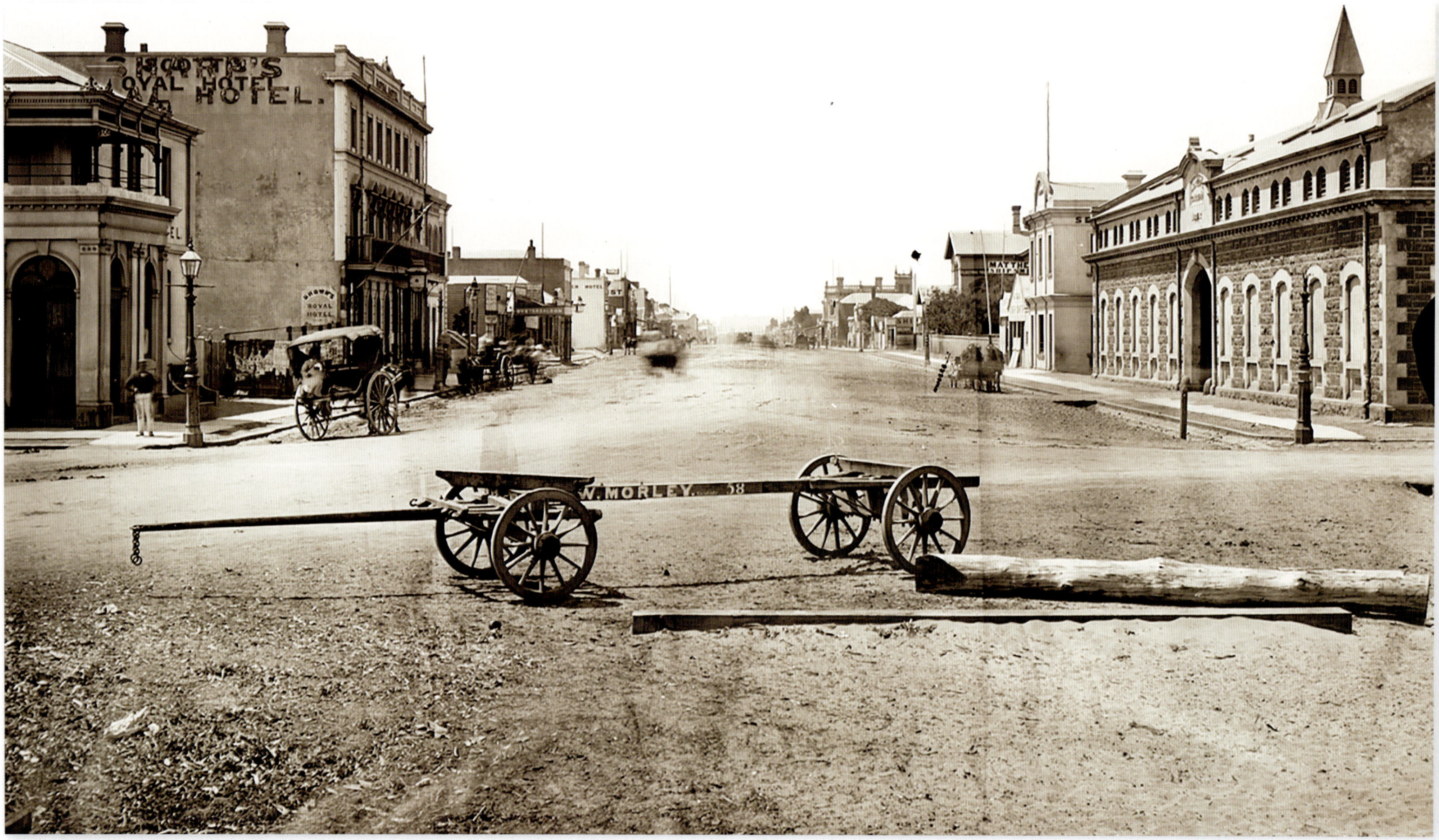

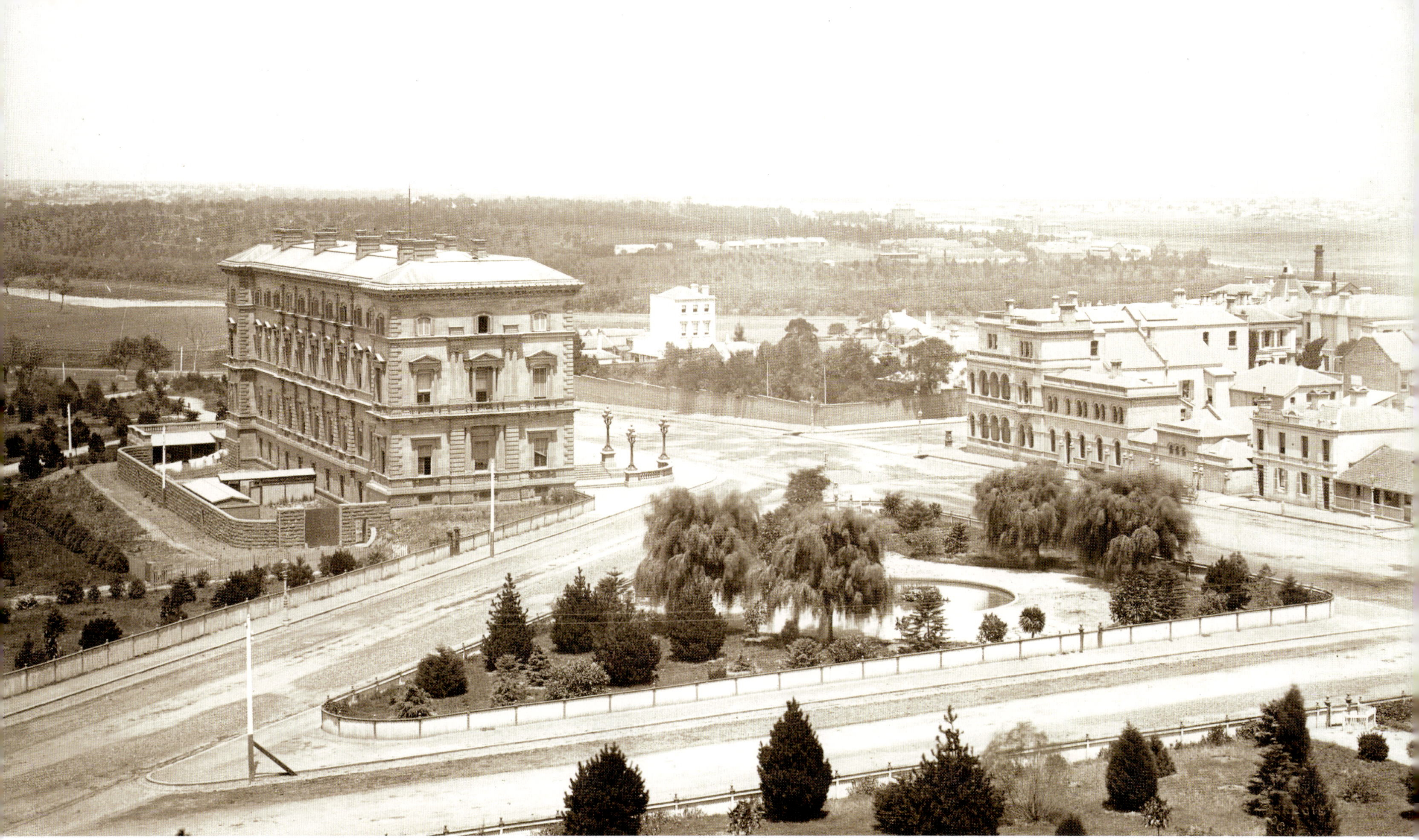

OLD TREASURY BUILDING

c. 1870

PHOTOGRAPHER: CHARLES NETTLETON

A splendid view over Macarthur and Spring streets, with the magnificent old Treasury Building to the left.

The building was completed in 1862. Even today it is considered one of Australia's finest Renaissance Revival buildings. Its intricate design and ornate details can be attributed to the wealth brought into the city during the Victorian gold rush.

The designer of this Melbourne icon was a nineteen-year-old architect named J. J. Clarke. The oldest-surviving designs of the building date back to 1857, and many of his drafts can be found on display throughout.

Clarke went on to design other famous buildings in Australia, such as the Brisbane Treasury in Queensland.

Though the Old Treasury Building was completed in 1862, the forecourt couldn't be completed until 1868 due to a funding shortage. A temporary staircase was ultimately replaced in 1868 with the grand forecourt that is still standing today.

MELBOURNE TOWN HALL

c.1870

PHOTOGRAPHER: DONALD MCDONALD

A view of the Melbourne Town Hall on the corner of Collins and Swanston streets.

This photo was taken shortly after the building was completed. On 11 August 1870 it was opened officially with an extravagant ball that was funded by the lord mayor himself, Samuel Amess (after whom Amess Street in Carlton North was named).

Over time, the town hall has been the location of some of our city's most monumental moments. It was here that Federation was debated, where the great Dame Nellie Melba debuted, and where The Beatles greeted their screaming fans in 1964.

It was also here in 1900 where the motion-picture film *Soldiers of the Cross* premiered. This was one of the first feature films in the world, and considered by some to be the first narrative-drama film presentation. Some glass slides of the production have survived.

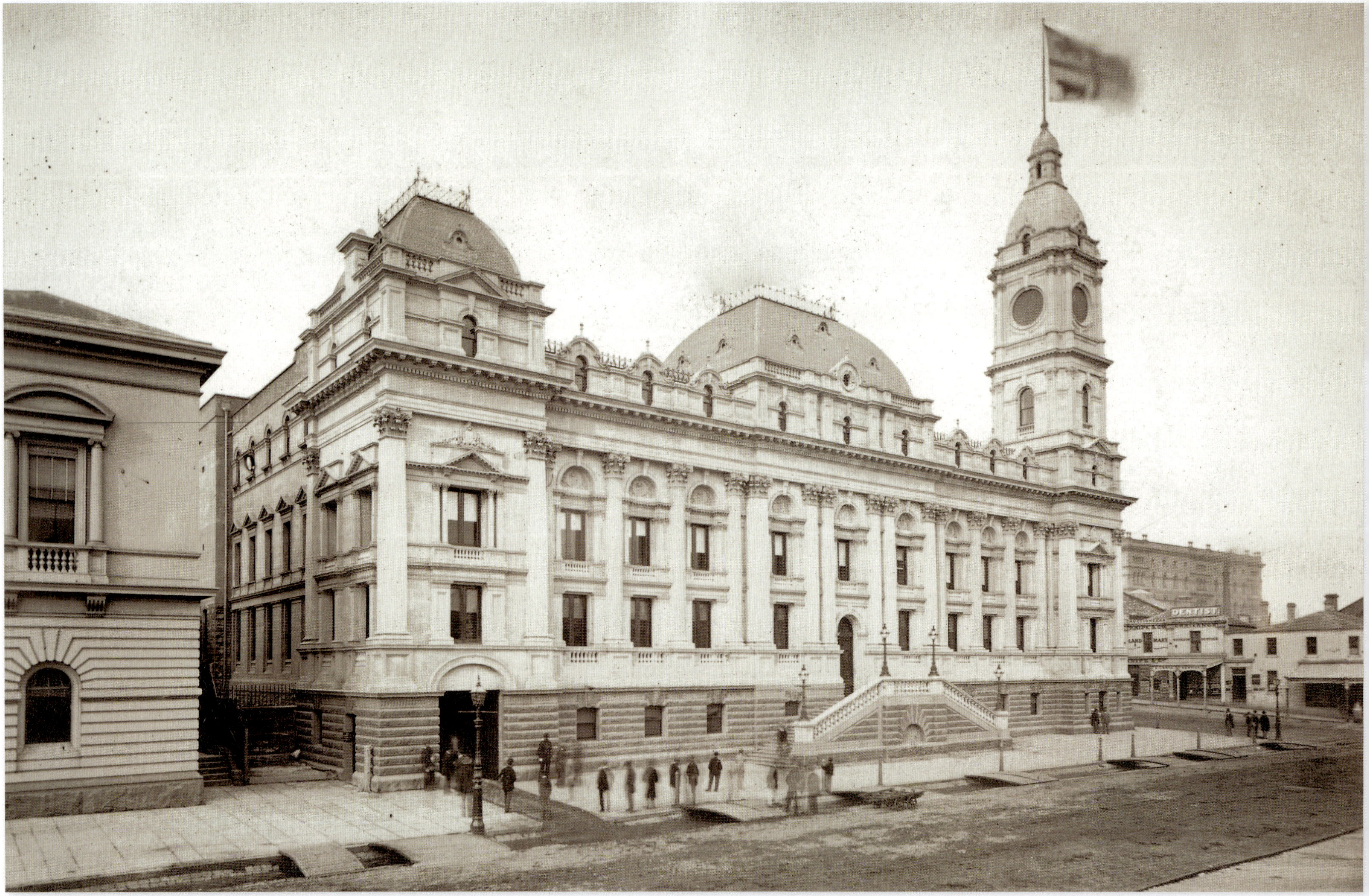

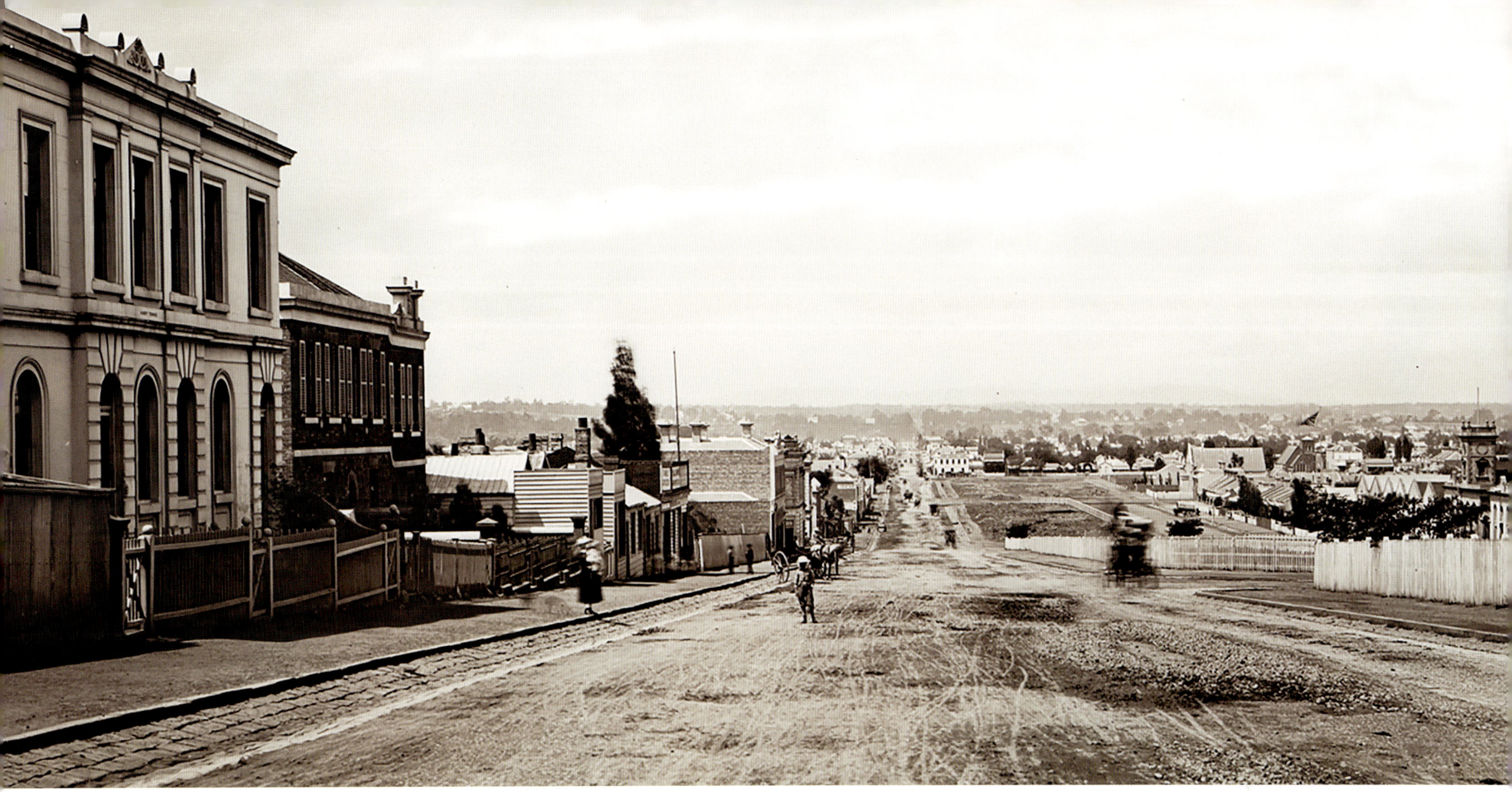

VICTORIA PARADE

c. 1870

PHOTOGRAPHER: AMERICAN & AUSTRALASIAN PHOTOGRAPHIC COMPANY (TOP IMAGE); CHRIS MACHERAS (BOTTOM IMAGE)
SOURCE: MITCHELL LIBRARY, STATE LIBRARY OF NEW SOUTH WALES

THEN AND NOW: Victoria Parade looking east towards Hoddle Street. Collingwood is on the left, and East Melbourne is on the right.

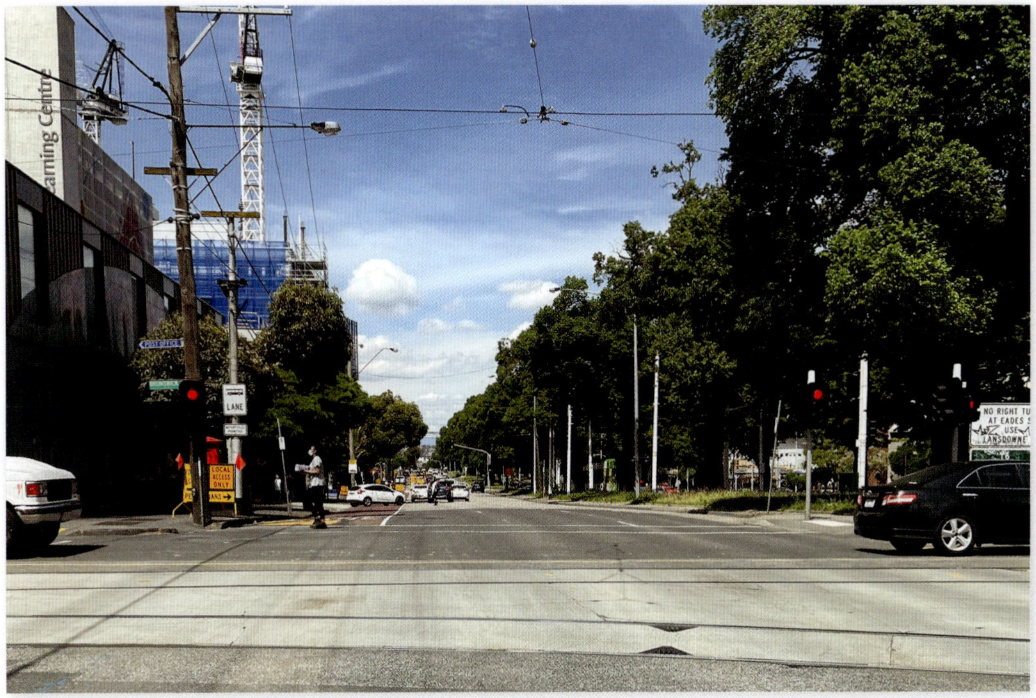

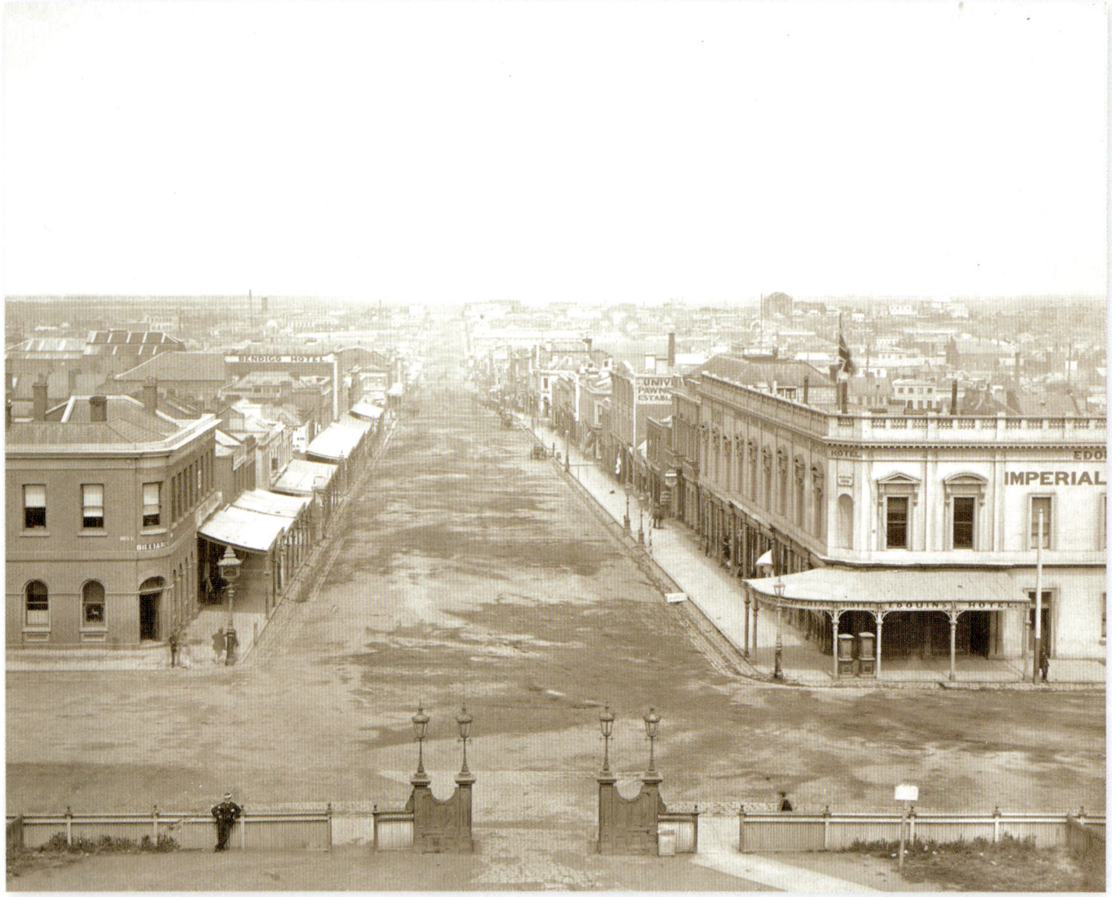

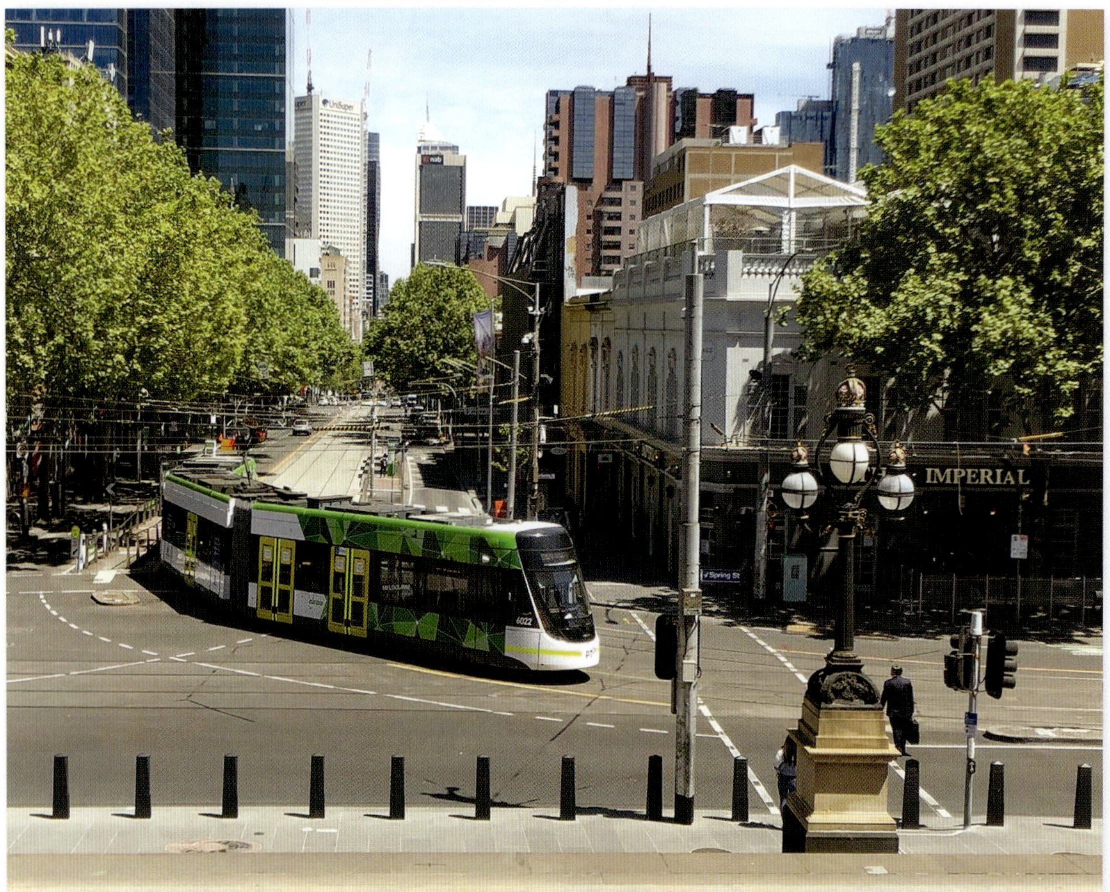

BOURKE STREET

c.1870

PHOTOGRAPHER: CHARLES NETTLETON (TOP IMAGE); CHRIS MACHERAS (BOTTOM IMAGE)

THEN AND NOW: A view of Bourke Street from the steps of Parliament House. Bourke Street was part of Robert Hoddle's 'Melbourne grid' design from 1837, and was considered to be 'out of town' until the 1840s. One thing to notice in the earlier image is just how incredibly wide the street is. Robert Hoddle, the great surveyor, had incredible foresight into the city that Melbourne would become.

He said at the time: 'I staked the main streets ninety-nine feet wide, and after having done so, I was ordered by the Governor to make them sixty-six feet wide; but upon my urging the Governor, and convincing him that wide streets were advantageous on the score of health, and convenience to the future city of Victoria, he consented to let me have my will. I therefore gave up my objection to the narrow lanes thirty-three feet wide.'

BURKE & WILLS MONUMENT

c. 1870

PHOTOGRAPHER: AMERICAN & AUSTRALASIAN PHOTOGRAPHIC COMPANY
SOURCE: MITCHELL LIBRARY, STATE LIBRARY OF NEW SOUTH WALES

The Burke and Wills monument at Collins and Russell streets.

Unveiled in 1865, the monument remained on Collins Street until 1886, when it was moved to Spring Street to make way for cable trams.

It was moved again in 1973 to the Carlton Gardens during the construction of the underground railway loop, and again in 1979 to the City Square.

In 1993 it underwent two months' restoration before being relocated to its fifth and most recent site.

It was moved again in 2017 for the Metro Tunnel project.

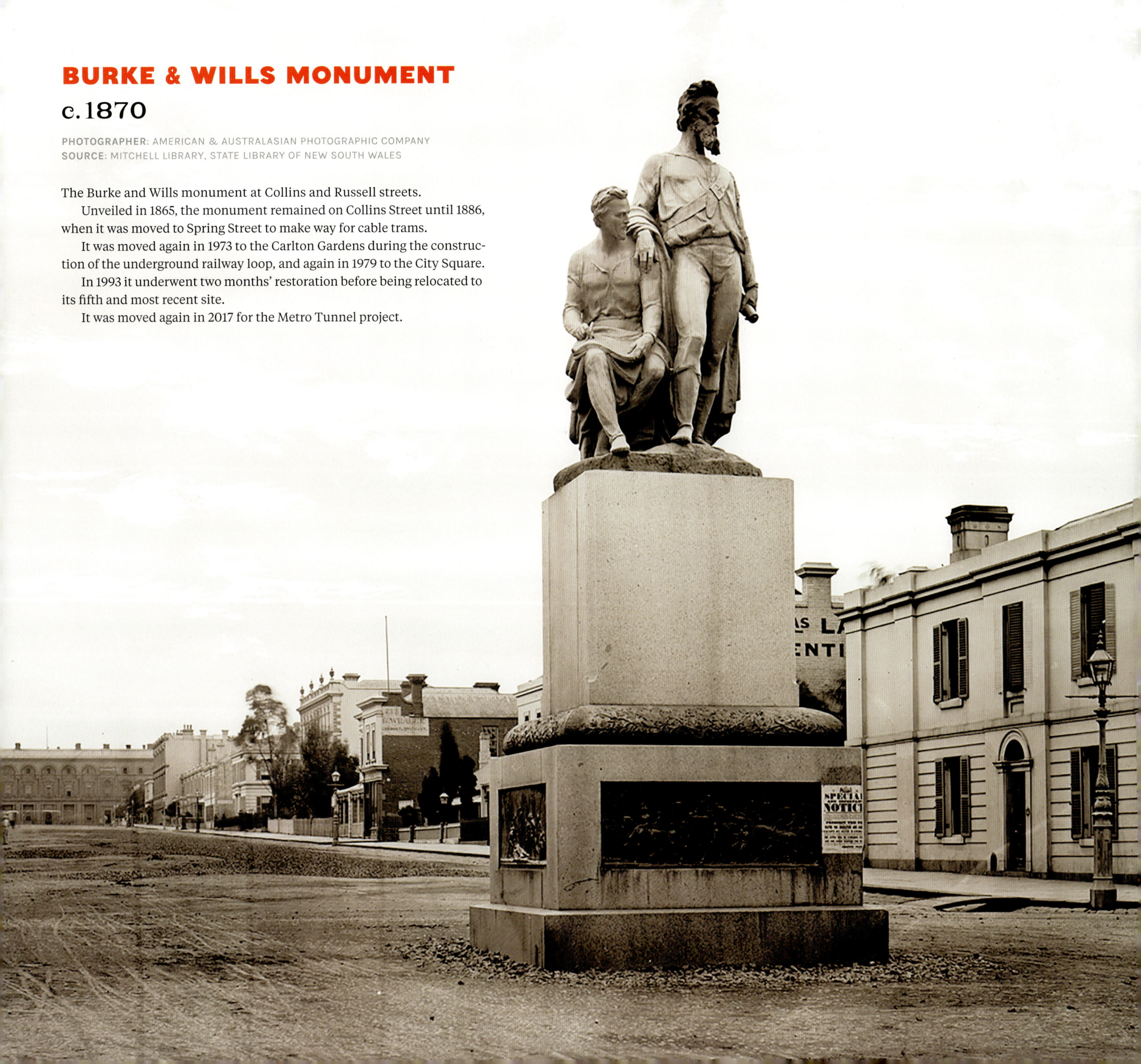

SPRING STREET

c.1870

PHOTOGRAPHER: CHARLES NETTLETON

The wide thoroughfare in the foreground is Spring Street, with a horse and cart standing on the corner of Little Collins Street.

We can see buildings, hotels, churches, and the names of businesses such as the Ulster Hotel, J. Eldridge Silk Dyer, the Standard Hotel, and the Scots Church. We can also see Port Phillip Bay in the distance.

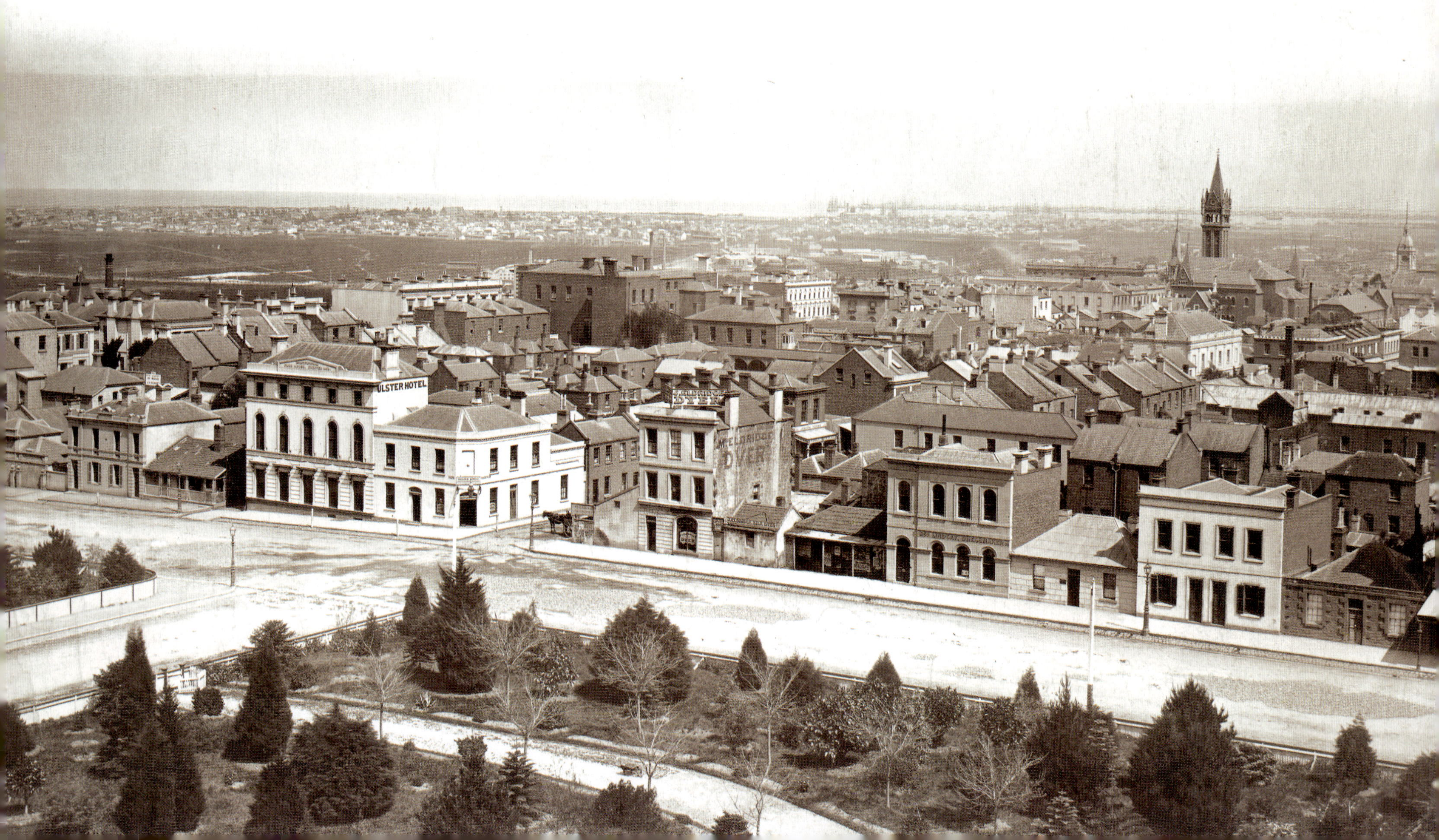

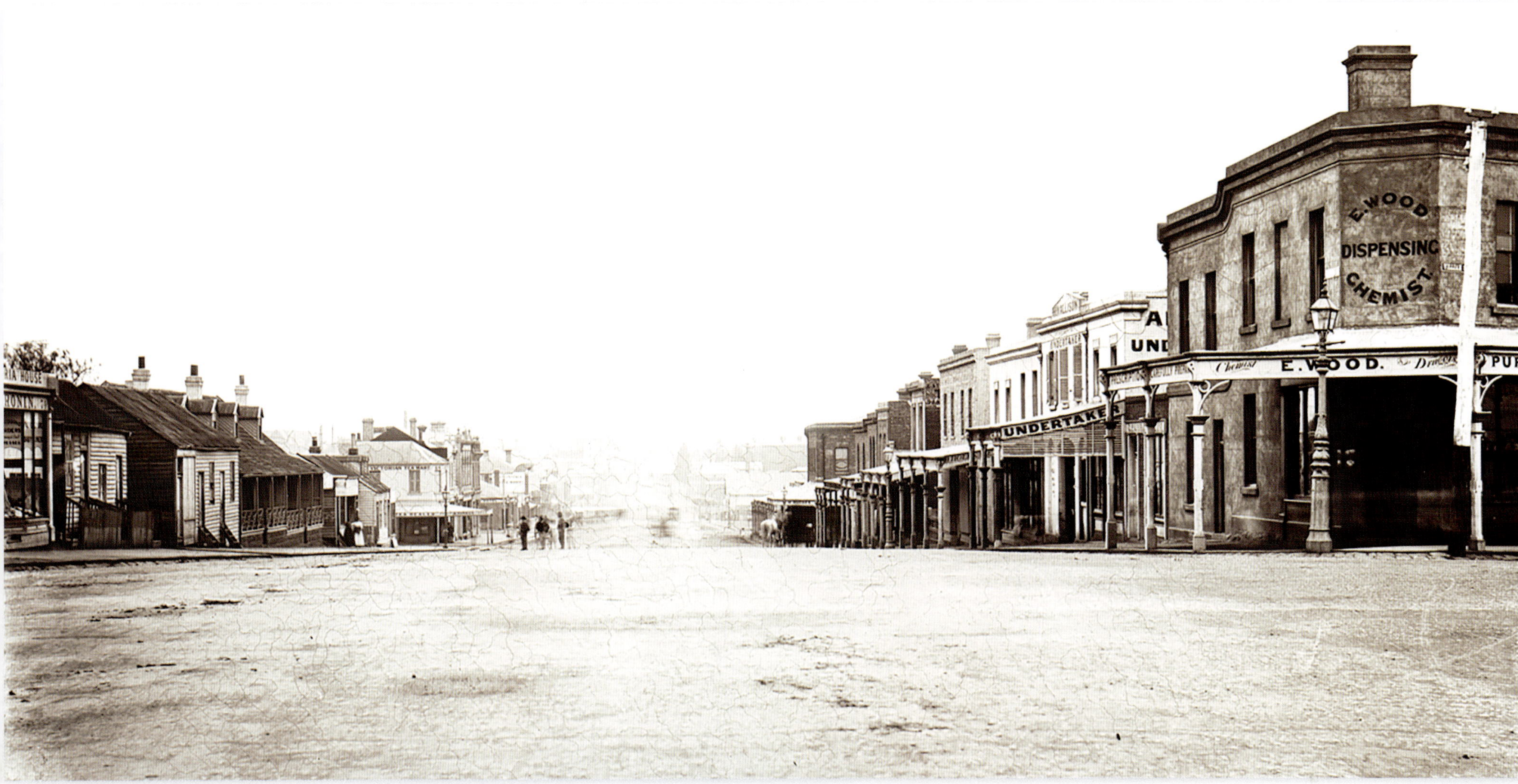

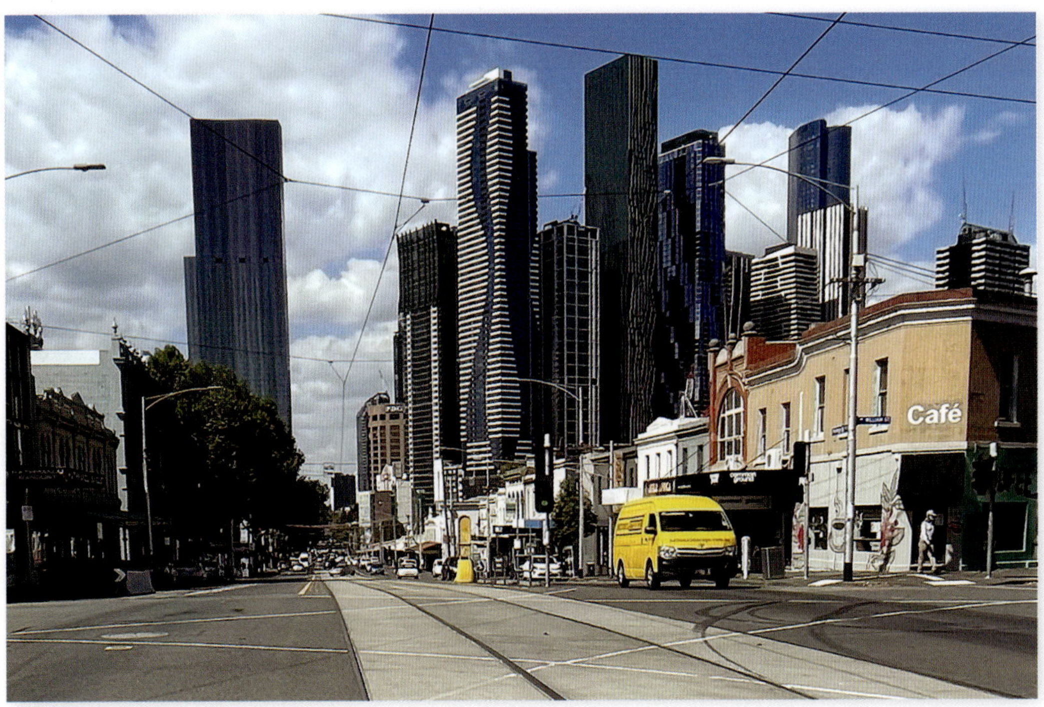

VICTORIA STREET, WEST MELBOURNE

c.1870

PHOTOGRAPHER: AMERICAN & AUSTRALASIAN PHOTOGRAPHIC COMPANY (TOP IMAGE); CHRIS MACHERAS (BOTTOM IMAGE)
SOURCE: MITCHELL LIBRARY, STATE LIBRARY OF NEW SOUTH WALES

THEN AND NOW: A 150-year difference! It's Victoria Street, West Melbourne, looking towards the city. To the left of the street is Hotham (North Melbourne), and on the right side is West Melbourne. Further down on the right is the Queen Victoria Market.

E. Wood operated a chemist on the righthand corner. The building is, quite astoundingly, still standing today, along with a few others on the right.

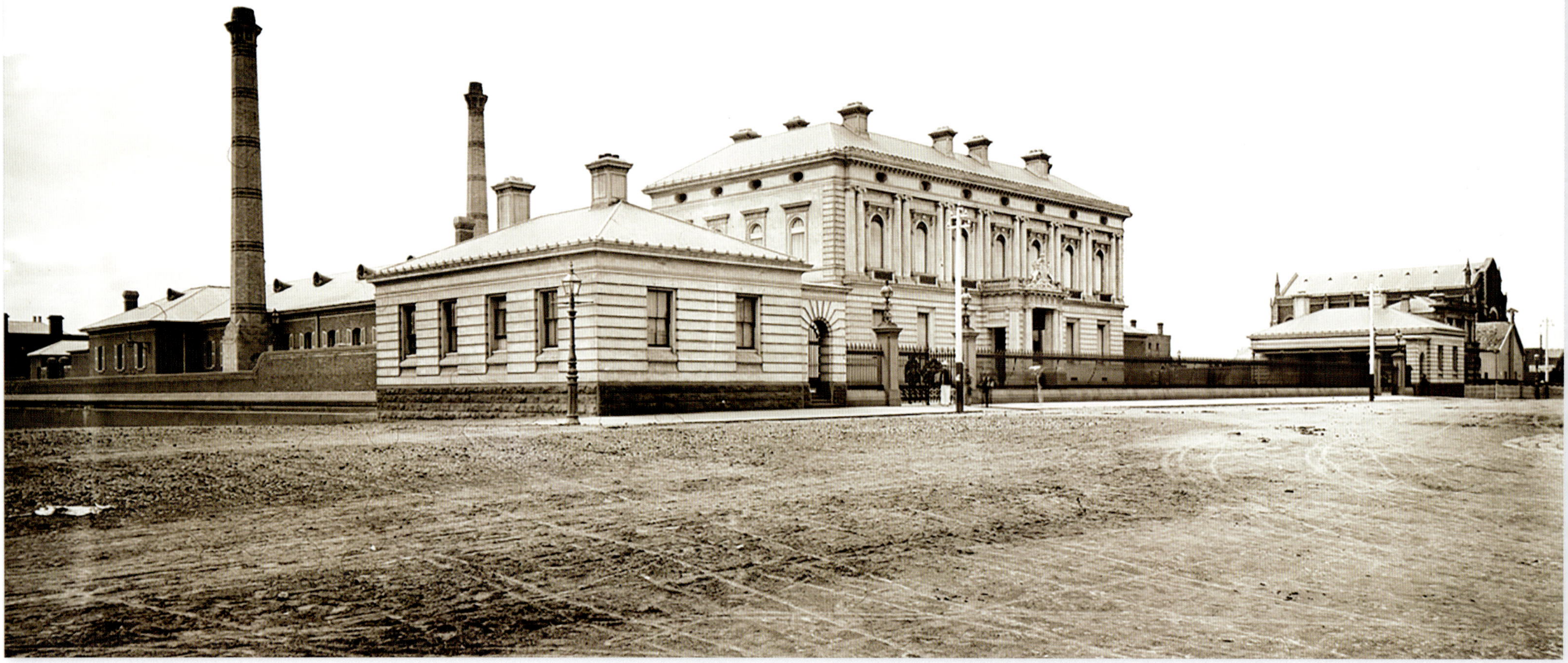

FORMER ROYAL MINT, WILLIAM STREET

c.1872

PHOTOGRAPHER: AMERICAN & AUSTRALASIAN PHOTOGRAPHIC COMPANY
SOURCE: MITCHELL LIBRARY, STATE LIBRARY OF NEW SOUTH WALES

Take a walk along William Street today, in Melbourne's legal district, and across from the Federal Circuit Court you will find the former Royal Mint building. Today it is home to the Hellenic Museum, showcasing an astonishing collection of ancient Greek artefacts. It's fitting that they are housed in a building of such opulence, with its own fascinating history.

As you can see, a factory complex with a large chimney once occupied the rear of the building. The Melbourne Mint opened in 1872, manufacturing gold coins at a time when Melbourne was growing at an exponential rate. J. J. Clark, the architect behind the Old Treasury Building, also designed this gem.

In 1969, the coin-minting equipment was demolished, and all coin production was moved to Canberra.

TEMPERANCE HALL, RICHMOND

c.1873

PHOTOGRAPHER: GEORGE ROSS REID (TOP IMAGE); CHRIS MACHERAS (BOTTOM IMAGE)

THEN AND NOW: The former Hibernian Hall at 316 Church Street, Richmond, was constructed in 1873. It was purposely built as a temperance hall for the newly formed Richmond Temperance Society. A number of temperance societies emerged at this time, advocating abstinence from alcohol.

By the 1930s the hall was being used as a meeting place for the Hibernian Australasian Catholic Benefit Society.

Next time you pass this location, look out for it. Not many are aware of the connection this grand hall had to the temperance movement for over fifty years.

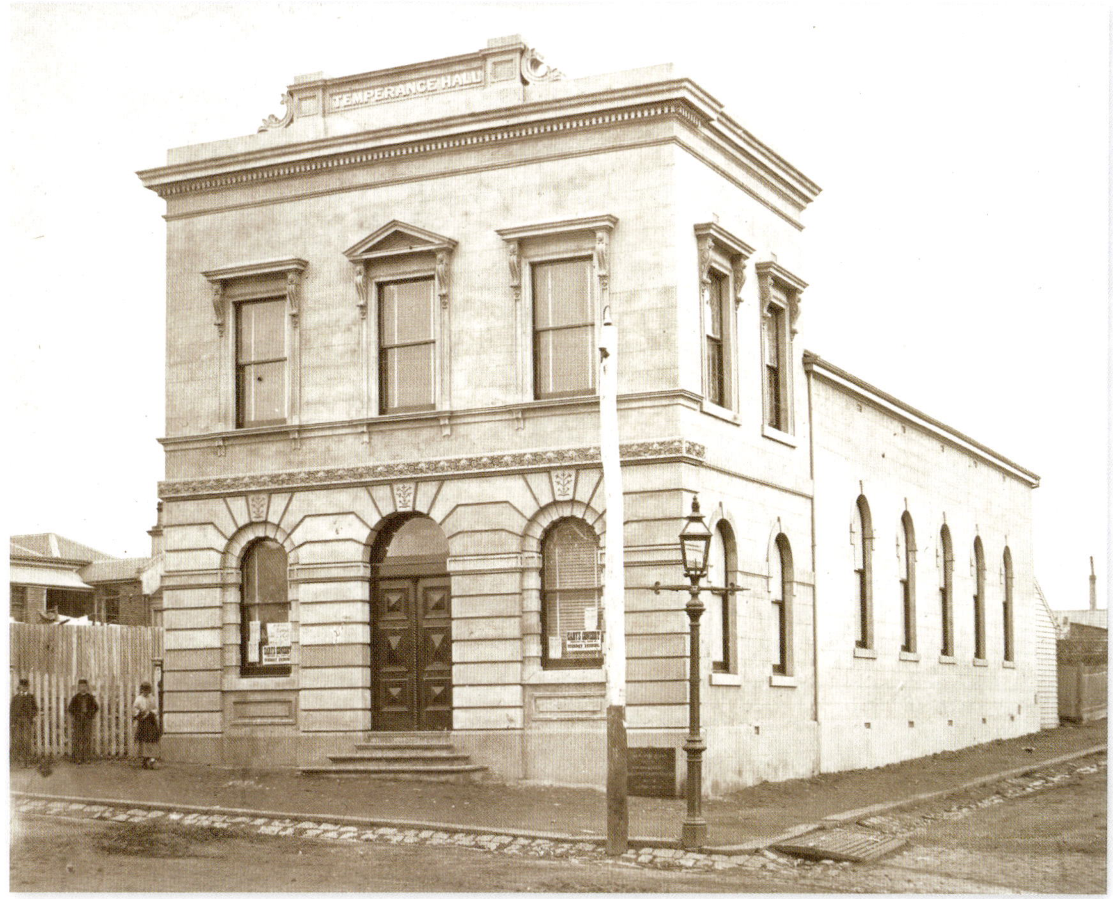

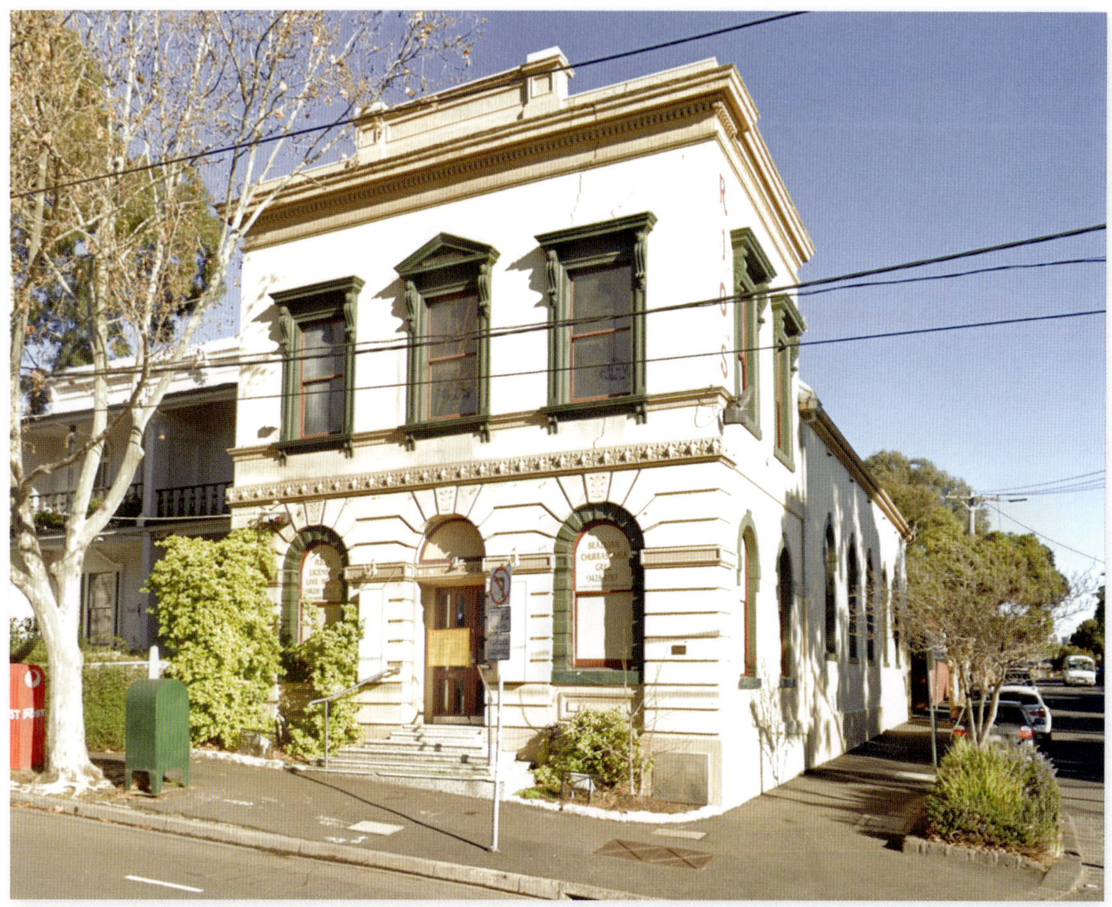

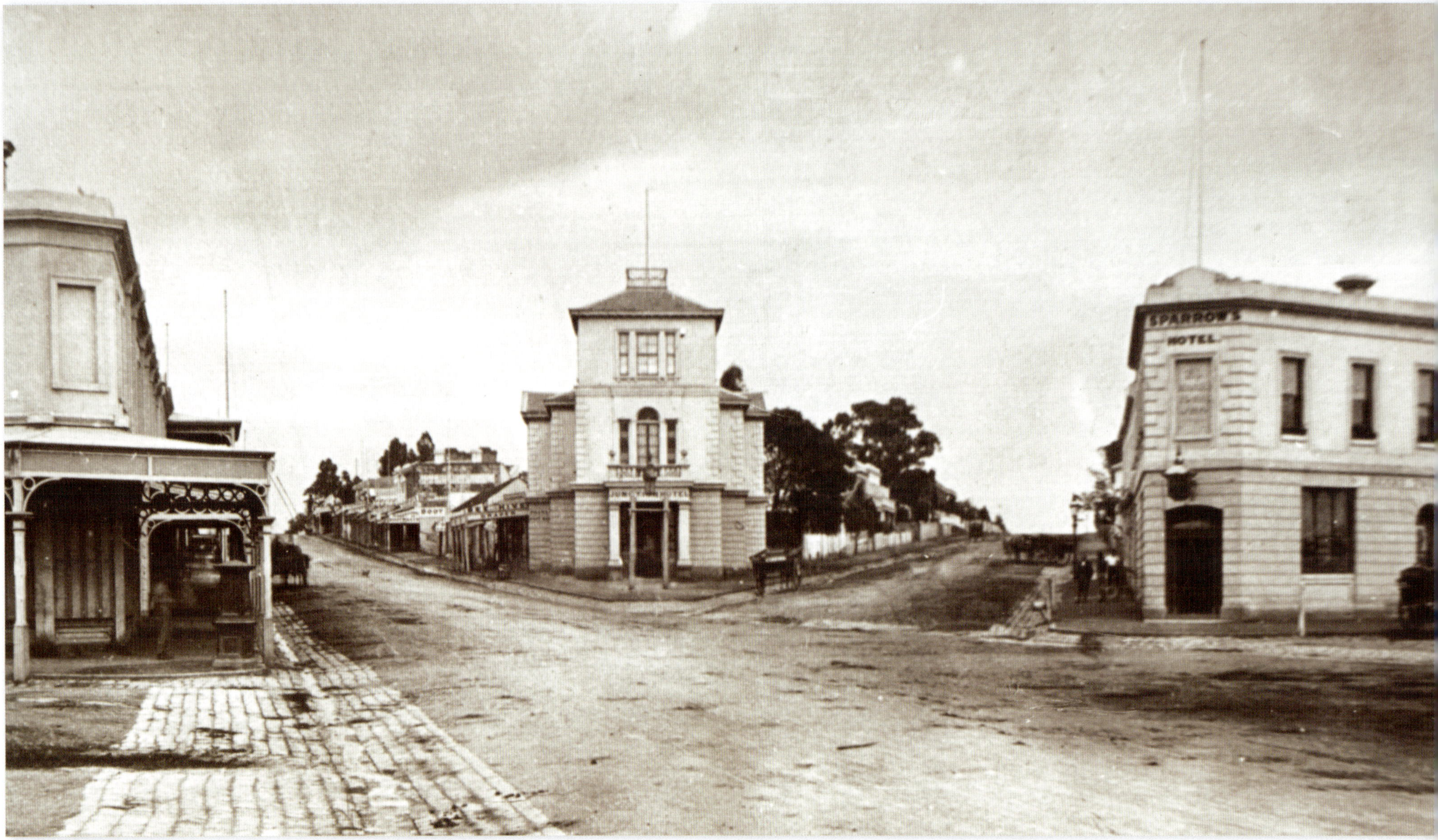

ST KILDA JUNCTION

c.1873

PHOTOGRAPHER: UNKNOWN

Gobsmacked. This is St Kilda Junction around 150 years ago.

The building in the middle is one of the earliest hotels in St Kilda, the original Grand Junction Hotel — famous for always flying the St Kilda flag high when the St Kilda Saints won a footy game, and for flying it at half-mast when they lost. The hotel was extensively rebuilt in a grander style, but was, sadly, demolished in 1973 when a city-planning decision was made to widen High Street. For many it was the end of an era in St Kilda, as the main bar, once abundant with photos of local sporting legends, was torn down.

Before 1966, St Kilda Junction comprised a tangled intersection of eight streets. In the late 1960s, the state government developed plans for a major revamp of the intersection, which ultimately led to the junction we recognise today.

LYGON & QUEENSBERRY STREETS, CARLTON

c.1875

PHOTOGRAPHER: CHARLES NETTLETON

Taken from St Andrew's Church, Carlton.

St Andrew's was an old bluestone church known as the Gaelic Church, which was established on the site in 1854. It was demolished in 1938, and the stone was used to build a church in Glen Iris. The former Presbyterian manse is still standing today on Rathdowne Street.

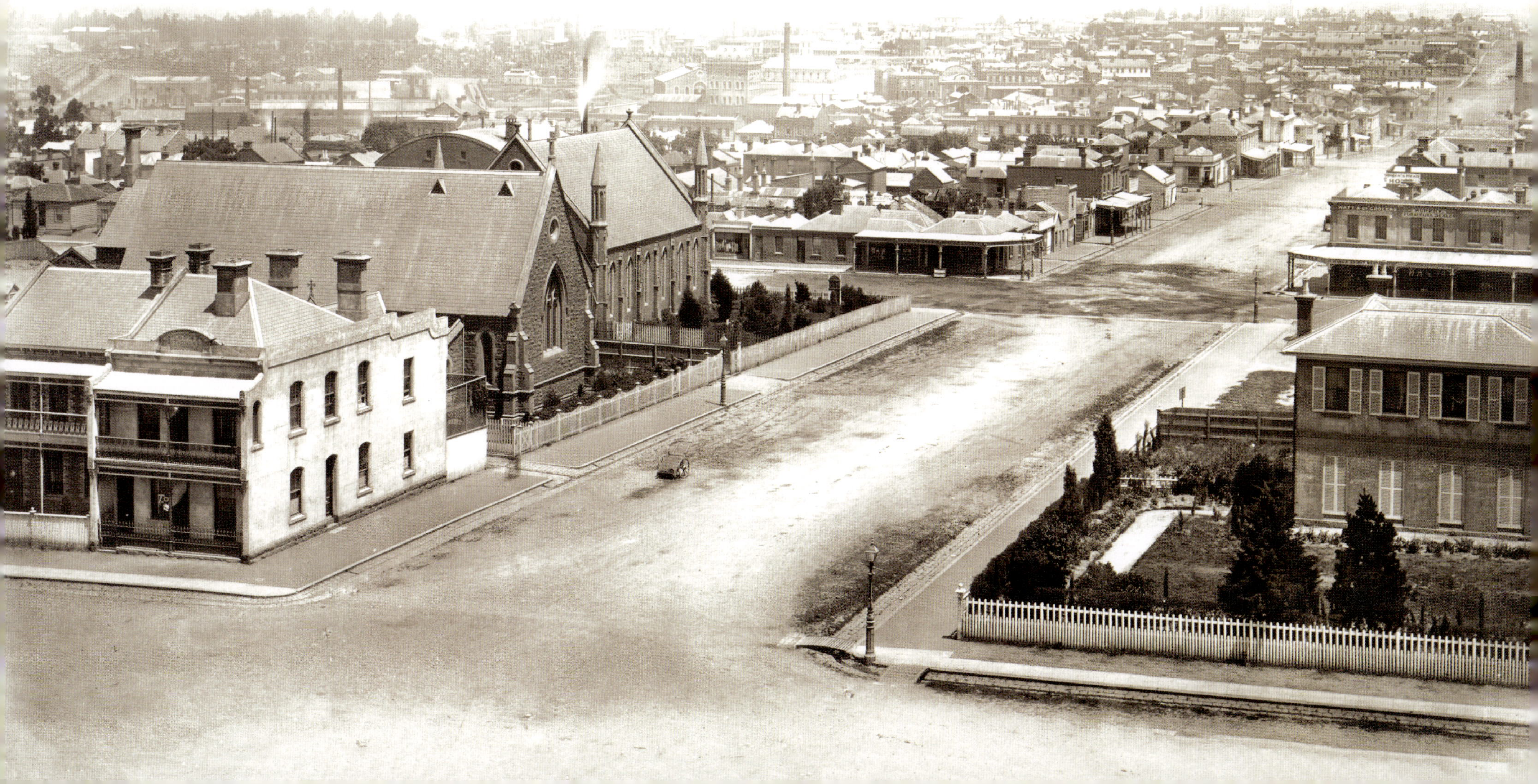

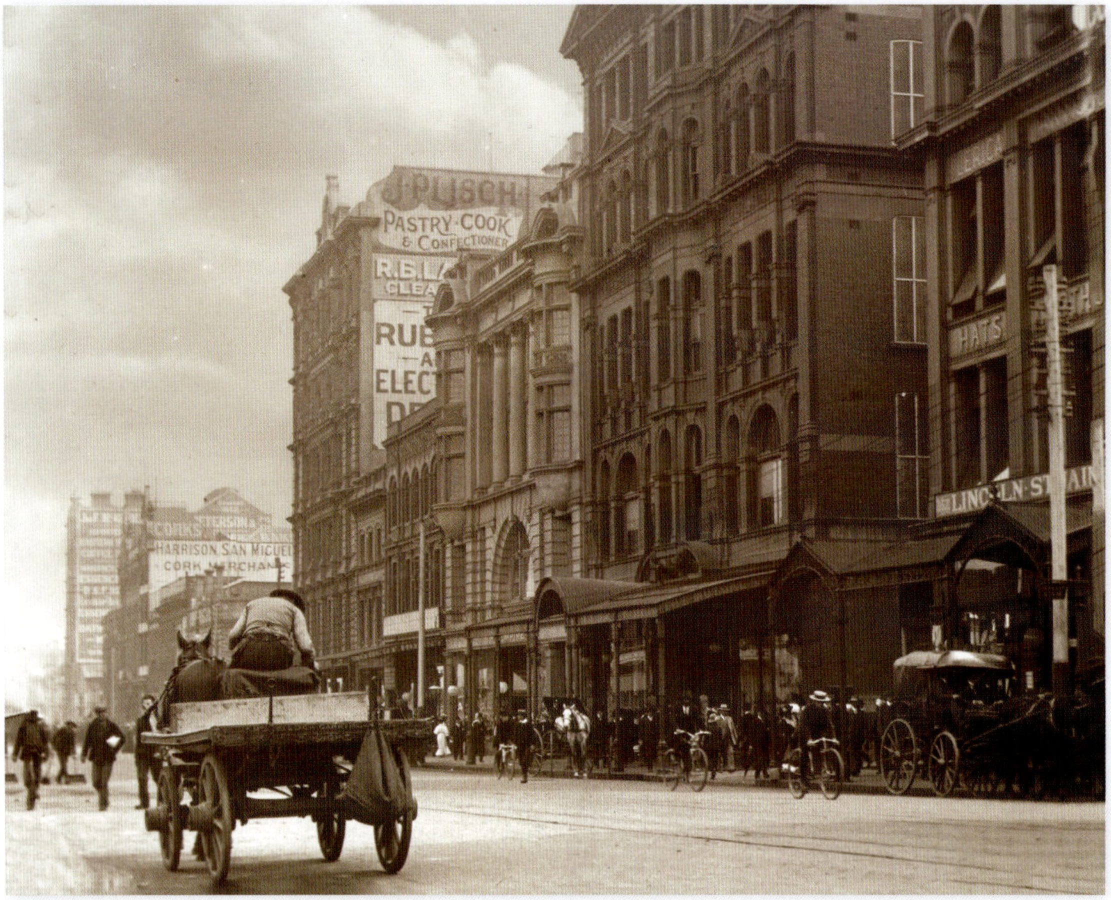

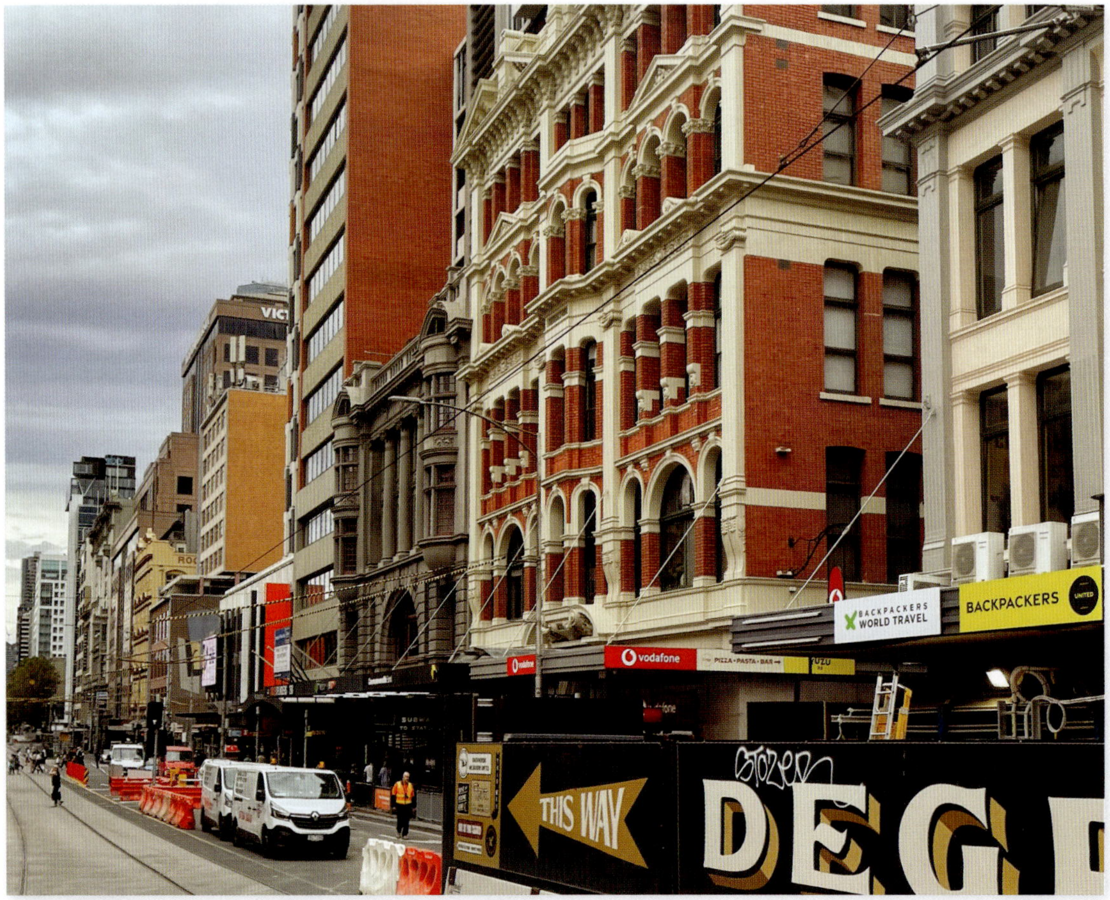

FLINDERS STREET

c. 1875

PHOTOGRAPHER: JOHN HENRY HARVEY (TOP IMAGE); CHRIS MACHERAS (BOTTOM IMAGE)

THEN AND NOW: A busy scene on Flinders Street as Melburnians go about their day beneath those exquisite verandas. The architecture of the time was very ornate, reflecting Melbourne's boom era during the gold rush.

The location appears to be at 242 Flinders Street, and the businesses include J. Plisch — Pastry Cook & Confectioner, which sounds delicious.

BOURKE STREET

c.1875

PHOTOGRAPHER: UNKNOWN

This is an incredible view of Bourke Street looking east from halfway between Elizabeth and Queen streets.

What almost looks like a castle in the distance is actually St Patrick's Cathedral in mid-construction.

Can you spot those three little children taking in the view? They are standing before the General Post Office (GPO) building, which is far shorter than it appears today.

With the rapid growth of Victoria following the gold rush, the GPO became overcrowded. Initially, the plan was to extend the building to Little Bourke Street. Instead, a third level, an attic level, and a taller and more ornate clock tower, all designed by Mr A.E. Johnson, were added.

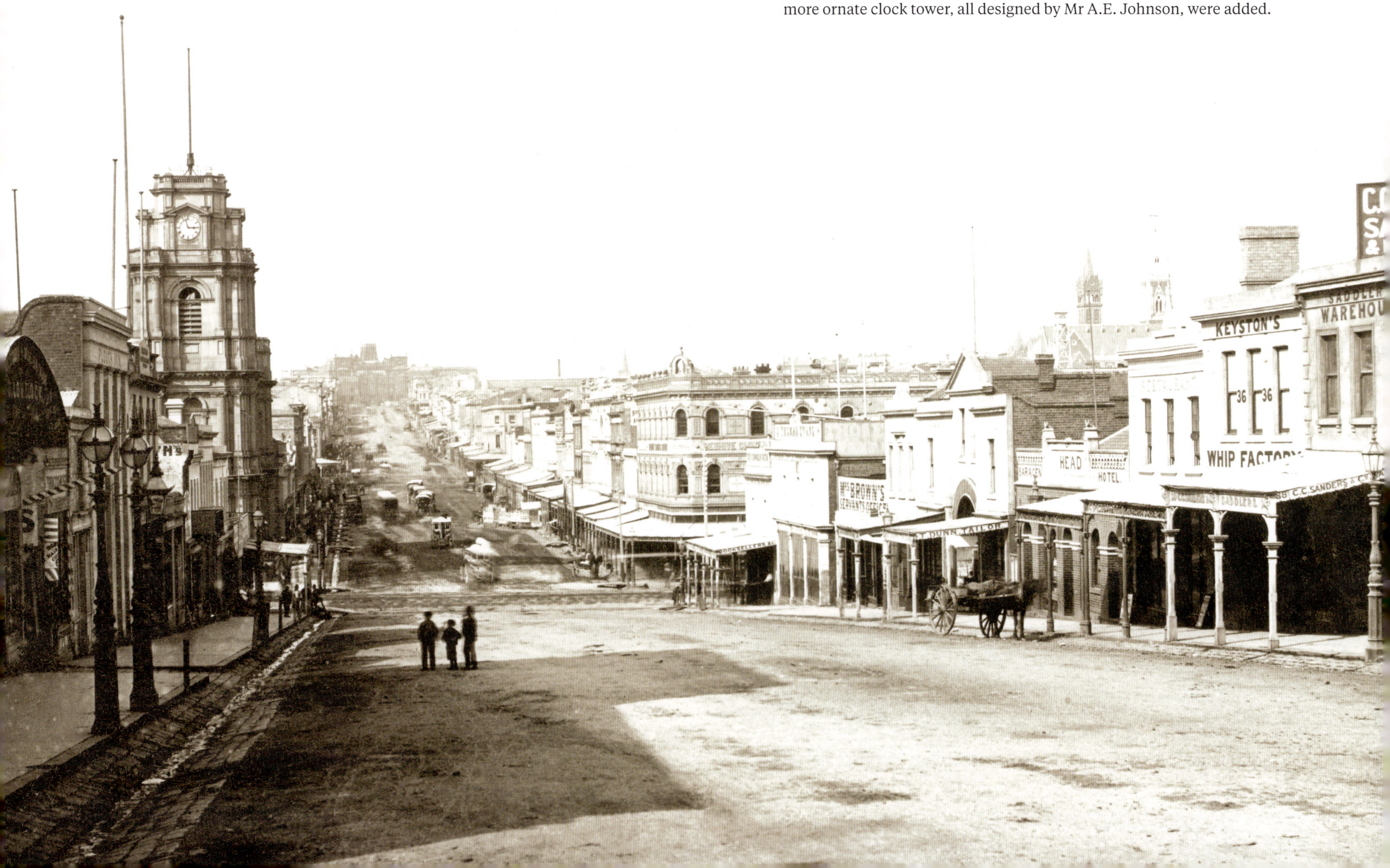

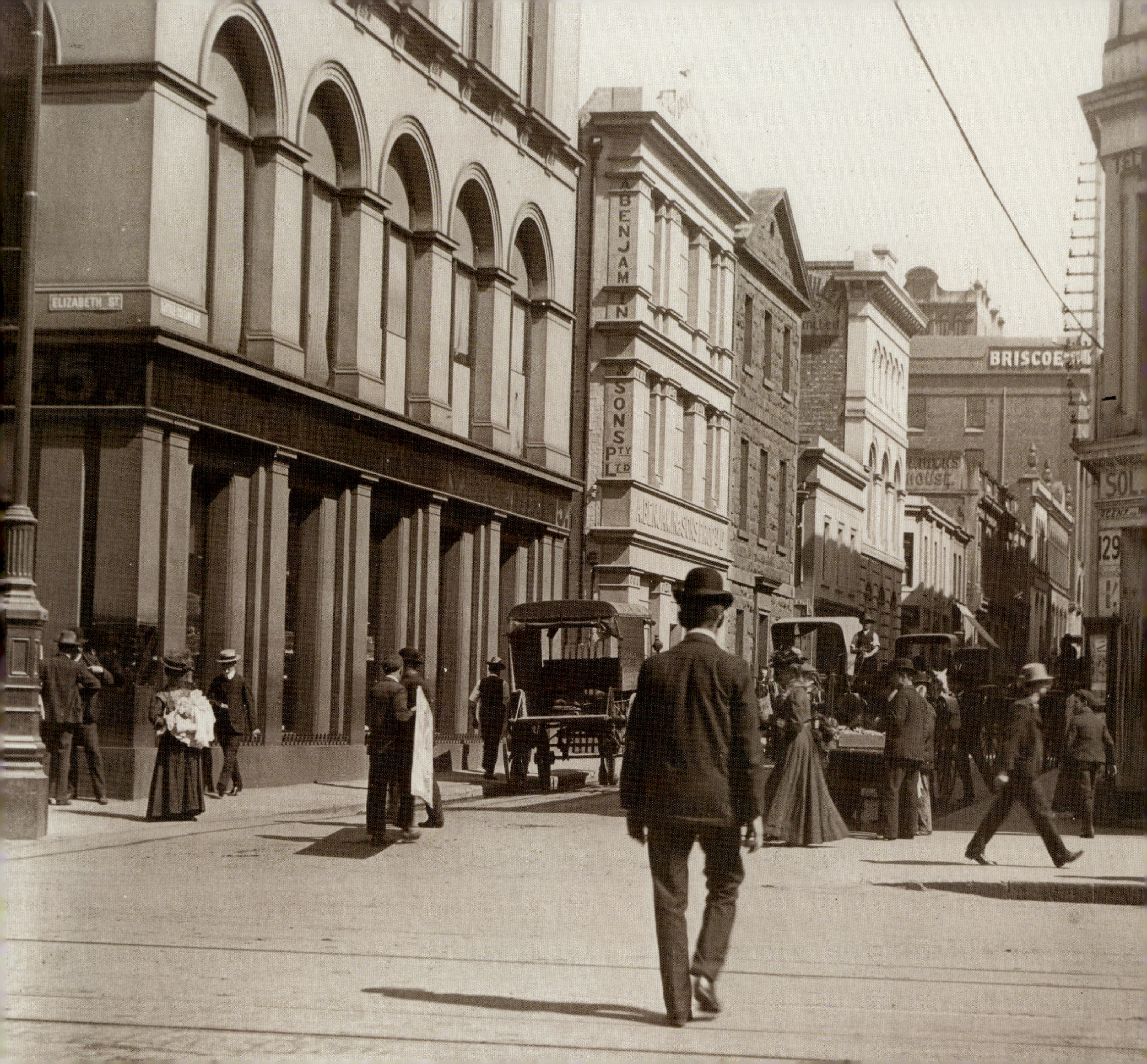
ELIZABETH ST
A BENJAMIN & SONS PTY LTD
BRISCOE

BOURKE STREET ▶

c.1875

PHOTOGRAPHER: AMERICAN & AUSTRALASIAN PHOTOGRAPHIC COMPANY (TOP IMAGE); CHRIS MACHERAS (BOTTOM IMAGE)
SOURCE: MITCHELL LIBRARY, STATE LIBRARY OF NEW SOUTH WALES

THEN AND NOW: The General Post Office building of today has additional levels and a taller and more ornate clock tower. These extensions were completed in 1887. The mansard roof originally intended for the central section of the Elizabeth Street facade was also constructed, as well as similar curved roofs as part of the tower, which, along with the increased height, gave the building much of its Parisian grandeur.

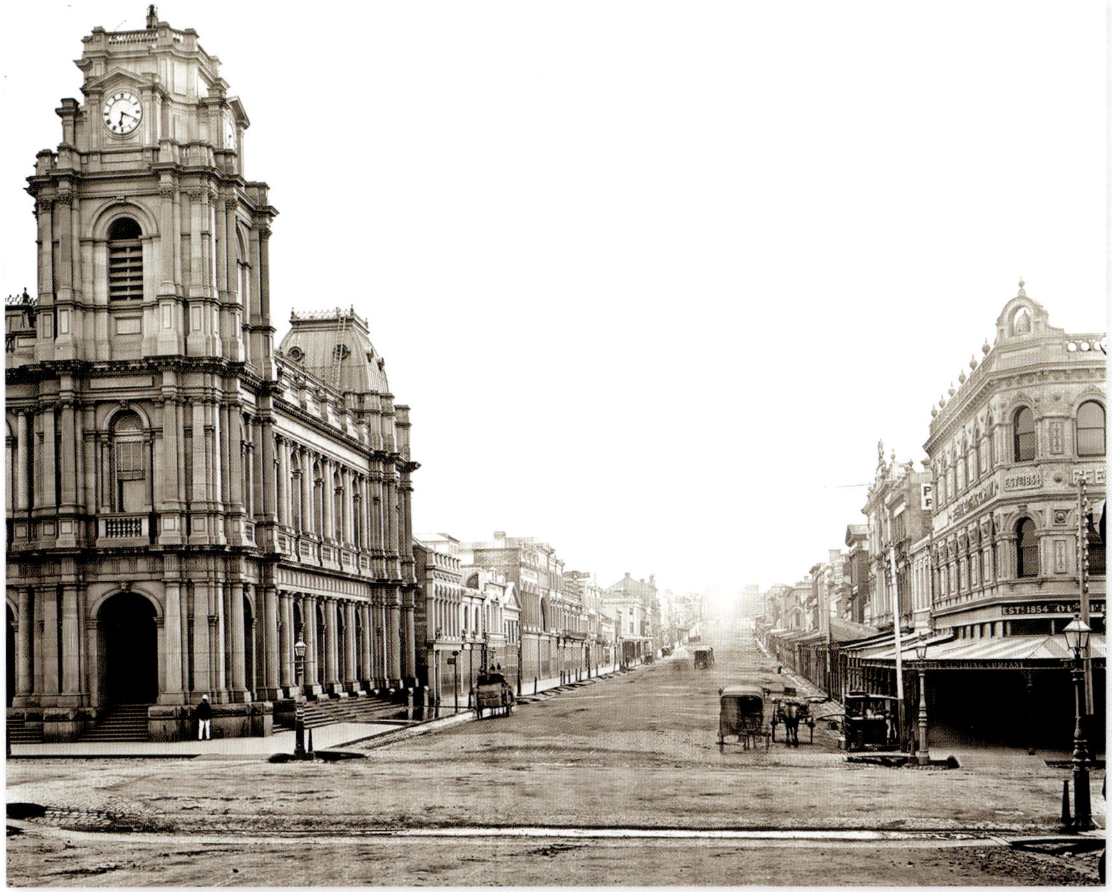

◀ LITTLE COLLINS & ELIZABETH STREETS

c.1875

PHOTOGRAPHER: JOHN HENRY HARVEY

A street scene at the corner of Little Collins and Elizabeth streets.

At 119–25 Little Collins Street, you can see signage for Iron Merchants and A. Benjamin & Sons Pty Ltd — an indication of Melbourne's industrial beginnings. I can't imagine walking down Little Collins Street today and popping into an iron merchant's factory.

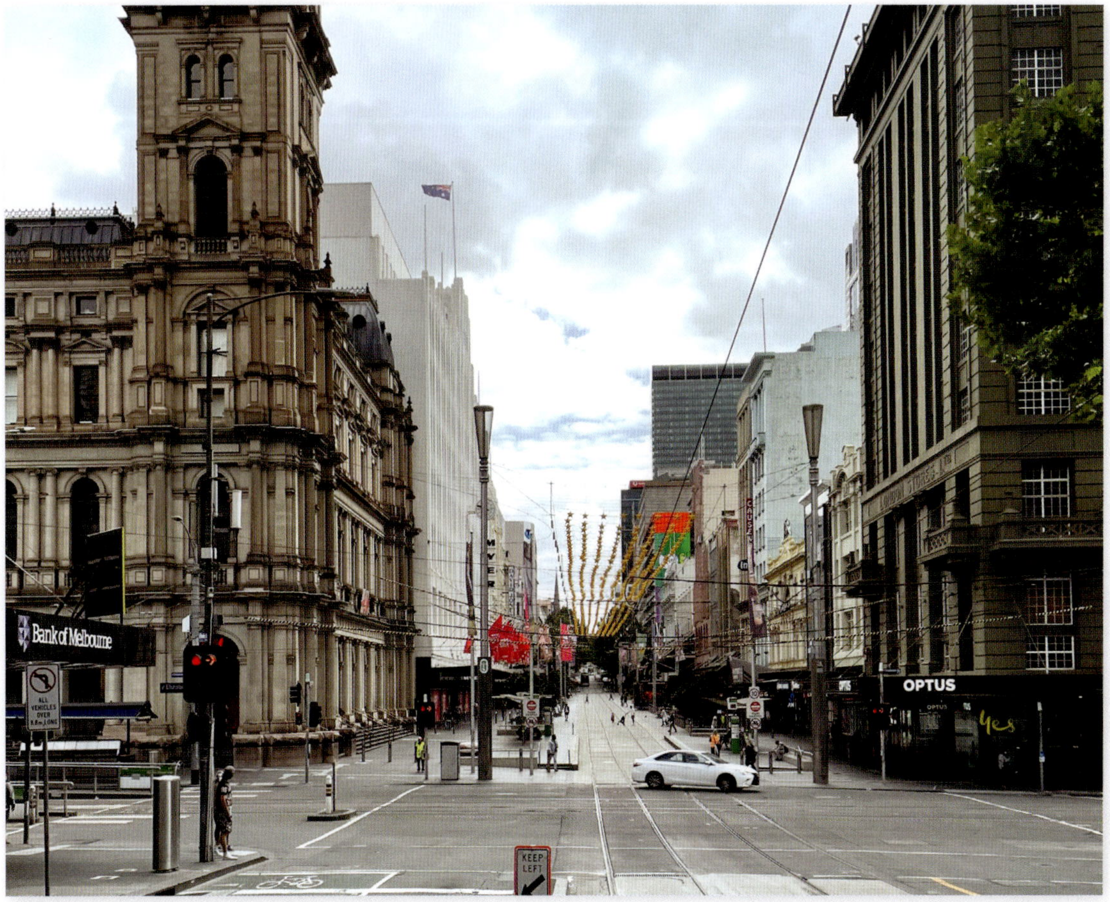

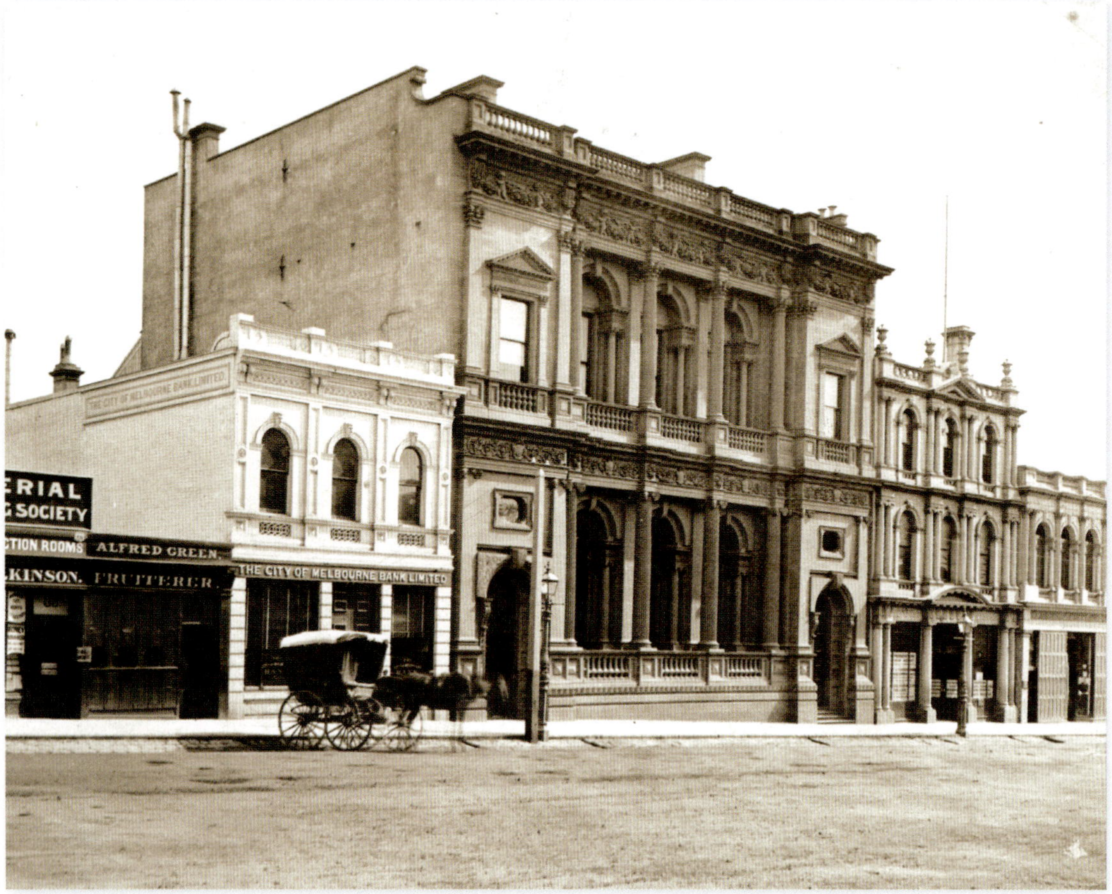

UNIVERSITY OF MELBOURNE, PARKVILLE

c. 1879 & 1954

PHOTOGRAPHER: J.W. LINDT (TOP IMAGE); MARK STRIZIC (BOTTOM IMAGE)

The University of Melbourne began its classes with just four professors and sixteen students in 1855. It is the second-oldest university in Australia.

The university itself was established in 1853 after the auditor-general, Hugh Childers, announced in his 1852 budget speech the setting aside of £10,000 for the establishment of a university. Childers went on to serve as the university's first vice-chancellor until 1857.

These images feature the Old Commerce Building. You may not be aware that this ornate facade wasn't always part of the campus at Parkville.

The building is pictured in the top image in around 1879, where it was front of house of the Bank of New South Wales on Collins Street. A series of structural problems were discovered just four years after its construction. Continuing concerns with the structural integrity, along with proposals made to expand the complex, resulted in a decision to demolish in 1932.

At the time, the public expressed collective concern over the demolition of many Victoria-era buildings in Melbourne. The decision was made to save the facade and donate it to the university. It was removed carefully by Whelan the Wrecker, a prominent demolition company.

In the late 1930s the facade was incorporated into the newly constructed Old Commerce Building; you can find it today fronting the even-newer Melbourne School of Design.

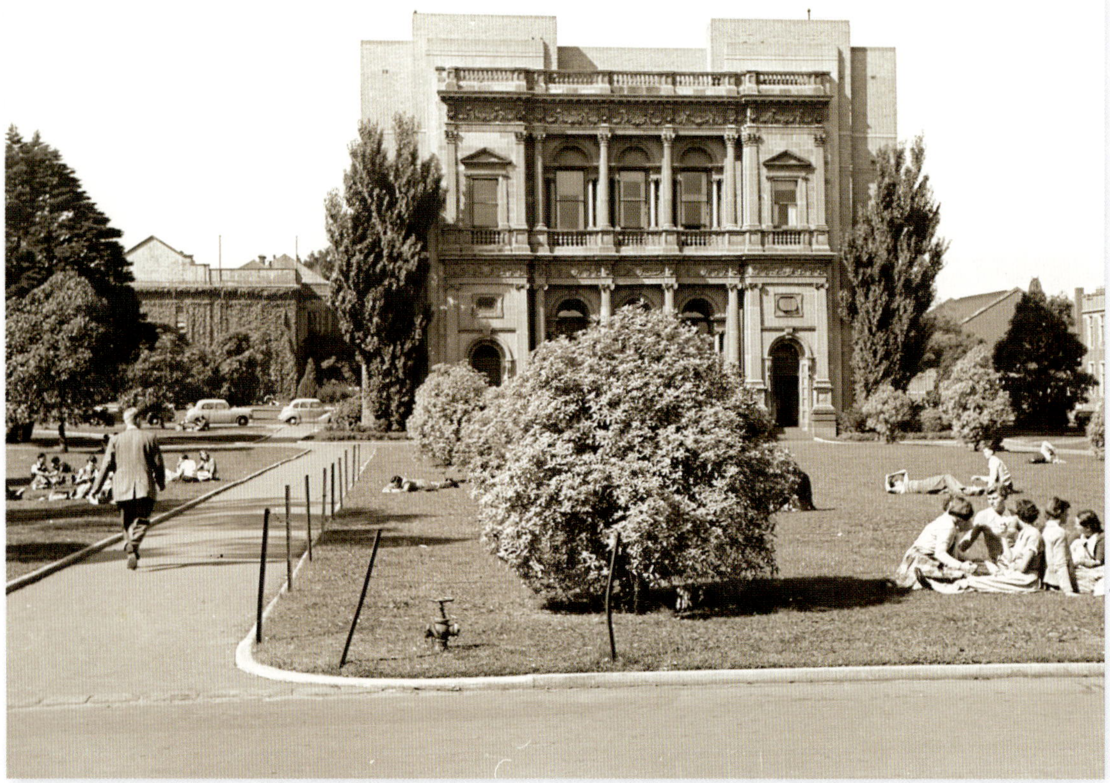

COLLINS & SPRING STREETS

c.1880

PHOTOGRAPHER: UNKNOWN

The view of Collins Street looking west from the steps of the Treasury Building. It looks pretty bare to me. Today, Collins Street is abundant in shade-giving trees.

The former townhouse on the left, at 61 Spring Street, has survived. It was built in 1877 for a wealthy pastoralist, William Campbell.

In 1901, the newly formed Commonwealth of Australia purchased the house, conveniently located close to Parliament House, to be used as ministerial and departmental offices. The office of the prime minister was located in the building from 1901 until 1912, after which it was relocated to a new purpose-built Commonwealth office block in Treasury Place.

Between 1901 and 1912, eight prime ministers occupied the building. They were Edmund Barton, Alfred Deakin (three times), Chris Watson, George Reid, and Andrew Fisher (twice), making the building of particular historical, architectural, and social significance to Melbourne and the State of Victoria.

As a side note, look at the man standing right in the middle of the street!

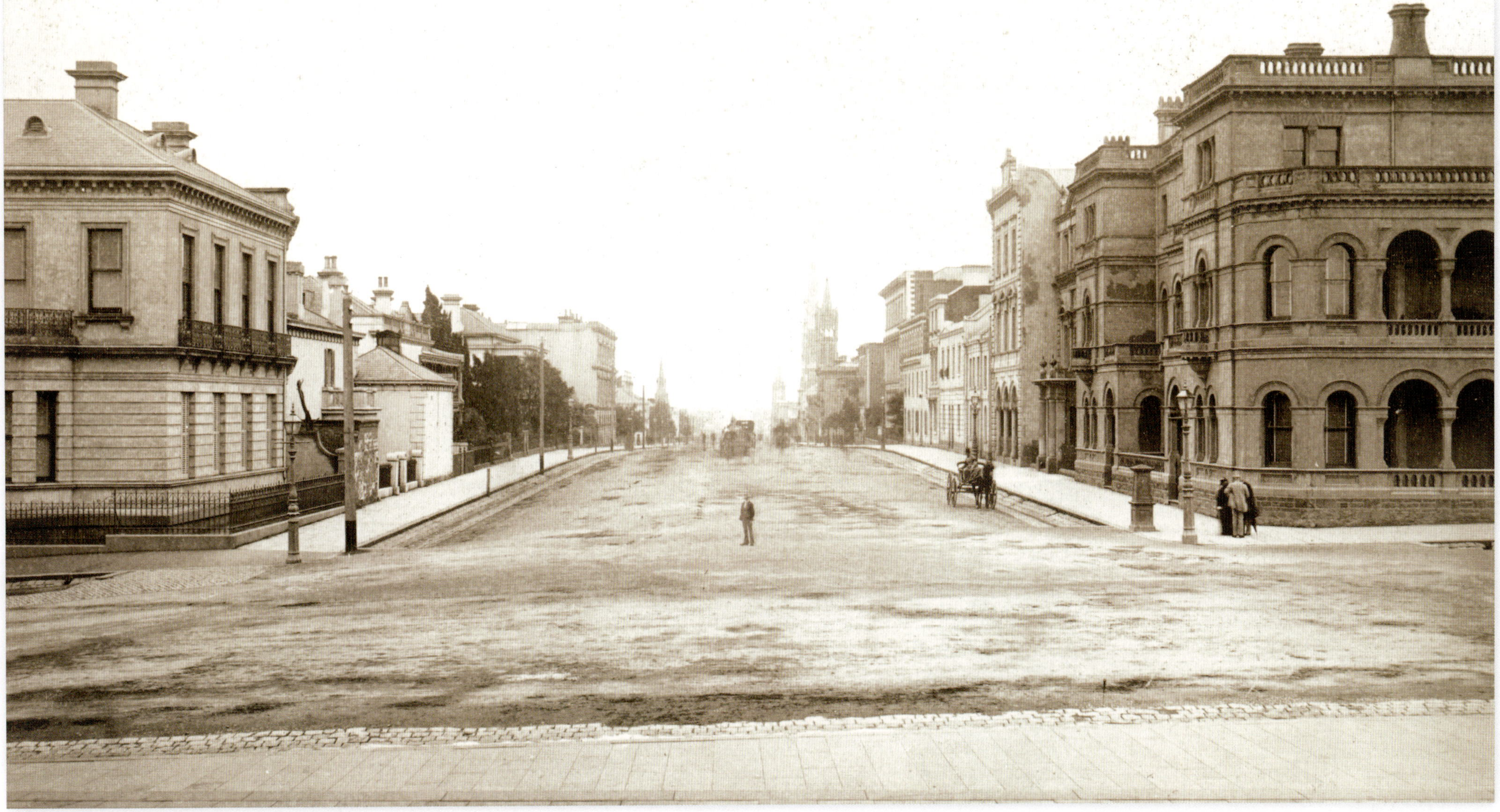

ROYAL EXHIBITION BUILDING

c. 1880

PHOTOGRAPHER: J.W. LINDT

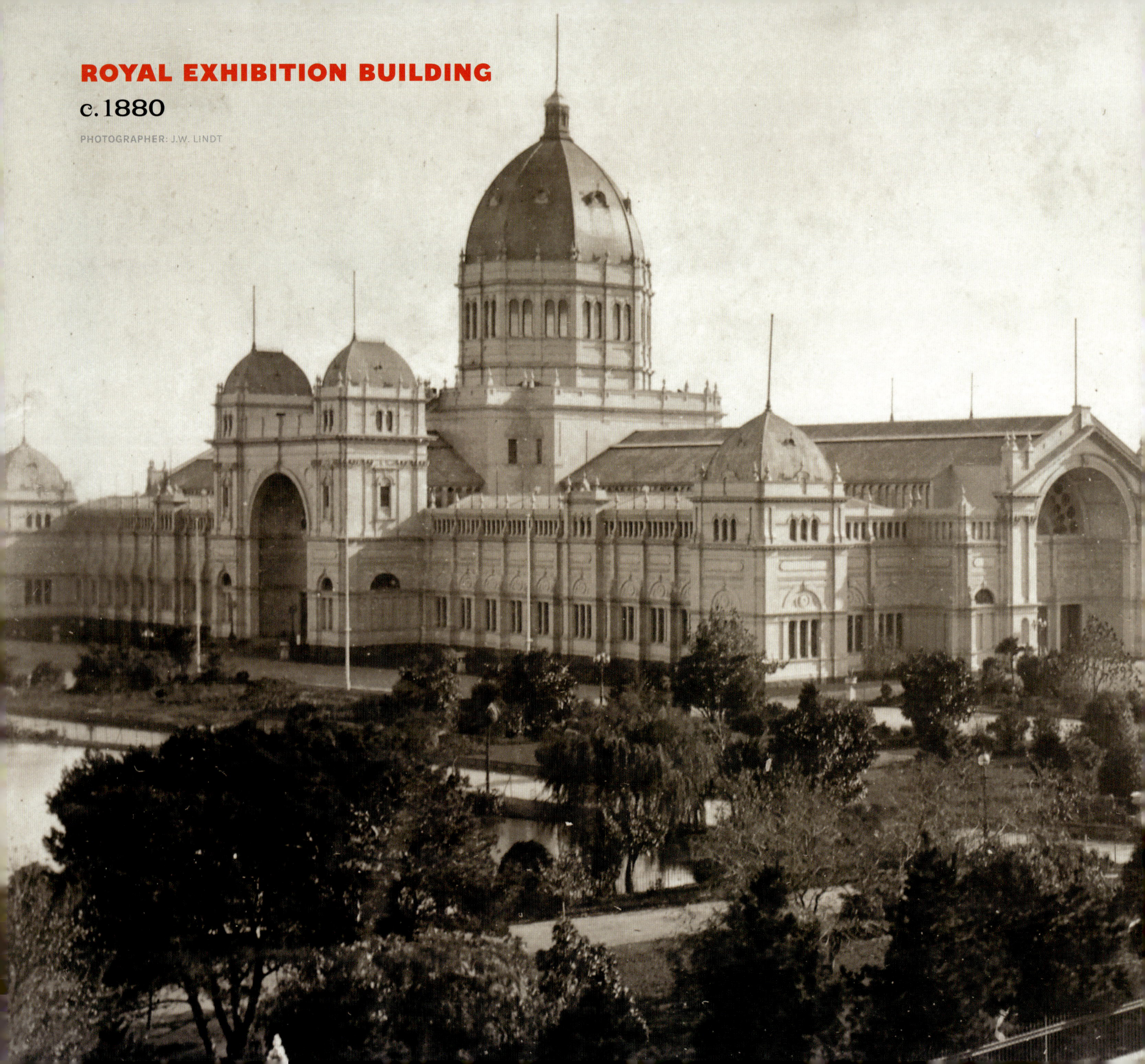

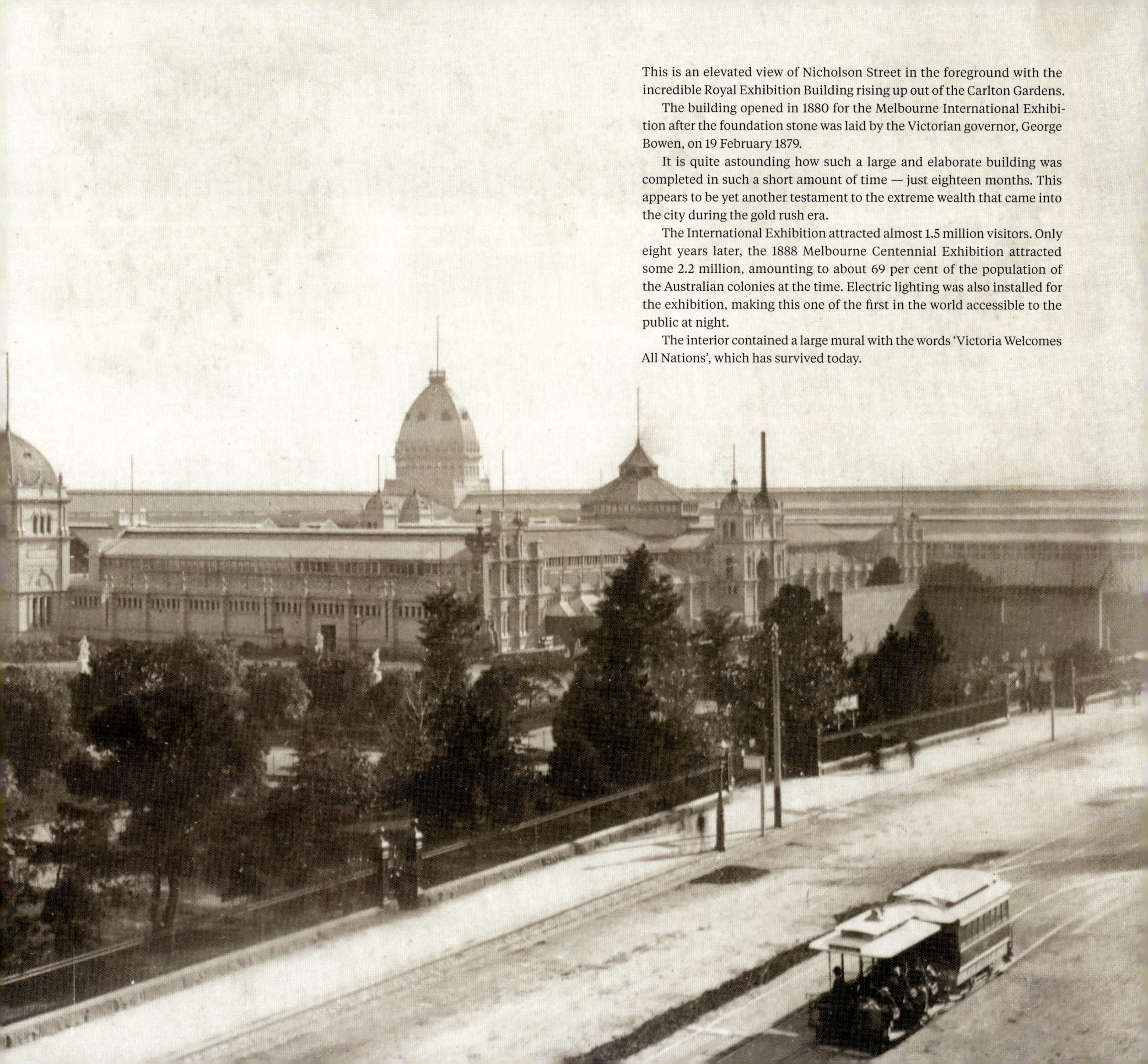

This is an elevated view of Nicholson Street in the foreground with the incredible Royal Exhibition Building rising up out of the Carlton Gardens.

The building opened in 1880 for the Melbourne International Exhibition after the foundation stone was laid by the Victorian governor, George Bowen, on 19 February 1879.

It is quite astounding how such a large and elaborate building was completed in such a short amount of time — just eighteen months. This appears to be yet another testament to the extreme wealth that came into the city during the gold rush era.

The International Exhibition attracted almost 1.5 million visitors. Only eight years later, the 1888 Melbourne Centennial Exhibition attracted some 2.2 million, amounting to about 69 per cent of the population of the Australian colonies at the time. Electric lighting was also installed for the exhibition, making this one of the first in the world accessible to the public at night.

The interior contained a large mural with the words 'Victoria Welcomes All Nations', which has survived today.

COLLINS STREET

c. 1880

PHOTOGRAPHER: UNKNOWN

A very unrecognisable Collins Street, looking west across Elizabeth Street.

Today, trams run through the open streets, and high-rise office buildings command the area to Queen Street and beyond.

This is Melbourne during the time of Ned Kelly, the commencement of the construction of the Royal Exhibition Building, the first use of a parachute in Australia, and the achievement of the eight-hour-day being pronounced a public holiday in Victoria.

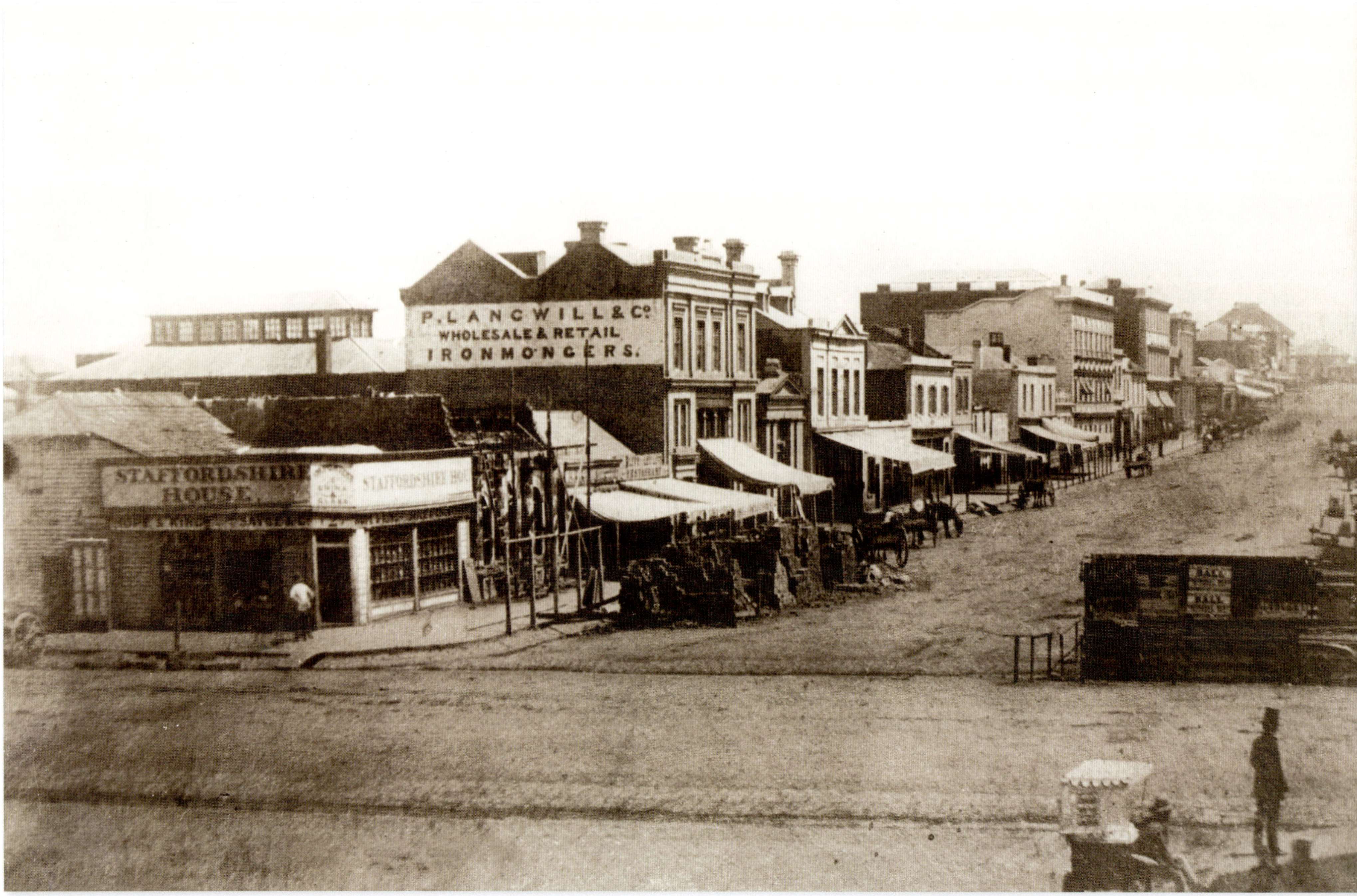

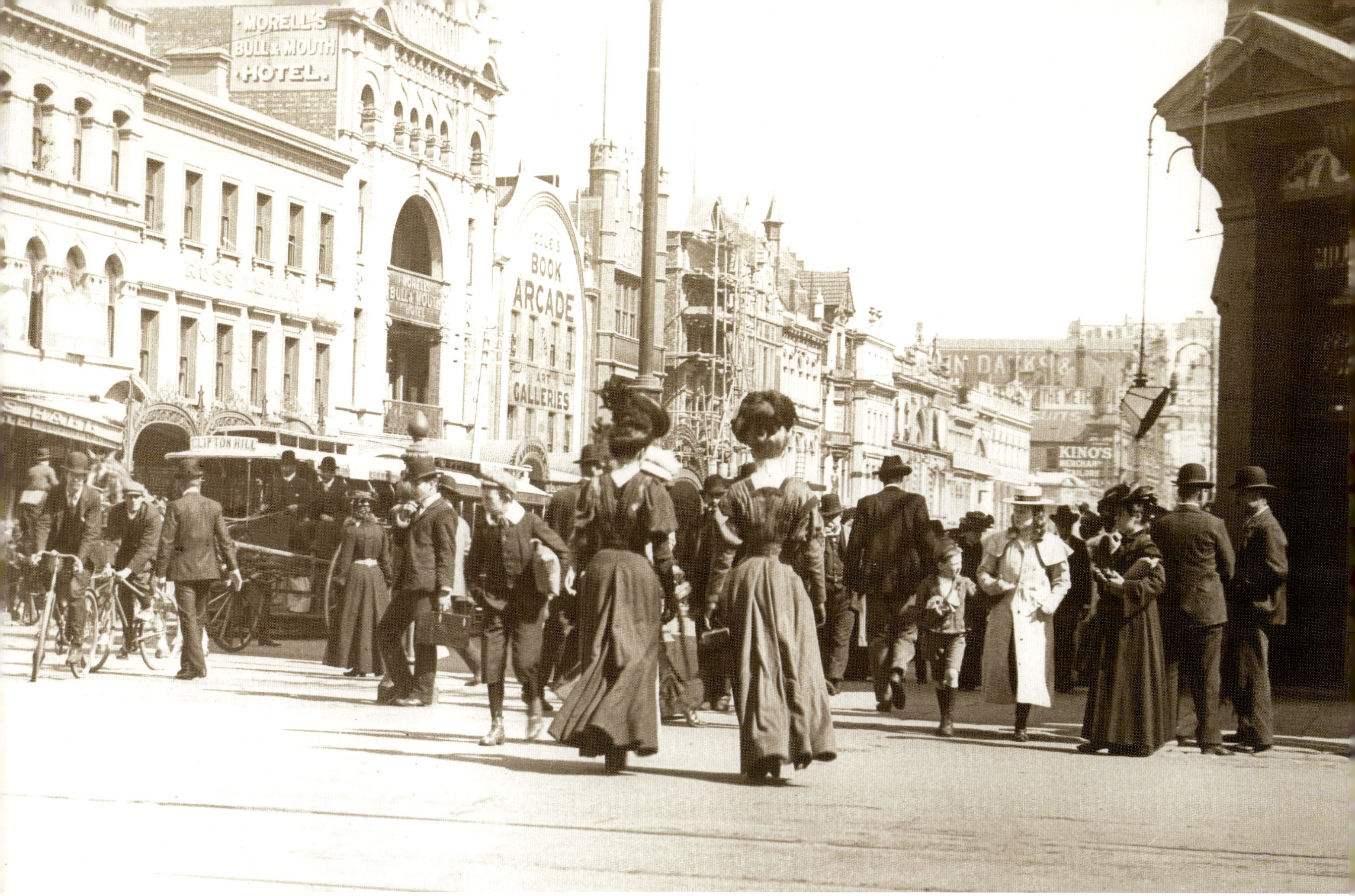

BOURKE STREET PEDESTRIANS

c.1880

PHOTOGRAPHER: JOHN HENRY

Busy street scenes on Bourke Street and Swanston Street.

What was hitting the headlines for these Melburnians?

Australia's first telephone exchange opened in Melbourne, and the Melbourne International Exhibition took place at the Royal Exhibition Building in Carlton.

In other news at the time, Melburnians learned about the capture of bushranger Ned Kelly at Glenrowan, who was subsequently hanged on 11 November 1880.

Strangely, Redmond Barry, the judge who sentenced Kelly to be hanged, died just twelve days later. Some have whispered that Ned held on a few days and took the judge with him.

'ROSTELLA', LONSDALE STREET

c.1881

PHOTOGRAPHER: CHARLES NETTLETON

Charles Nettleton, the man behind so many of these earlier depictions of Melbourne, took this panoramic shot from the tower of the Supreme Court.

The elevated view shows us just how residential the city was in those days. The opulent Victorian mansion in the foreground is 'Rostella', at 486 Lonsdale Street. This was the home of Sir Thomas Fitzgerald, an eminent surgeon. Why this well-to-do gentleman built his home at this location is unknown — it was not considered to be a prestigious part of town at the time.

Unfortunately, Rostella was demolished in 1972 to make way for a car park. (Painful, I know.)

To add a little context however, today you will find the County Court to the left, and, while the building no longer exists, the fine cast-iron gates remain. Next time you are near the intersection of Lonsdale and William streets, have a look.

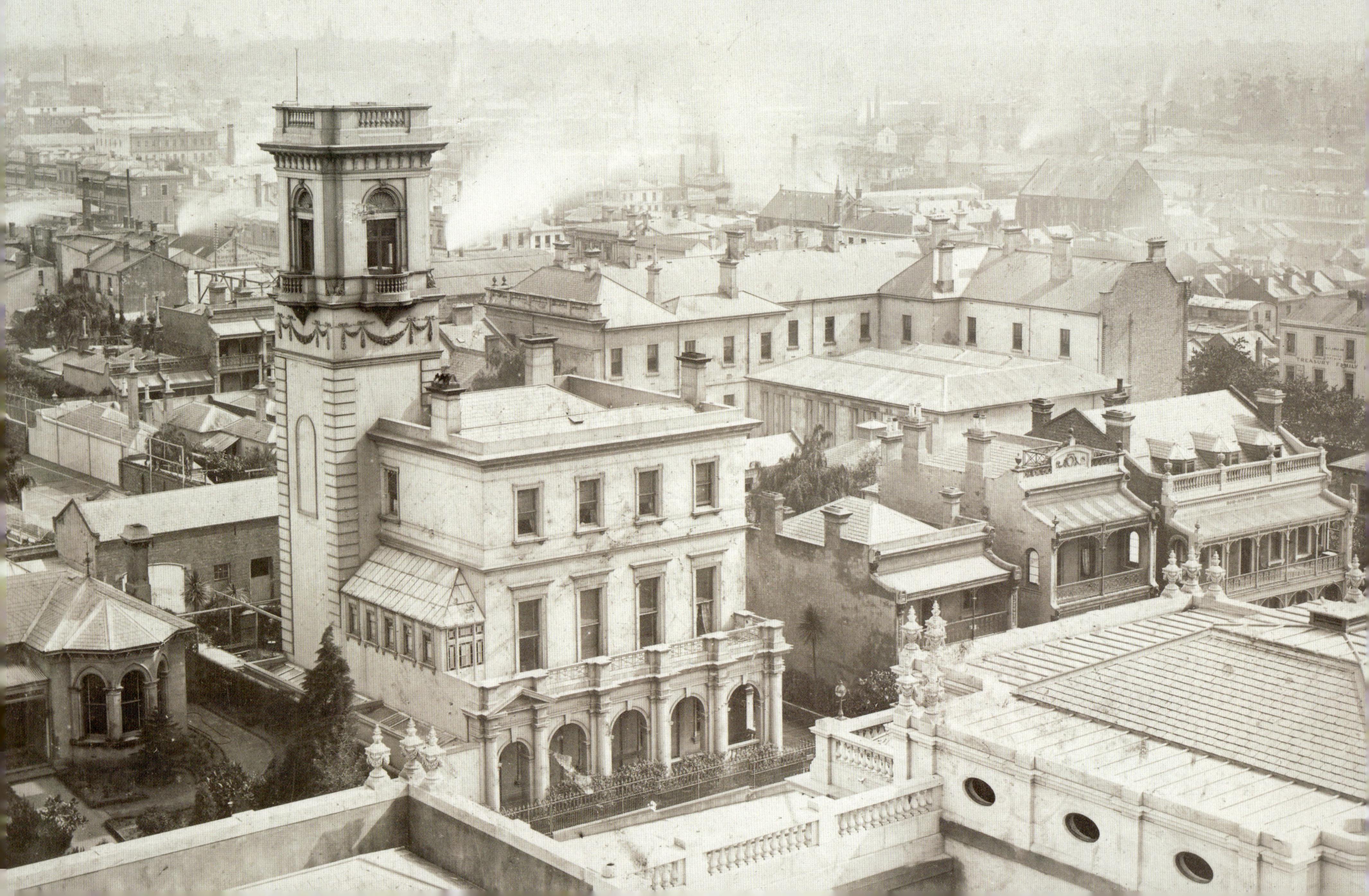

NELSON PLACE, WILLIAMSTOWN

c.1881

PHOTOGRAPHER: ANDREW RIDER (TOP IMAGE); CHRIS MACHERAS (BOTTOM IMAGE)

THEN AND NOW: These shots feature the former English, Scottish and Australian Bank at 139 Nelson Place, Williamstown. Also known as the Mission to Seamen, this building was the first major purpose-built bank branch in Williamstown. Look at the incredible contrasting views, 140 years apart.

Did you know that Williamstown was initially considered, along with the sites that became known as Geelong and Melbourne, for the capital of the new colony at Port Phillip? Although Williamstown offered excellent proximity to anchorage sites, Melbourne was ultimately chosen because of its abundance of fresh water.

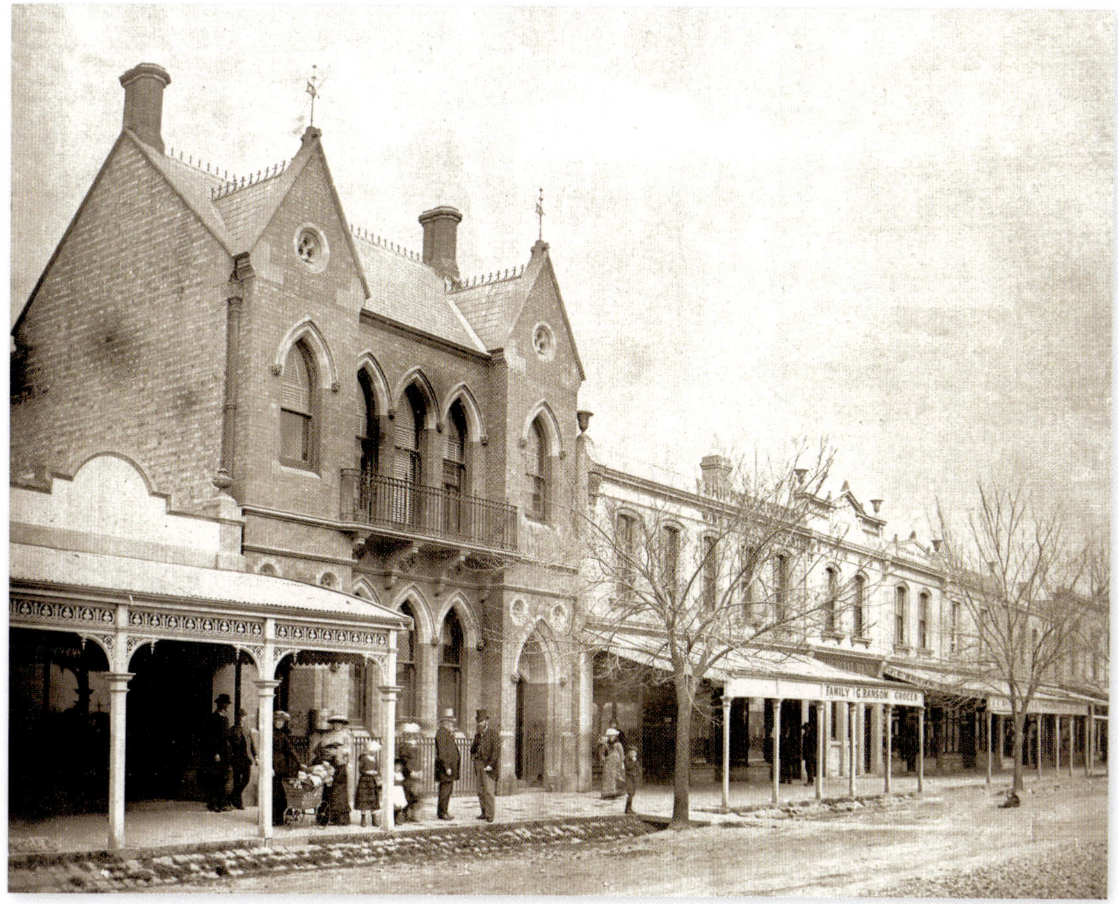

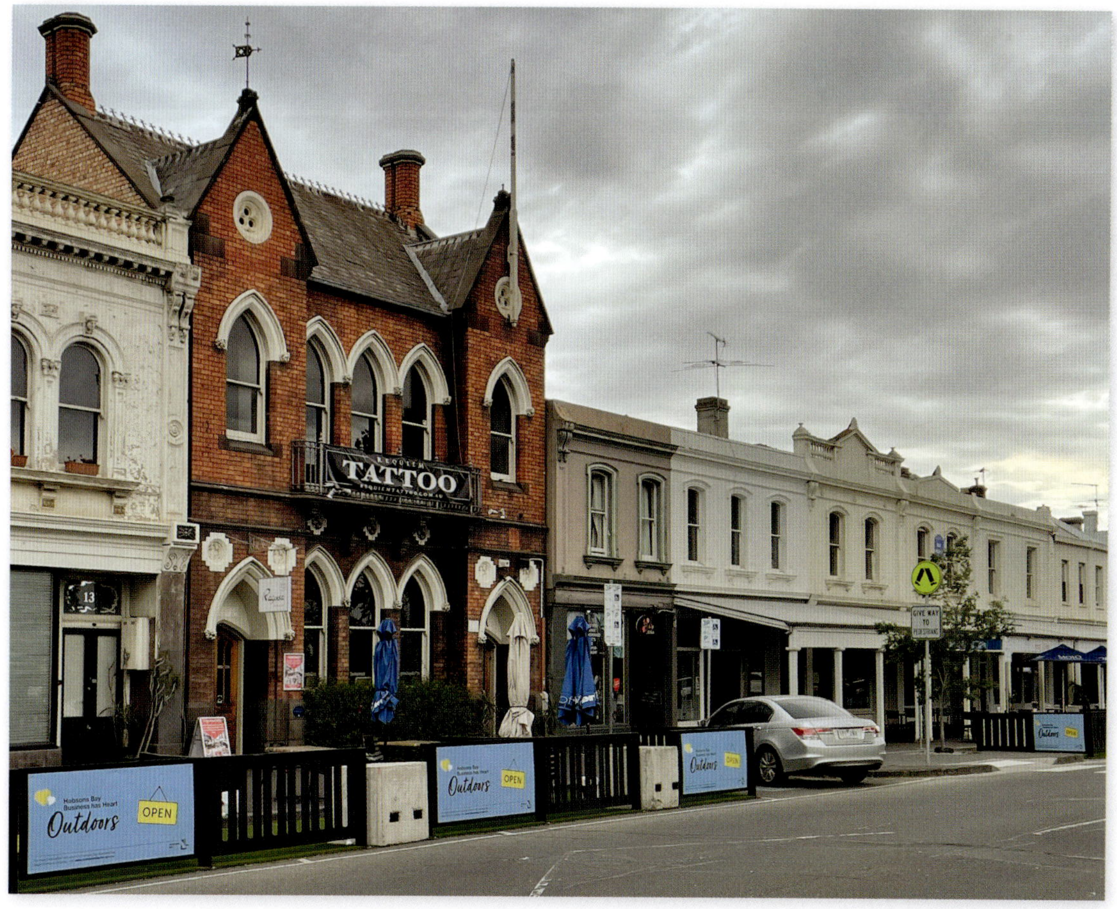

COLLINS & ELIZABETH STREETS

c. 1885

PHOTOGRAPHER: UNKNOWN

The view from the corner of Collins and Elizabeth streets, looking east along Collins Street.

Road works are being undertaken, possibly to lay tramlines. What's Melbourne without its iconic trams, after all!

The first cable tramline opened in Melbourne on 11 November 1885. At its most extensive, this was one of the largest cable-tram systems in the world.

From 1924 the cable trams were progressively converted to electric trams, or abandoned in favour of buses. Records show that the last Melbourne cable tram ran its course on 26 October 1940.

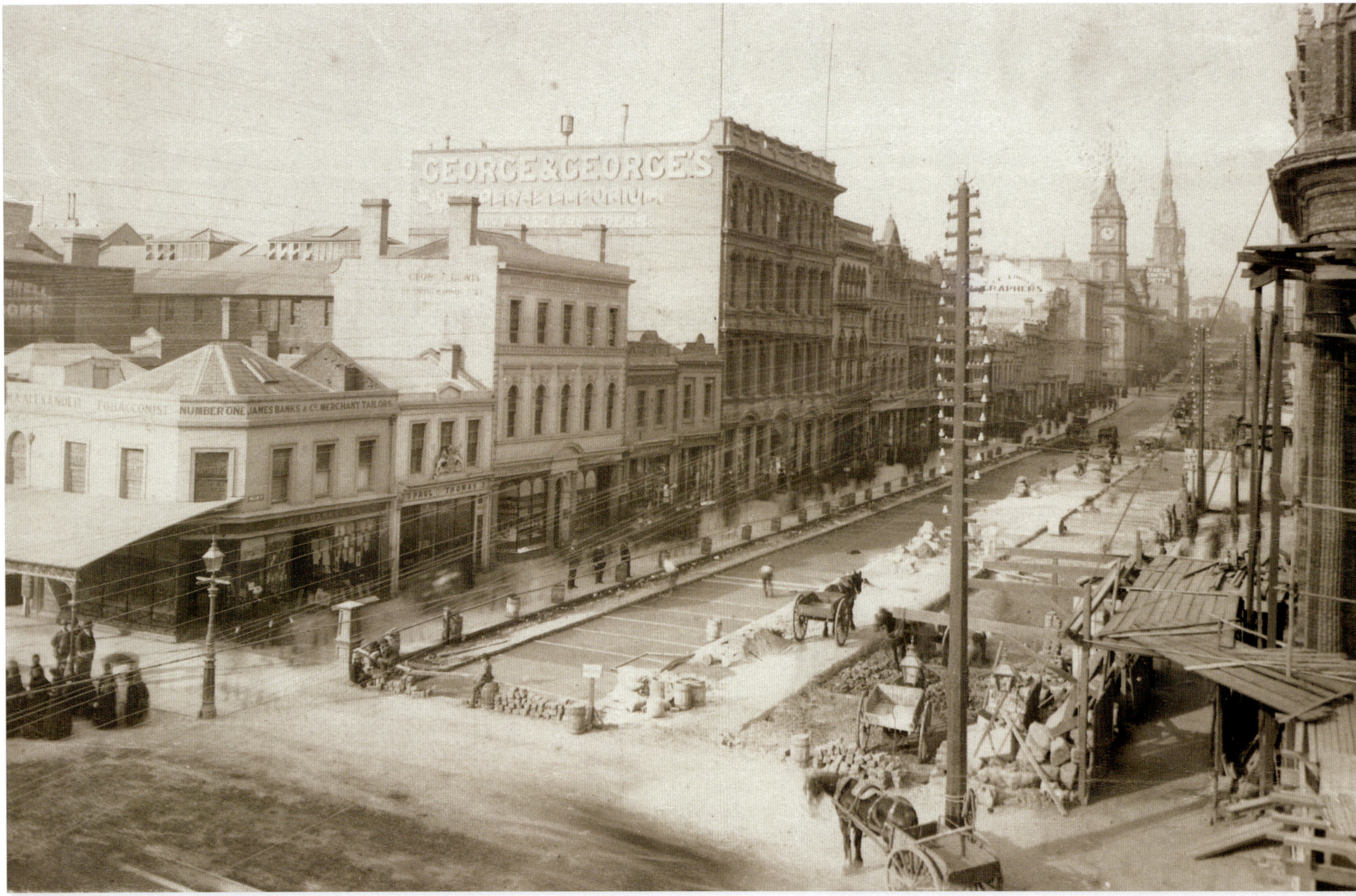

HODDLE STREET, COLLINGWOOD

c. 1886

PHOTOGRAPHER: H. HUME

Hoddle Street, Collingwood, appears to be much narrower than we're now used to, with very few trees in sight. The street was widened in the 1970s, with many of the buildings in this image demolished to extend the width of the road by about 40 metres.

On the left, you might also notice that the Collingwood Town Hall has no clocks in its tower. They had not yet been completed.

The clocks were rumoured to have been those once installed in the GPO building, which was extended in 1888. The rumour, however, has since been myth-busted. They were in fact ordered from Gaunt & Co., clockmakers, and were made to be similar to the clocks at the GPO.

Ordered in April 1888, they were reportedly on display at the 1888 Melbourne Centennial Exhibition.

The clock bell was cast by Mears and Stainbank at the Whitechapel Foundry in London in 1890.

Put the traffic aggravation aside next time you're stopped there, and remember this image.

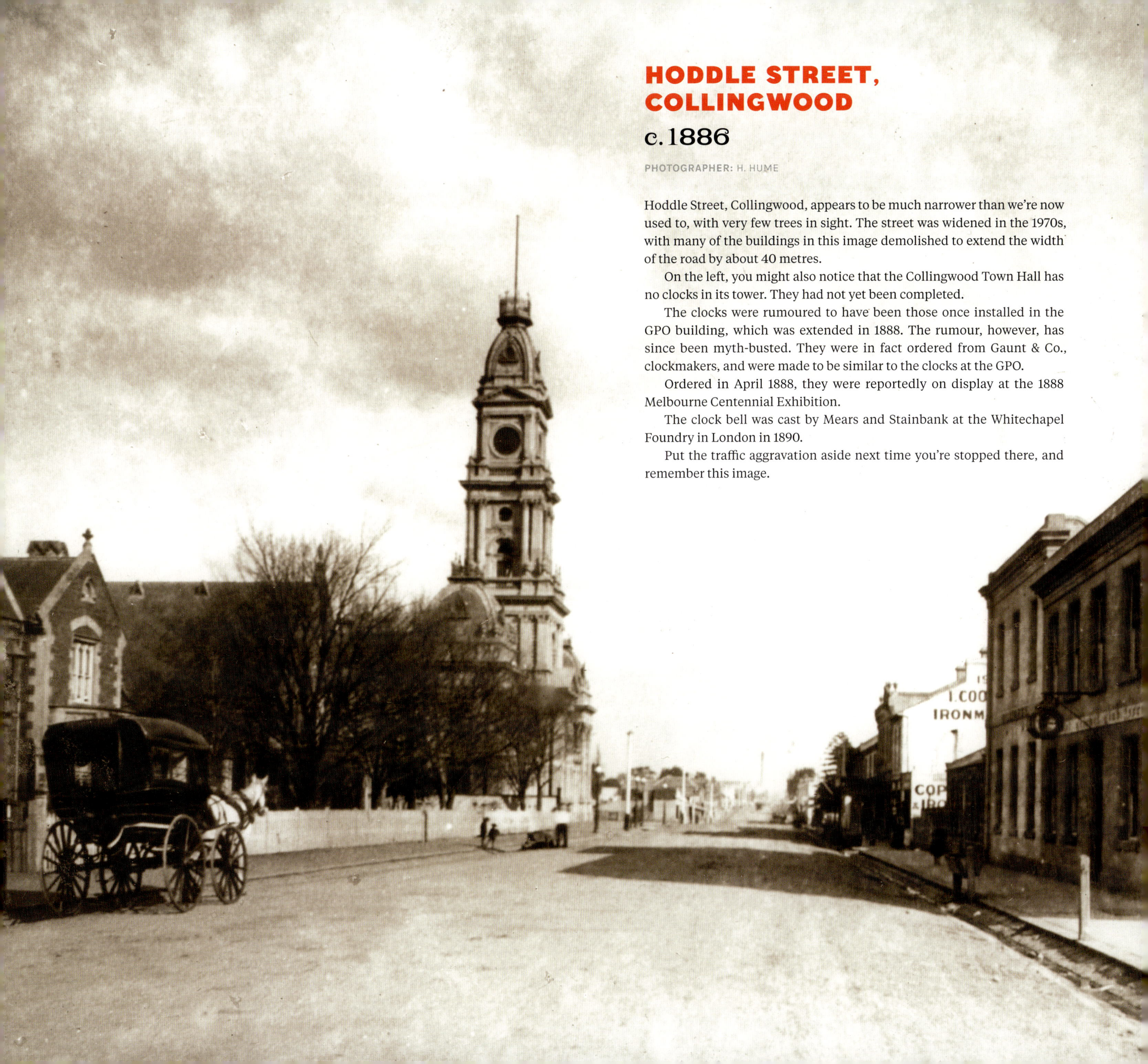

PRINCESS THEATRE, SPRING STREET

c.1888

PHOTOGRAPHER: N.J. CAIRE

Here is a view down Spring Street, with the Burke and Wills statue on the front right and the Hotel Windsor in the distance on the left.

In the centre is the spectacular Princess Theatre, as it still looks today. The theatre dates back to the mid-1800s, during the gold rush, when it was called Astley's Amphitheatre and apparently looked like a large barn.

By 1885 the existing theatre was so run down that plans were put forward to demolish it. Construction began on the new theatre shortly thereafter, and was completed in 1886 at a cost of £50,000.

The opening performance was Gilbert and Sullivan's *The Mikado*. In this image, the central roof is being used to advertise Essie Jenyns, the renowned Australian actress best known for her Shakespearean roles.

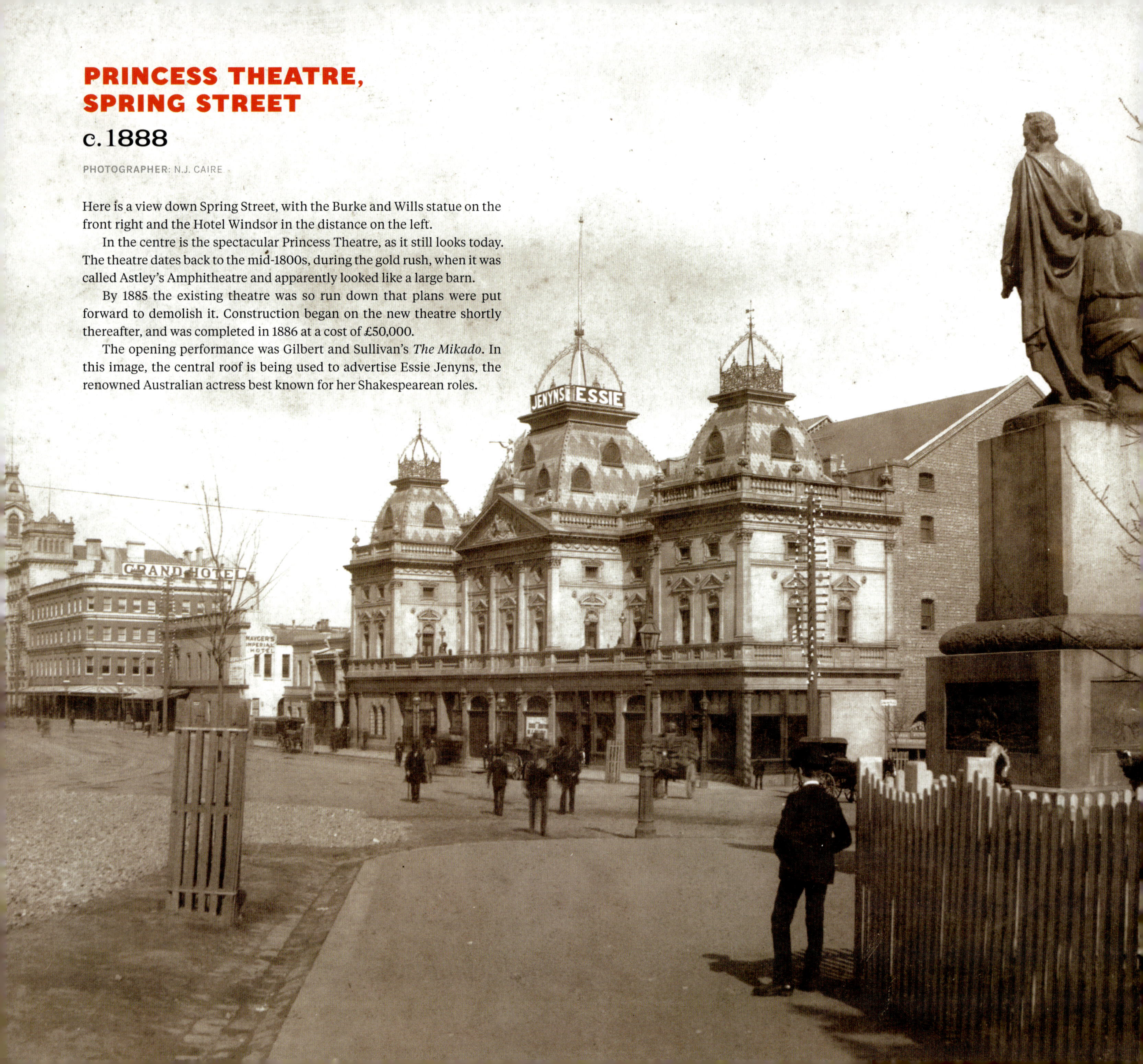

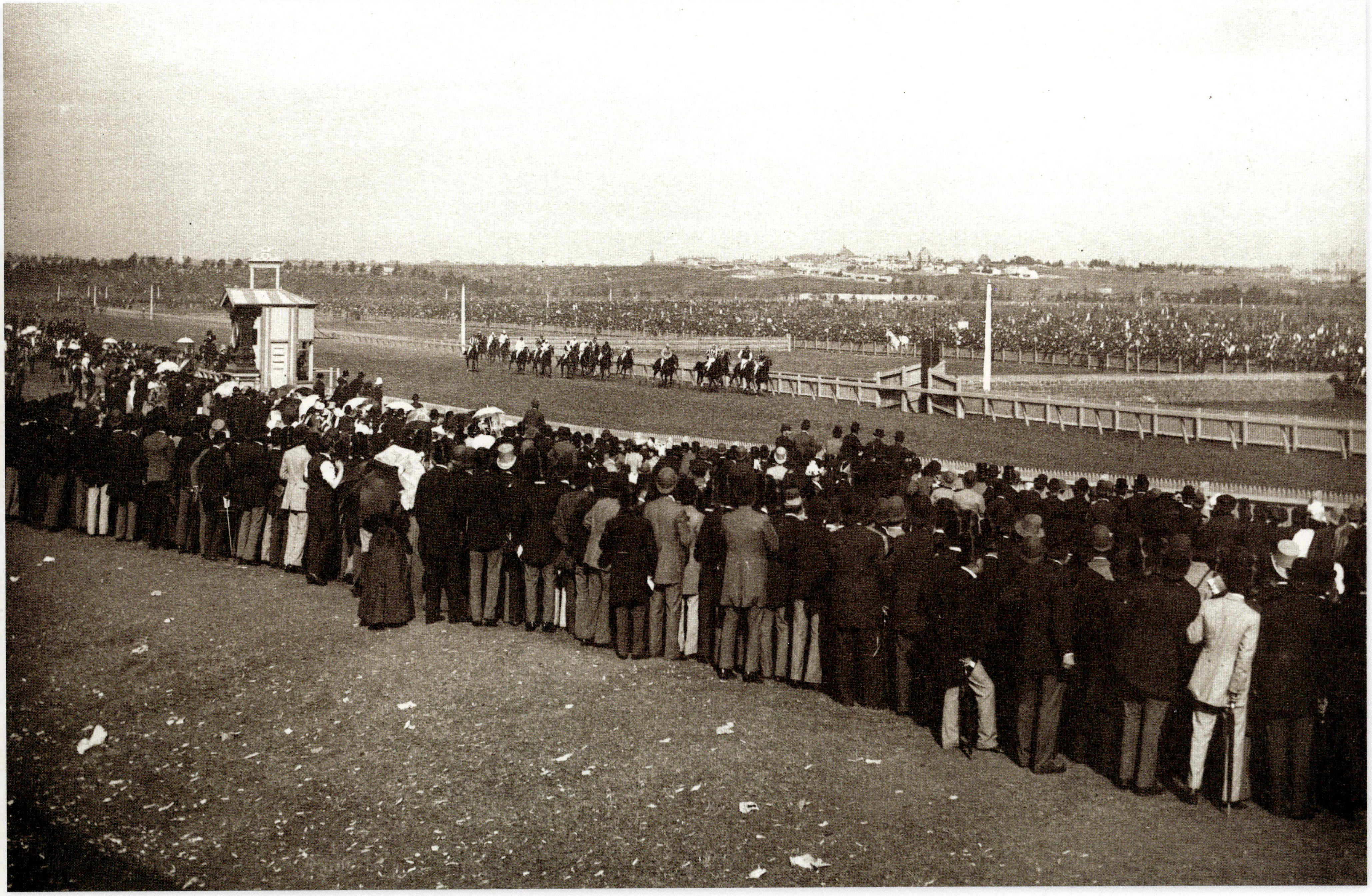

MELBOURNE CUP

1889

PHOTOGRAPHER: J.F.C. FARQUHAR

Spectators watching the Melbourne Cup with anticipation at Flemington Racecourse. The winner that year was a horse named Bravo.

The Cup tradition extends back to 7 November 1861, when seventeen horses raced for the rather modest prize of 710 gold sovereigns (£710 cash) and a hand-beaten gold watch — winner takes all!

ST KILDA PIER

c. 1889

PHOTOGRAPHER: JOHN STEEL

Dressed to impress on St Kilda Pier.

You can see St Kilda's iconic Esplanade Hotel, aka the 'Espy', in the distance, which had been built about a decade earlier in 1878. It was one of the largest and most renowned nineteenth-century resort hotels in Victoria, and had the reputation of hosting world-famous celebrities such as the great French stage actress Sarah Bernhardt and Mark Twain, who was said to have stayed there in the 1880s under his real name, Samuel Clements.

Music has been at the core of this venue's soul from the very beginning. Before it was the Esplanade Hotel, the site was home to the New Bath Hotel, a music venue. Charles Wedel, the licensee, introduced string music in the 1860s to capitalise on the entertainment value of the location.

Thomas Symington Carlyon renovated the hotel and transformed it into a premier jazz venue in the 1920s, heavily influenced by the jazz scene in the United States.

During the 1930s and 1940s, big bands were all the craze, with jazz and be-bop taking over well into the 1950s and 1960s. The 1970s saw the introduction of disco fever, before blues and country took centre stage during the 1980s.

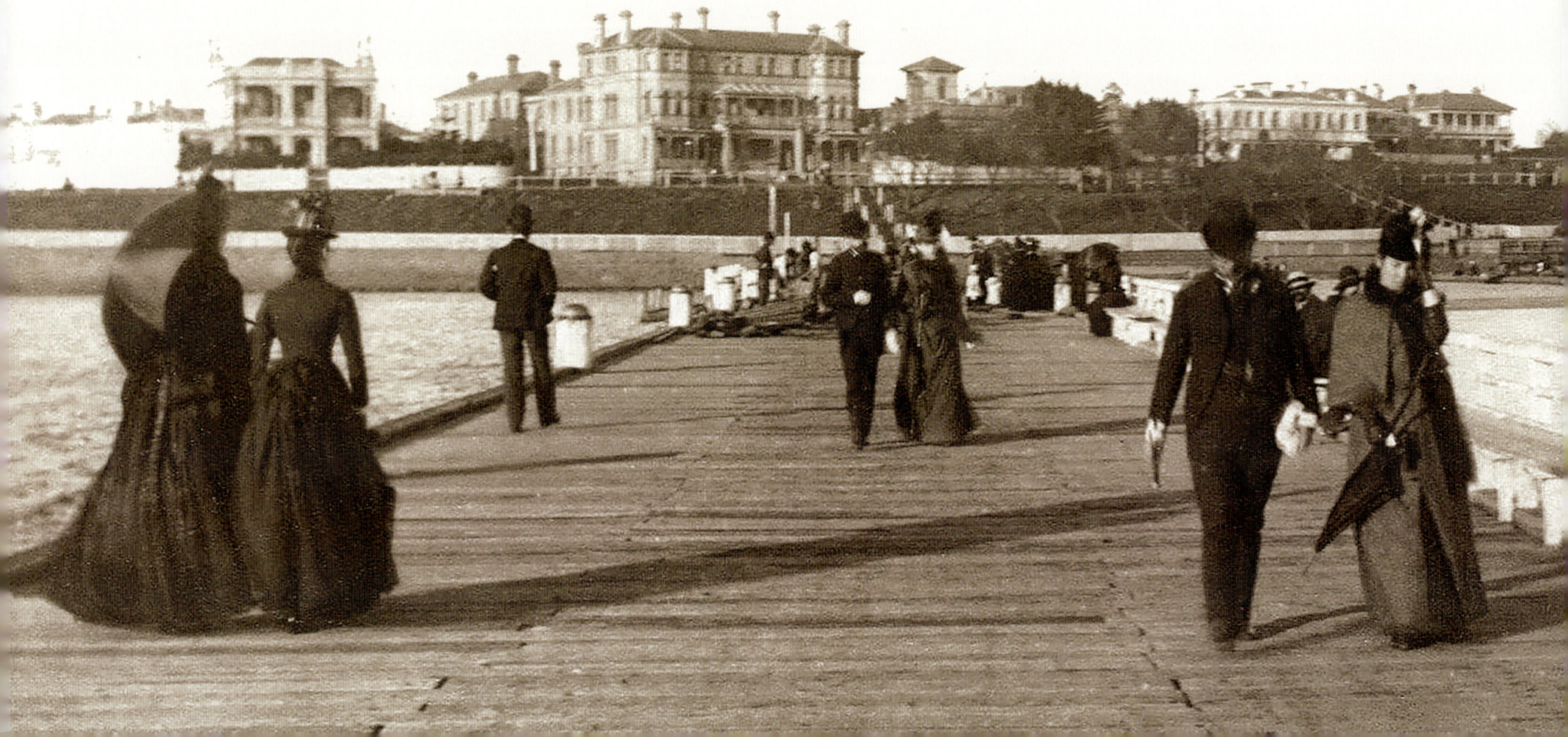

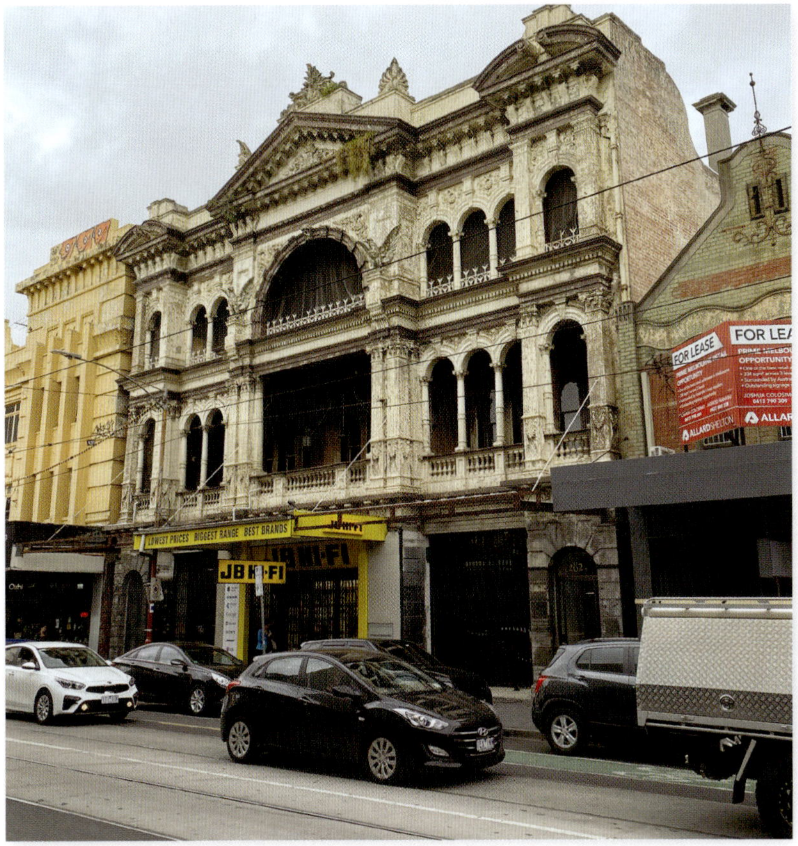

PRAHRAN ARCADE

c. 1890

PHOTOGRAPHER: TOBY-JON WILSON (TOP IMAGE); CHARLES RUDD (RIGHT IMAGE)

THEN AND NOW: Built in 1889 for a Mrs Elizabeth Delaney, the arcade originally incorporated Turkish baths, a hotel, a fancy cafe, and billiard rooms.

From the 1920s it was known as The Centreway, and from the 1960s the entire building was used by a wine seller named Mr Dan Murphy. (It was, in fact, the very first Dan Murphy's.) The original mansard roof was, unfortunately, removed in the 1950s, and the ground-level facade altered. As you can see, it now operates as a JB Hi-Fi store.

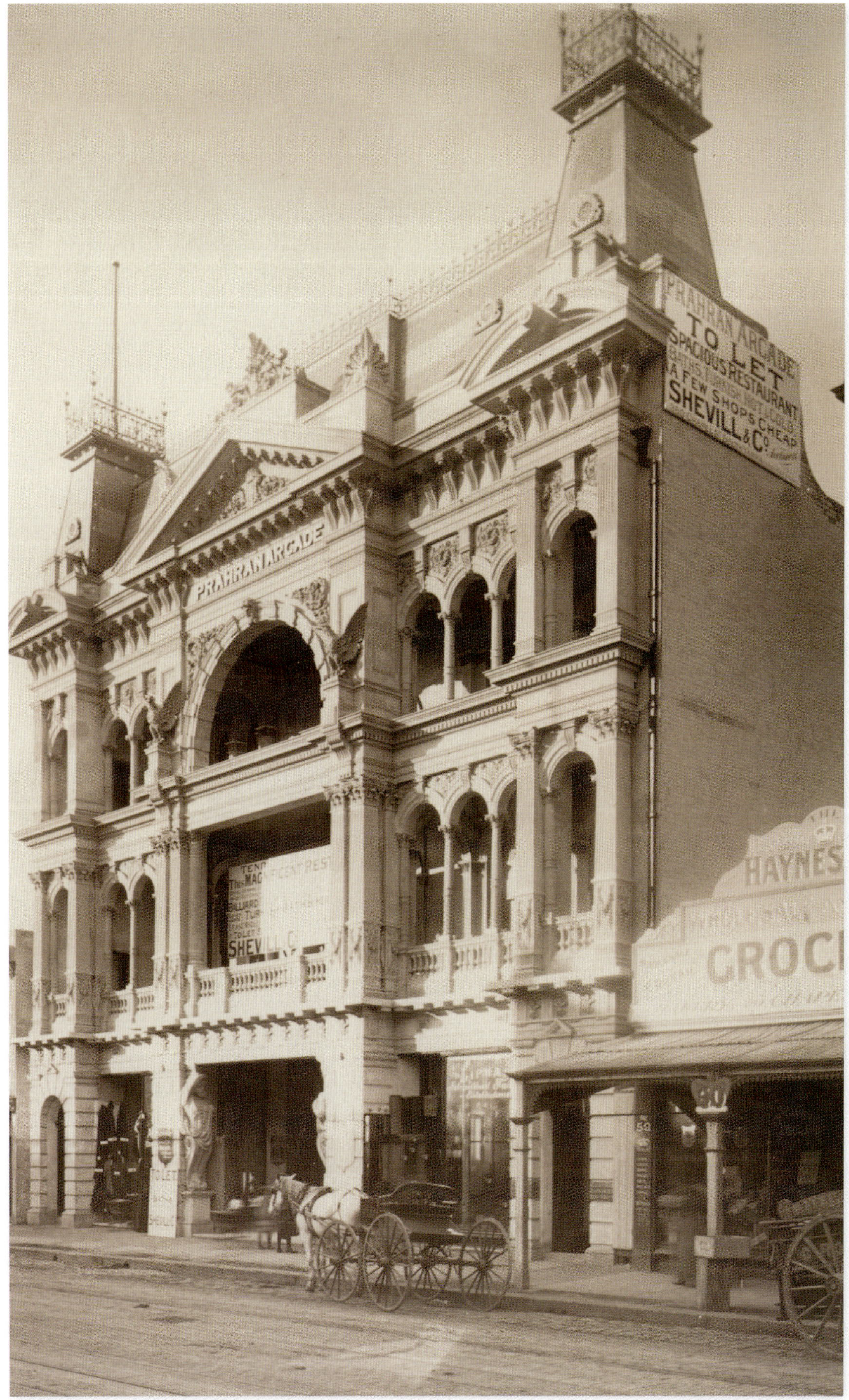

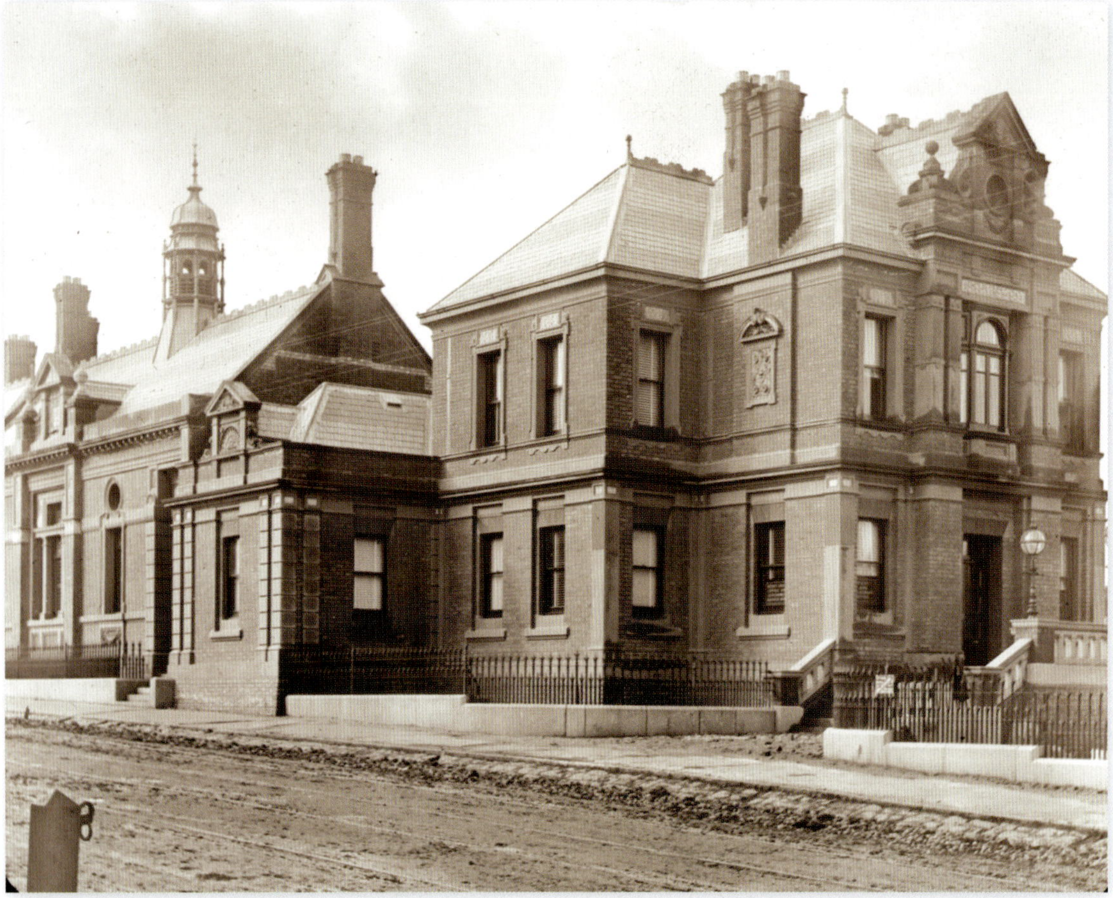

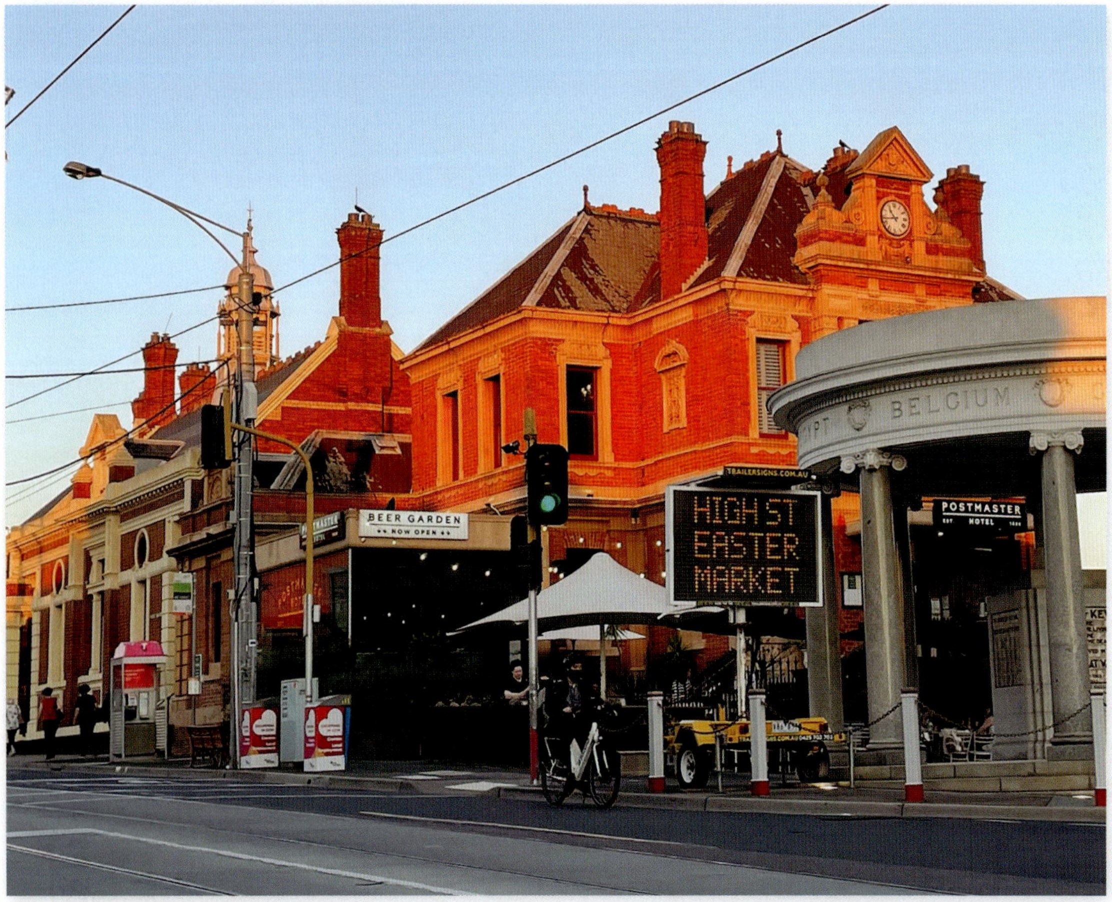

KEW POST OFFICE, POLICE STATION & COURT HOUSE

c. 1890

PHOTOGRAPHER: JOHN HENRY HARVEY (TOP IMAGE); CHRIS MACHERAS (BOTTOM IMAGE)

THEN AND NOW: Exterior view of the former Kew Post Office, Police Station, and Court House, on the corner of Cotham Road and High Street, Kew. The buildings were completed in 1888.

In the 1840s, the region was named the Parish of Boroondara. Boroondara means 'a place of shade' in the Aboriginal Woiwurrung language. The first Crown land sales in the area were recorded in 1851, and one of the purchasers was Nicholas Fenwick, who named the region Kew based on his memory of Kew in England.

COLLINS STREET

c. 1890

PHOTOGRAPHER: UNKNOWN

There is a lot to take in from this majestic shot of Collins Street.

You can see that the renowned George's Emporium has two locations. George's was a Melbourne-based department store established in 1880, which closed in 1995.

The motto of the store was *Quod facimus, Valde facimus* ('What we do, We do well'). And this was very much the reputation that carried George's through to the mid-1990s: impeccable service and luxurious, high-quality goods.

A year before this image was taken, their 280 Collins Street location had been destroyed by a fire. It was restored and replaced by the first stage of the Block Arcade, after which the owners simply rebranded the 162–68 Collins Street location.

Moreover, you can see the Treasury Building, the Town Hall, Scots Church, and the Hotel Windsor. Even further in the distance, you can see the half-completed spire of St Patrick's Cathedral.

What a gorgeous city. No wonder it rivalled London and New York at the time.

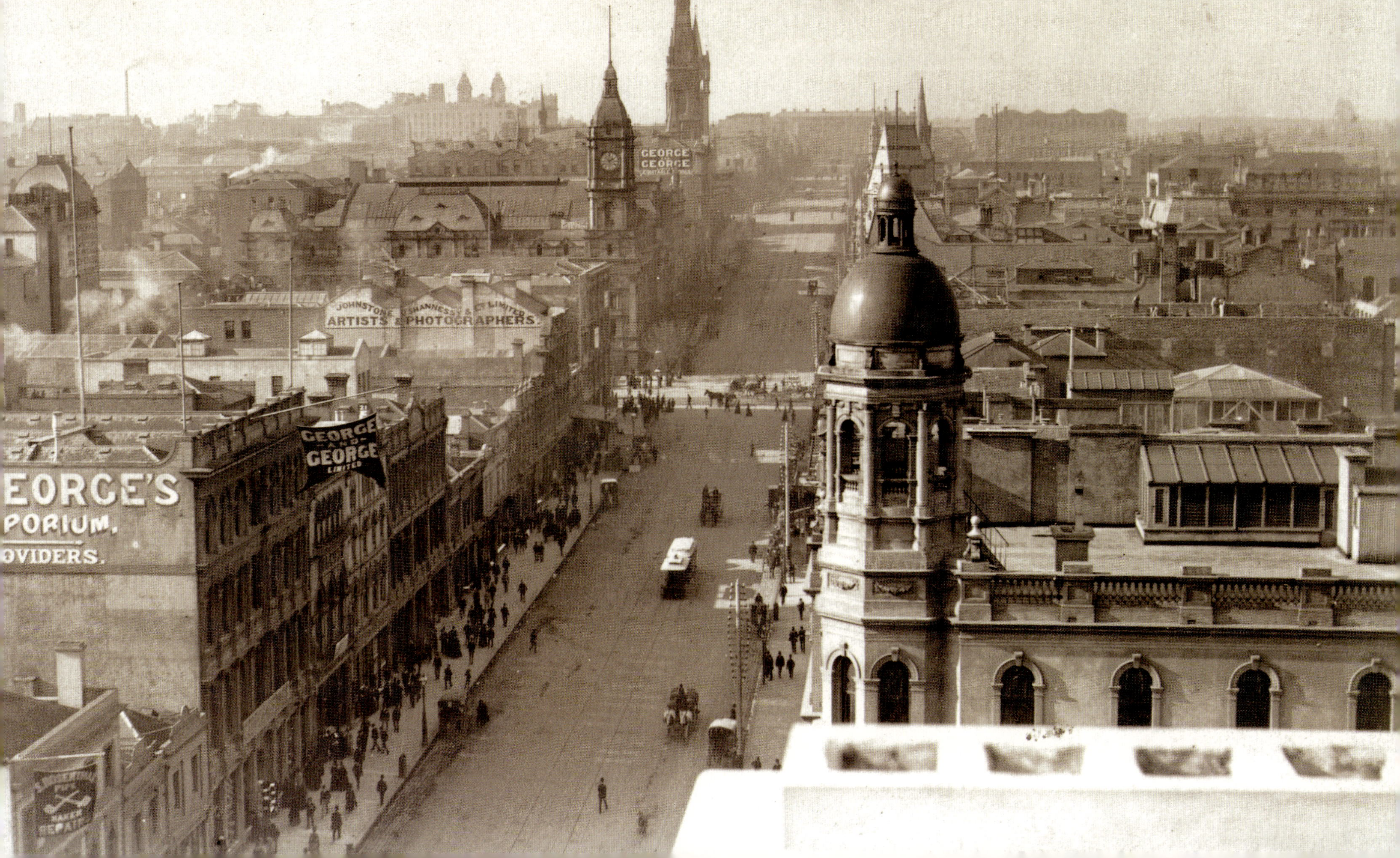

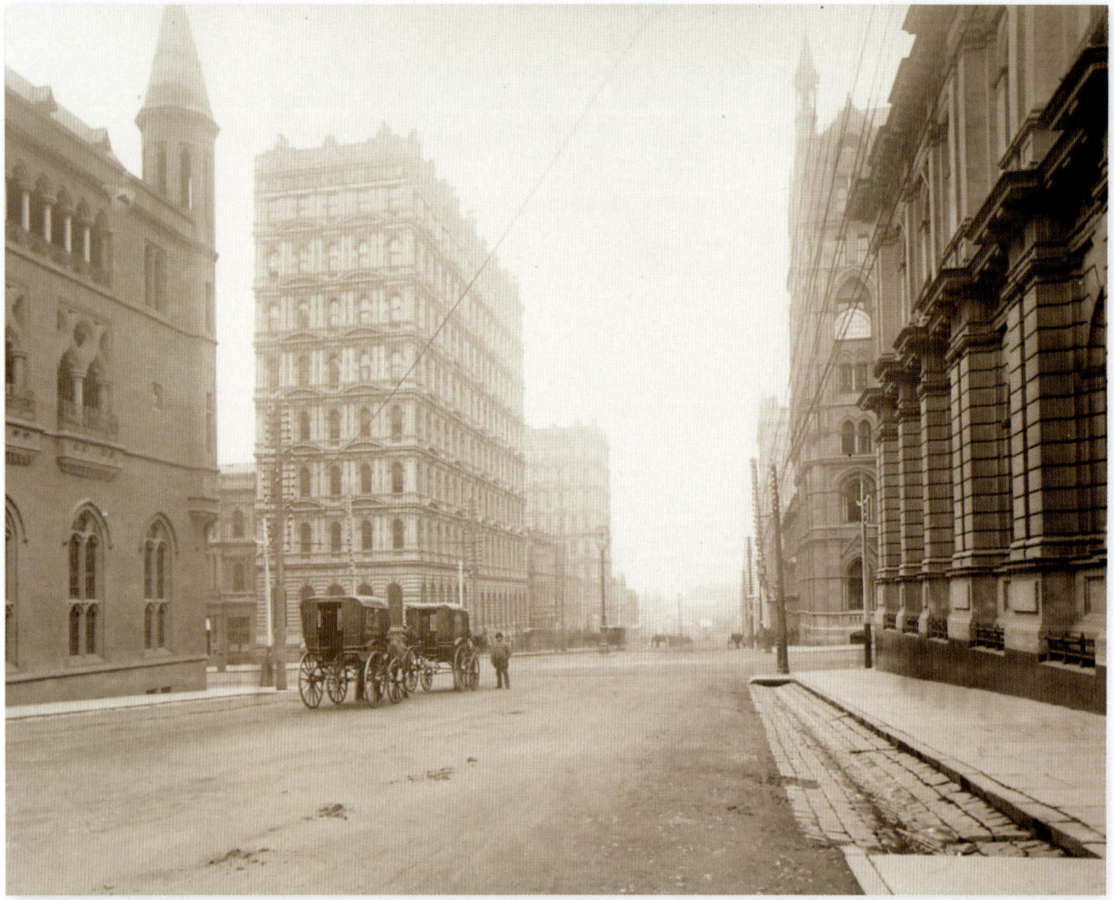

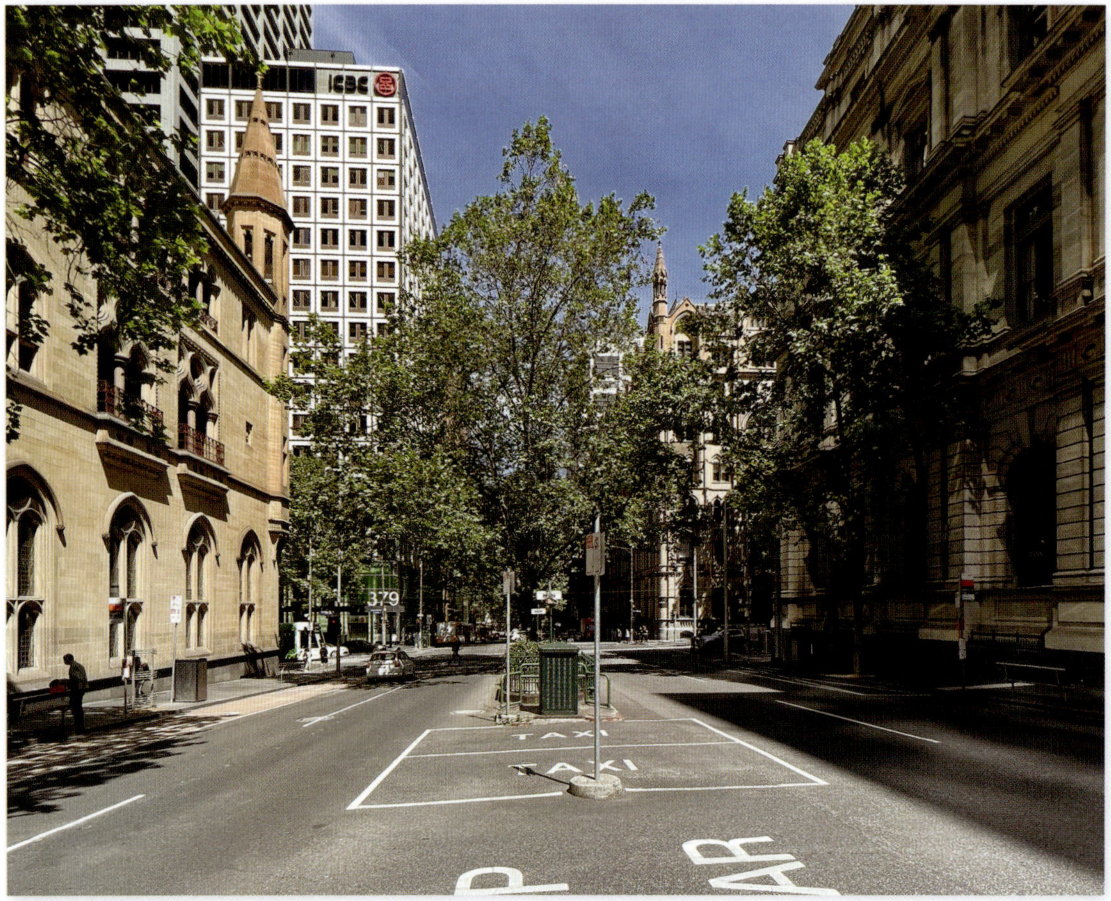

QUEEN & COLLINS STREETS

c.1890

PHOTOGRAPHER: NETTLETON & ARNEST PHOTOGRAPHIC STUDIO (TOP IMAGE); CHRIS MACHERAS (BOTTOM IMAGE)

THEN AND NOW: Of particular significance to the left is the ANZ's 'Gothic Bank', completed in 1887 and very new in the top photo.

It was built for the ES&A Bank as a residence, known as the 'Verdon Chambers', for the bank's general manager, George Verdon. Talk about a job perk! Verdon oversaw the building's construction, essentially supervising the building of his own home — which probably explains why it's so opulent (cheeky old George ...).

The bank purchased the site for £61, with the build itself costing £77,393 (double the budget). The Reserve Bank of Australia's pre-decimal inflation calculator indicates that in 2020 terms, the land site would have cost around $10,000, and the build over $12 million.

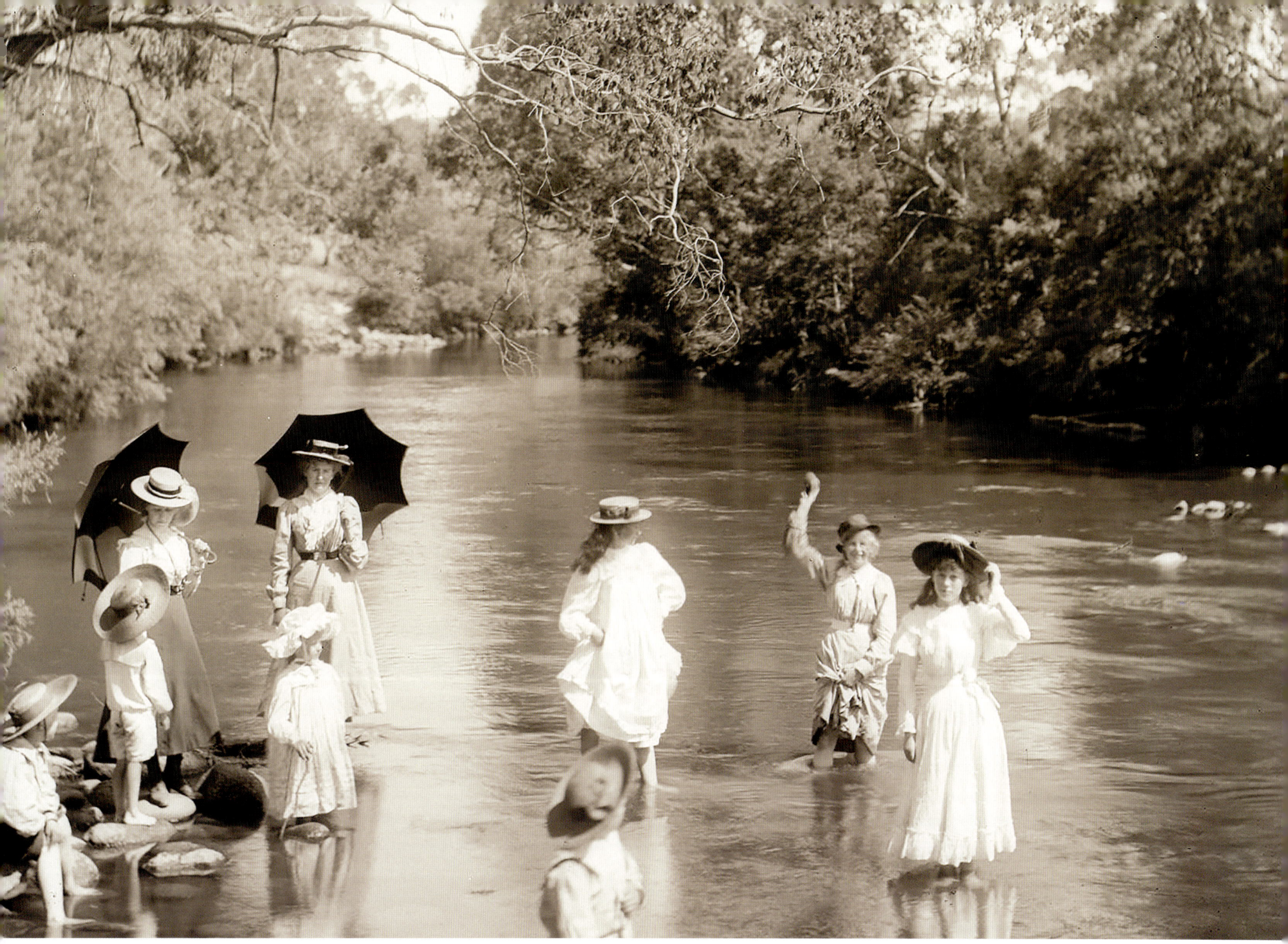

YARRA RIVER, WARRANDYTE

c.1890

PHOTOGRAPHER: UNKNOWN

Ladies and children frolic in the Yarra on a summer's day in Warrandyte.

For some context, at the time of this photo it is likely that Banjo Paterson was writing his poem 'The Man from Snowy River', published in April that year.

Did you know that in 1851, gold was first discovered in Victoria, in Warrandyte? A man named Louis Michel discovered it at Anderson's Creek. In 1938, a cairn was erected at the location to mark the find.

BURGUNDY STREET, HEIDELBERG

c. 1890

PHOTOGRAPHER: W.H. FERGUSON

Who would have thought that this was Burgundy Street, Heidelberg, around the year 1890? Today you will find the Austin Hospital to the right of this image.

Heidelberg has an interesting history. The land that makes up the suburb today was sold by Crown auction in 1838, making it one of the earliest rural allotments in Australia. Melbourne had been founded only three years before this!

At the time, the township was known as Warringal, the Aboriginal term for an eagle's nest. For a reason unknown, a land agent changed the name from Warringal to Heidelberg, after the German city. After World War I, there was a growing resentment of Germany, and a number of locals, including those on the city council, proposed the name be changed to something more British. The most popular suggestion was Georgetown, after the British prime minister David Lloyd George. However, after many public debates and a community naming competition, the name Heidelberg remained.

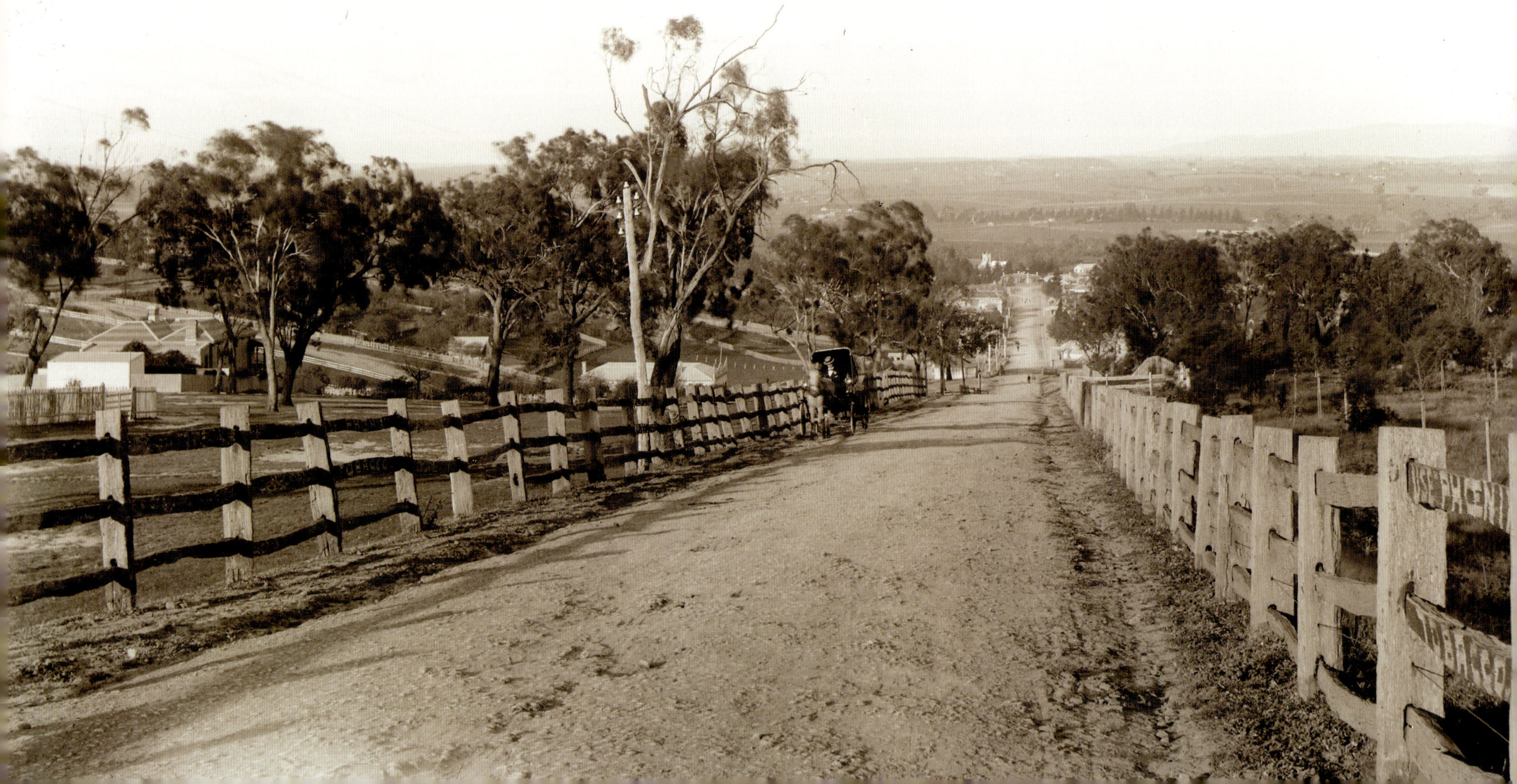

VICTORIA PARADE & BRUNSWICK STREET, EAST MELBOURNE

c. 1891

PHOTOGRAPHER: J.W. LINDT (TOP IMAGE);
CHRIS MACHERAS (BOTTOM IMAGE)

THEN AND NOW: A Melbourne tram passing the corner of Brunswick Street and Victoria Parade. You can see the former Belvidere Hotel, built in 1853.

In 1856, the hotel served as the headquarters of the 'Eight Hour Movement', an industrial movement that saw stonemasons walk off the job in protest over their employers' refusal to accept demands for reduced working hours. This brought the employers to the negotiating table and led to an agreement whereby stonemasons worked no more than an eight-hour day. It was the first of a long, hard-fought series of victories that led to Australia having one of the most progressive and sophisticated labour-law systems in the world by the early twentieth century. Campaigners chanted: 'Eight hours to work, Eight hours to play, Eight hours to sleep, Eight bob a day, A fair day's work, For a fair day's pay.'

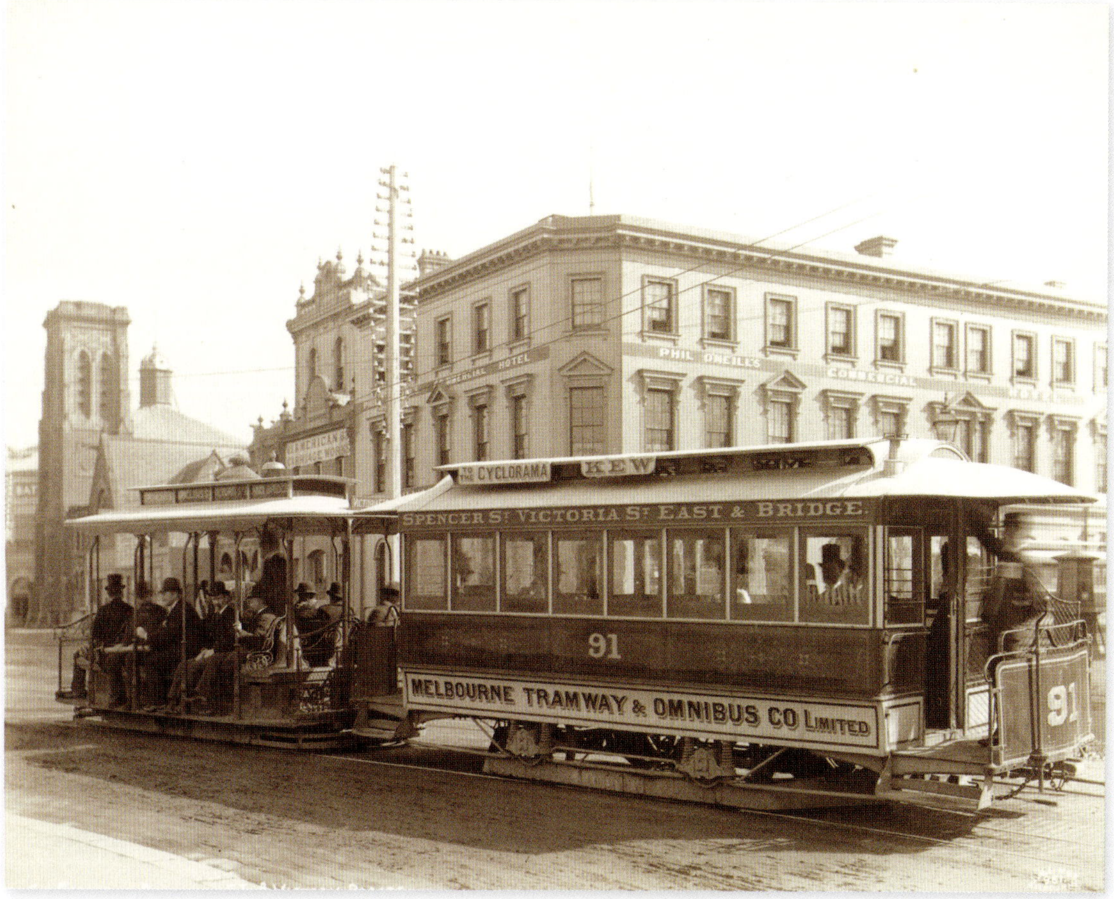

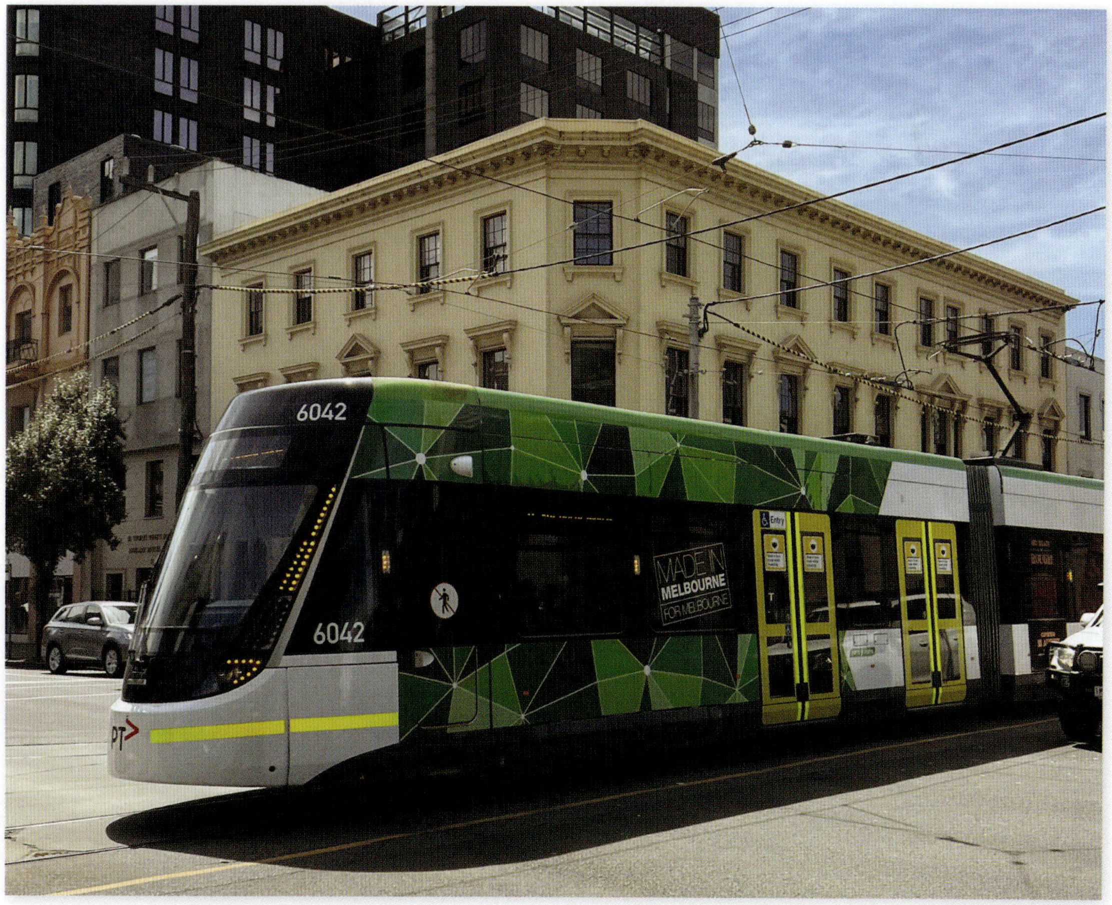

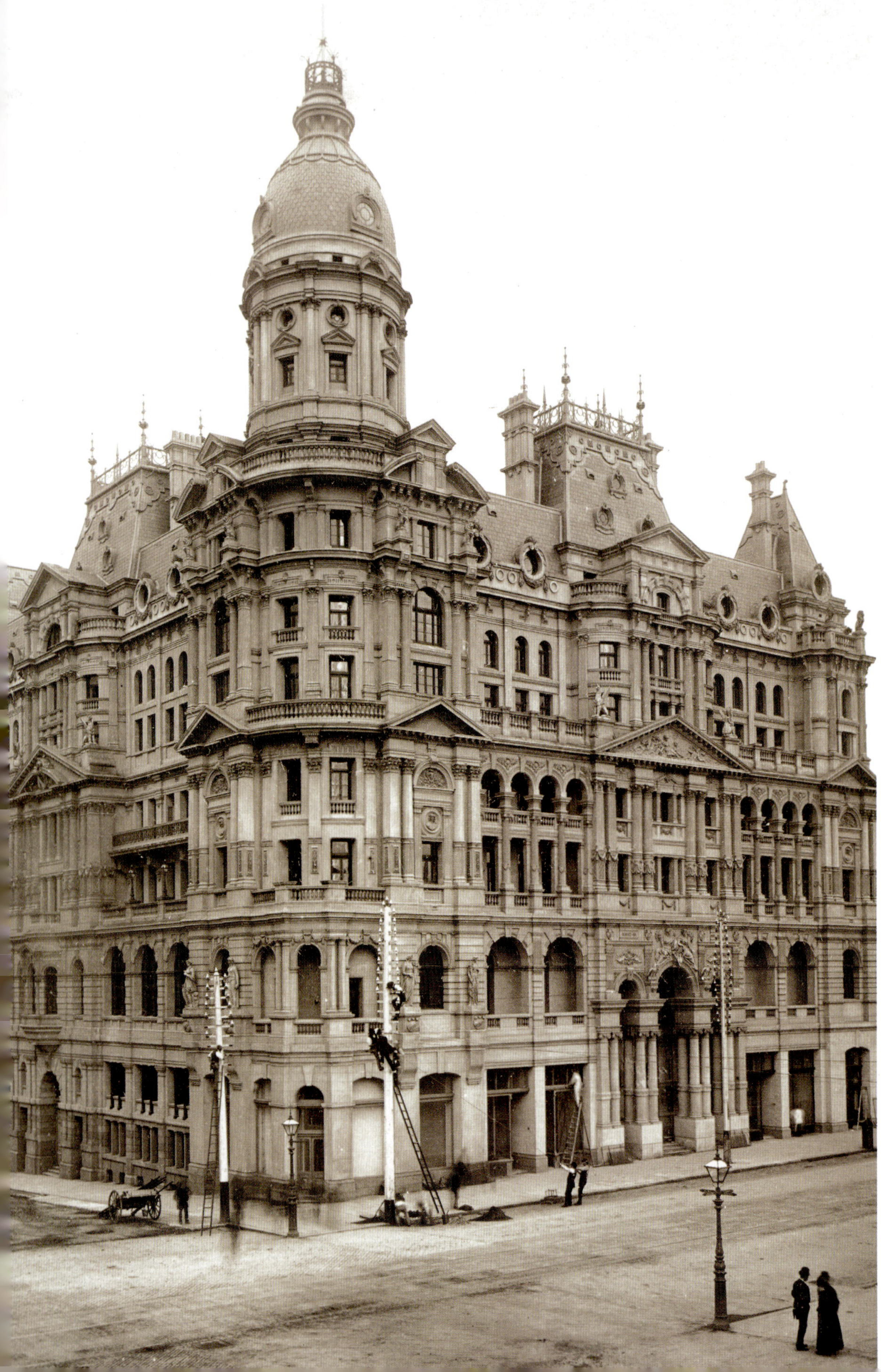

FEDERAL COFFEE PALACE

c.1892

PHOTOGRAPHER: J.W. LINDT

Melbourne's stunning Federal Coffee Palace at 555 Collins Street (on the corner of King Street, near Spencer Street Station).

The building opened in July 1888, in time for Melbourne's Centennial Exhibition.

A coffee palace was often a large and elaborate residential hotel that served coffee, not alcohol. A number were built in Australia during the boom years of the 1880s.

The Federal Coffee Palace was by far the largest and grandest, though it had to compete with establishments that sold alcohol. Eventually, in 1923, it became fully licensed, and was renamed the Federal Hotel.

The building was tragically torn down in 1973 — Melburnians have remained loud in their disapproval of its demolition.

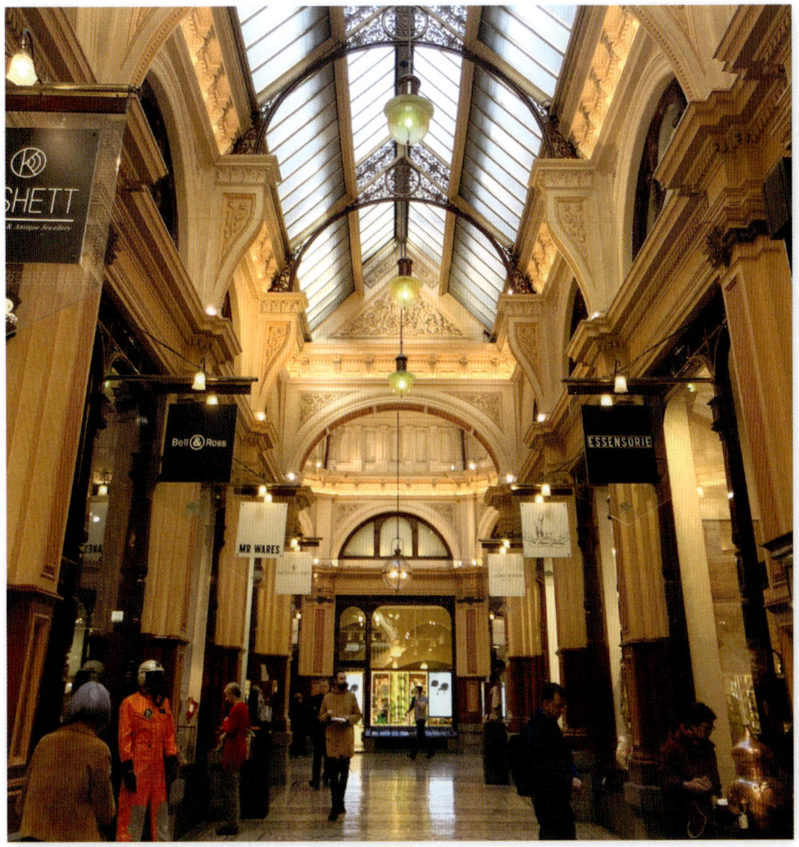

BLOCK ARCADE

c. 1893

PHOTOGRAPHER: UNKNOWN (RIGHT IMAGE);
CHRIS MACHERAS (TOP IMAGE)

THEN AND NOW: The interior of the Block Arcade.

Originally called 'Carpenters Lane', it was renamed in response to the popular saying 'doing the block'. This referred to the activity, undertaken by fashionable Melburnians, of parading around this section of Collins Street.

The site was originally purchased by Henry Batman, the brother of the founder of Melbourne, John Batman.

When the arcade opened, with its stunning Victorian-era features, shops included fifteen milliners, three lace shops, a photographer, and the Hopetoun Tea Rooms. Yes, the tea rooms have been there since it opened!

The Block Arcade remains one of Melbourne's most iconic locations.

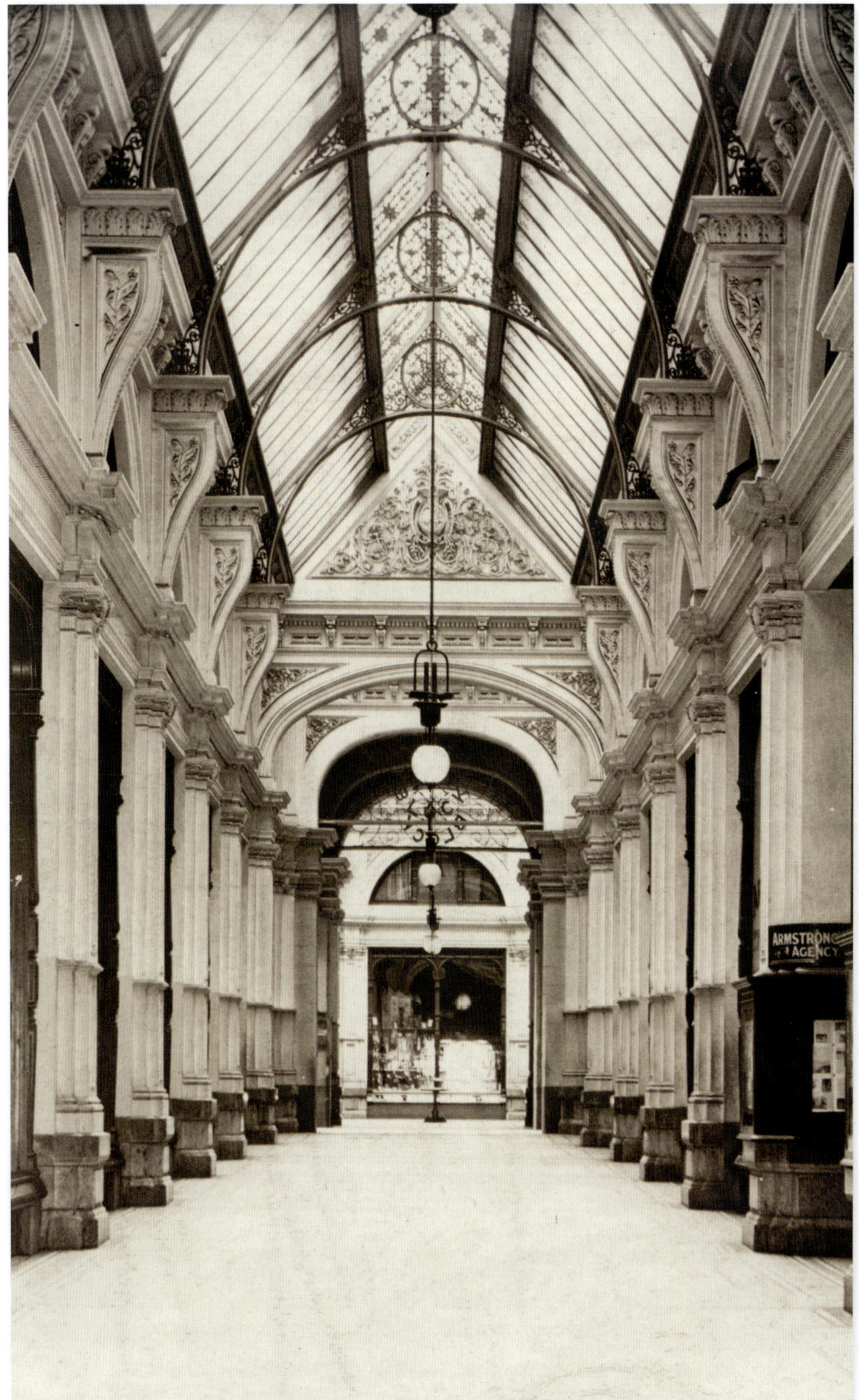

FLINDERS STREET FISH MARKET

c. 1900

PHOTOGRAPHER: UNKNOWN

Here's a location I bet many of you wouldn't recognise. Does 'Meet me under the clocks' ring a bell? This is actually the corner of Swanston Street and Flinders Street, the current site of the iconic Flinders Street Station.

In this image, you can see the original train station to the left, with St Kilda, Port Melbourne, Coburg, Preston, Brighton, Essendon, and Williamstown lines advertised above the clocks.

The large building in the centre housed the old Fish Market. In 1900, H.B. Hanson leased much of it for a vegetable market and bicycle stable, as the signs on the building indicate.

The Flinders Street Station that we all recognise commenced construction in 1906, so this may very well be one of the very few images taken of this corner before it was demolished.

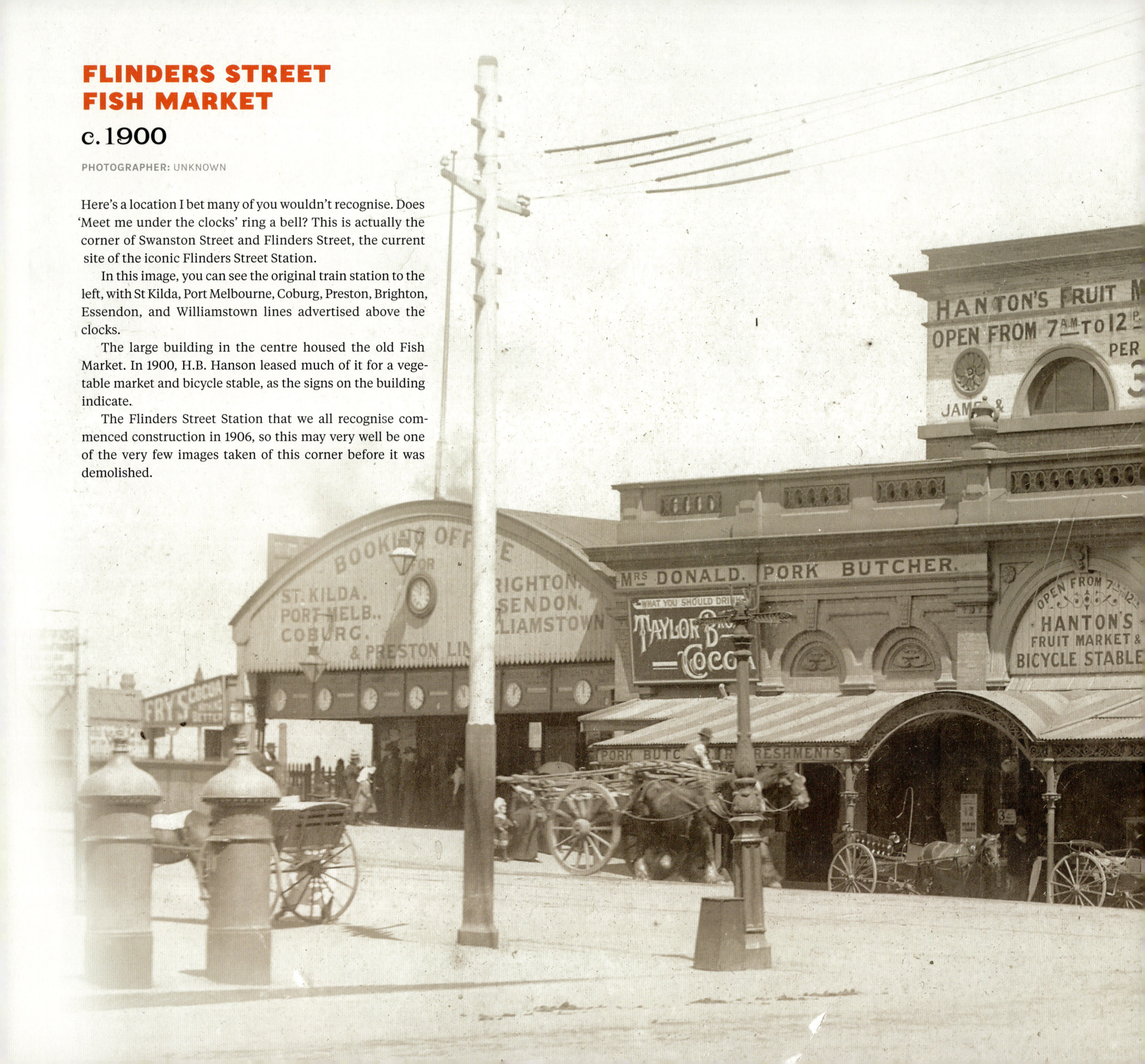

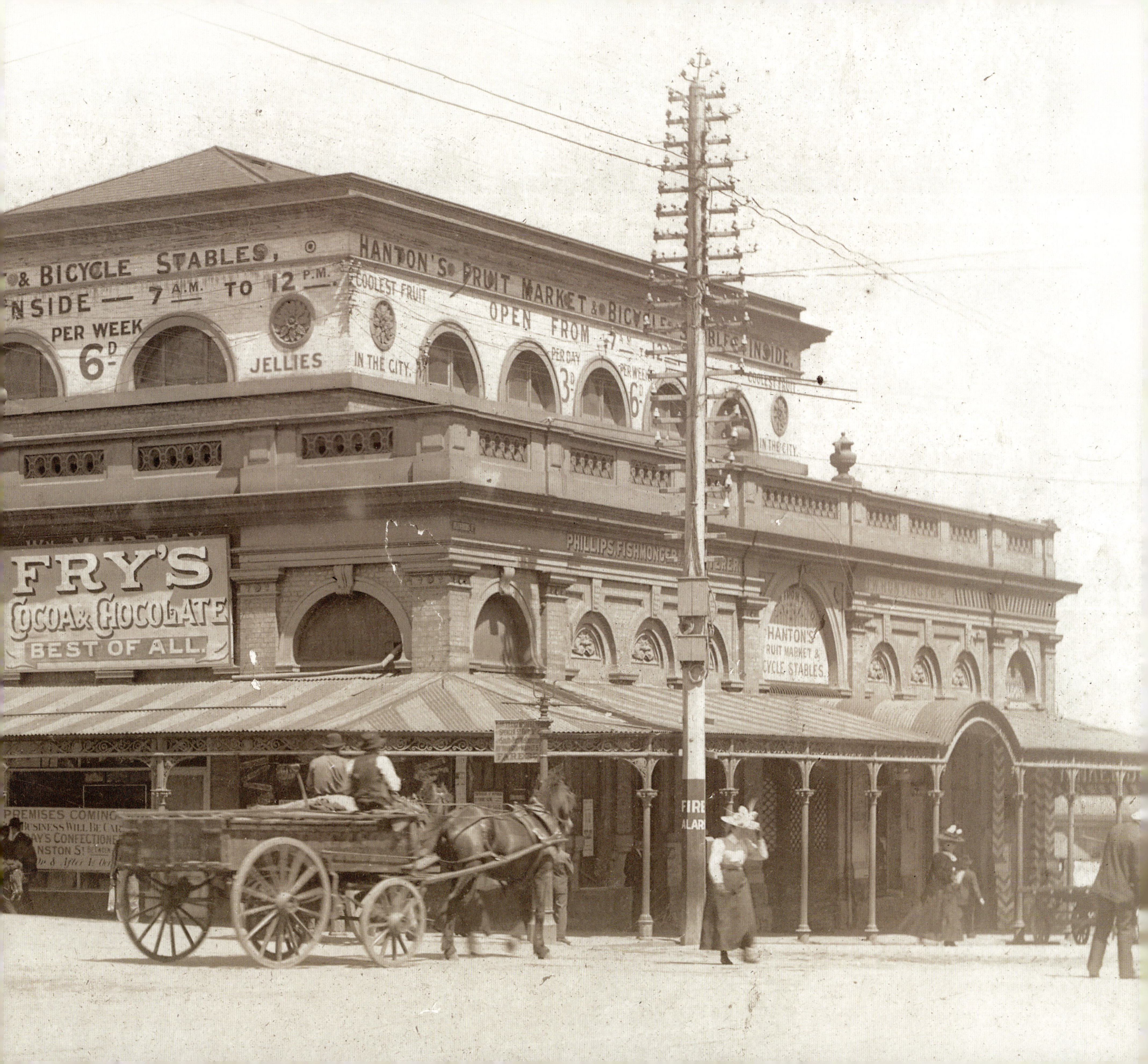
& BICYCLE STABLES,
7 A.M. TO 12 P.M.
PER WEEK 6D
JELLIES
COOLEST FRUIT IN THE CITY.
HANTON'S FRUIT MARKET
OPEN FROM
PER DAY 3D
PER WEEK 6D
FRY'S
COCOA & CHOCOLATE
BEST OF ALL.
PHILLIPS, FISHMONGER
HANTON'S FRUIT MARKET &
PREMISES COMING
FIRE

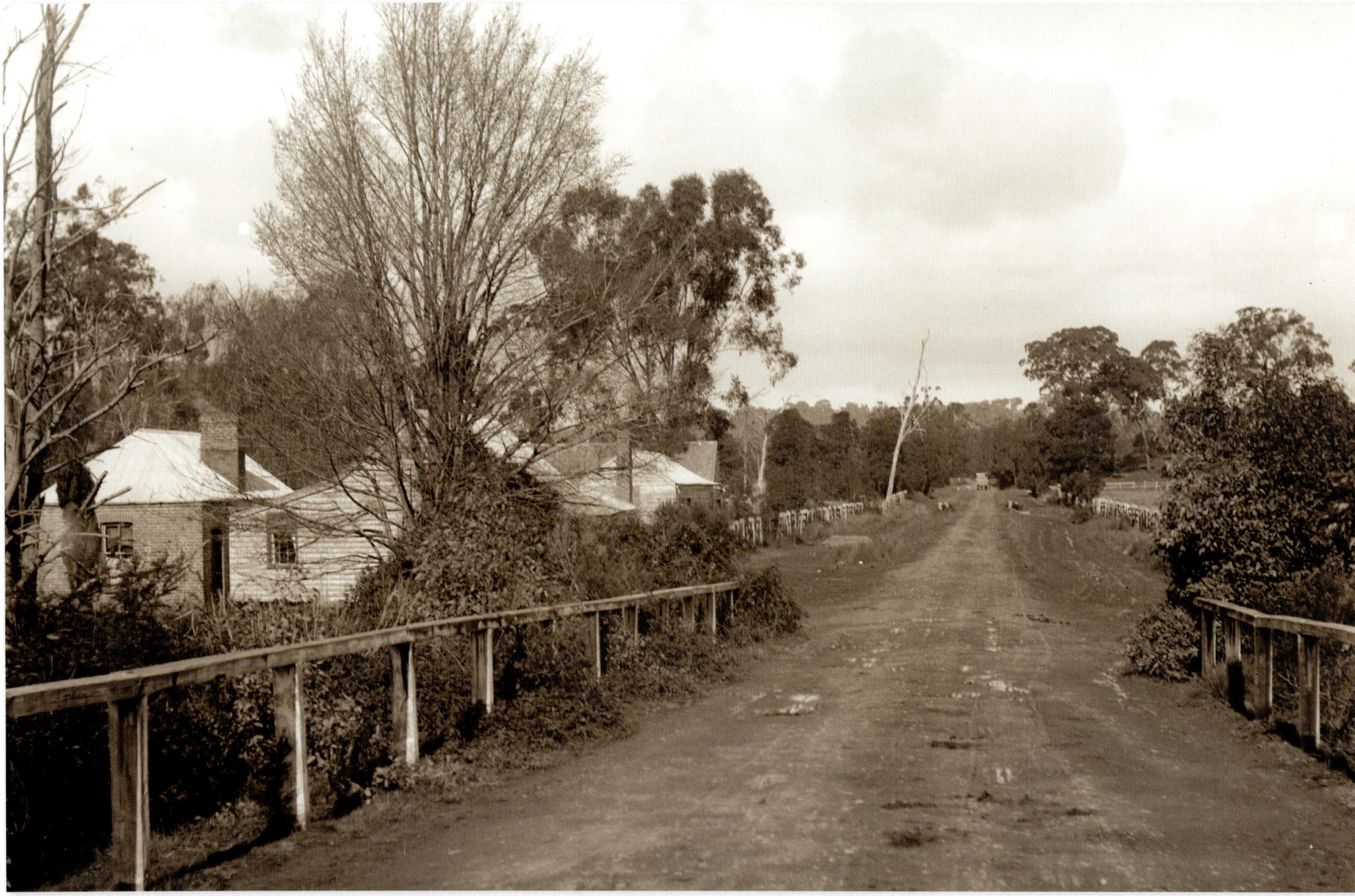

LOWER FERNTREE GULLY

c. 1900

PHOTOGRAPHER: MARK JAMES DANIEL

Here is a country road in the ten-year-old shire of Ferntree Gully. It might be Burwood Highway today.

Prior to the arrival of Europeans, Ferntree Gully was home to the Wurundjeri people. It was known for its abundance of ancient fern trees and lush flora. This idyllic scenery attracted visitors to the area from as far back as the 1870s.

From this point onwards, new arrivals to Melbourne began settling in Ferntree Gully. A local church, hotel, and primary school were established, with growth continuing once the railway line was extended to the area from Ringwood in 1889.

ELIZABETH STREET

c.1900

PHOTOGRAPHER: UNKNOWN

A Brunswick tram amidst the busy scene on Elizabeth Street.

Sadly for many of us who feel strongly about the preservation of our city's history, this pocket of the city is renowned for having lost much of its heritage charm. A large number of the buildings in this image have been demolished.

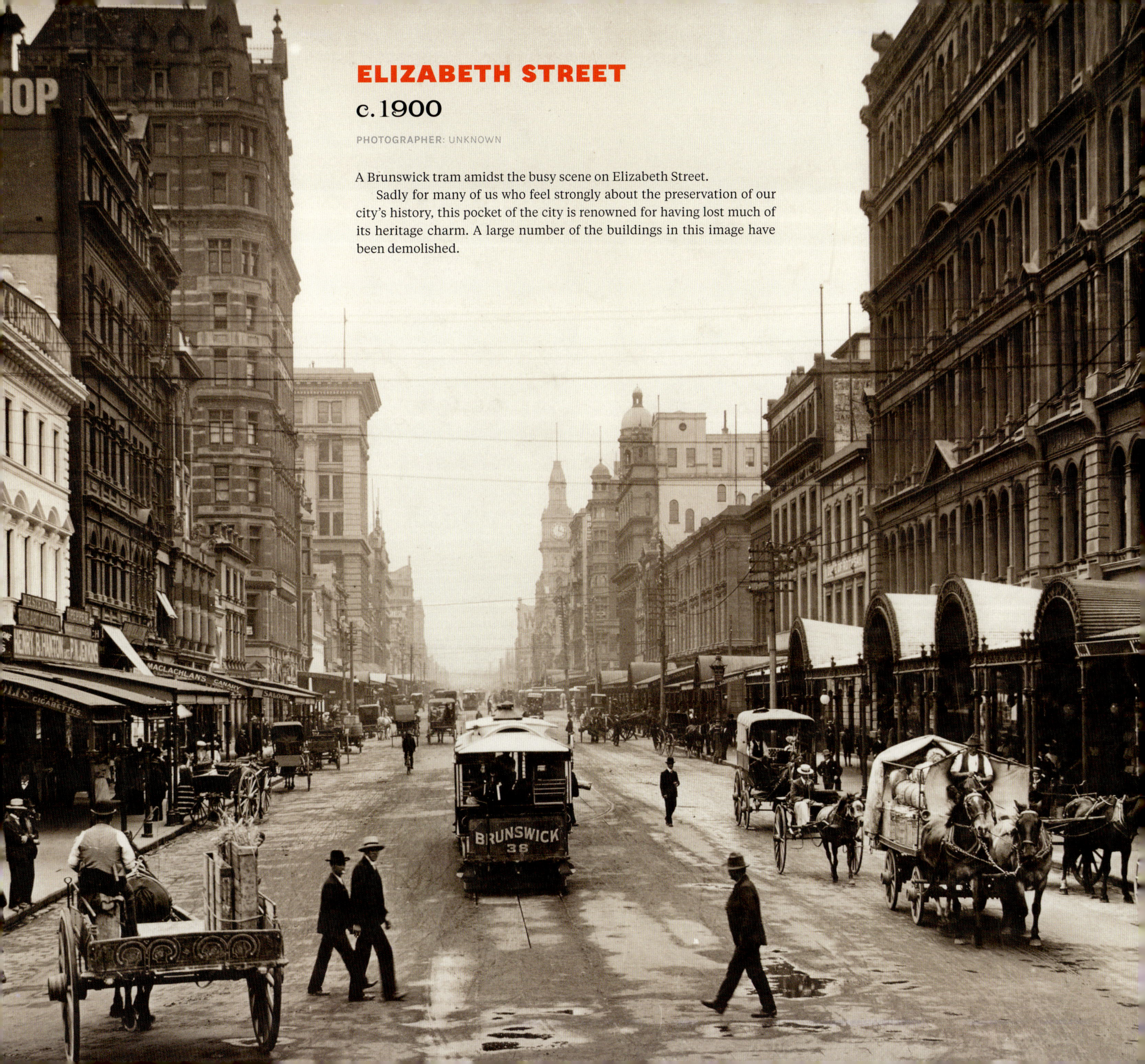

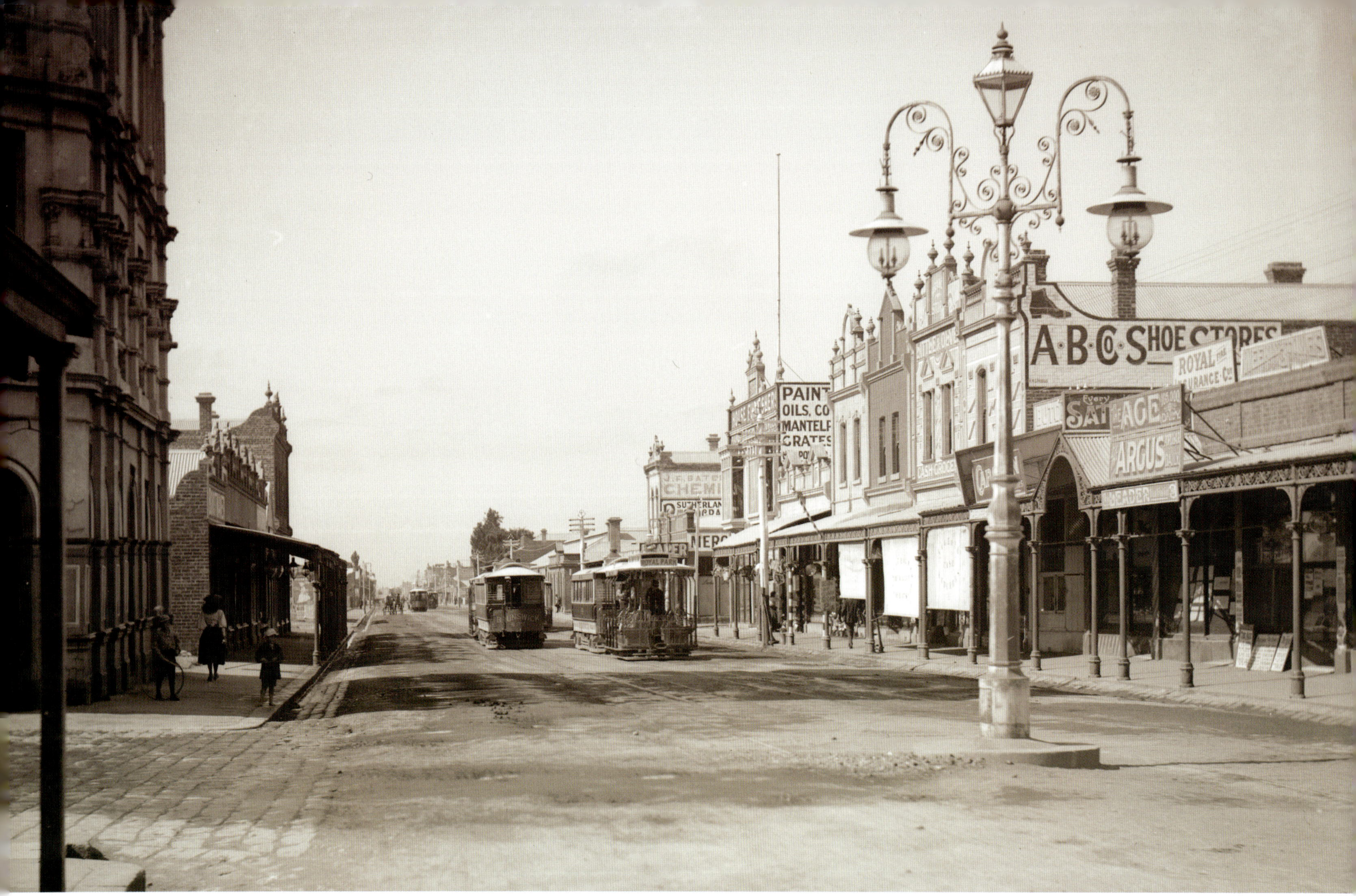

MORELAND ROAD, BRUNSWICK

c. 1900

PHOTOGRAPHER: GABRIEL KNIGHT

This intersection, right in the middle of Brunswick and Coburg, features an incredible light pole.

Coburg was first surveyed in 1837 by Robert Hoddle, who marked out a 327-acre village with two roads for the district: Bell Street and Pentridge Road, later called Sydney Road.

Dr Farquhar McCrae, a wealthy surgeon, purchased 600 acres in the area, which he called Moreland.

In 1841 he also bought land called La Rose in what is now Pascoe Vale South. The house he built there in 1842 is known as Wentworth House. It's the oldest-known private dwelling still standing on its original site, as well as the fifth-oldest building, in Victoria.

COLLINS STREET LOOKING TO SWANSTON STREET

c. 1900

PHOTOGRAPHER: JOHN HENRY HARVEY (TOP IMAGE); CHRIS MACHERAS (BOTTOM IMAGE)

THEN AND NOW: Comparing the images, we can see noticeable differences in architecture, fashion, and technology. But the town hall to the right remains unchanged, as do the stone tiles on the footpath. Note the information plaque at the far left in the present-day shot: it contains a history of the town hall, with an accompanying photo taken in 1910.

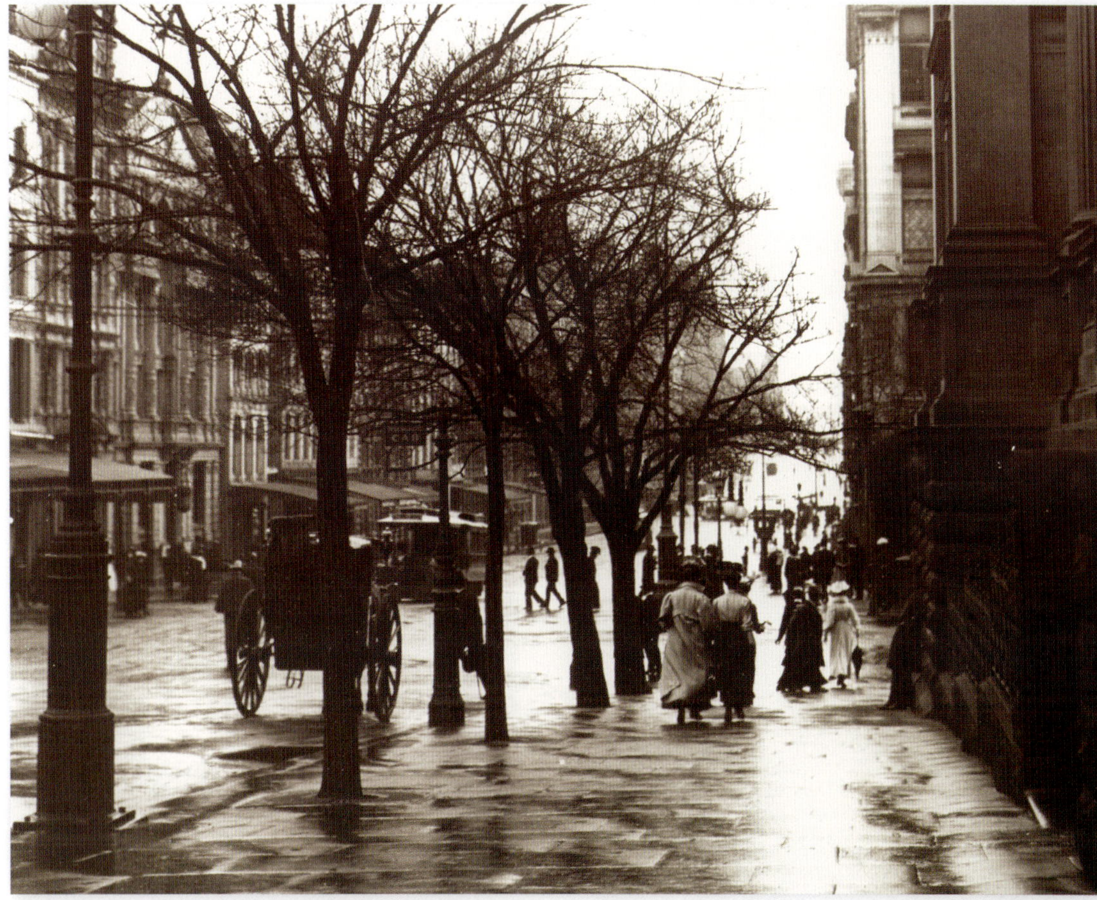

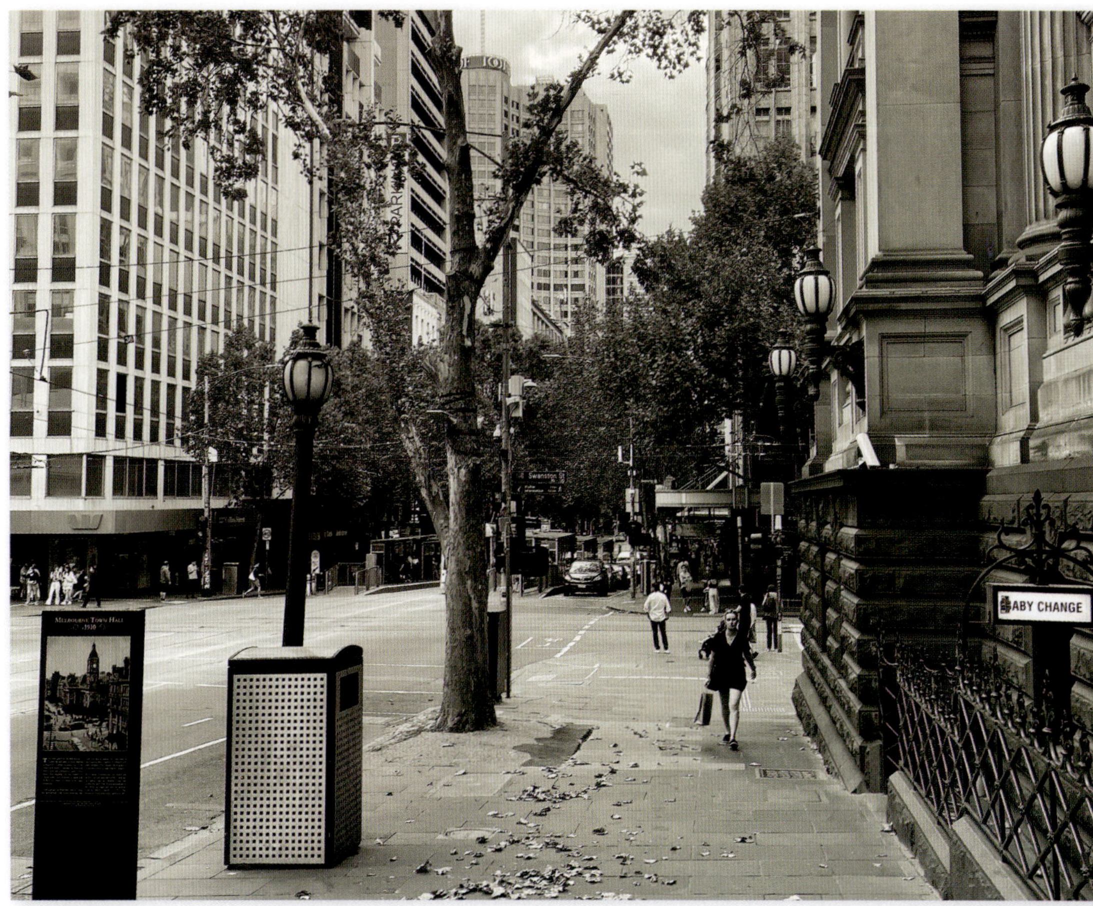

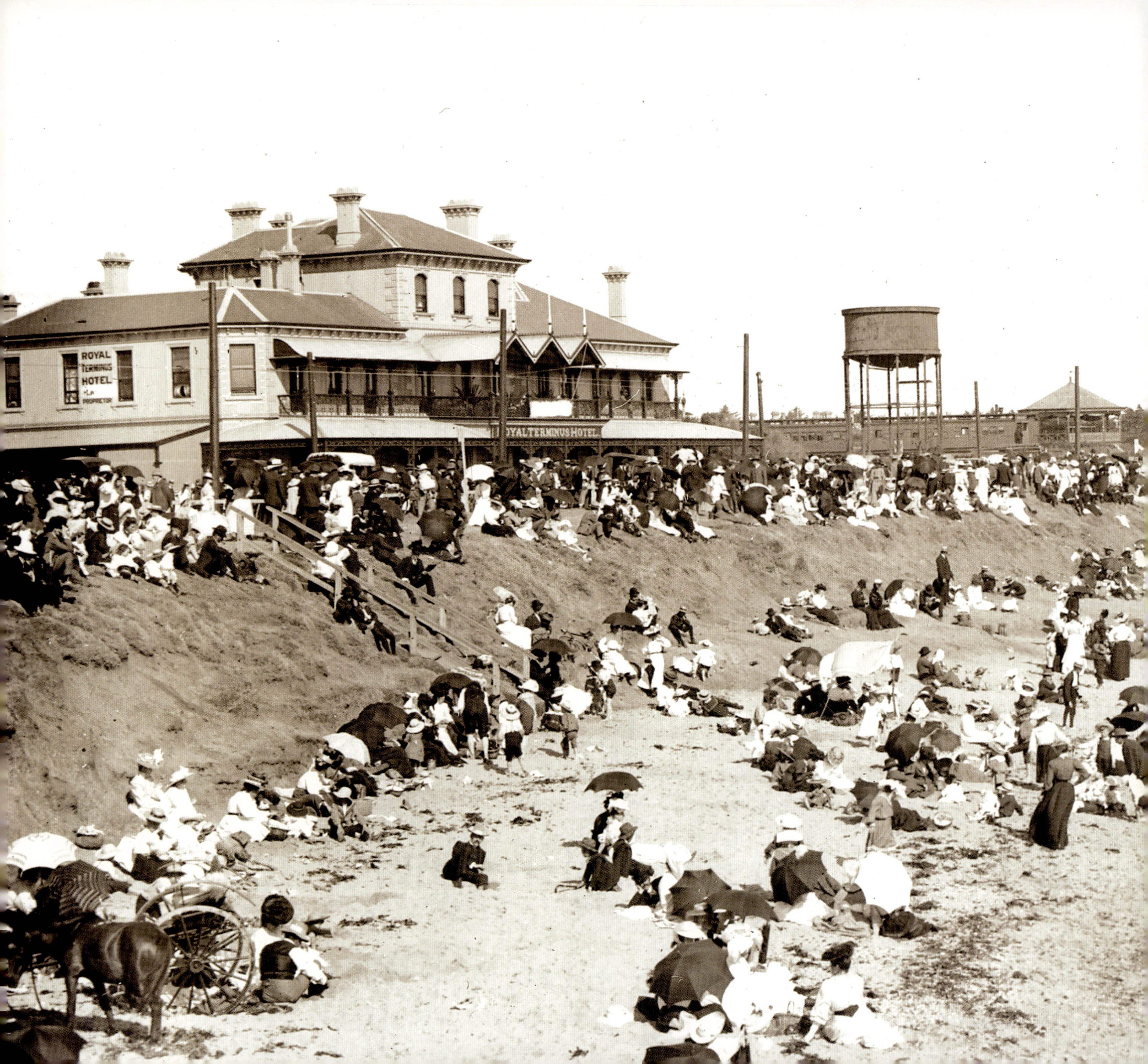
ROYAL
TERMINUS
HOTEL
ROYAL TERMINUS HOTEL

BRIGHTON BEACH

c.1900

PHOTOGRAPHER: VICTORIAN RAILWAYS

The area known as Brighton today was originally called Dendy's Special Survey.

In 1840, a man named Henry Dendy purchased over 5,000 acres of land in the Brighton area. He purchased it for only £1 per acre before even travelling to Australia to claim his land.

By the late 1840s, a vast array of lavish homes were built overlooking the beach. Ever since, Brighton has maintained its reputation as a high-status suburb.

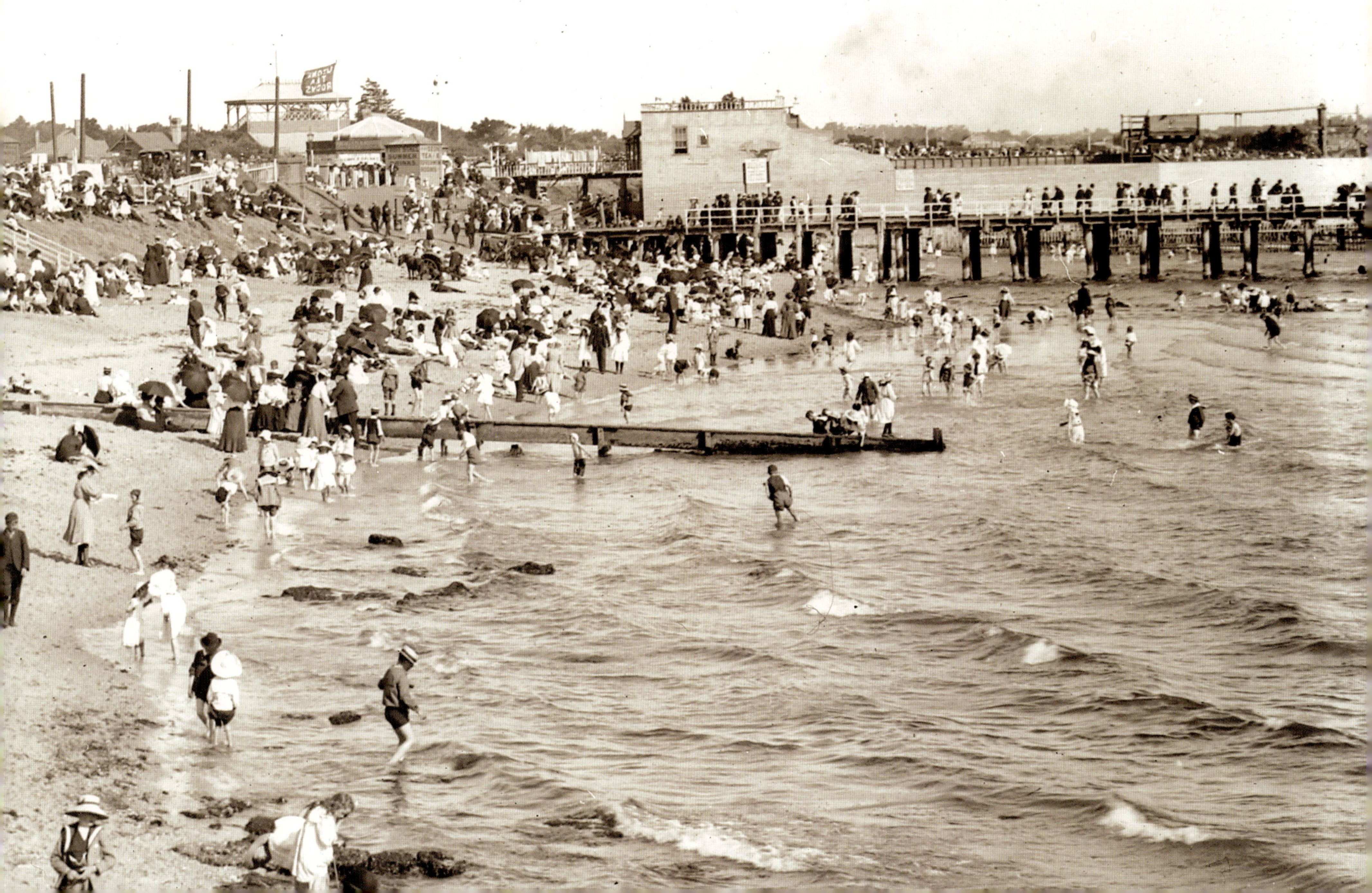

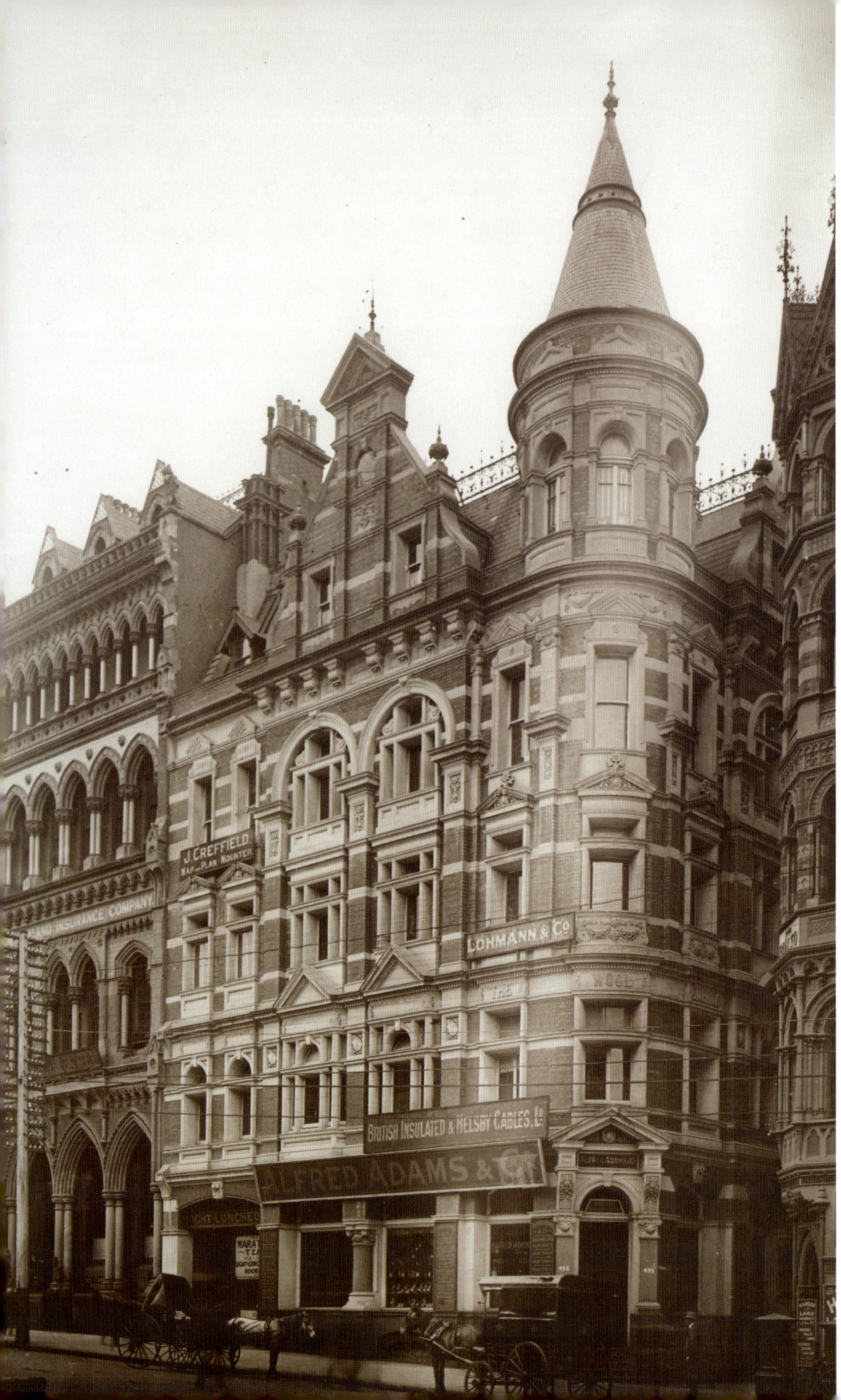

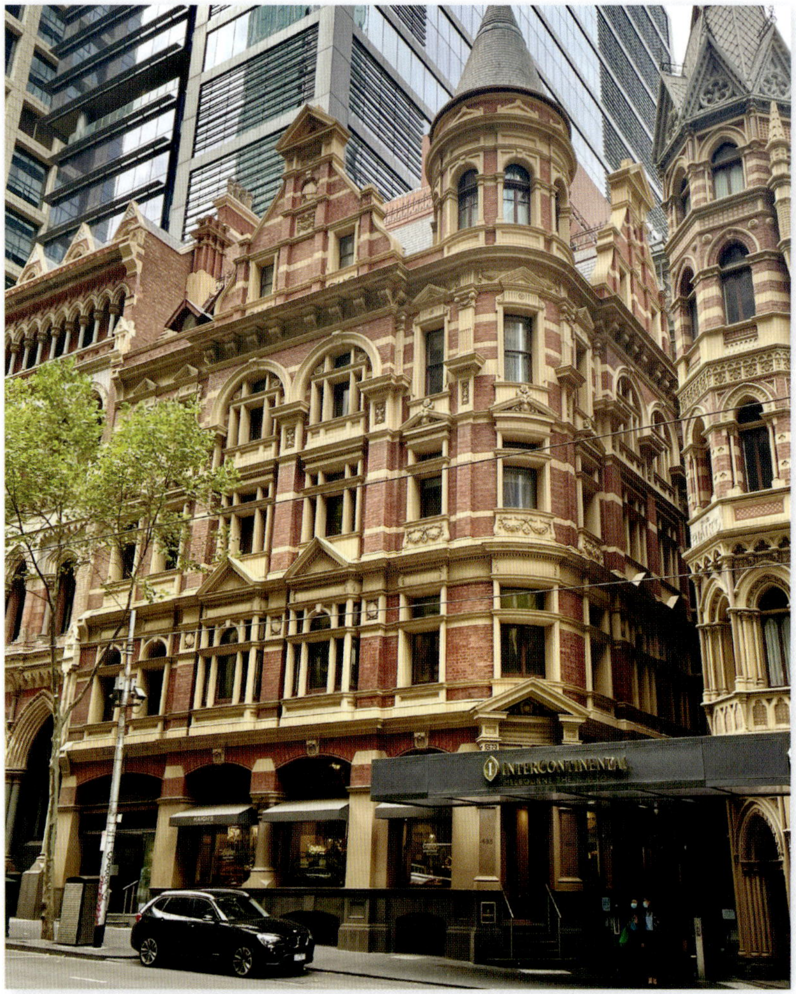

WINFIELD BUILDING, COLLINS STREET

c. 1900

PHOTOGRAPHER: ALGERNON DARGE (LEFT IMAGE); CHRIS MACHERAS (TOP IMAGE)

The Winfield Building at 487–95 Collins Street was built in 1891. Formerly the Will Exchange Building, it became known by its current name in the mid-1920s.

It is believed to have been built for J.R. Murphy, the owner of Murphy's brewery.

From 1892 to 1894, the building was the site of Melbourne's first amalgamated wool exchange, and included an auction hall, which brought together all the Melbourne wool sales.

The front section on Collins Street is all that remains of the former, much larger complex, although it has retained its original facade.

The rear of the building was replaced by a large fourteen-storey extension in 1984, as part of the redevelopment of the site as a hotel.

HOTEL WINDSOR, SPRING STREET

c.1900

PHOTOGRAPHY: CHARLES NETTLETON

The grand Hotel Windsor was originally called just 'The Grand'. Built by the wealthy shipping tycoon George Nipper, it was completed in 1884.

In 1886, a company headed by James Munro ran the hotel. He was the fifteenth premier of Victoria, and a man of strict Christian morals, who spearheaded the temperance movement. Mr Munro famously burned the hotel's liquor licence in public, and operated the venue as a coffee palace.

Unfortunately for him, Munro was overcome by a mountain of debt and declared bankrupt in 1893, after which a new owner took over. Attacked and beaten unconscious by a man who had been ruined in the crash of the 1890s, Munro left a less-than-favourable legacy as the most notoriously corrupt politician in Melbourne's land-boom era.

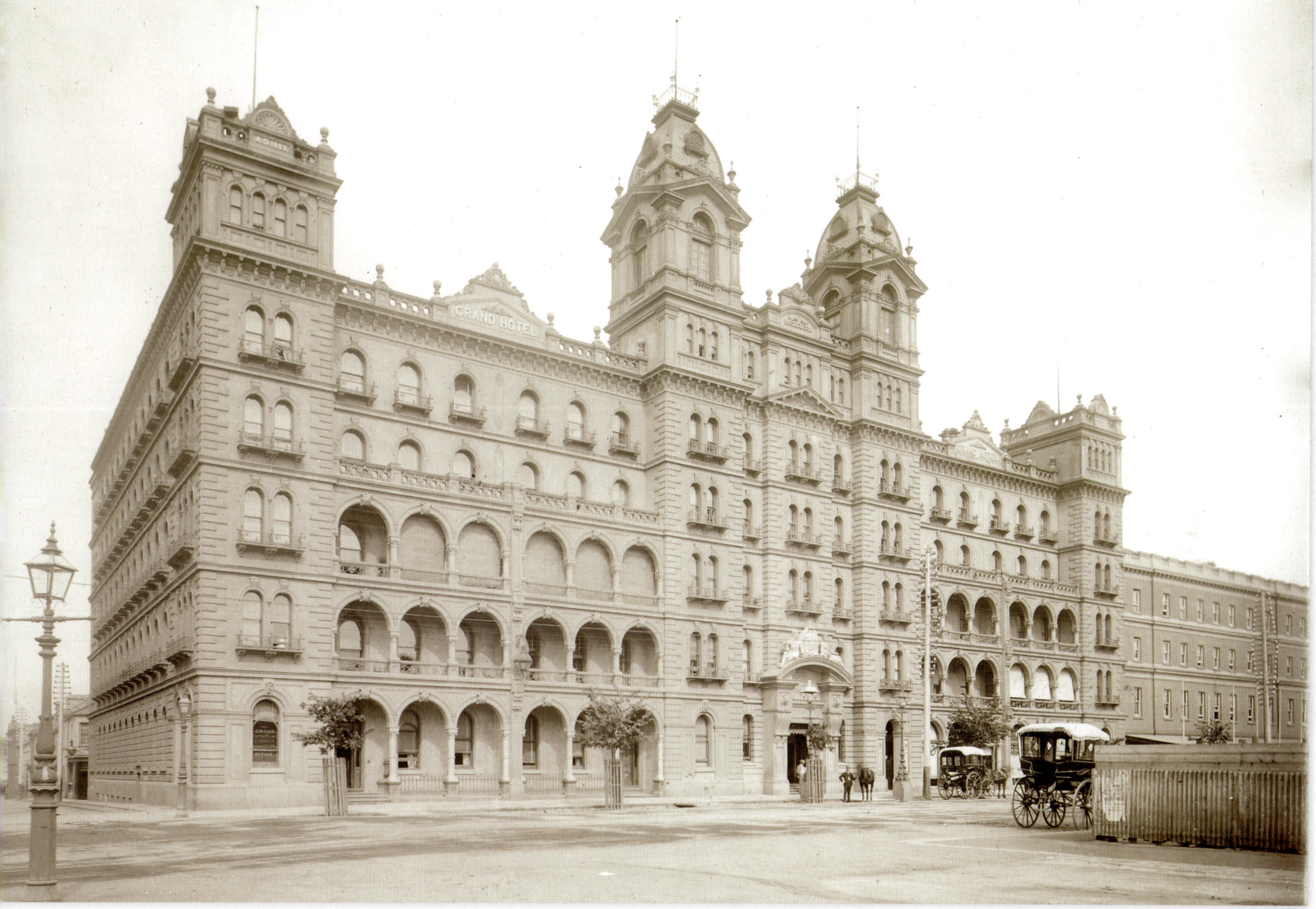

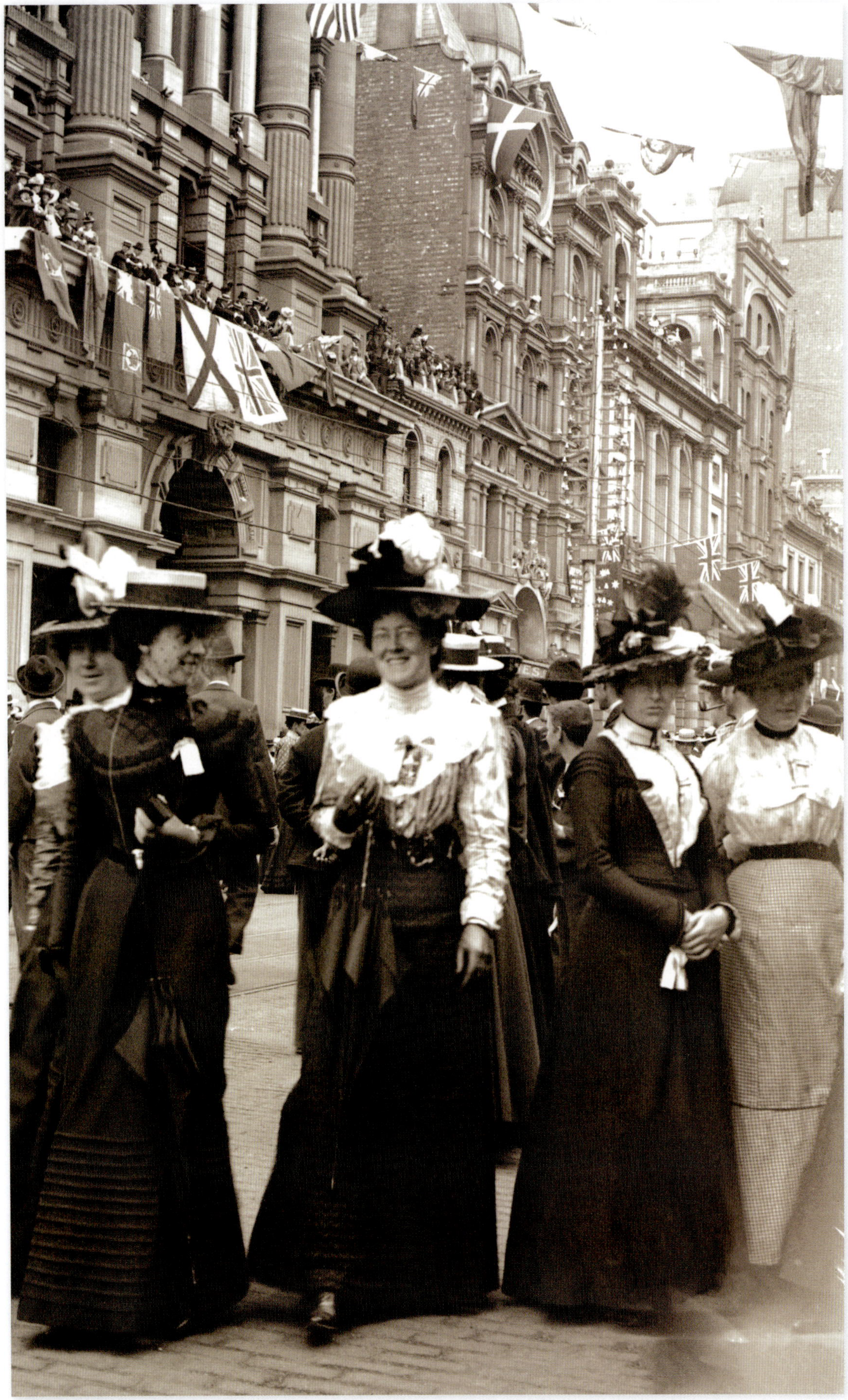

RELIEF OF MAFEKING PROCESSION, COLLINS STREET & BOURKE STREET

c.1900

PHOTOGRAPHER: JAMES FOX BARNARD

Photos from the procession on Collins Street (left) and Bourke Street (right). The procession was held to celebrate the British army's lifting of the 217-day siege of Mafeking in the Second Boer War.

The fashion of the time astounds me, especially the hats. It would appear that wearing a hat was very much the norm for both men and women of the time.

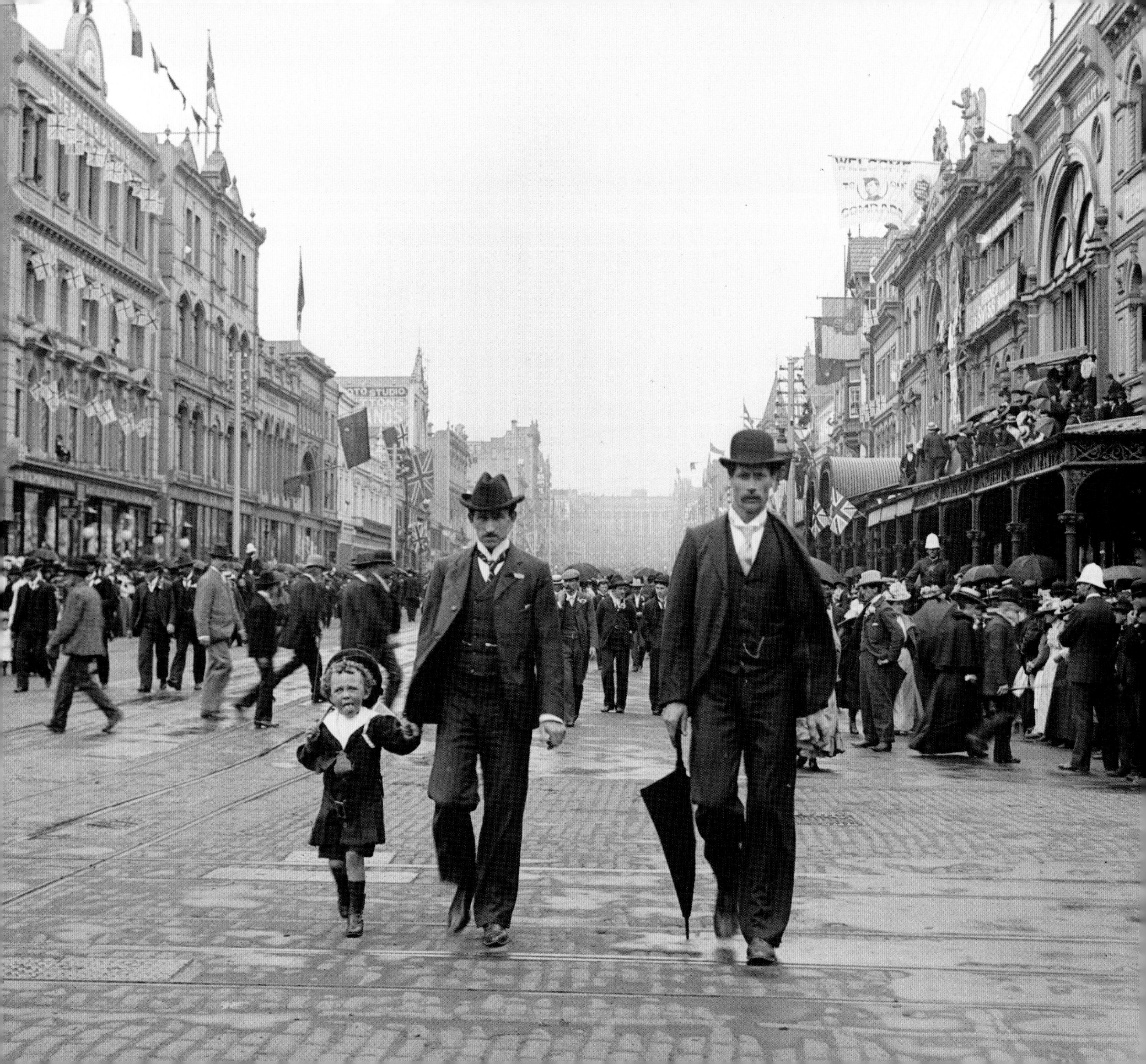
WELCOME

COLLINS STREET

c.1900

PHOTOGRAPHER: RUTH HOLLICK

Collins Street, looking east towards Elizabeth Street.

Collins Street was nothing short of majestic, full of ornate and opulent structures. At the end of the street, you can just make out the Treasury Building. I love the way people looked at cameras a century ago — with such intrigue!

This fabulous shot was taken by Ruth Hollick, who became famous for her portraits of children. She had a studio at 167 Collins Street.

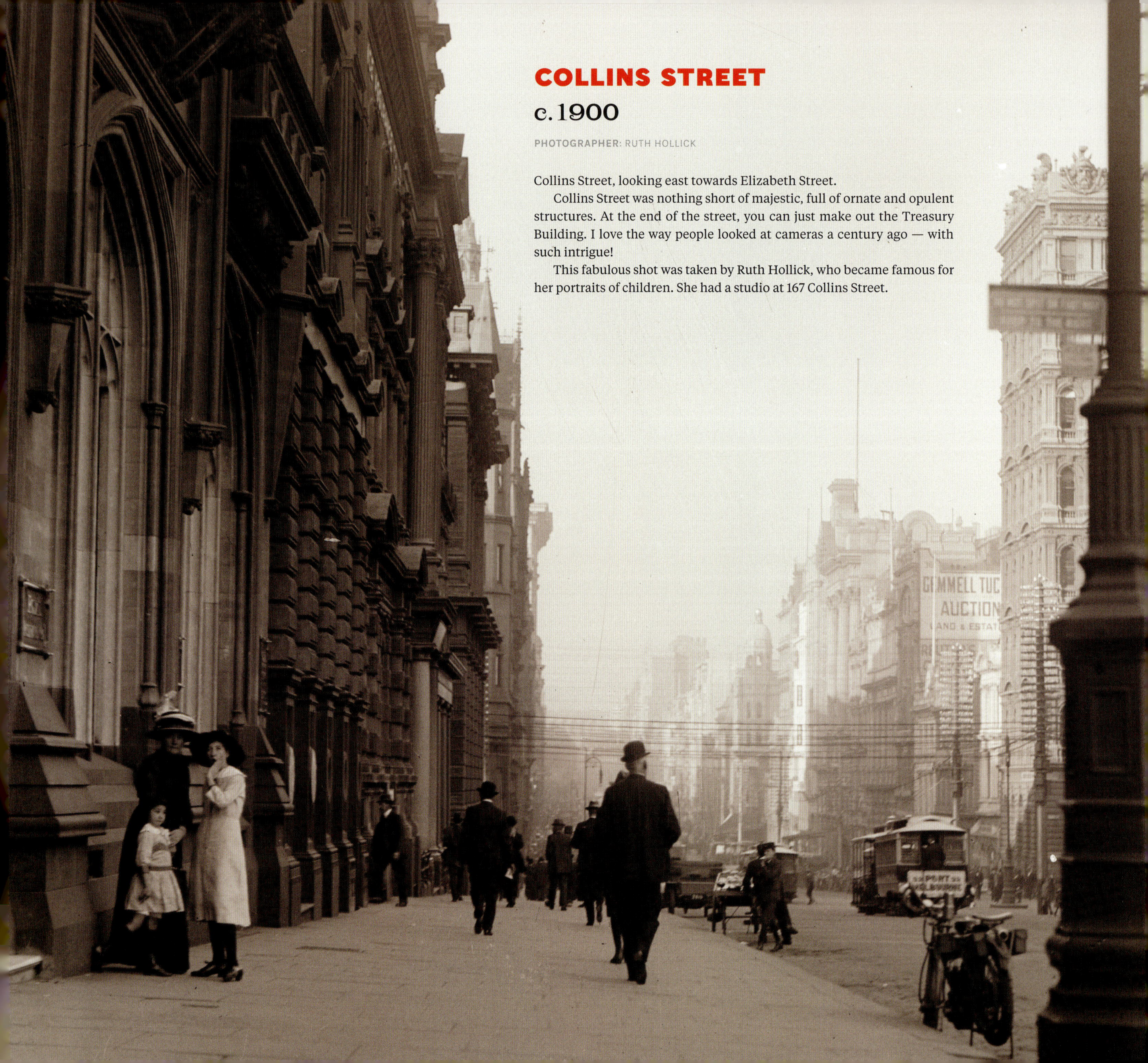

ELIZABETH STREET

c. 1905

PHOTOGRAPHER: UNKNOWN (TOP IMAGE); ALLAN WILKINSON (BOTTOM IMAGE)

THEN AND NOW: Laying of cable-tram tracks on Elizabeth Street, looking towards the Flinders Street Station clock tower.

The first clock was known as the 'Water Tower Clock', after a wooden-framed water tower was erected on the site in 1853. The tower remained in place until 1905, when work began on the new station and the clock tower was moved to outside Princes Bridge Station. The clock itself can still be seen on display at Southern Cross Station. Next time you're there, look out for it!

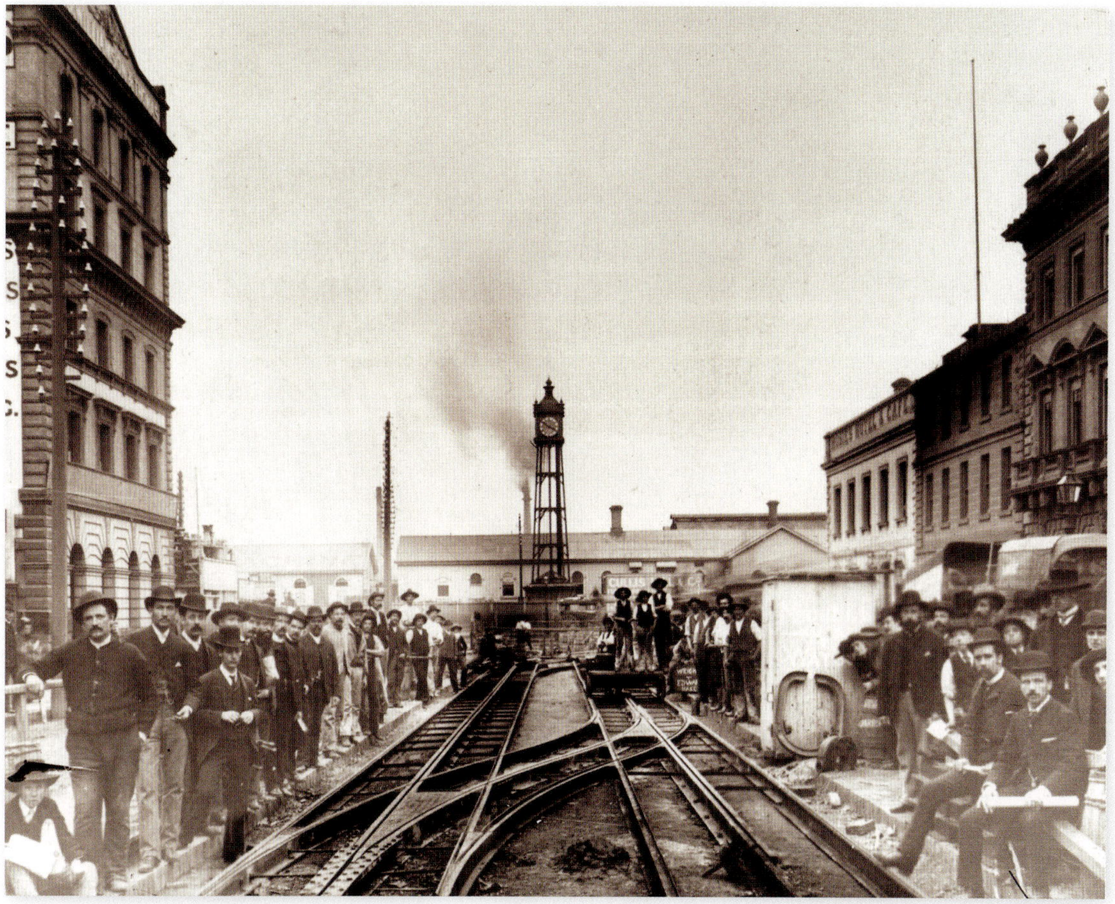

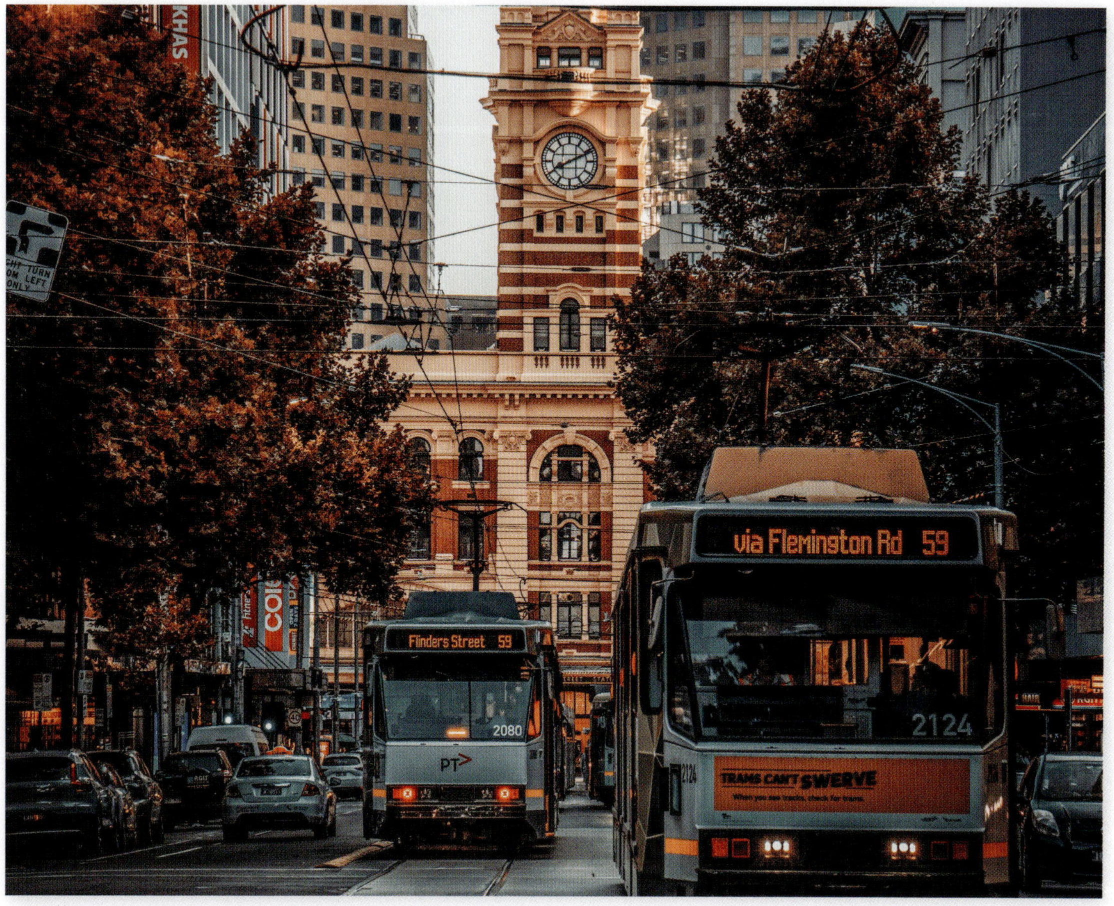

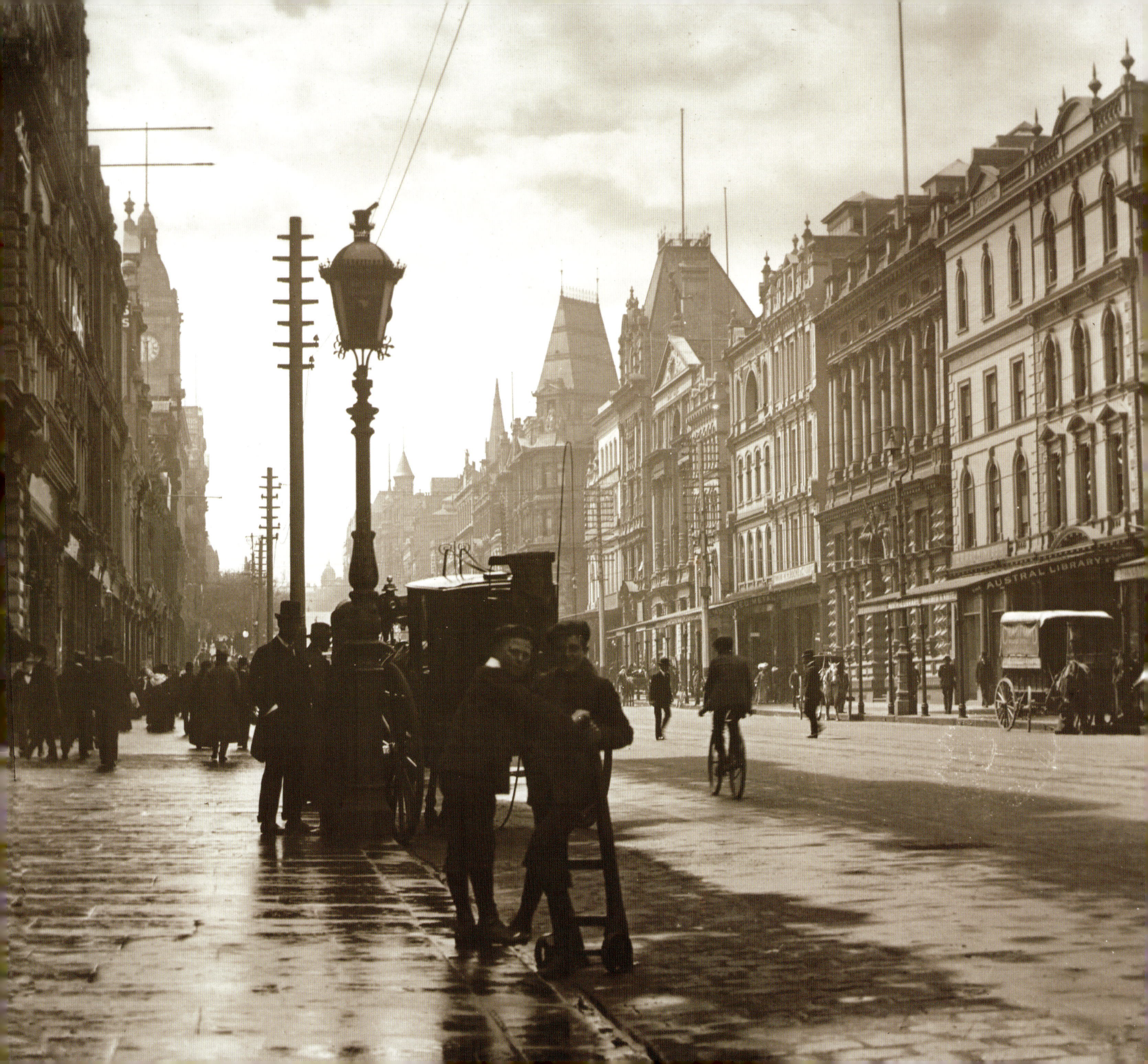
AUSTRAL LIBRARY

FLINDERS STREET STATION ▸

c. 1906

PHOTOGRAPHER: UNKNOWN

A pretty rare shot of Flinders Street Station still under construction. Work on the central dome began in 1906, so I date this photo to that year. The building in front looks like a temporary office of sorts.

Initially, the architects intended the front facade to be stone-faced. After some deliberation, the state government decided that this was too costly. The design was amended, with the since-famous red brick and cement render substituted.

The first electric-train service operated from Flinders Street to Essendon in 1919. By 1923 it was thought to be the world's busiest passenger station, servicing 2,300 trains and 300,000 passengers daily — surpassing Gare Saint-Lazare in Paris, Grand Central Terminal in New York, and Liverpool Street Station in London.

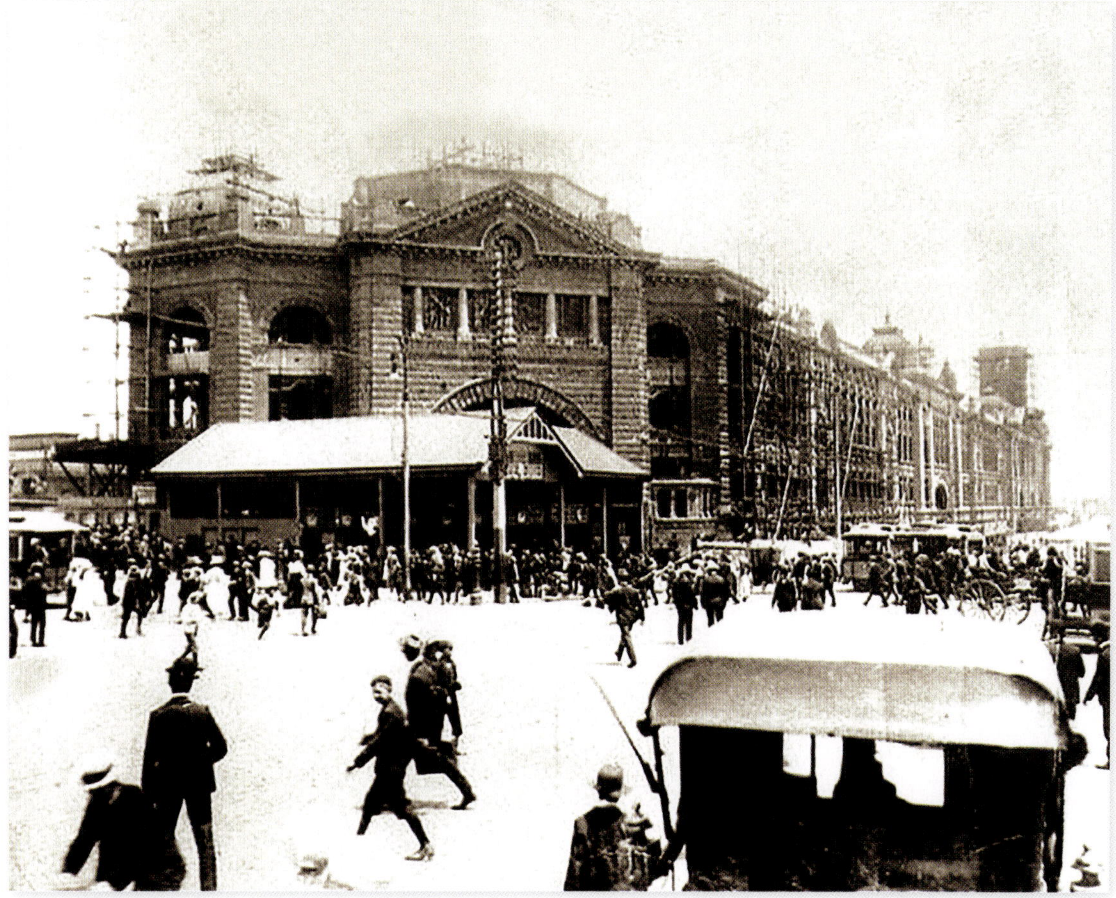

◂ COLLINS STREET

c. 1905

PHOTOGRAPHER: JOHN HENRY HARVEY

Two young lads, intrigued, are looking directly at the camera. You wonder what direction their lives took, especially whether they joined the front lines of the Great War only a decade later.

Behind them you can see the wonderfully opulent buildings of Collins Street.

When writer George Sala coined the term 'Marvellous Melbourne' during his 1885 visit, Melbourne was the largest and wealthiest city in the British Empire after London.

The city was given an array of nicknames, including 'New Gold Mountain' and the 'Land of the Golden Fleece', referring to a booming metropolis of ornate architecture, hotels, theatres, cathedrals, galleries, restaurants, and residences.

MELBOURNE CUP PARTY, MALVERN

1906

PHOTOGRAPHER: SEARS' STUDIOS

Fine ladies and gentlemen pose for a photo during a Melbourne Cup party at Government House, Malvern, in November 1906.

Now known as the Stonington mansion, at the time of this photo it was the residence of the governor of Victoria. It was purchased by the state in 1928, and functioned as Government House until 1931.

During that time, many famous people were hosted at the mansion, such as Dame Nellie Melba, the Duke and Duchess of York (later King George VI and Queen Elizabeth), the Prince of Wales (later King Edward VIII), Lord and Lady Baden-Powell, Lord Kitchener, Sir John Monash, Keith Murdoch, and Ernest Shackleton.

In 1925, the nine-year-old son of the then governor, Christopher Rous, tragically died of leukaemia and was buried within the grounds of the property. There have been modern accounts of his ghost haunting the premises.

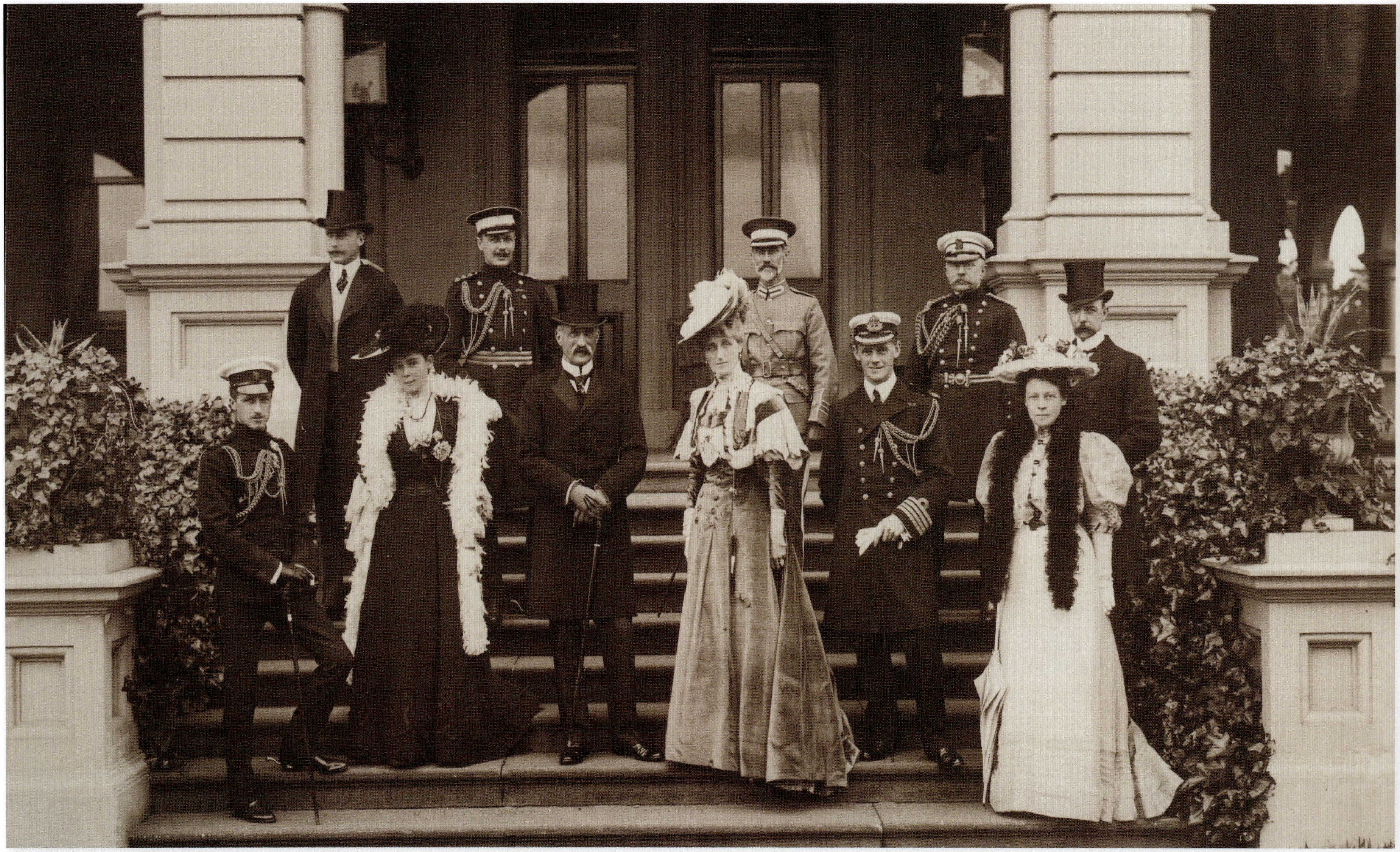

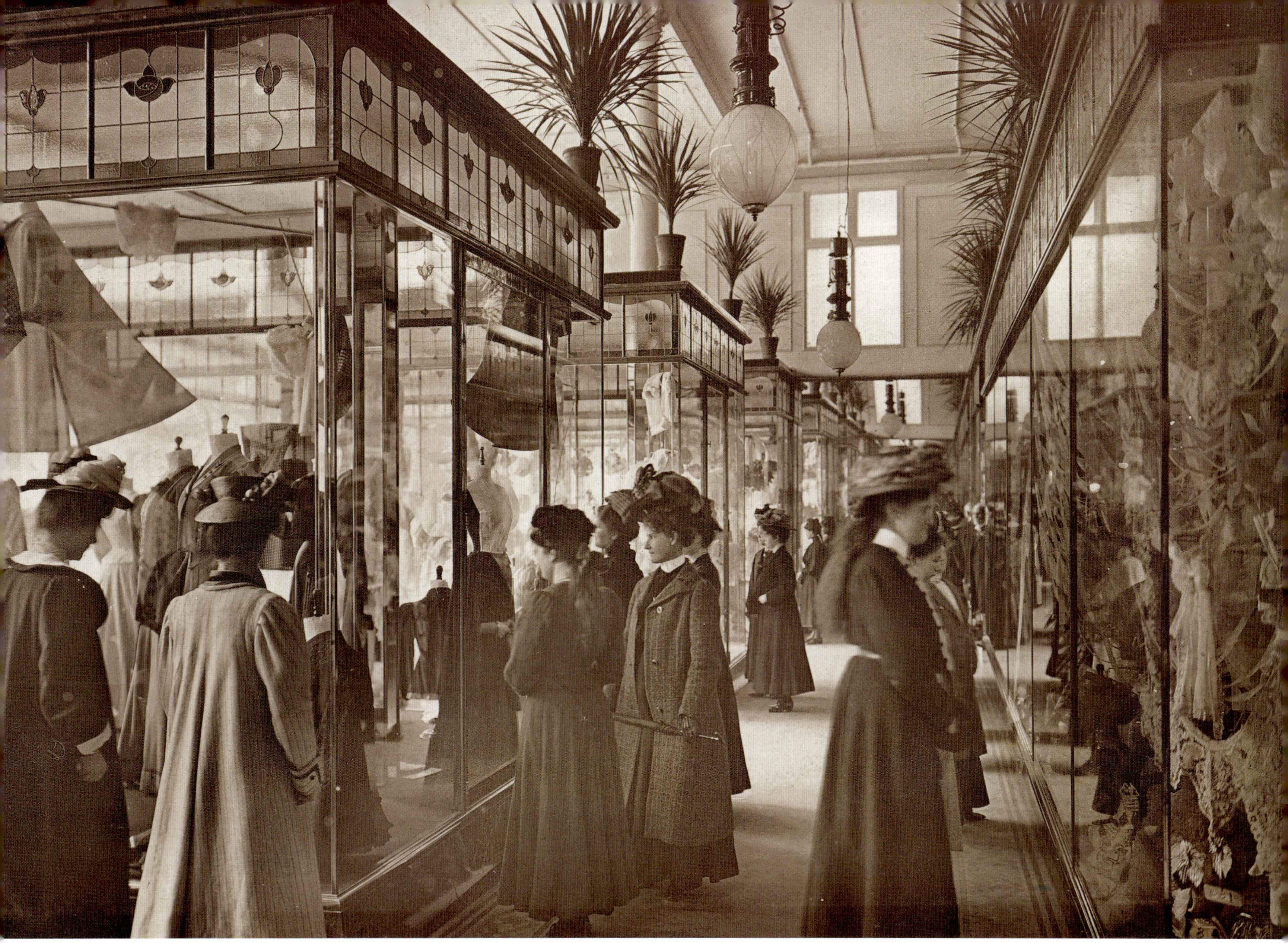

GEORGES, COLLINS STREET

c. 1908

PHOTOGRAPHER: SEARS' STUDIOS

Here is a fascinating insight into Melbourne's first island windows, at Georges department store.

Melbourne is known as a major fashion hub today. Back in the late 1800s, the rise of the rag trade was already evident along Flinders Lane.

In the age of Marvellous Melbourne and the economic booms with which it is associated, Melbourne's elite prided themselves on their awareness and adoption of the latest fashions from Paris and London.

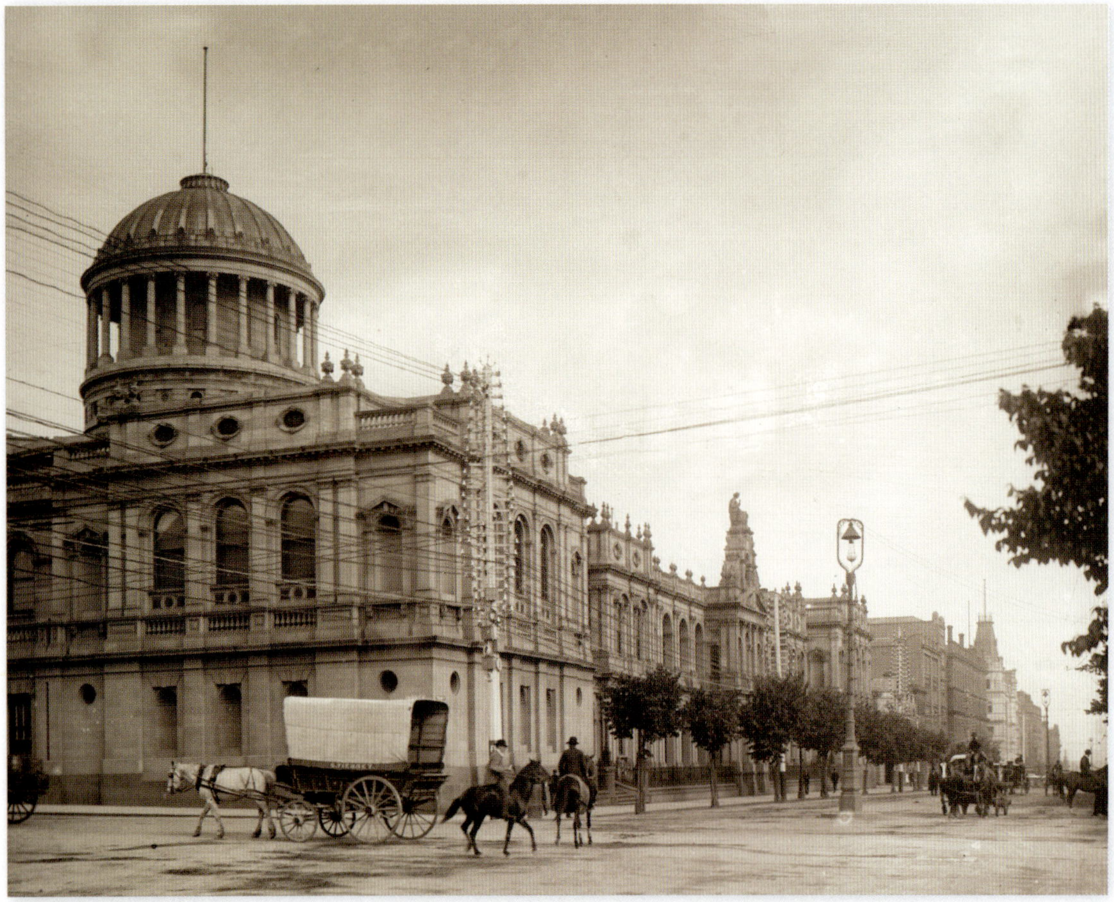

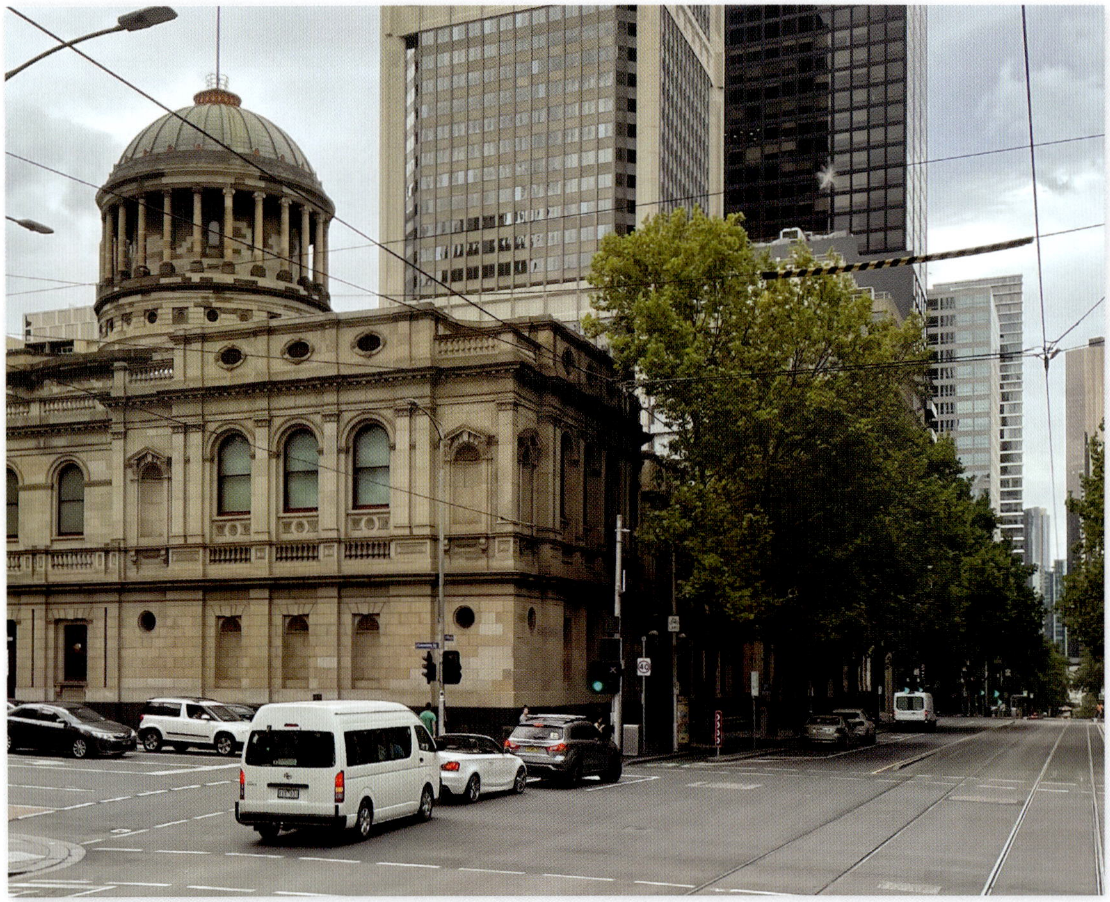

SUPREME COURT OF VICTORIA

c.1910

PHOTOGRAPHER: UNKNOWN (TOP IMAGE); CHRIS MACHERAS (BOTTOM IMAGE)

THEN AND NOW: Same shots, 110 years apart, featuring the Victorian Supreme Court in 1910 and in 2020, on the corner of Lonsdale and William streets. I can't help but wonder if those are the same trees.

The Supreme Court building was completed in 1884. Its design was determined via a competition. The Public Works Department judged the contest, with architects Alfred Louis Smith and Arthur Ebden Johnson being victorious. Much controversy surrounded the competition, however, because Mr Johnson was also on the judging panel. This was somewhat ironic, given that they were designing the highest court of law in the state! The Victorian Supreme Court remains to this day the largest single-design network of court buildings in Australia.

SOUTH PRESTON

c. 1910

PHOTOGRAPHER: UNKNOWN

The northern suburb of Preston in the pre-Northland era.

This shot appears to have been taken from the corner of High Street and Gower Street, Preston, likely from the Preston Town Hall.

Looking up High Street, it appears that the church on the left is the Greek Orthodox Church of Saint Cyril and Saint Methodius on Yann Street. Built in 1888, and formerly a Methodist church, it was passed to the Greek Orthodox Archdiocese at a combined Methodist–Greek Orthodox service in 1967, due to dwindling attendances.

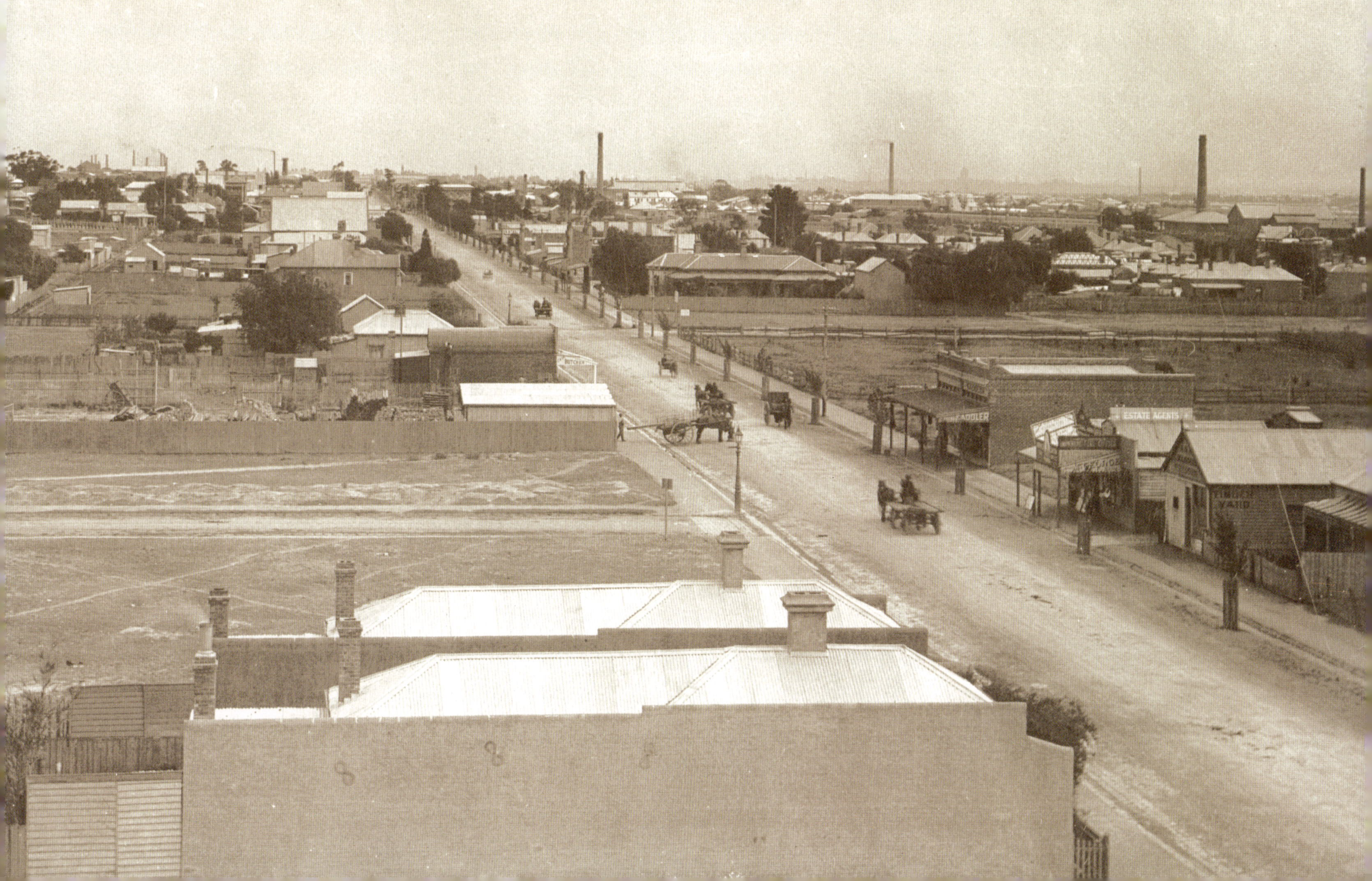

FLINDERS STREET FISH MARKET

c. 1910

PHOTOGRAPHER: UNKNOWN

The Fish Market on Flinders Street was a grand nineteenth-century palace with copper spires that resembled witches' hats.

It was built in 1890 to replace the market on the corner of Flinders Street and Swanston Street (where the current Flinders Street Station stands). The market also featured a huge clock tower.

Between 1958 and 1960, in what is now widely regarded as an act of great vandalism, the market was demolished. Its demolition was well documented.

All that remains are faded photographs and the wrought-iron gates, now at the entrance to Fawkner Cemetery.

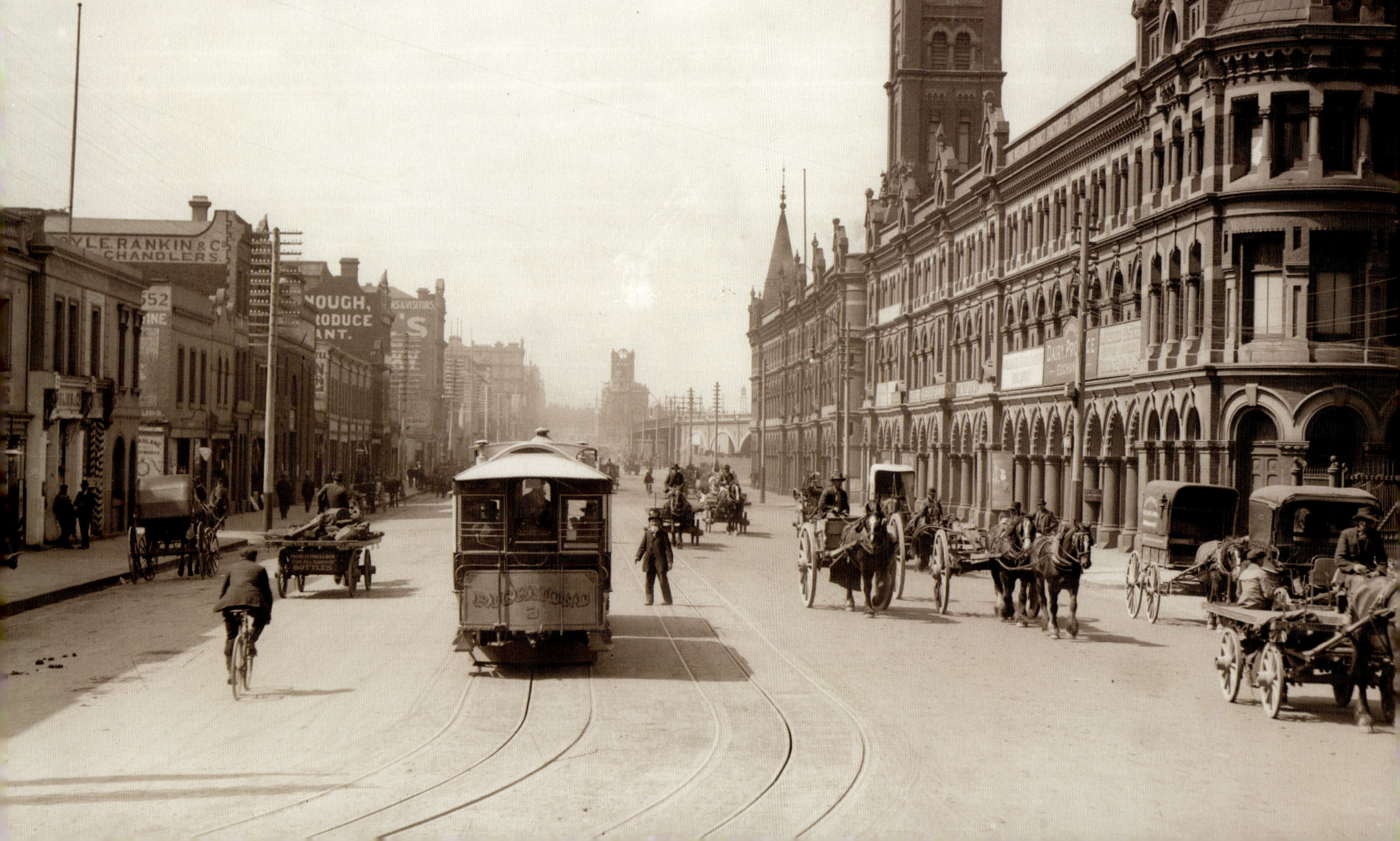

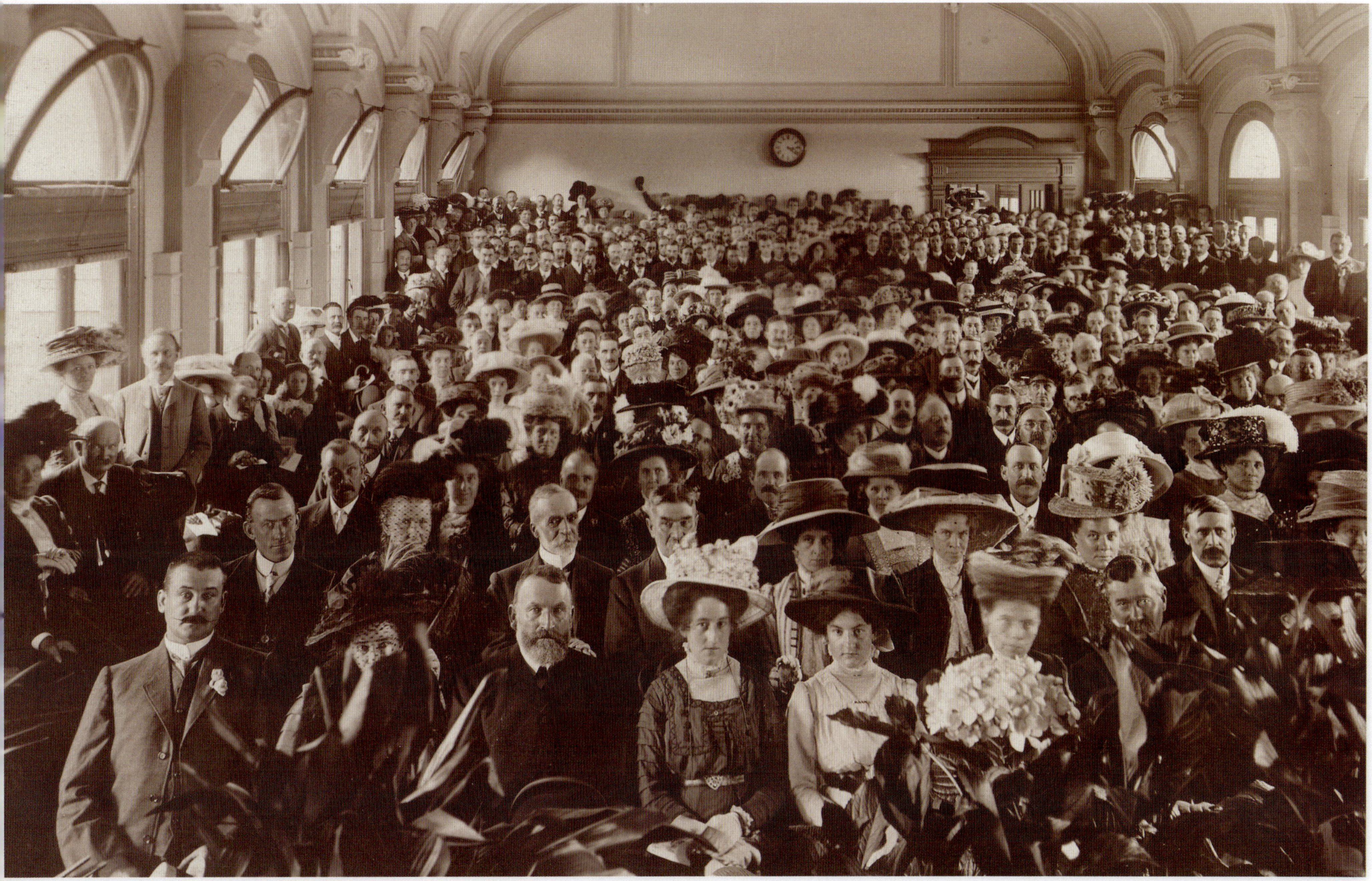

FLINDERS STREET STATION BALLROOM

c.1910

PHOTOGRAPHER: UNKNOWN
SOURCE: ALFRED GALBRAITH COLLECTION, STATE LIBRARY VICTORIA

I just love looking at all the facial expressions in this photograph. These are members of the Victorian Railways Institute attending an event in the Upper Hall (the Ballroom) of Flinders Street Station in 1910 — the year the building opened!

The institute was a source of education and social activity for railways employees. It offered classes in bookkeeping and specific technologies, which provided its employees with opportunities for advancement. It also operated a large lending library and concert hall, which doubled as a ballroom, and organised various sporting teams. Alfred Galbraith was one of its founding members.

Though this photo reminds me of the final scene in *The Shining*, I hope plans to restore the ballroom come to fruition soon. I'd love to go up there and have a look around.

FLINDERS STREET

c. 1910

PHOTOGRAPHER: UNKNOWN

A jaw-dropping shot of Flinders Street looking west past the intersection with Swanston Street.

The newly built, freshly painted Flinders Street Station commands the left of the image. The building closer to us on the left, with the tobacco advertisement, would one day become the Visitors' Centre. This is now an area under construction as part of the Metro Tunnel project.

Across the road from the station stands the iconic Young and Jackson Hotel, established in 1861 and listed on the Victorian Heritage Register.

The large billboard-like advertisement that reads 'Sargood Bros' pertains to a business that imported and sold soft goods. The company was involved in a significant tariffs and duties legal case that went before the High Court in *Sargood Bros v Commonwealth*, a case that is still cited and referenced today.

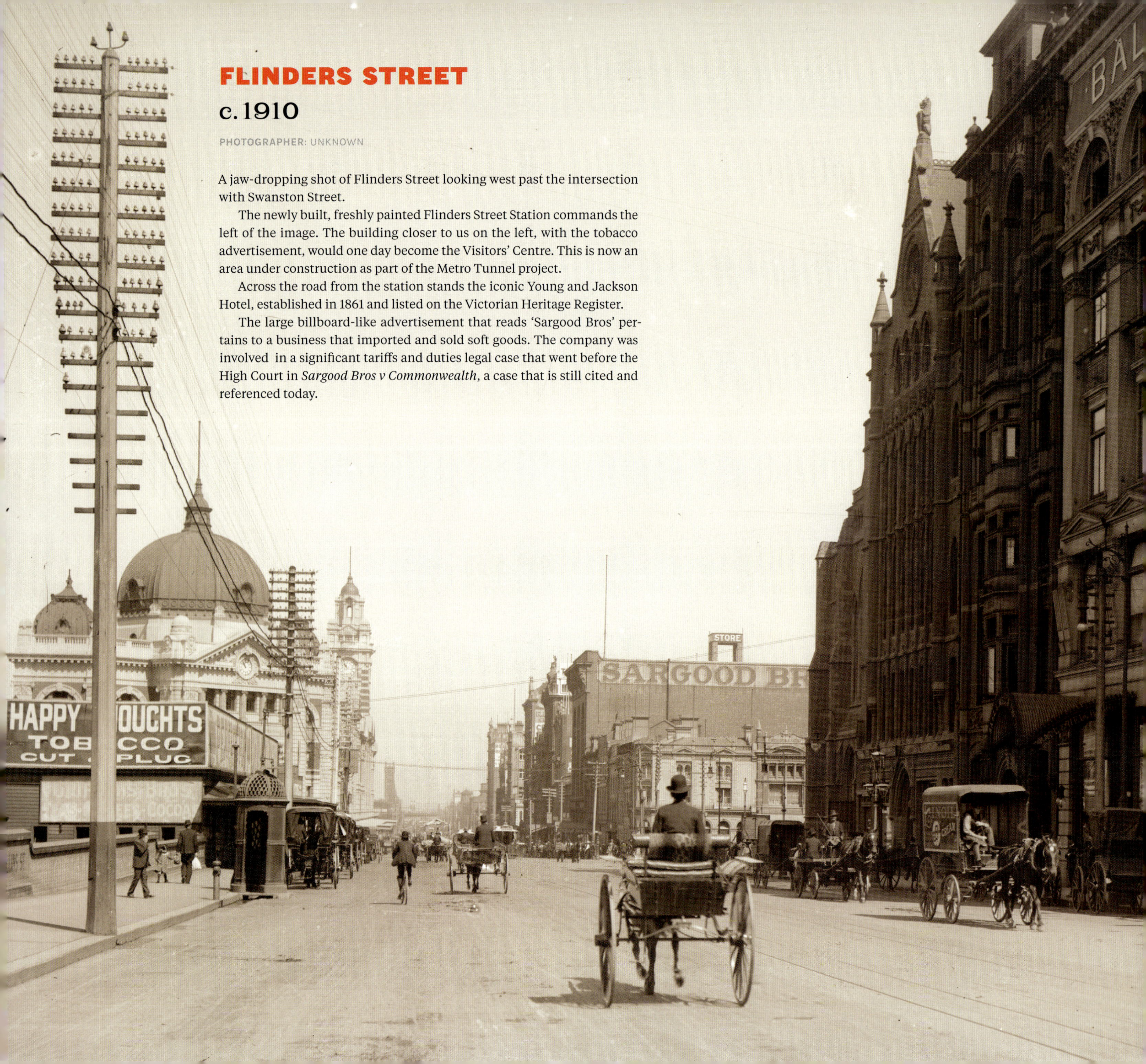

DAYLESFORD POST OFFICE

c. 1910

PHOTOGRAPHER: UNKNOWN (TOP IMAGE);
CHRIS MACHERAS (BOTTOM IMAGE)

THEN AND NOW: Daylesford, originally named Wombat, and traditionally inhabited by the Dja Dja Wurrung people, is a spa town 108 kilometres north-west of Melbourne. The local gold rush came about when gold was struck in the area now covered by Lake Daylesford.

The post office depicted here opened in 1858. Over time, many of the town's historical buildings have survived, making it not only a quaint and picturesque town, but one that offers a fascinating look into the past.

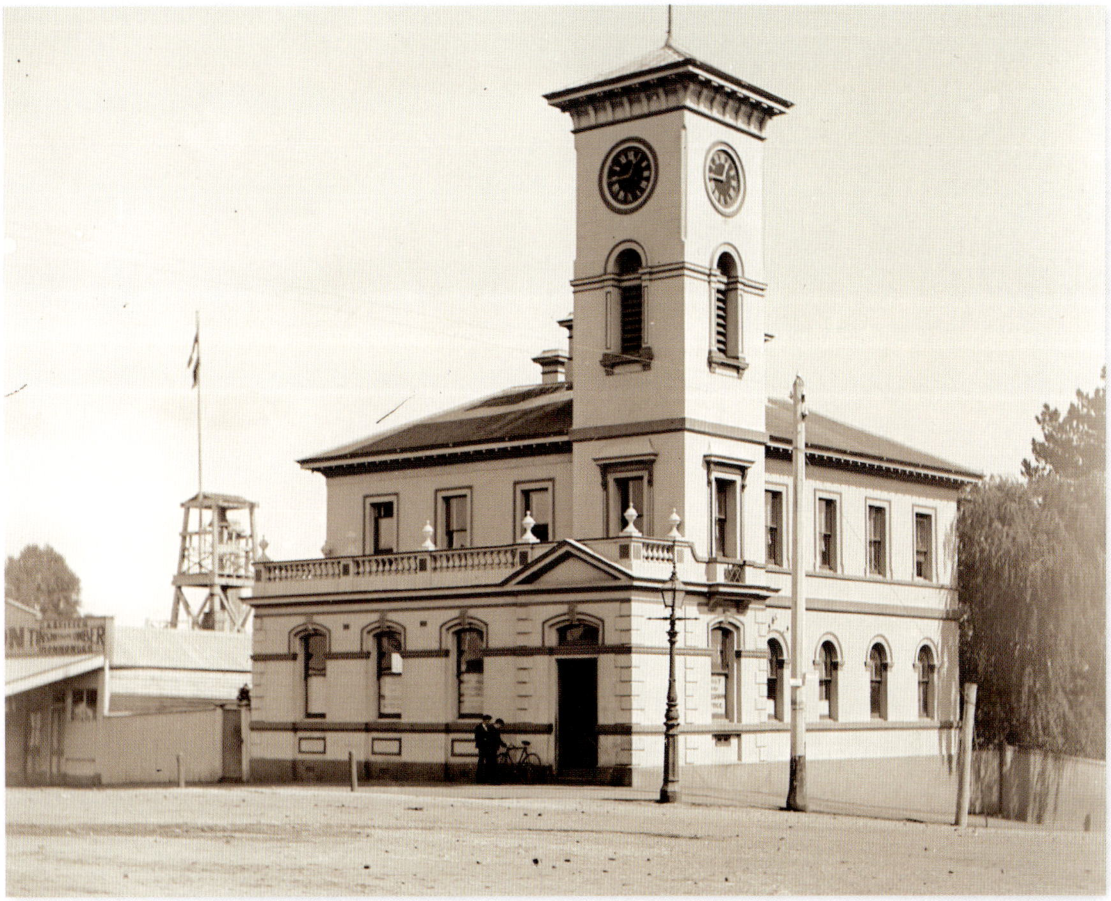

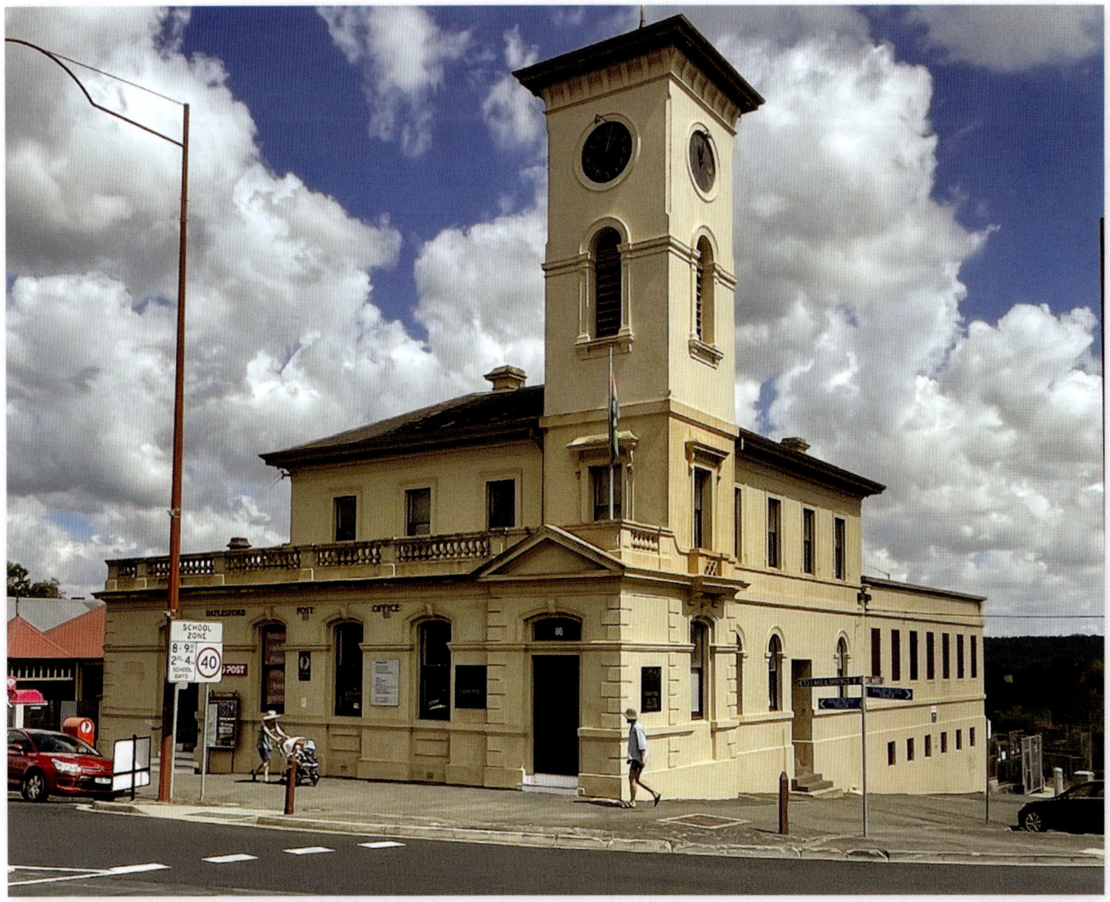

FLINDERS STREET STATION CLOCK TOWER

c.1910

PHOTOGRAPHER: UNKNOWN

This image of the clock tower on Flinders Street was taken from Elizabeth Street, near its intersection with Flinders Lane.

The current clock in the tower was built by F. Zeigler, a Melbourne clockmaker, and installed in the newly finished clock tower in 1907. The clock now operates electrically, but can still be wound by hand.

In 1962, the minister for transport and HKJ Pty Ltd signed an agreement for a £30 million redevelopment of the station that would have resulted in the demolition of the clock tower and its replacement with a 'modern' sixty-storey office building. Thanks to strong opposition, the project fell through, and aren't we lucky it did? I cannot bear the thought of a 1960s office building replacing that iconic clock tower!

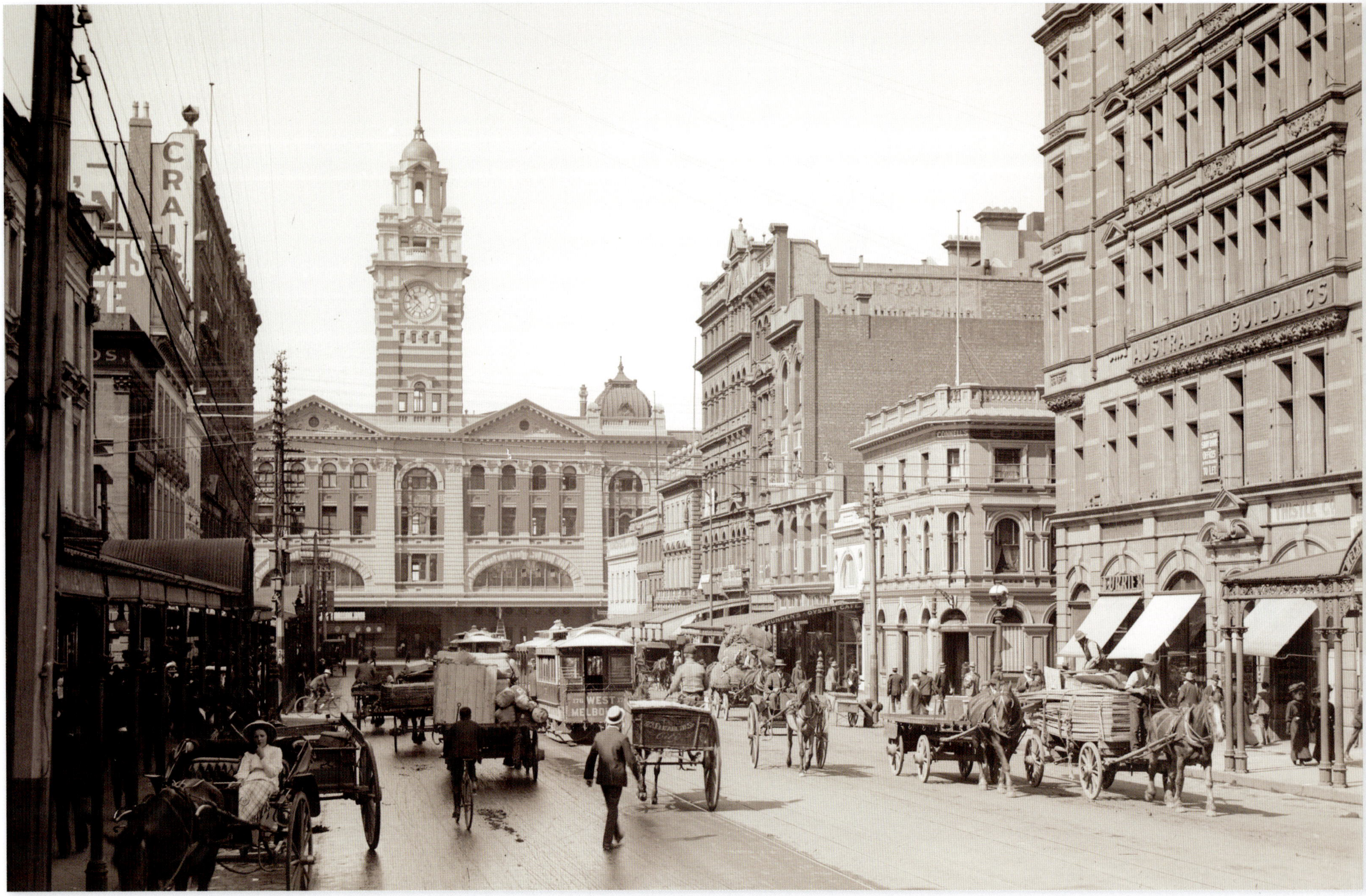

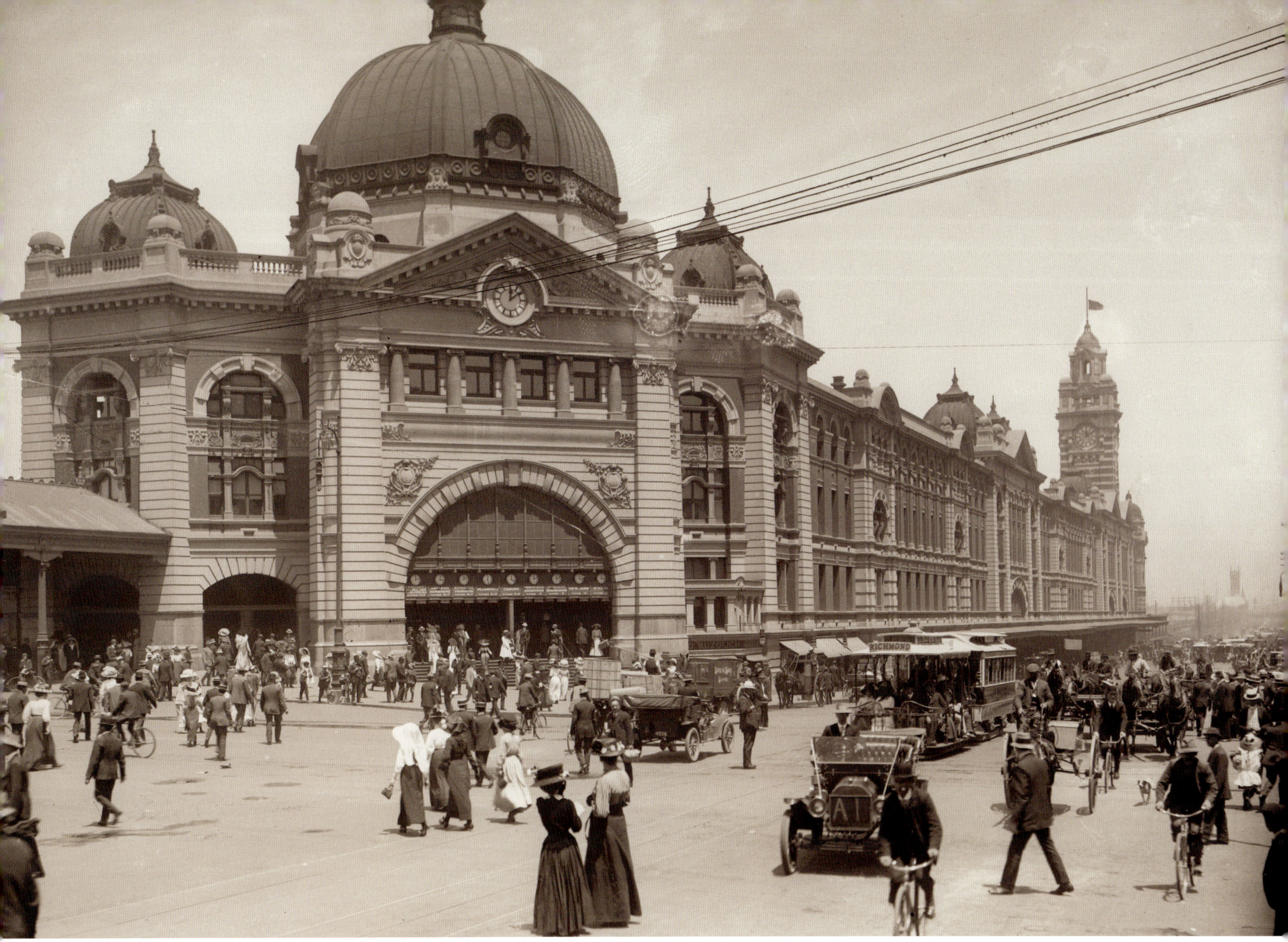

FLINDERS STREET STATION

c.1910

PHOTOGRAPHER: UNKNOWN

A busy street scene at the intersection of Flinders and Swanston streets.

Melbourne's instantly recognisable greatest landmark, Flinders Street Station, opened within months of this photo being snapped.

From the trams, to the fashion, to the Fish Market tower in the distance, this image is iconic.

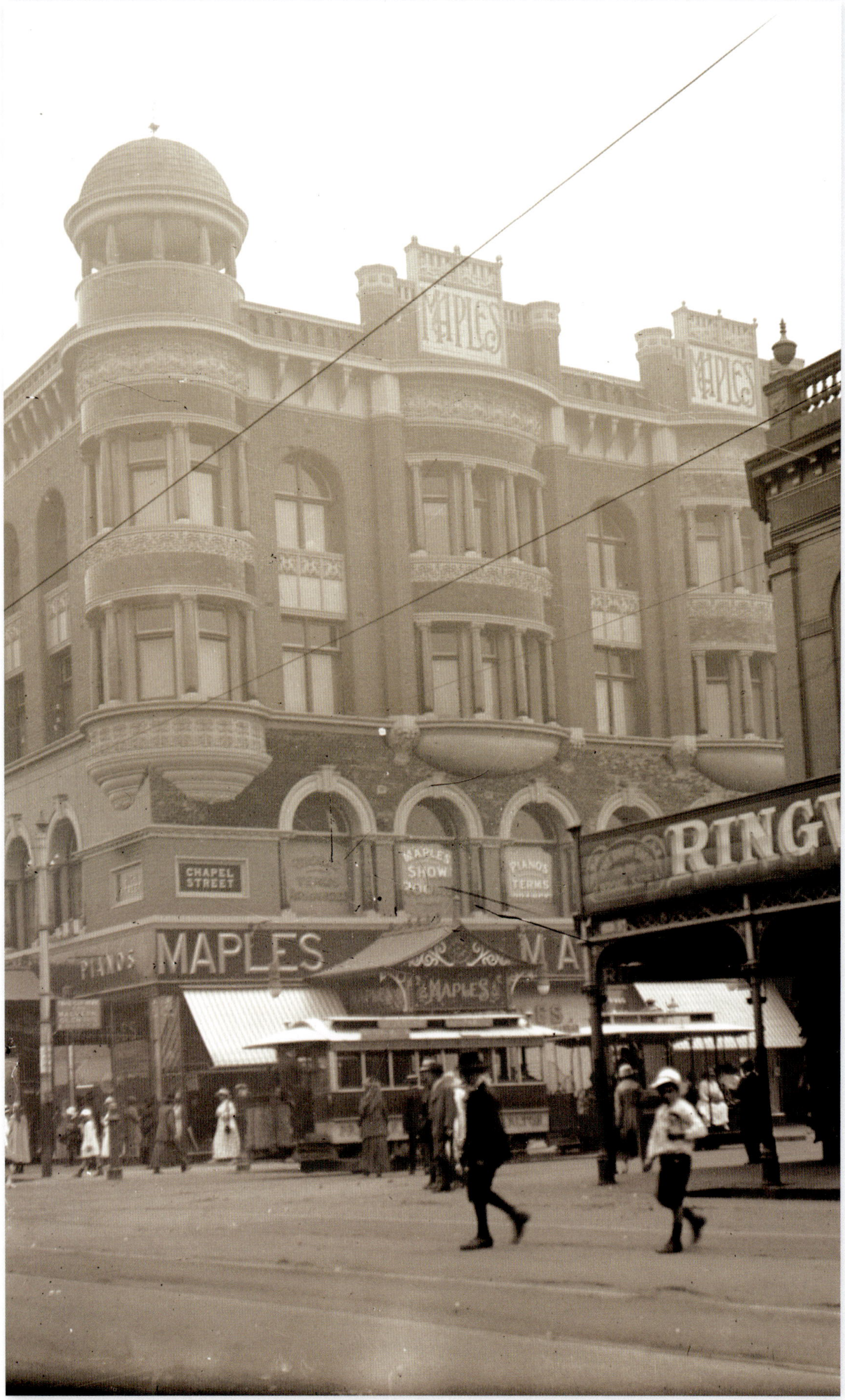

CHAPEL STREET, PRAHRAN

c.1910

PHOTOGRAPHER: KELYNAK FAMILY

We are looking at the north-west corner of Chapel and High streets, Prahran.

You can clearly see the Maples store, at 181–95 Chapel Street, in the year it was built.

Maples was a furniture emporium that opened along with other large department stores of the time, such as Love and Lewis, Read's, and The Big Store. The buildings remain, but the department stores themselves are long gone.

The Maples store was converted into offices in the 1980s. It was around then that a renovation took place, and many deteriorating decorative features were replaced with what some would say were less-attractive postmodern elements.

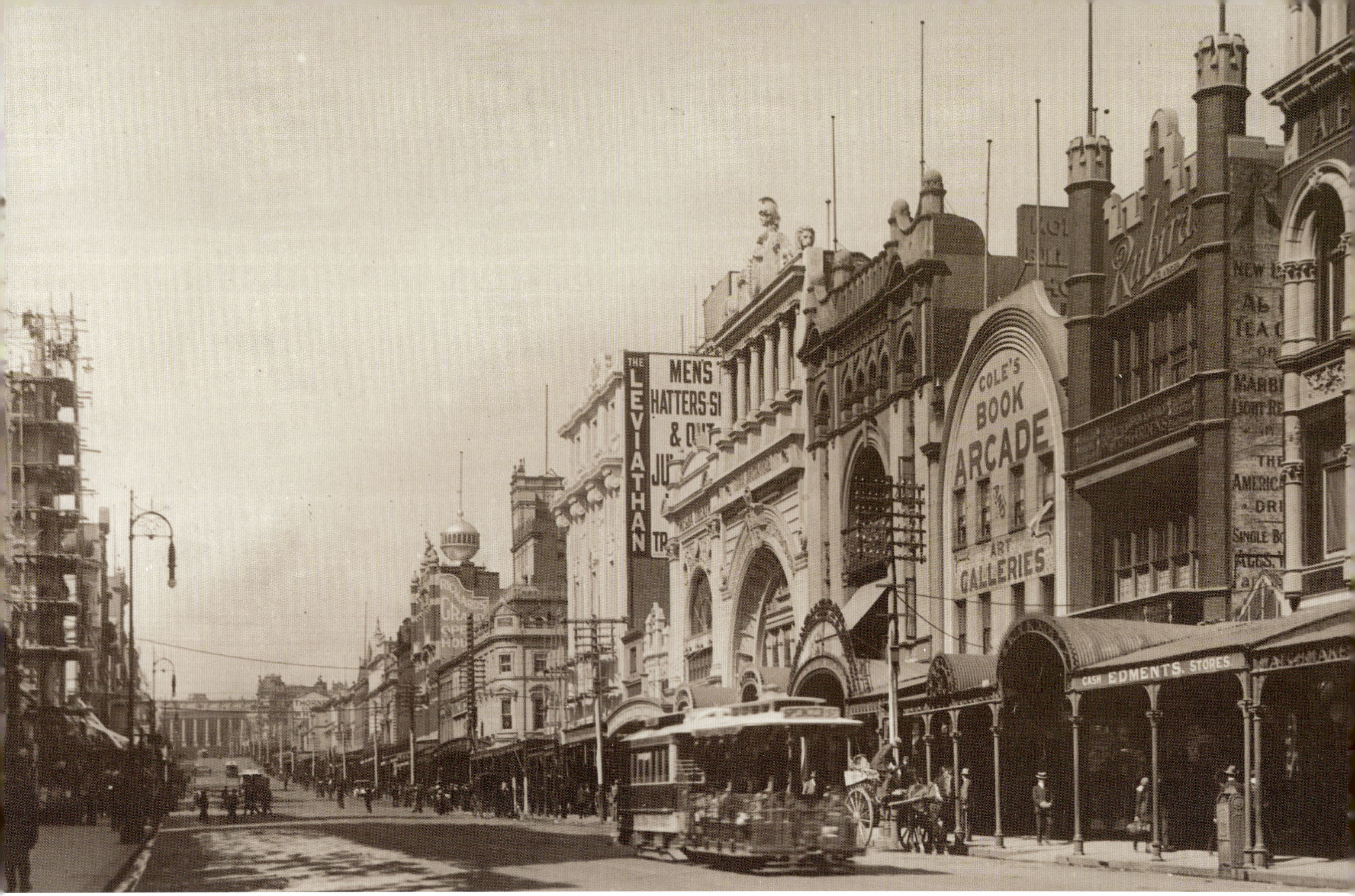

COLE'S BOOK ARCADE

c.1912

PHOTOGRAPHER: UNKNOWN

Bourke Street around 1912 — the year that the great *Titanic* sank to the depths of the Atlantic Ocean.

On the right is the extraordinary Cole's Book Arcade. With around two million books on its shelves, it was also known as the Palace of Intellect, and was reputedly the largest bookstore in the world.

This was one of the iconic 'must visit' Melbourne stores in the late-nineteenth and early-twentieth centuries, and was so well known that both Rudyard Kipling and Mark Twain visited during their travels to Australia.

LUNA PARK

1912

PHOTOGRAPHER: UNKNOWN
SOURCE: SHIRLEY JONES COLLECTION OF VICTORIAN POSTCARDS, STATE LIBRARY VICTORIA

Crowds form near the entrance of Melbourne's iconic Luna Park, which opened in December 1912. This might very well be a shot from the opening day. Luna Park has been operating continuously since then.

Although it's a quintessentially Melbourne institution, Luna Park was built by four American showmen — James Dixon Williams and three brothers by the name of Harold, Leon, and Herman Phillips. They even brought out experts from Coney Island, New York, to drive its design. It is generally accepted by historians that Melbourne's Luna Park was named after Coney Island's Luna Park, which opened in 1903.

Williams returned to the United States in 1913, and helped found First National Pictures, which was subsequently absorbed by Warner Brothers. The Phillips brothers stayed on and ran the park until their deaths in the 1950s.

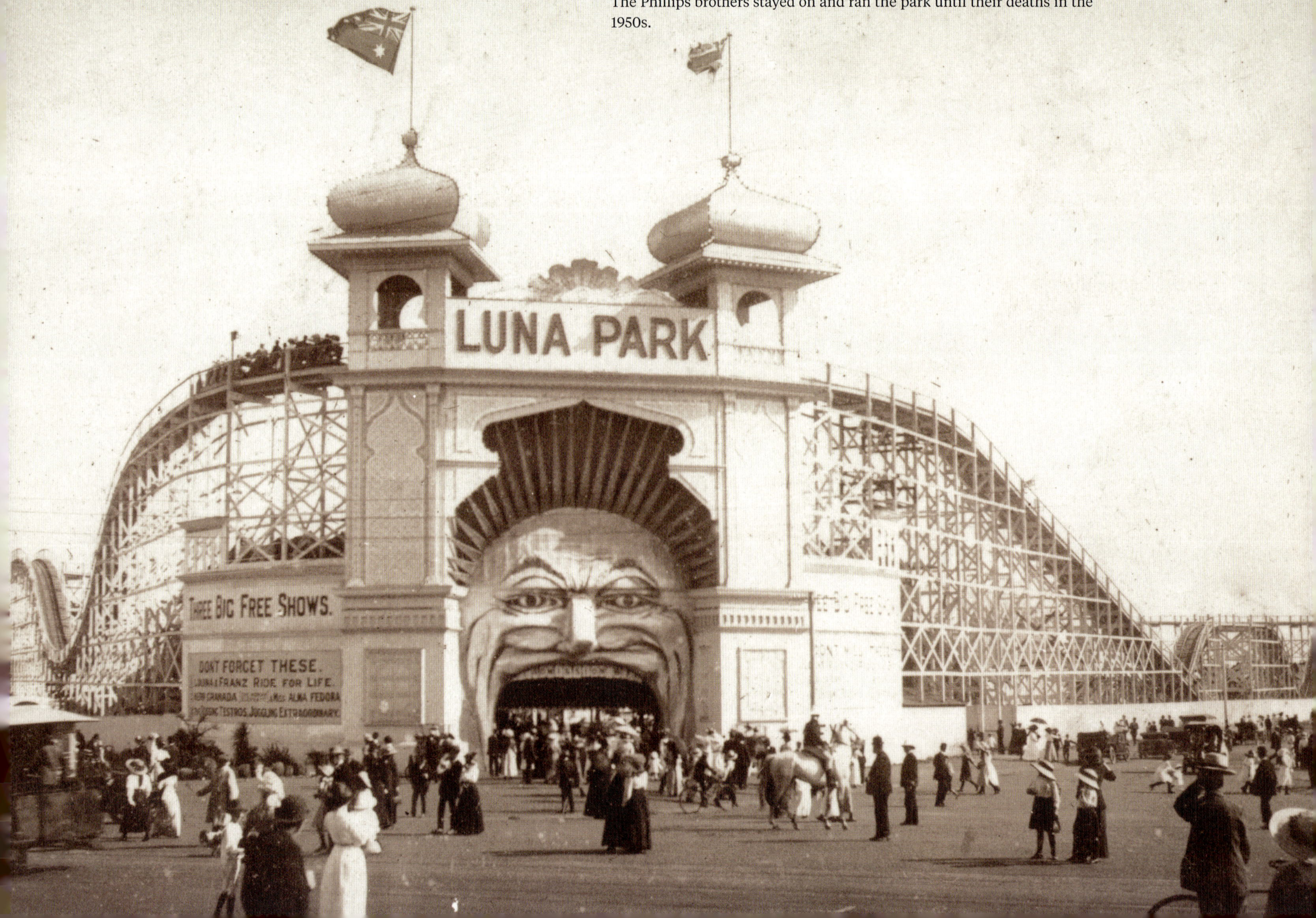

FLINDERS STREET

c. 1913

PHOTOGRAPHER: UNKNOWN

Here is a spectacularly clear view of Flinders Street looking east, taken from atop Flinders Street Station.

You can see the Metropolitan Gas Co. offices, Princes Bridge railway station, and the Flinders Street railway yards.

St Paul's Cathedral, at the very left, looks rather strange without its spires. The cathedral was completed in 1891, but construction of the spires didn't start until 1926. Once the central spire was completed, the cathedral became the tallest structure in central Melbourne, dominating the city's skyline when viewed from the south.

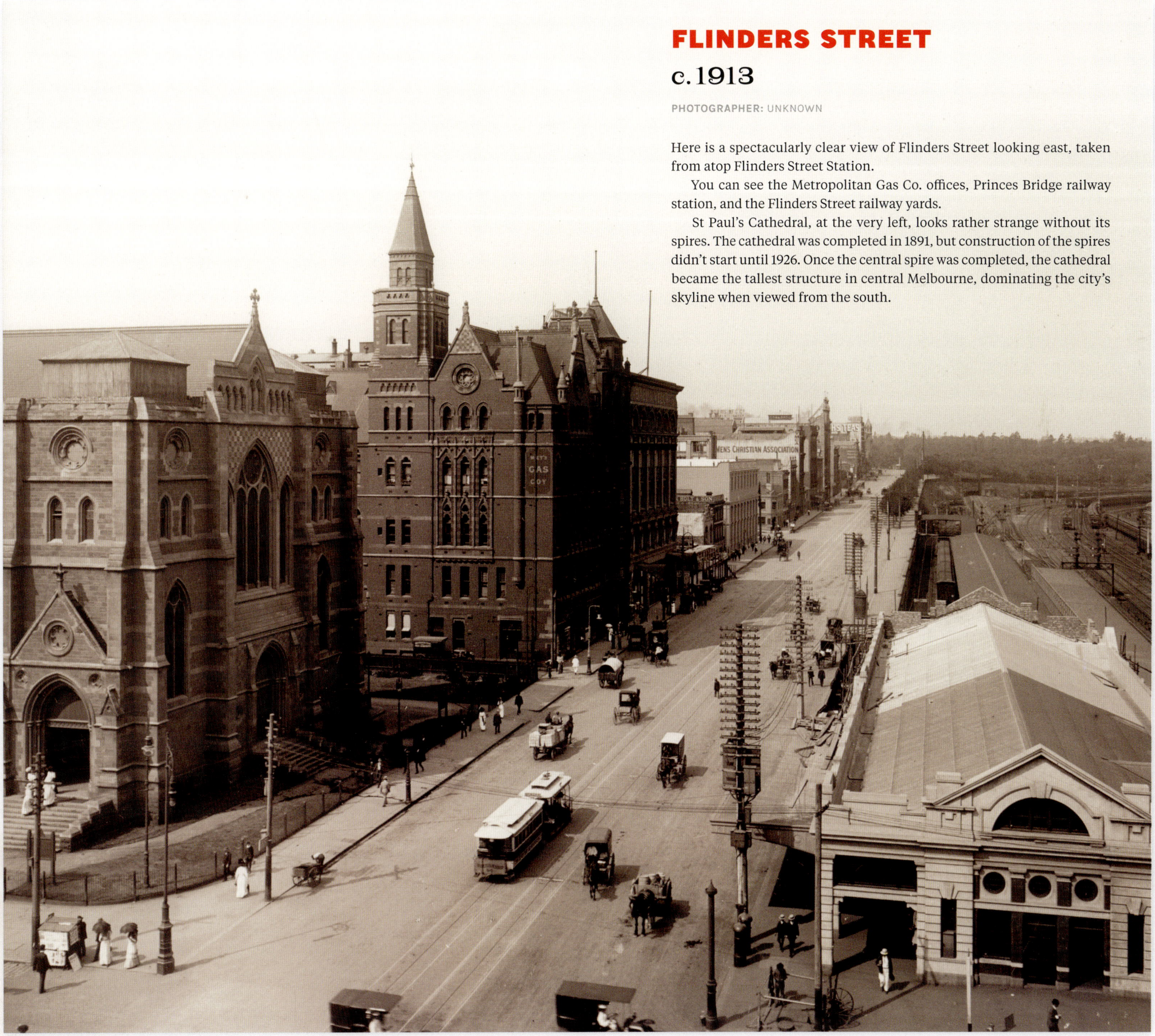

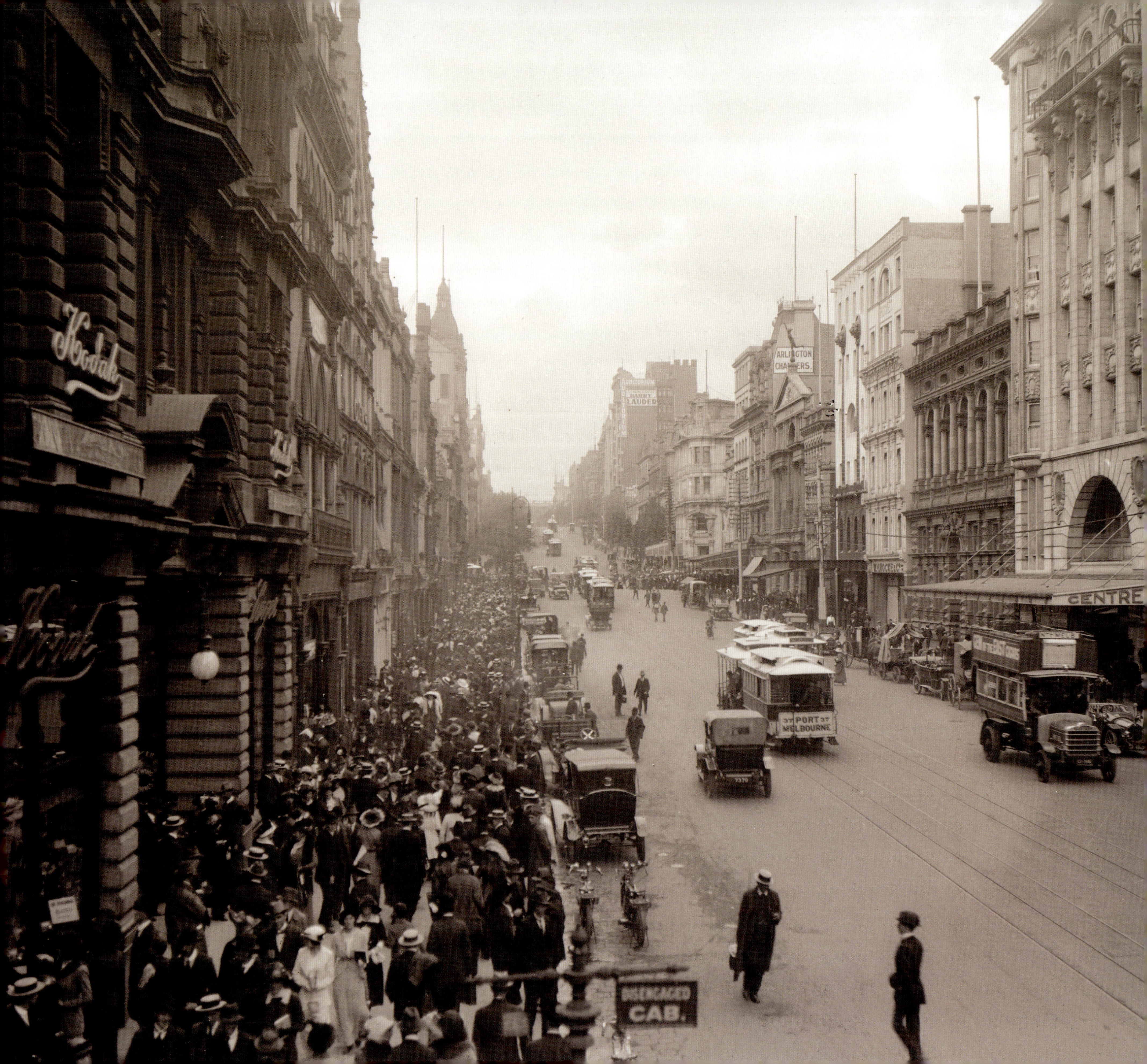
Kodak
ARLINGTON CHAMBERS
HARRY LAUDER
CENTRE
PORT MELBOURNE
DISENGAGED CAB.

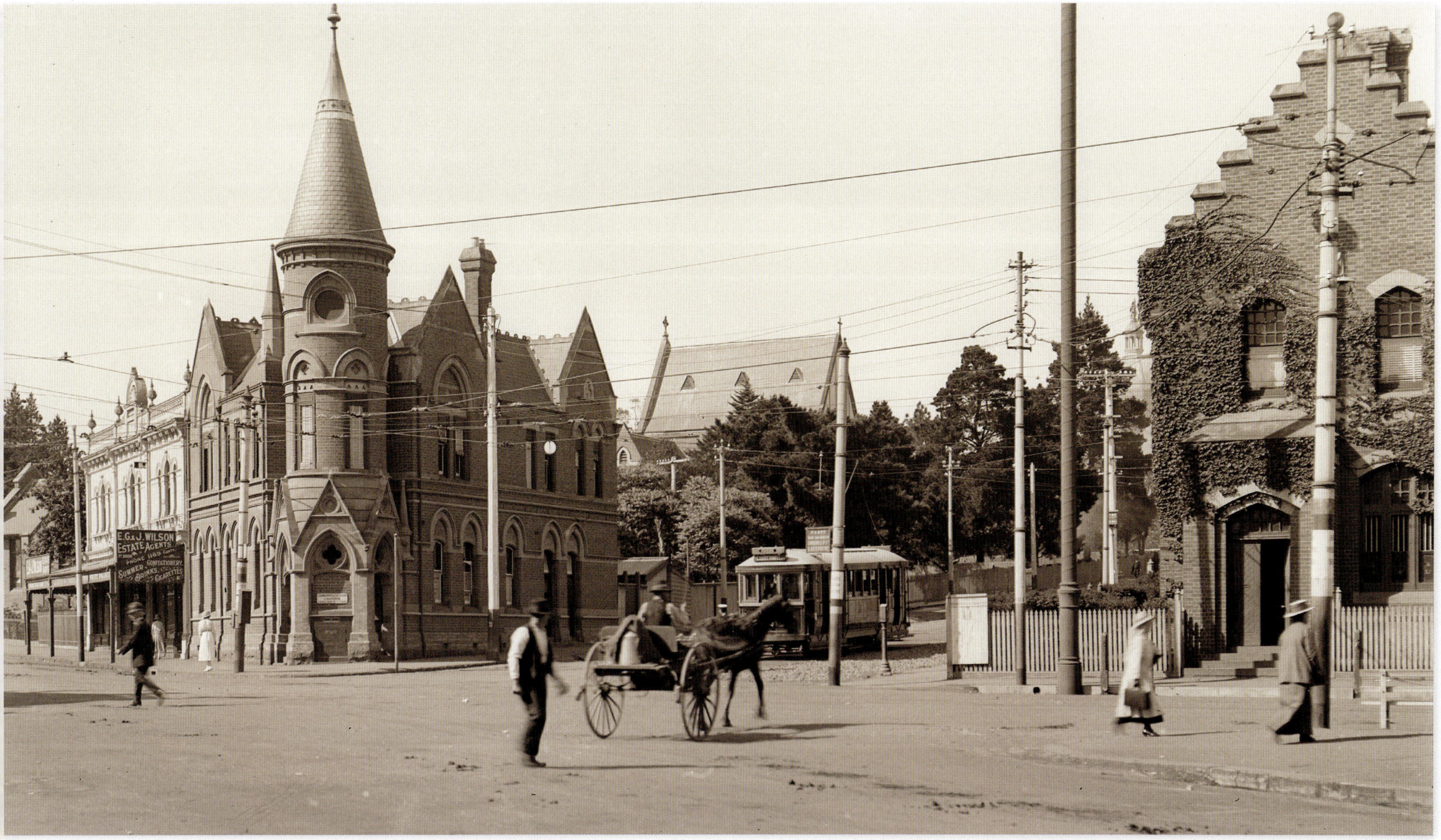

◀ BLOCK ARCADE, COLLINS STREET

c.1913

PHOTOGRAPHER: UNKNOWN

Fashionable Melburnians 'doing the block' on Collins Street, at the front entrance of the Block Arcade.

As the years went on, fashion changed, but one thing remained: this was where you went to be seen.

CAMBERWELL JUNCTION ▲

c.1914

PHOTOGRAPHER: ROSE STEREOGRAPH CO.

Camberwell Junction contained some historic buildings, some of which remain and some of which have been demolished.

The exquisite building to the left is the Camberwell Post Office. The original post office opened in 1864; the one pictured was built in 1890 and demolished in 1963.

To the right is the former English, Scottish and Australian (ES&A) Bank, erected in 1885. It remains today, and operates as the Meat and Wine Co. restaurant.

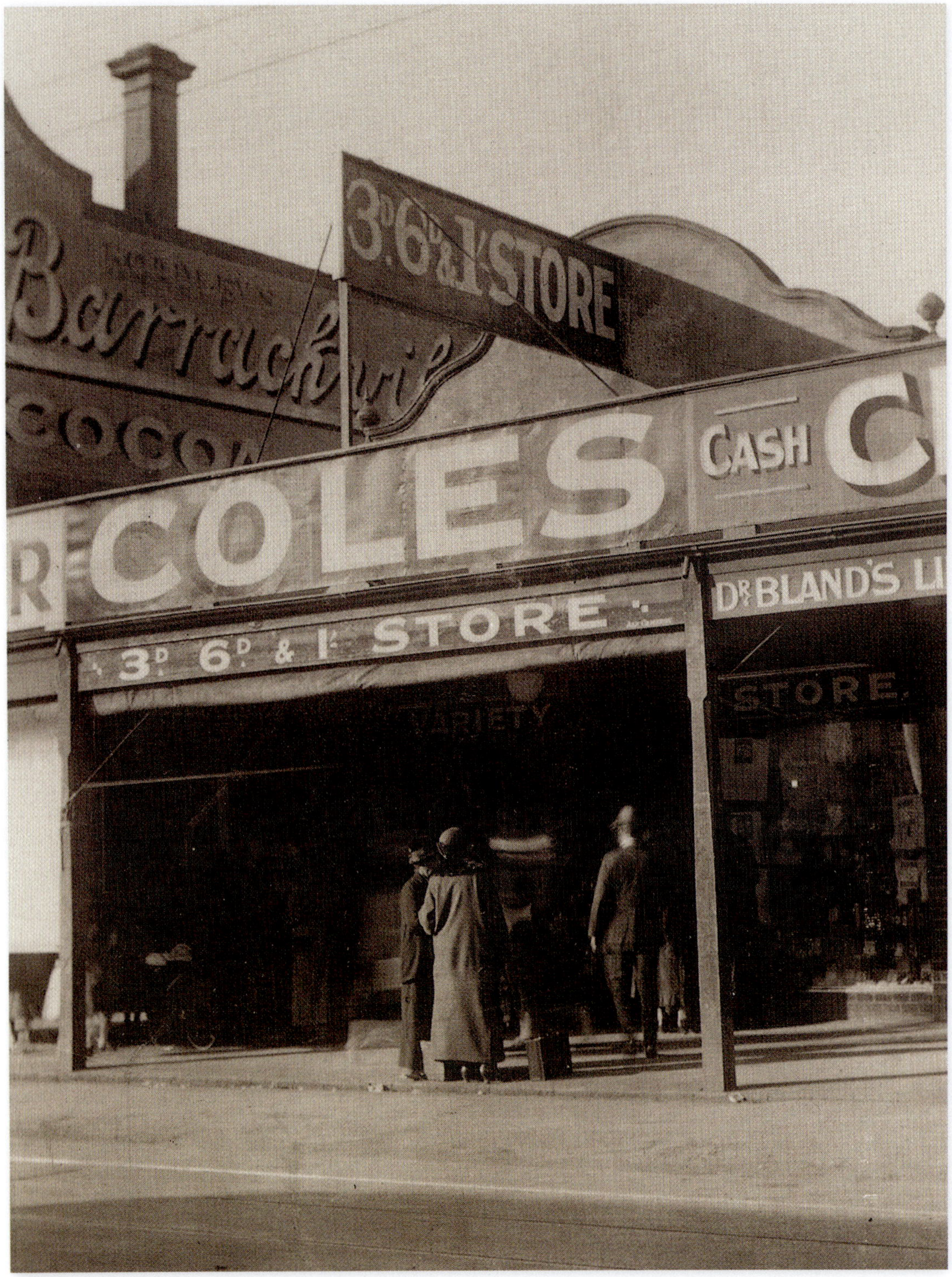

◀ COLES, SMITH STREET

c.1914

PHOTOGRAPHER: UNKNOWN
SOURCE: COLLINGWOOD LOCAL HISTORY PHOTOGRAPH COLLECTION, STATE LIBRARY VICTORIA

This is the very first Coles supermarket. It was opened on 9 April 1914, as the Coles Variety Store, by a young man named George James Coles on Smith Street, Collingwood.

Coles learned the retail trade while working at his father's Coles Store from 1910 to 1913. Arguably, this was the original Coles, located in Wilmot, Tasmania. The historic store was tragically lost after a devastating fire in 2014.

Immediately before the Smith Street shop opened, George James set down his thoughts about the task ahead. 'A proprietor has to have a happy home life,' he wrote, 'he has to have a contented staff; he has to have a store he would be proud of; he has to earn the respect of his fellow men, and to do all this he must also operate a business that would be successful.' Little did he know of the empire that was to follow.

The business duly expanded, and Coles' interest in food retailing increased significantly in 1958 when it acquired fifty-four John Connell Dickins grocery stores. It then acquired the Beilby's chain in South Australia in 1959, and 265 Matthews Thompson grocery stores in New South Wales in 1960.

Today, Coles is a multi-billion-dollar supermarket giant that employs over 100,000 people.

MELBOURNE CRICKET GROUND ▶

c.1914

PHOTOGRAPHER: G.G.M.

A day out at the 'G' around 1914. Here is the view from the grandstand of the Melbourne Cricket Ground (MCG) looking across the crowd and out towards the oval.

The MCG was founded in 1853, and today it is the largest stadium in the southern hemisphere, by volume and capacity.

Before the stadium's construction, the fifteen-year-old Melbourne Cricket Club was based in South Melbourne. The government of the time was building Australia's first steam train, which was set to pass through the South Melbourne site. As a result, the club moved to its current location at Jolimont.

Since then, the MCG has had an illustrious history, hosting a plethora of international cricket matches (including the first ever Test and the 1992 World Cup final), VFL and AFL grand finals, and, of course, the Olympic Games in 1956.

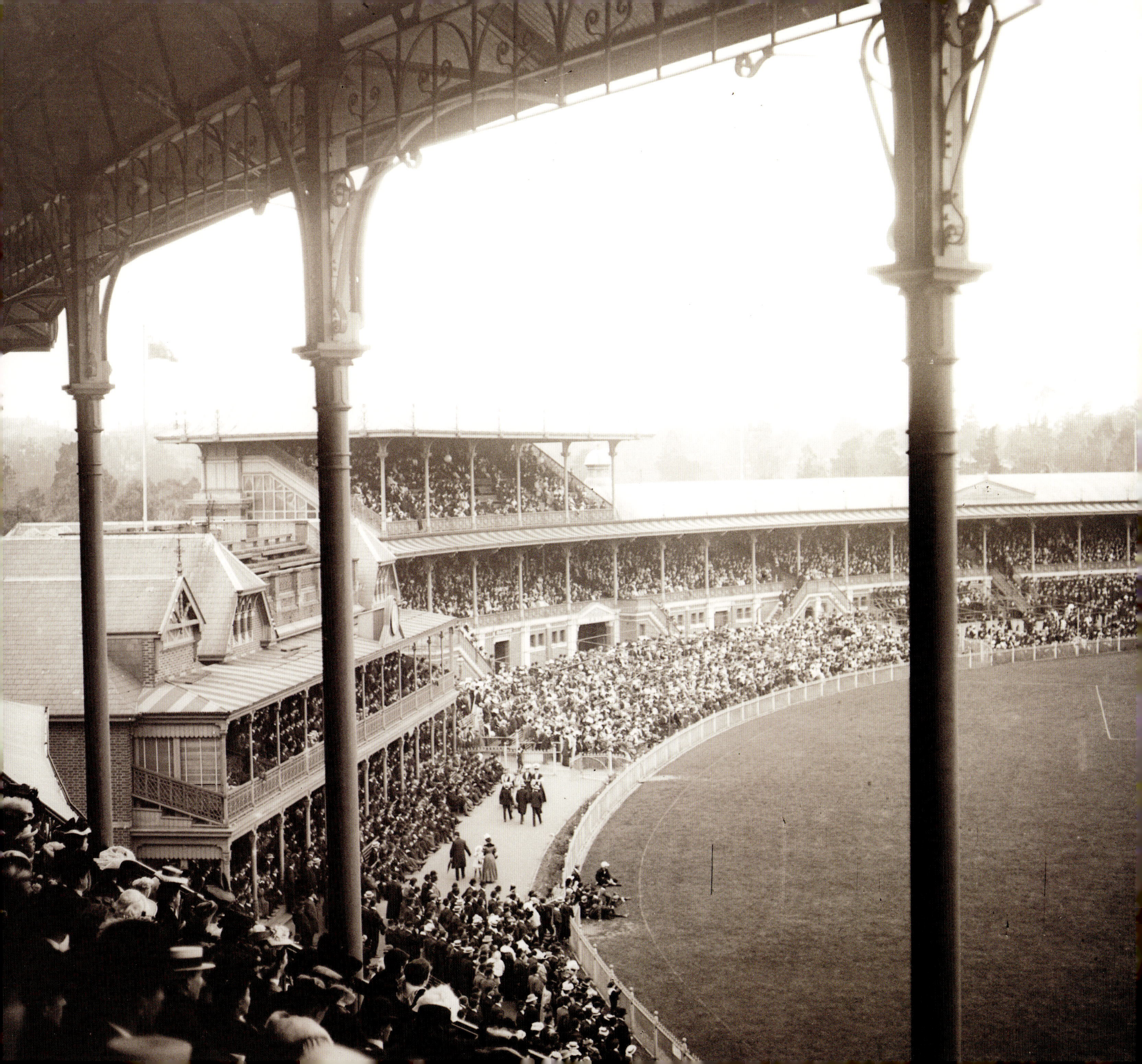

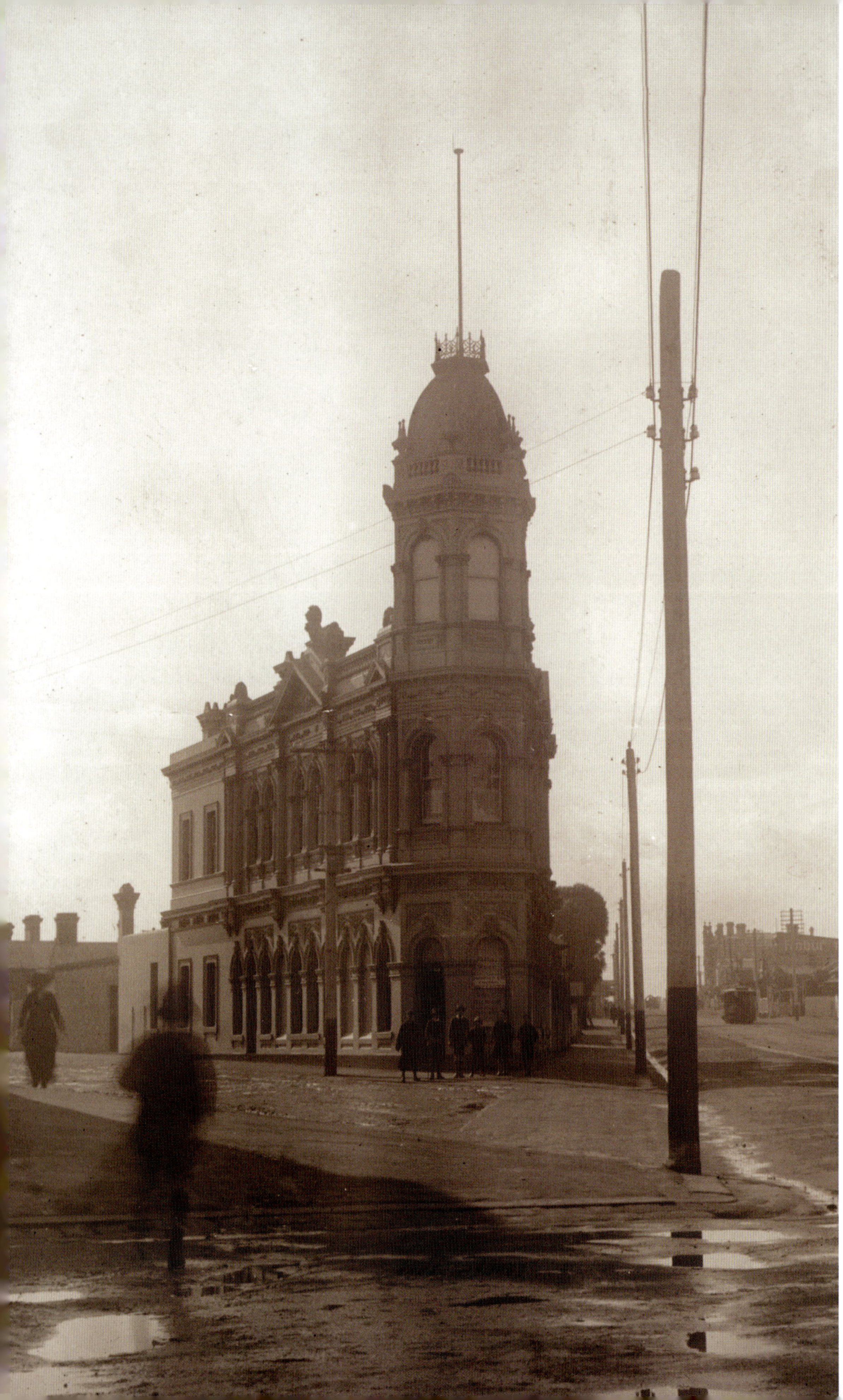

NORTH FITZROY POST OFFICE

c.1914

PHOTOGRAPHER: GEORGE REID ROSS (LEFT IMAGE); CHRIS MACHERAS (BOTTOM IMAGE)

THEN AND NOW: The North Fitzroy Post Office appears to have had its head chopped off since the photo on the left was taken.

Built in the late 1800s, the building was originally the suburb's land office. Locals would climb to the top floor, and from there point out which spot of land they were after. It operated for many years as a post office, before being turned into an antique shop.

More recently, you will know it as The Fitzroy Pinnacle, a renowned Fitzroy pub.

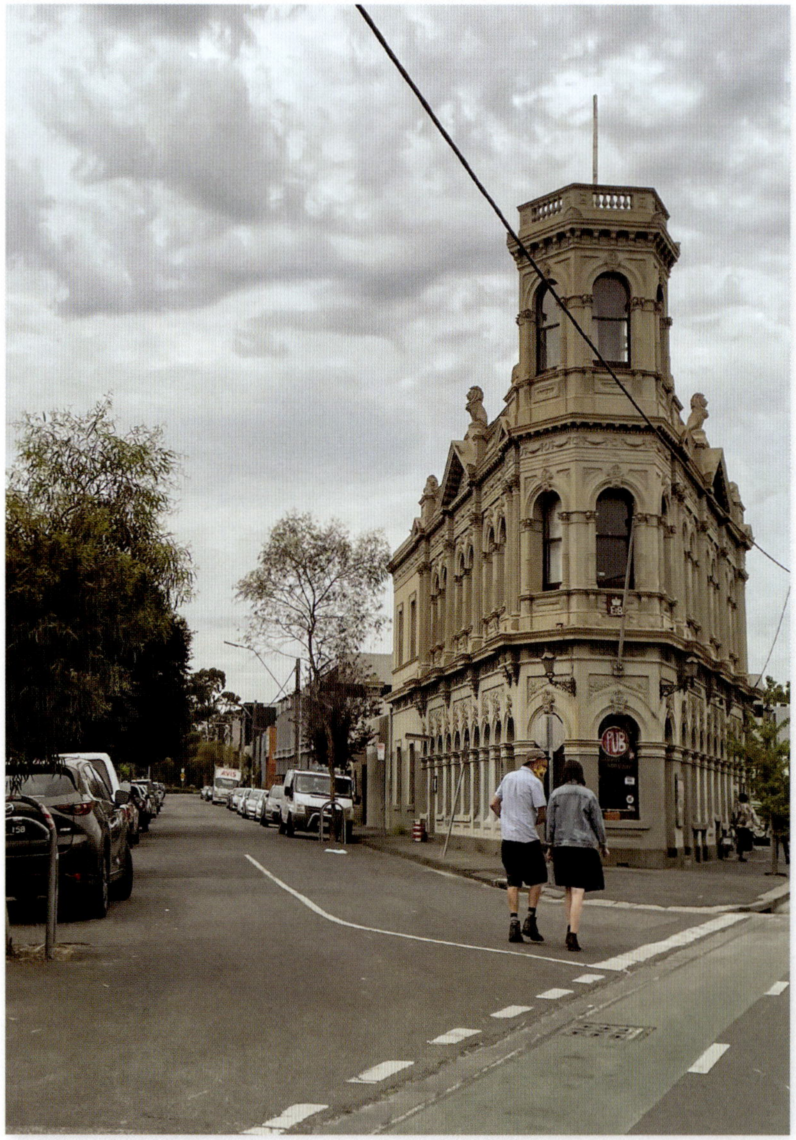

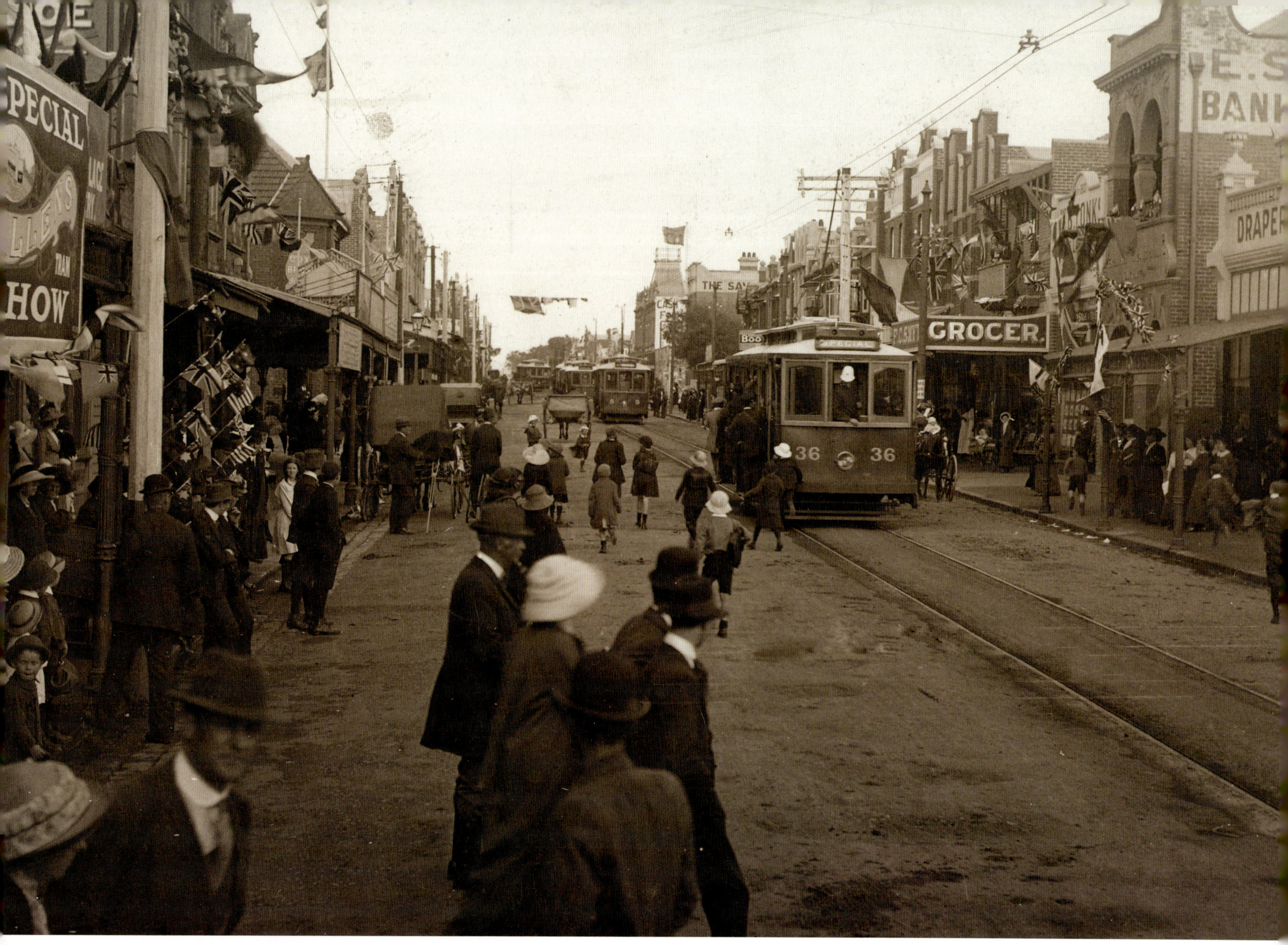

GLEN HUNTLY ROAD, ELSTERNWICK

c. 1914

PHOTOGRAPHER: UNKNOWN

The decorations are in place to celebrate the new electric-tram service along Glen Huntly Road, operated by The Prahran and Malvern Tramways Trust. The service, which previously ended at Caulfield and St Kilda, was extended to Elsternwick in 1914.

Although the Number 36 tram depicted here didn't survive, the Number 35 did. One is currently on display at the Ballarat Tramway Museum.

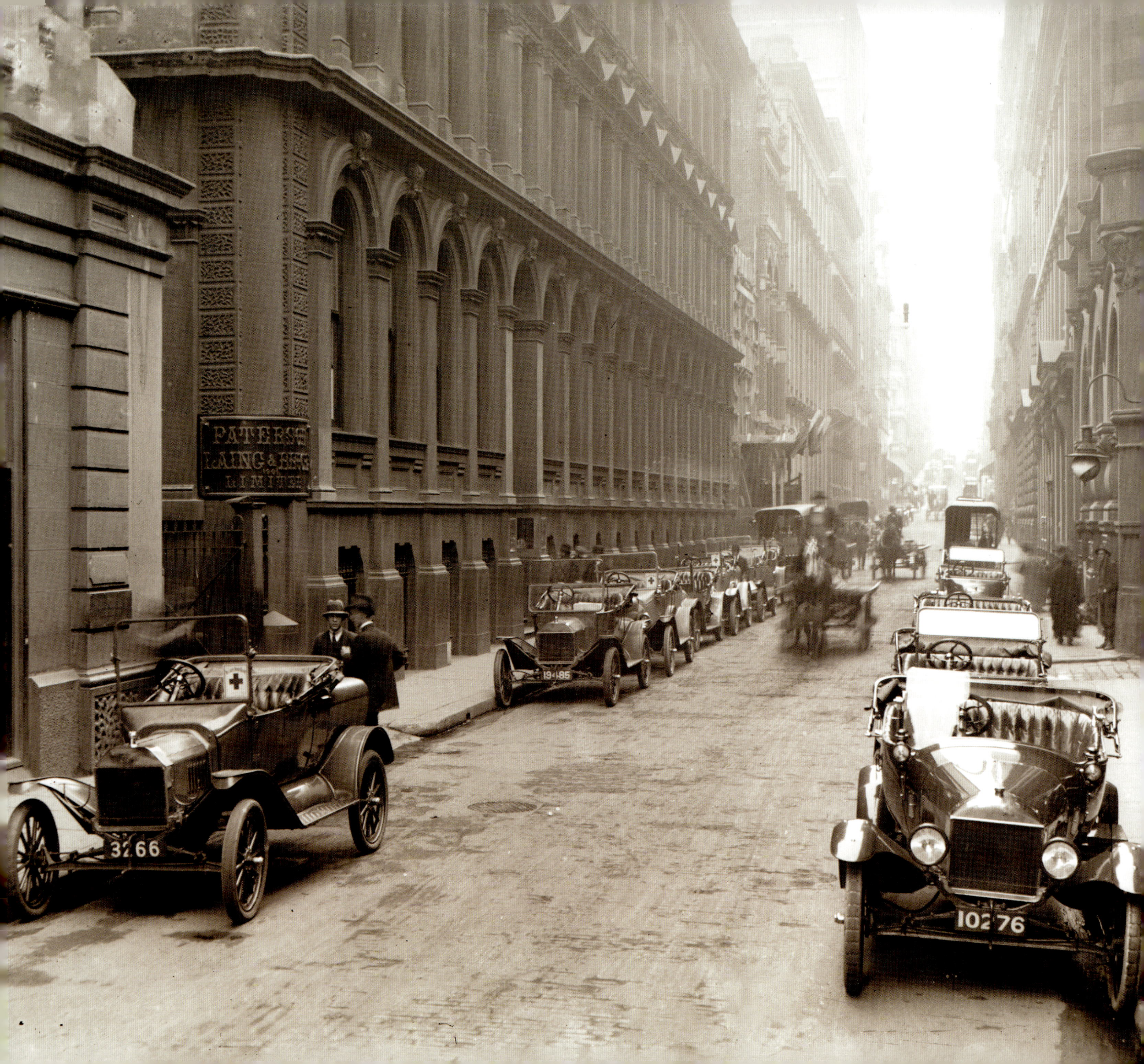

LAING &
3266
10276

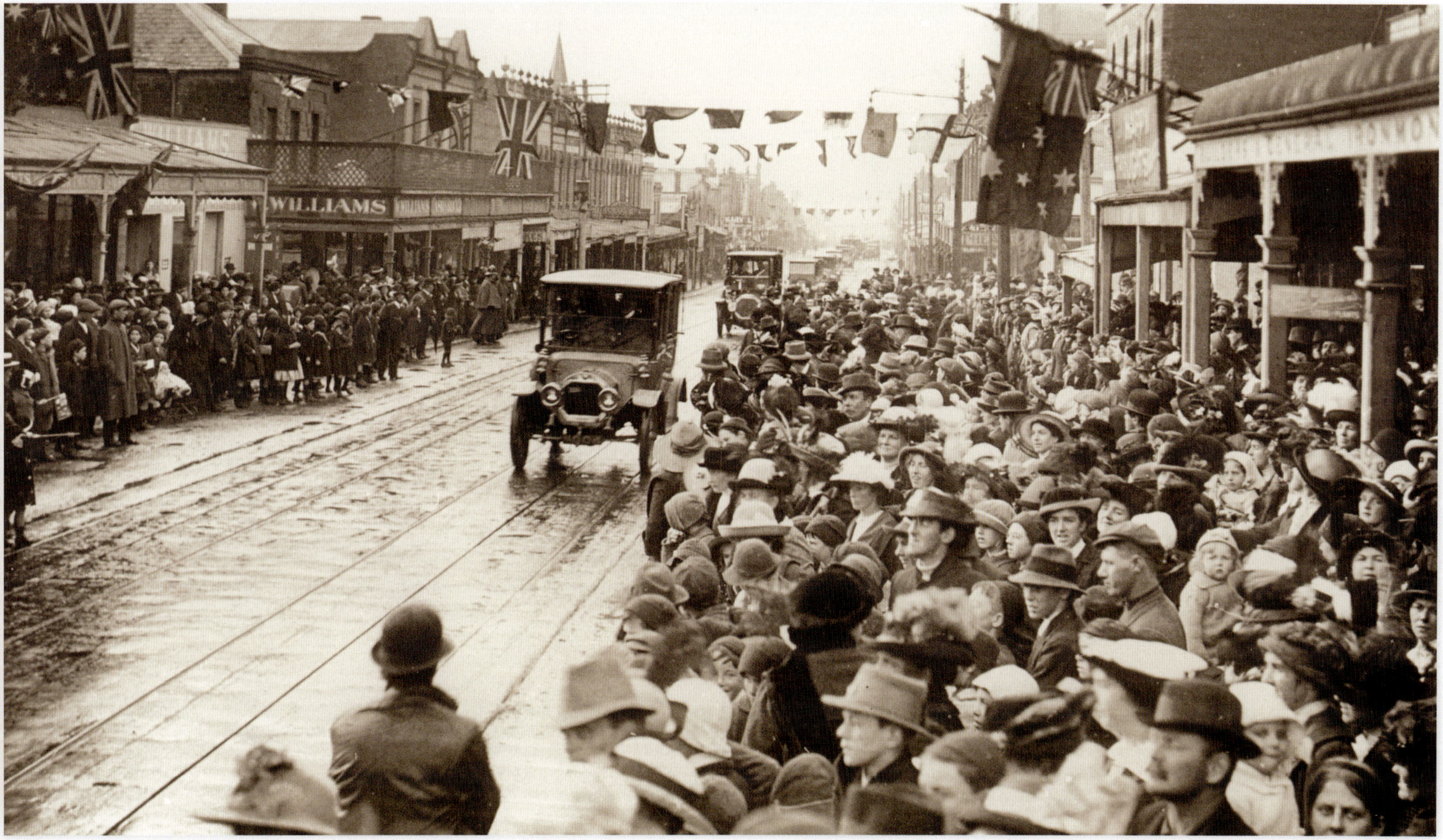

◀ FLINDERS LANE

c.1914

PHOTOGRAPHER: UNKNOWN

First-generation motorcars are lined up on narrow Flinders Lane.

You may know this part of town for its restaurants and boutiques. But in the 1880s, Flinders Lane was the centre of Melbourne's garment trade.

Clothing and textiles manufacturers built large warehouses here because of its close proximity to wharves, railway stations, and the city centre.

For over 100 years, buyers would pop down and 'do' the lane, visiting all the warehouses, many of which were owned by Jewish migrants.

The number of clothing firms on Flinders Lane reached 610 in 1939. This is how it remained until the early 1960s, after which businesses began to close due to changing requirements for space, and the pressures of rising labour costs, rents, and traffic congestion.

HIGH STREET, NORTHCOTE ▲

1914

PHOTOGRAPHER: ALLAN STUDIO

This is pretty cool, especially if you are familiar with Melbourne's north.

Northcote was severed from the city of Melbourne and incorporated as a borough on 25 May 1883. It became a town on 12 September 1890, and was proclaimed a city in 1914.

This image shows the proclamation day of the city, on 27 May 1914. As you can see, some of the original buildings remain, including the Northcote Theatre on the right. This might even pre-date Lambs on High Street.

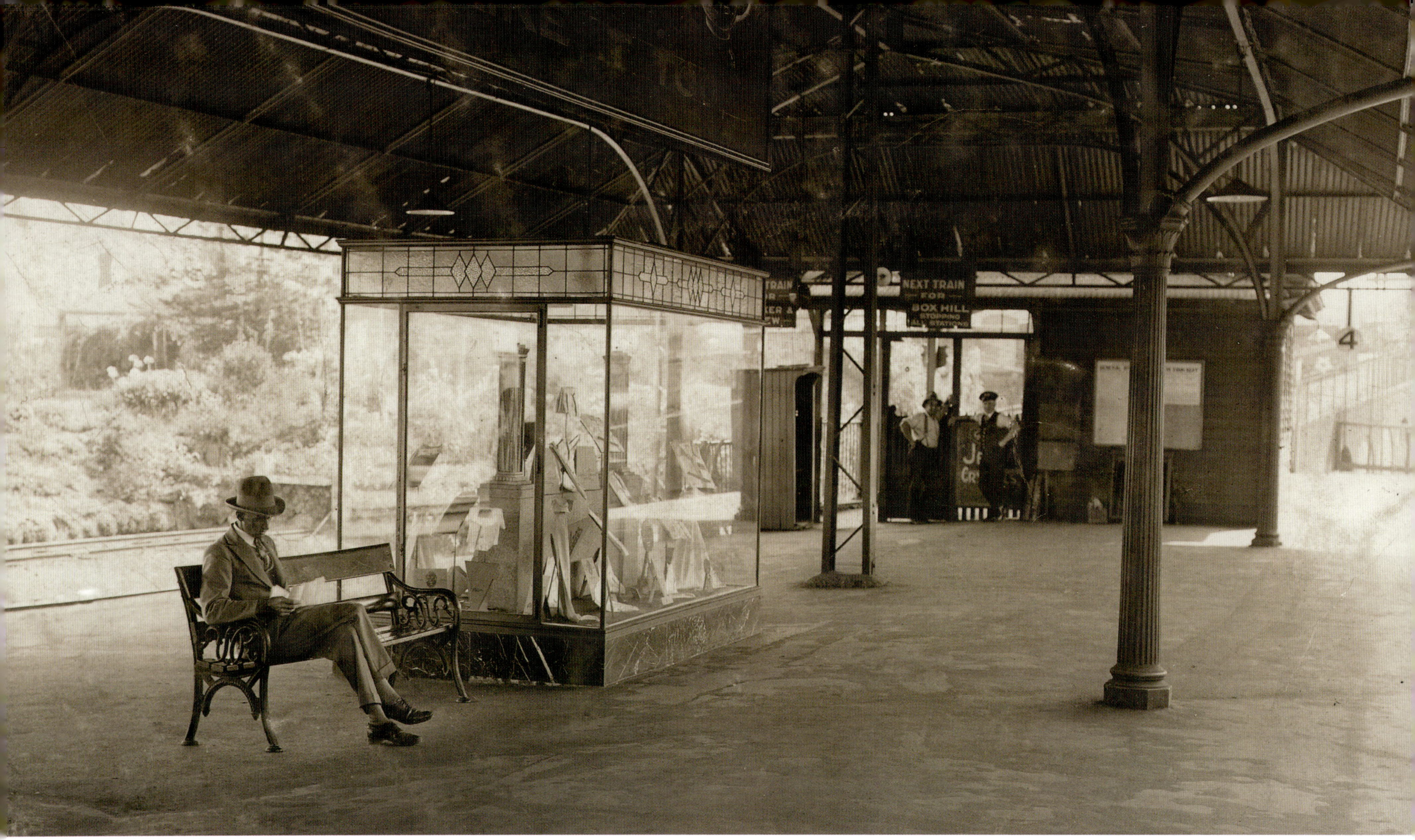

HAWTHORN TRAIN STATION

c. 1914

PHOTOGRAPHER: UNKNOWN

On the platform, which is covered by a corrugated-iron roof, is a man seated on a bench seat reading a letter as he waits for his train to arrive.

The sign above him is advertising 'Robur Tea', and there are two men standing at the gate in the background. The sign above them reads 'Next train for Box Hill stopping all stations'.

What also stands out is the magnificent glass cabinet advertising various products. Unfortunately, it's difficult to make out what's in there.

RAMSDEN STREET, CLIFTON HILL

c. 1915

PHOTOGRAPHER: UNKNOWN

Mr John Conway Gibson out the front of his bootmaking business in Ramsden Street, Clifton Hill.

The confluence of the Yarra River and the Merri Creek was an important area for the local Indigenous community, the Wurundjeri-willam.

The area we know today as Clifton Hill was given that name in 1871. By 1855 the area had been settled by contractors, who used the local bluestone to build houses for themselves.

Most residential development took place later in the nineteenth century and twentieth century. Almost the whole of Clifton Hill is covered by two Heritage Overlays.

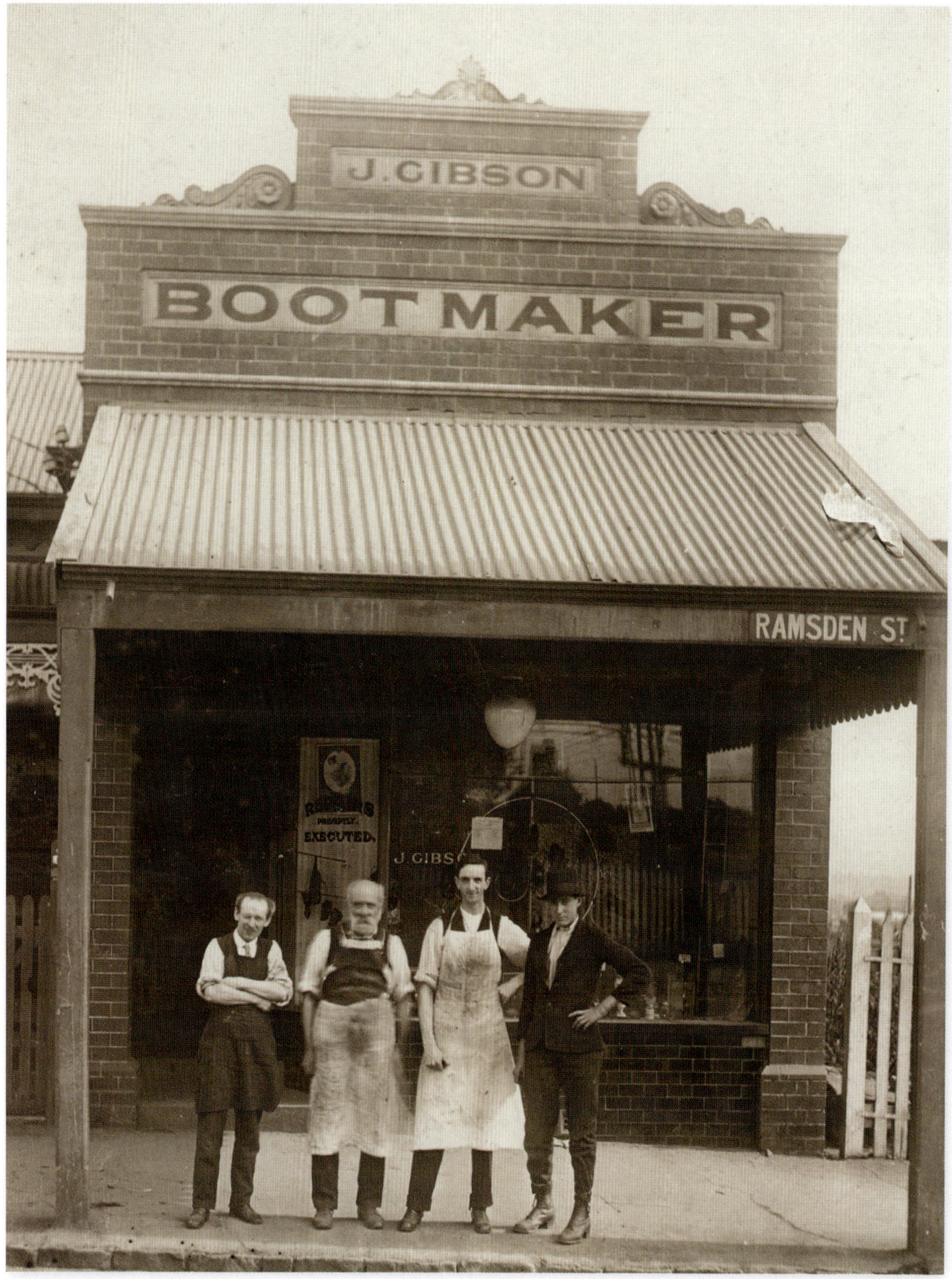

ELIZABETH STREET

c.1916

PHOTOGRAPHER: UNKNOWN

An elevated view of Elizabeth Street looking north, likely taken from the clock tower of Flinders Street Station.

The tall building on the left is the APA Building, at 49 Elizabeth Street. This was a skyscraper at the time — twelve storeys high, and rising 53 metres to the top of the corner spire. Originally known as the Australian Building, it was the tallest commercial building in the country when it was built in 1888.

The building lost its status as the tallest building in Australia in 1912 when it was surpassed by the Culwulla Chambers in Sydney. It remained Melbourne's tallest building until 1929, and was demolished in 1981.

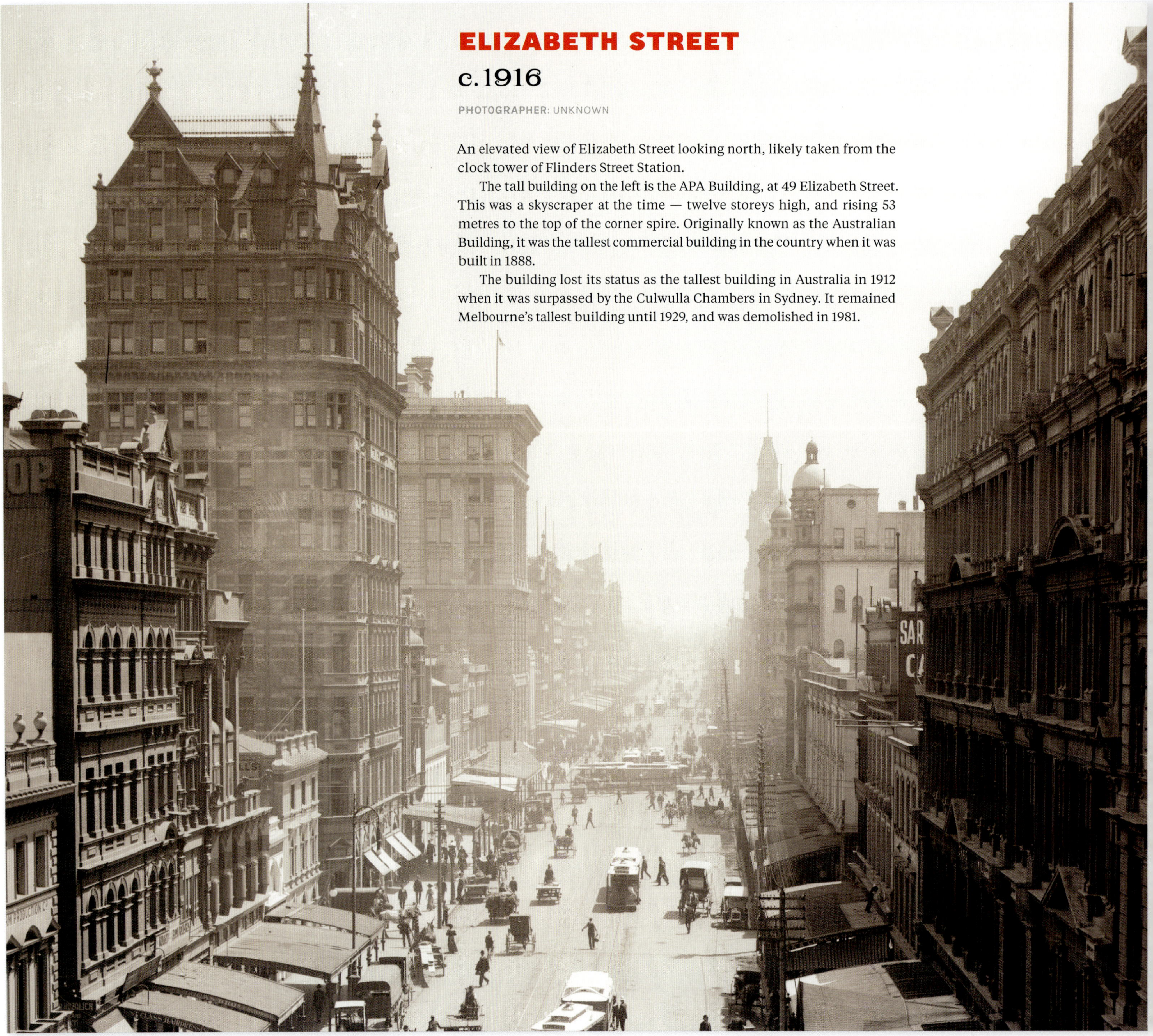

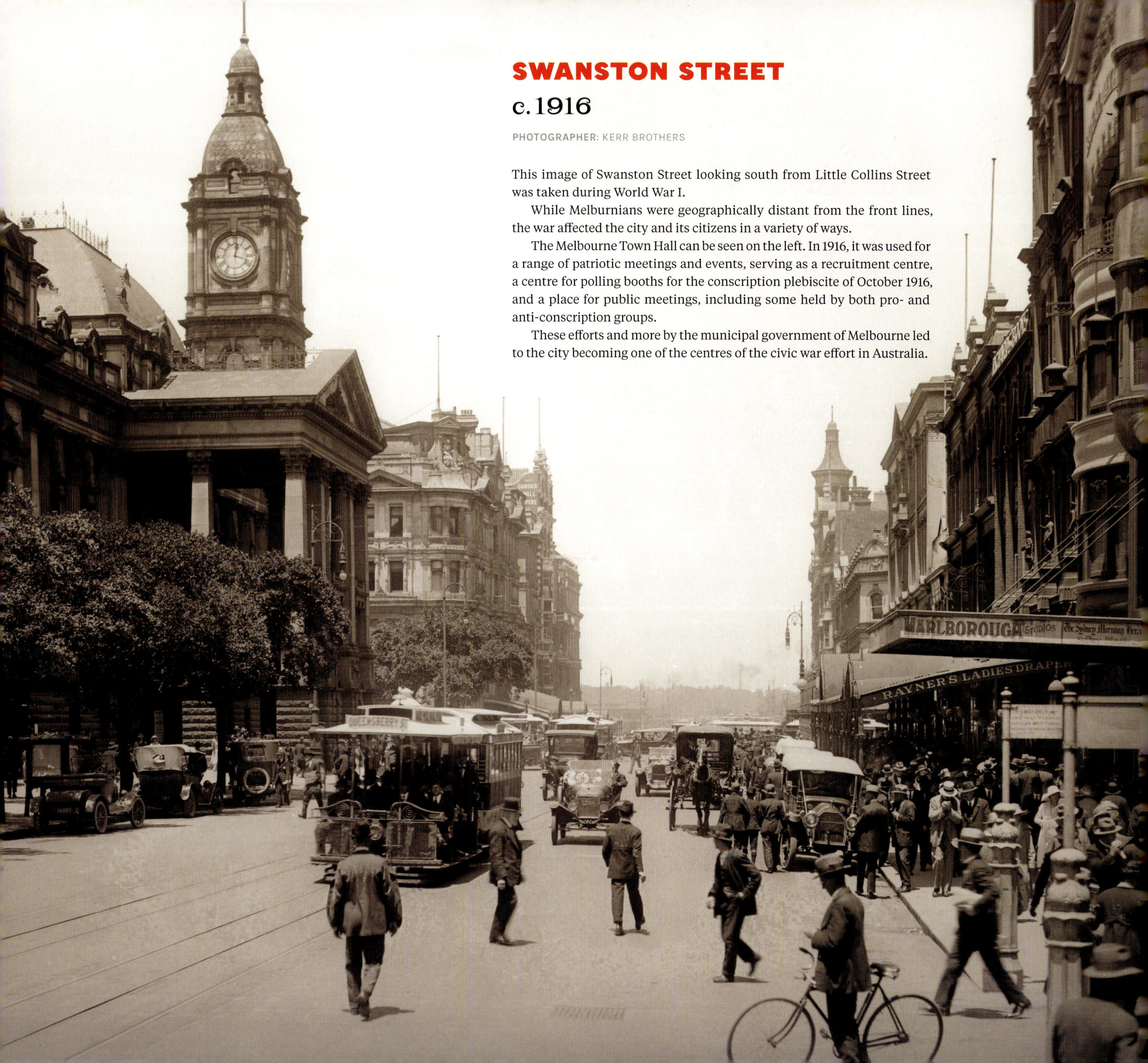

SWANSTON STREET

c. 1916

PHOTOGRAPHER: KERR BROTHERS

This image of Swanston Street looking south from Little Collins Street was taken during World War I.

While Melburnians were geographically distant from the front lines, the war affected the city and its citizens in a variety of ways.

The Melbourne Town Hall can be seen on the left. In 1916, it was used for a range of patriotic meetings and events, serving as a recruitment centre, a centre for polling booths for the conscription plebiscite of October 1916, and a place for public meetings, including some held by both pro- and anti-conscription groups.

These efforts and more by the municipal government of Melbourne led to the city becoming one of the centres of the civic war effort in Australia.

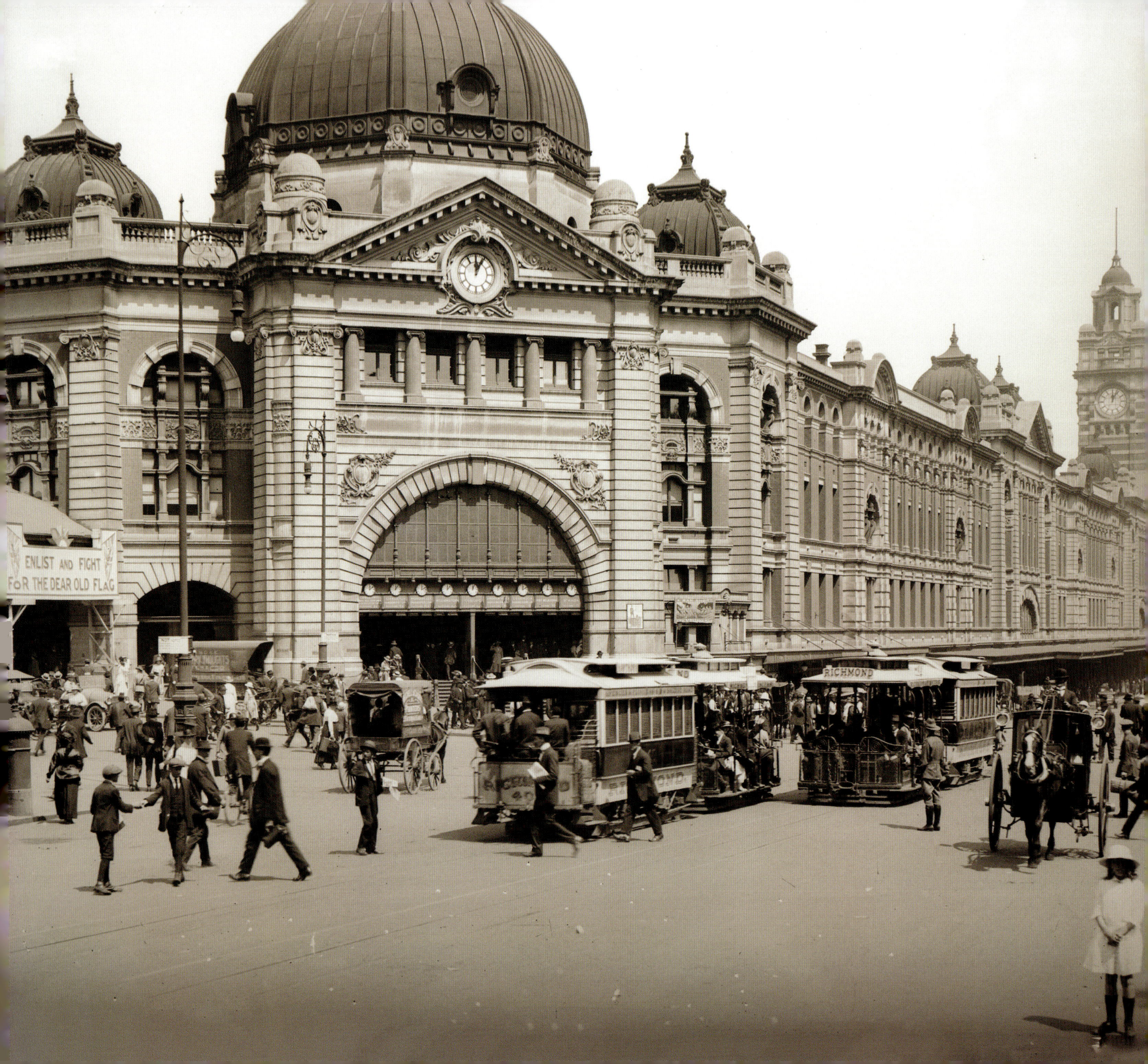
ENLIST AND FIGHT
FOR THE DEAR OLD FLAG
RICHMOND

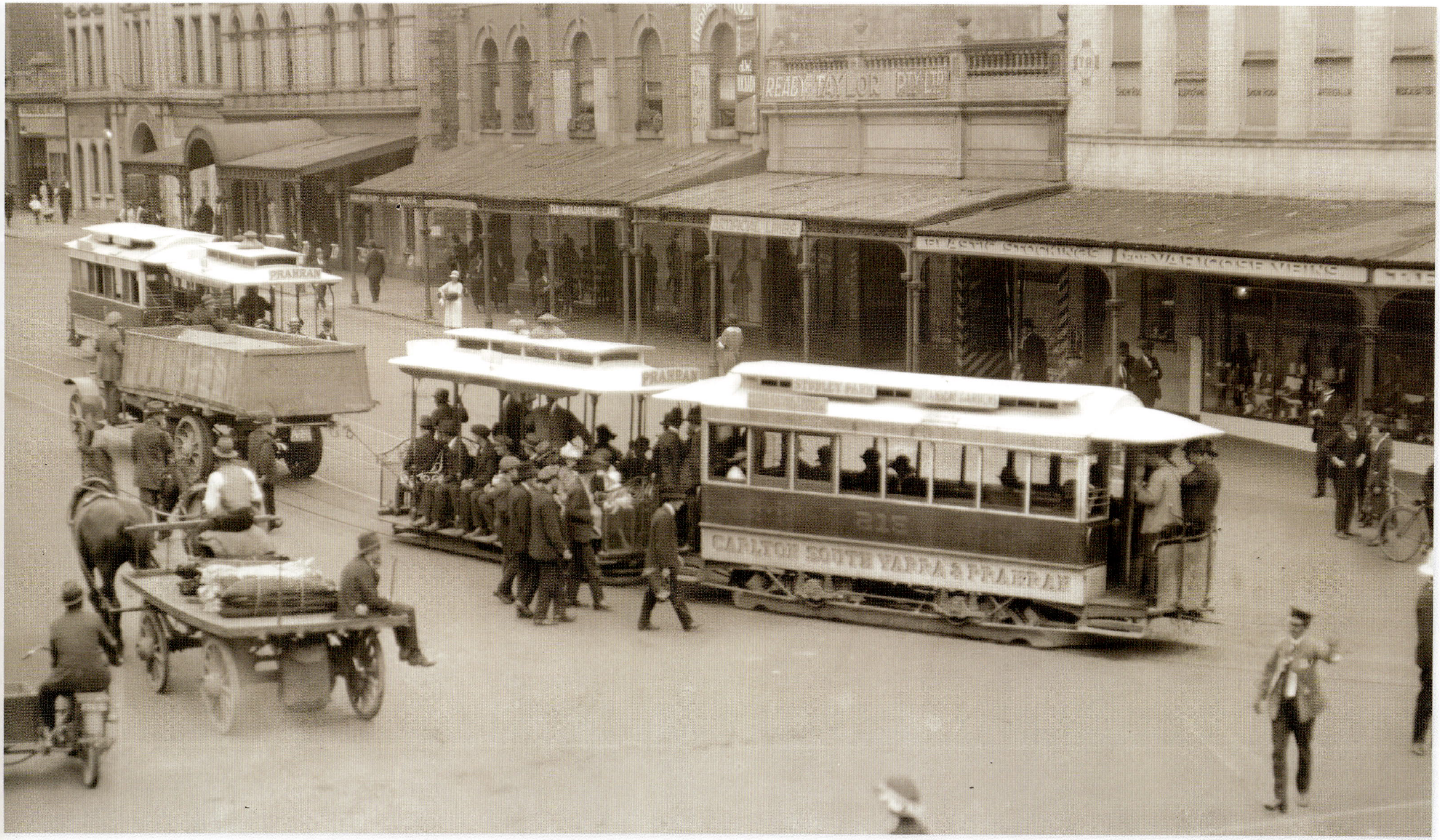

◀ FLINDERS STREET STATION

c.1916

PHOTOGRAPHER: KERR BROTHERS

A spectacular shot of a street scene outside Flinders Street Station. It's hard to fathom that the station building was only six years old at the time.

In the age of COVID-19, the midday rush never looked so different. Notice the sign above the left entrance to the station, which reads 'Enlist and Fight for the Dear Old Flag' — it's a World War I recruiting banner.

The design of the old Melbourne trams is rather fabulous. Wouldn't you love to see a few of them making their way through the city today?

Finally, draw your attention to the curious young girl in the bottom right. She seems to be rather intrigued with the camera. I can't help but get horror-film vibes!

TRAM TOWING ▲

c.1918

PHOTOGRAPHER: E.J. FRAZER

A group of young men hold on for the ride as a tram is towed down what looks like Swanston Street. The trams are branded with the suburb names 'Prahran' and 'Carlton South Yarra & Prahran'.

The shopfronts include Reaby Taylor Pty Ltd and the Melbourne Cafe.

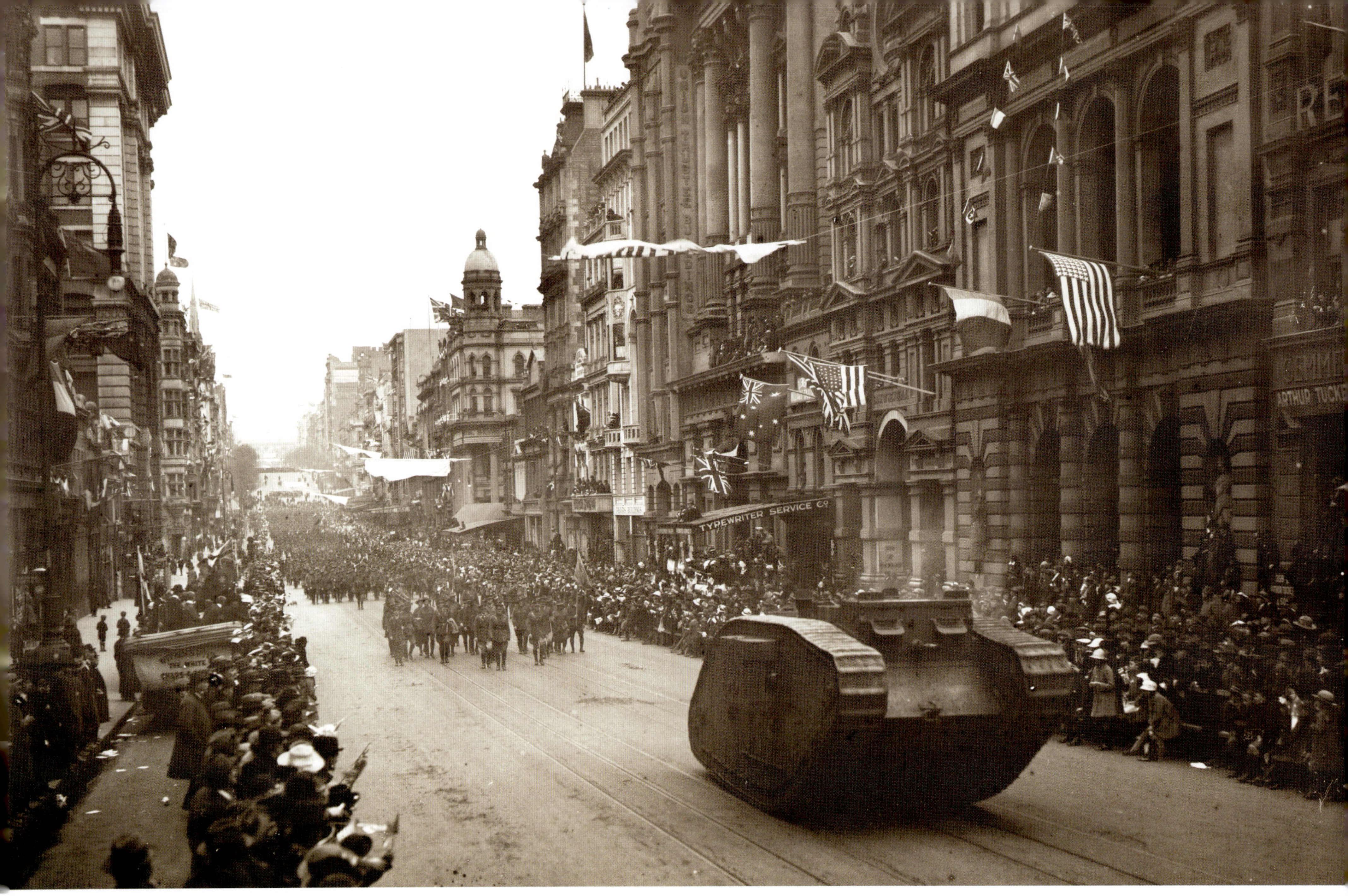

VICTORY PARADE, COLLINS STREET

1919

PHOTOGRAPHER: KERR BROTHERS

A view of Collins Street looking east, near the junction with Queen Street.

The image depicts a victory parade that took place on 19 July 1919, through Melbourne. Historic peace celebrations were held in three states, and practically every unit of the Australian Imperial Force was represented.

The Treaty of Versailles had been signed on 28 June 1919, less than a month earlier, formally ending World War I. To mark the end of 'the war to end all wars', the day was declared 'Peace Day' throughout the British Empire.

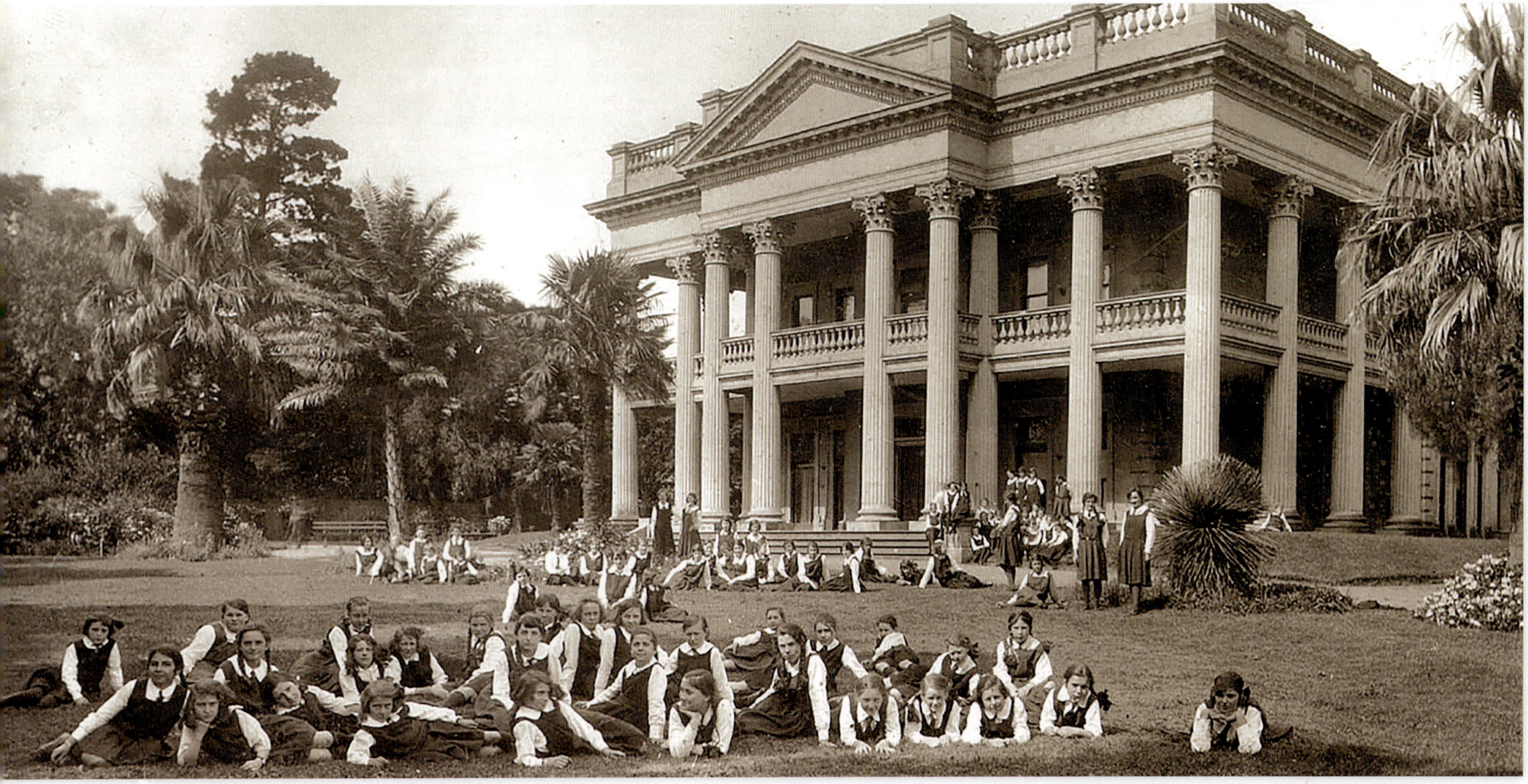

LOWTHER HALL ANGLICAN GRAMMAR SCHOOL, ESSENDON

1920

PHOTOGRAPHER: UNKNOWN (TOP IMAGE);
MARK FARRELLY PHOTOGRAPHY 2019 (BOTTOM IMAGE)
SOURCE: LOWTHER HALL ANGLICAN GRAMMAR SCHOOL ARCHIVES (TOP IMAGE)

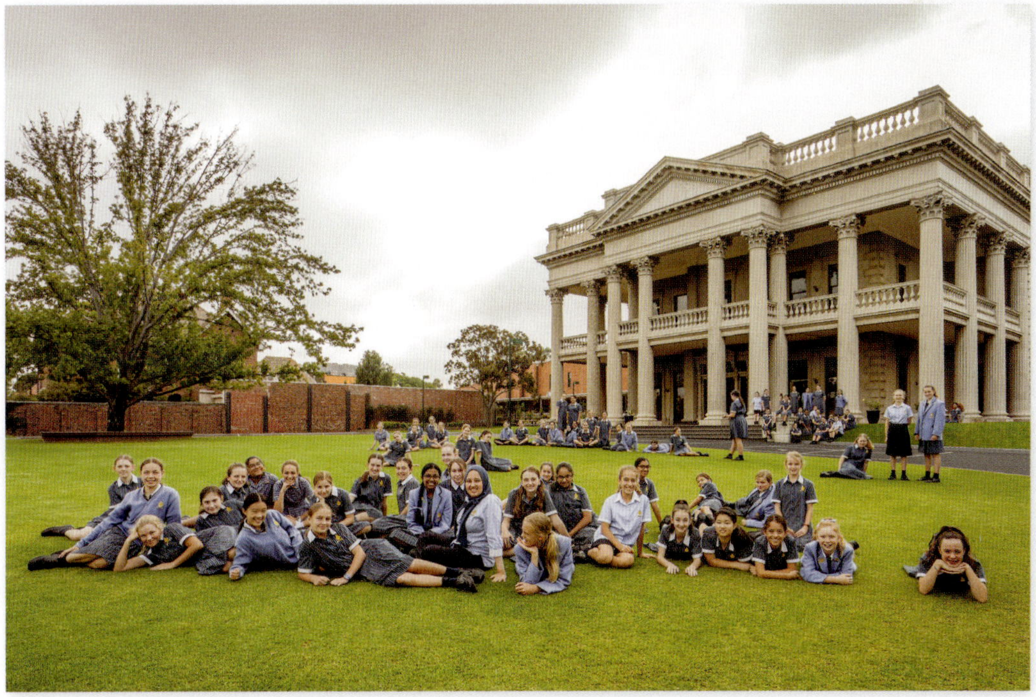

THEN AND NOW: Check out this incredible re-enacted photo of students at Lowther Hall Anglican Grammar!

The 'Mansion' building at the school was built in 1890 by Coiler McCracken as a family home, then known as Earlsbrae Hall.

It was later home to prominent Melburnian Edward Cole, the man behind Cole's Book Arcade and Cole's Funny Picture Book. Cole bequeathed Earlsbrae Hall to the Church of England for the purposes of education, and Archbishop Henry Lowther Clarke acquired the property and turned it into the school it is today.

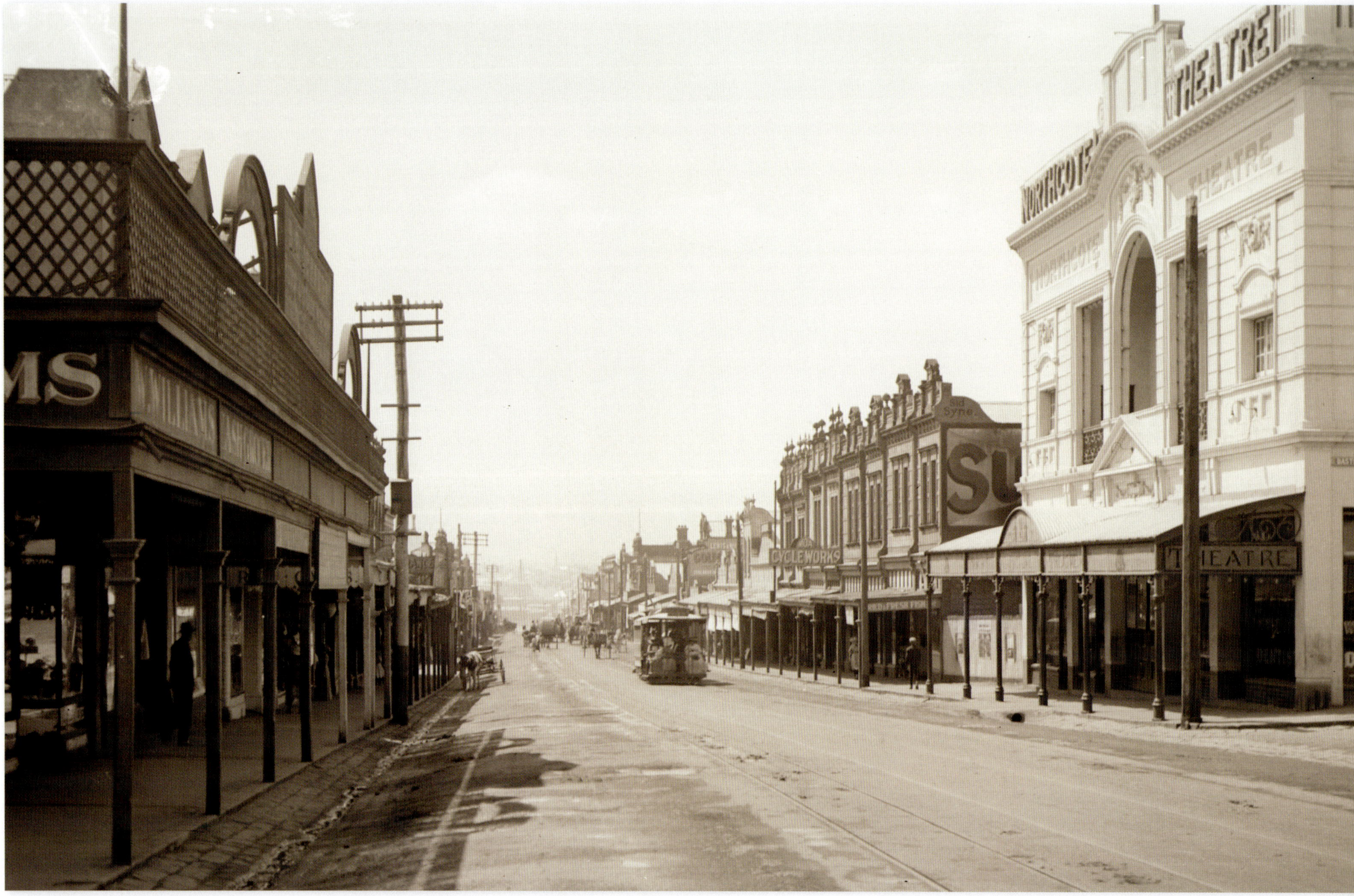

HIGH STREET, NORTHCOTE

c. 1920

PHOTOGRAPHER: ROSE STEREOGRAPH CO.

The Northcote Theatre on the right opened in June 1912. Perhaps the earliest surviving picture theatre designed in Victoria, it was the first public building in Northcote to be illuminated with electricity. While operating as a cinema, it was used as the setting for the film *Night Club* in 1952. The cinema closed in 1960, and today operates as a reception venue.

MELBOURNE PUBLIC LIBRARY, LATROBE STREET

c.1920

PHOTOGRAPHER: THOMAS MAHOOD

An elevated view depicting the Melbourne Public Library (now State Library VIctoria). To the right is Coop's Shot Tower, which you may recognise today from its incorporation into the Melbourne Central complex, where it towers beneath the iconic conical glass roof.

The library was established in 1854, making it one of Melbourne's founding institutions, Australia's oldest public library, and one of the first free libraries in the world. Today, it is Australia's busiest library and, as of 2018, the fourth-most-visited library in the world.

When it first opened, the library was enclosed by a wooden fence, surrounded by paddocks with trees and shrubs. The wooden fence was replaced by a wrought-iron fence in 1873, which was removed in 1939.

Until around 1920, two ornate bronze lions sat atop the front steps. In 1925 they were relocated to the Melbourne Zoo, where they were put on display until the early 1960s. They were removed during a preservation clean up, and have never been seen since!

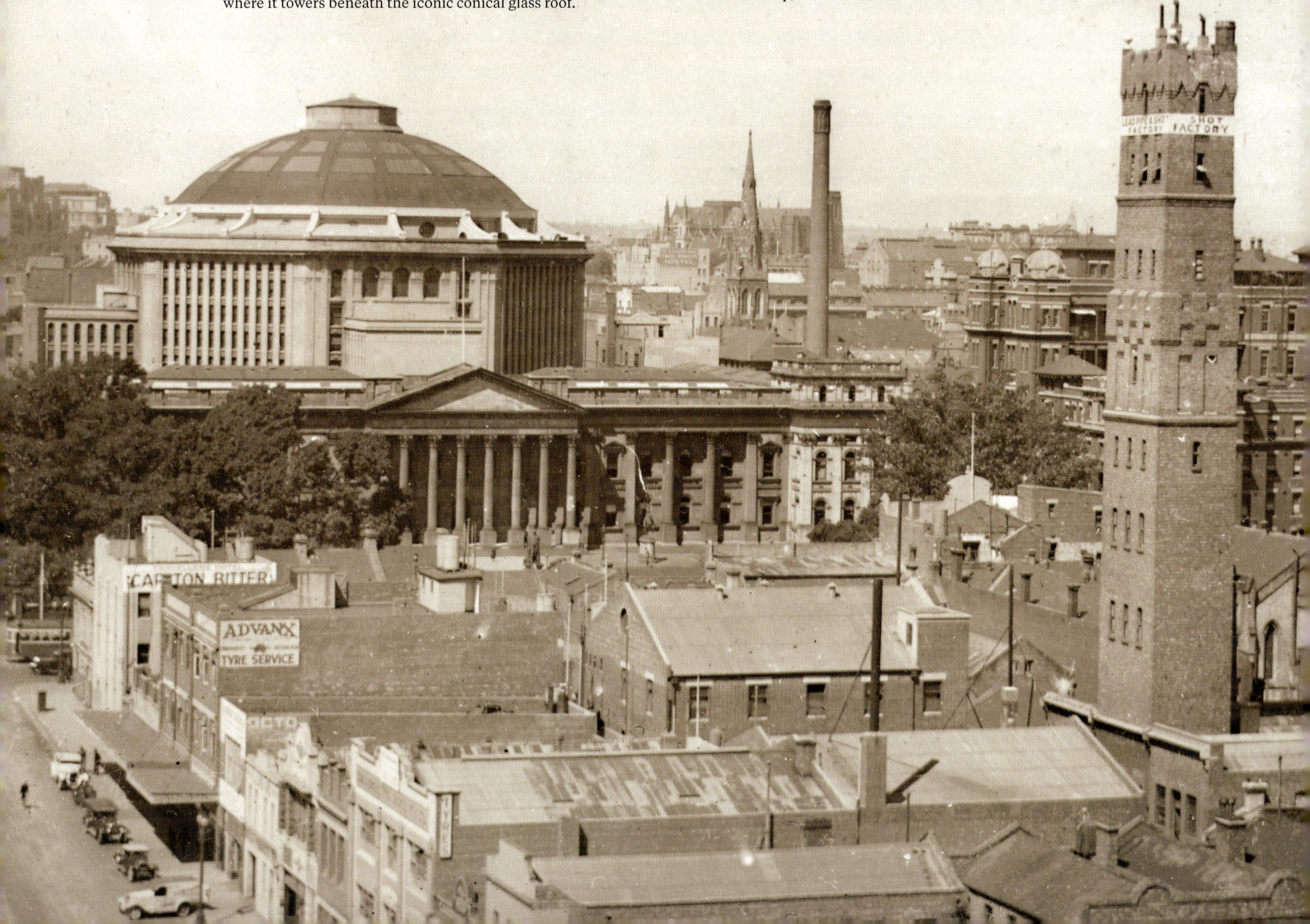

PRINCES BRIDGE

c.1920

PHOTOGRAPHER: JOHN HENRY HARVEY

A remarkable photo of fruit and vegetable sellers in the early 1920s on Princes Bridge near Flinders Street.

Many European migrants occupied these stores, and were among some of the early Greek, Italian, and Turkish migrants in Australia.

In the background is a spireless St Paul's Cathedral. The cathedral's spires were constructed between 1926 and 1932.

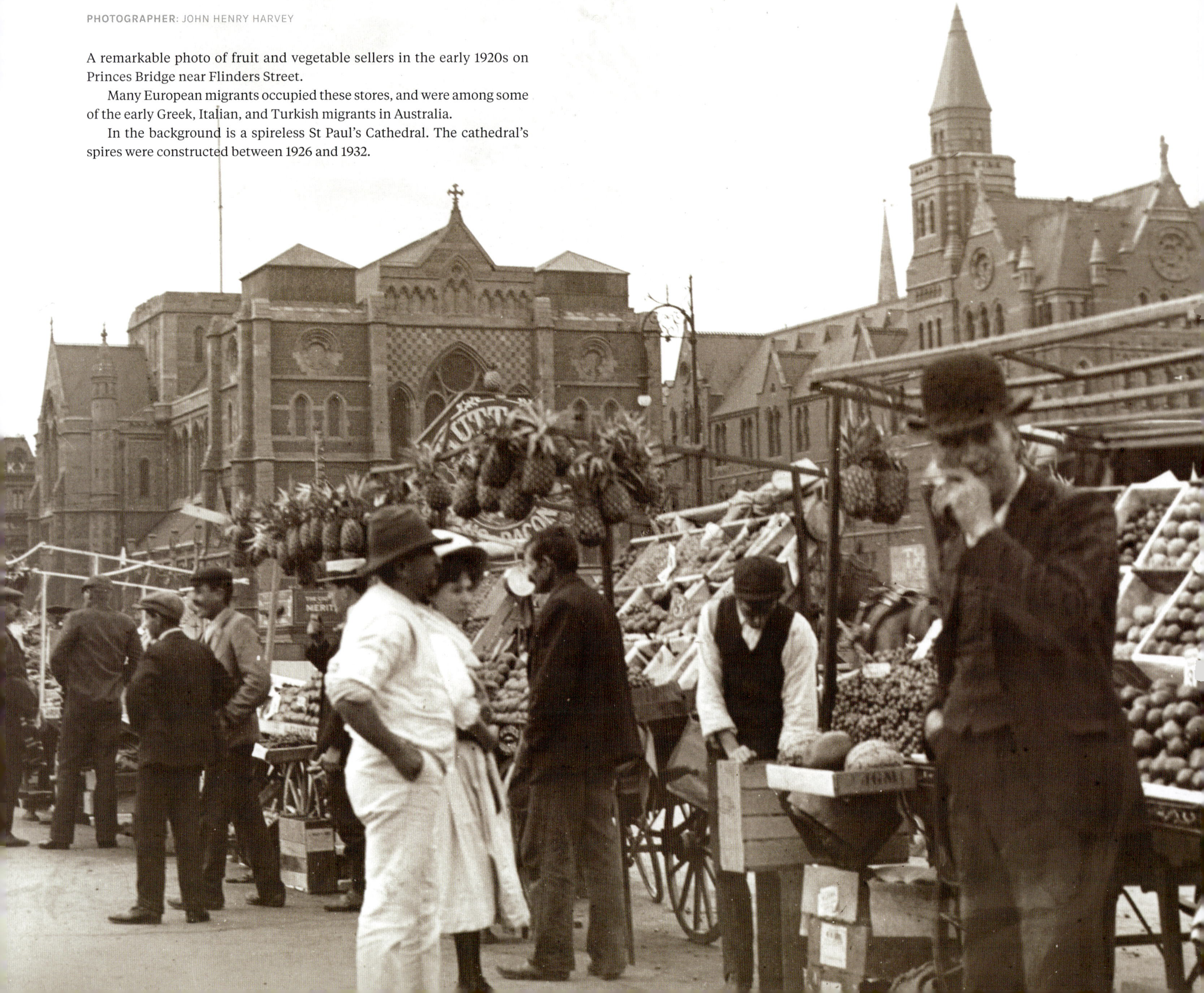

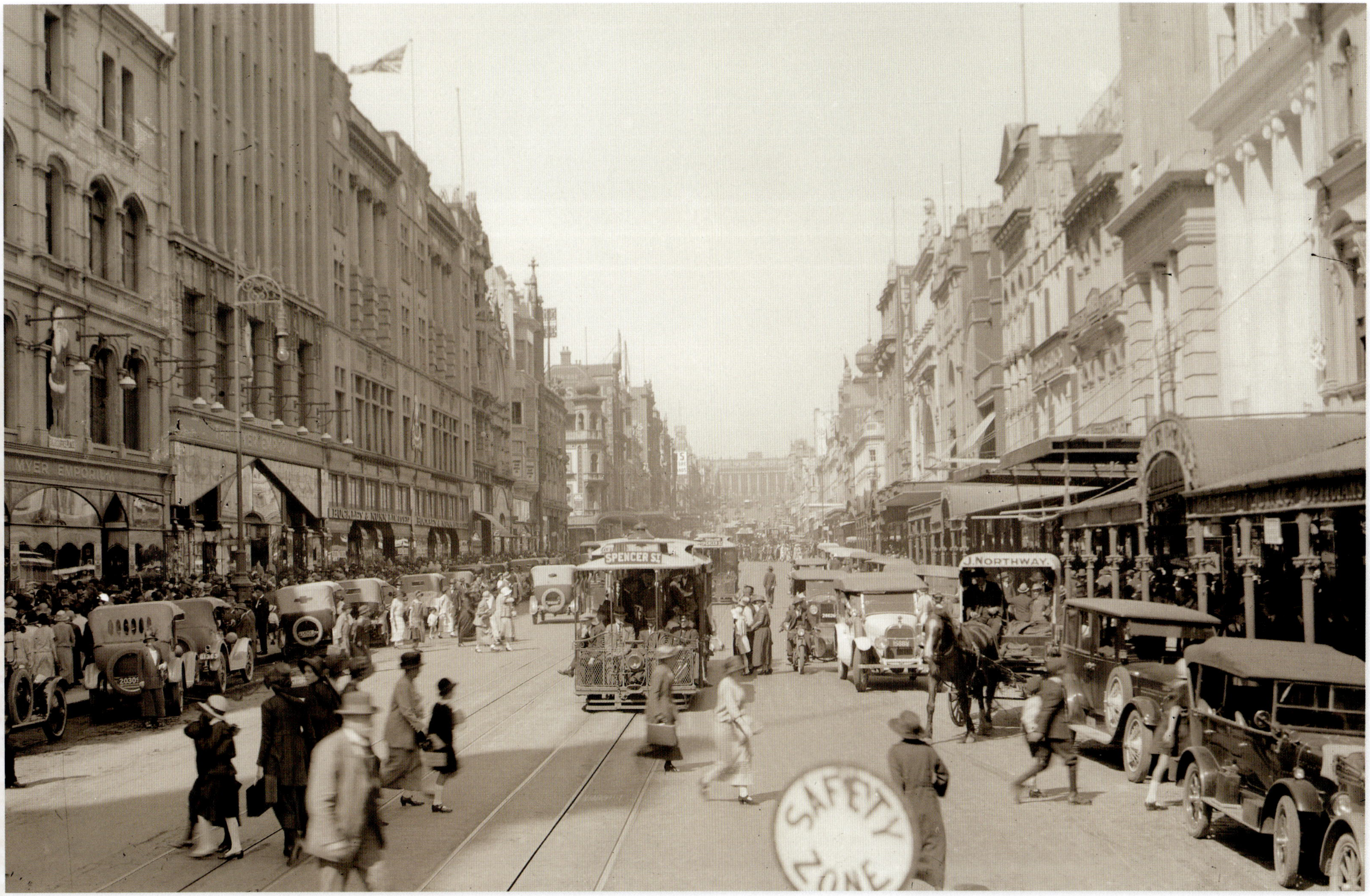

BOURKE STREET

c.1920

PHOTOGRAPHER: LYLE FOWLER

A fabulous Christmas street scene on Bourke Street. To the right you can see the newly built Myer Emporium.

The renowned Myer department store was founded by Sydney Myer (born Simcha Myer Baevski), a Russian immigrant. He migrated to Melbourne in 1899 during Victoria's gold rush era, with very little money and little knowledge of English.

In 1900 he opened the first Myer store with his brother in Bendigo. After much success, the Bourke Street store was opened in 1914.

From this base in Melbourne, Myer built Australia's largest chain of department stores — the only chain with stores in all Australian states.

VIEW OF MELBOURNE FROM SOUTH MELBOURNE

c.1920

PHOTOGRAPHER: CHARLES NETTLETON

A rare elevated view of Melbourne from South Melbourne.

As you can see, the foreground is largely agricultural. In the distance, beyond some large white tents, is the Yarra River and Flinders Street.

Quite noticeable to the left is the old Customs House, now the Immigration Museum. While the city looks relatively populated with buildings, it is quite astounding to realise what little growth has occurred on the south side of the Yarra. As time went on, this area remained very industrial, in contrast to areas north of the river.

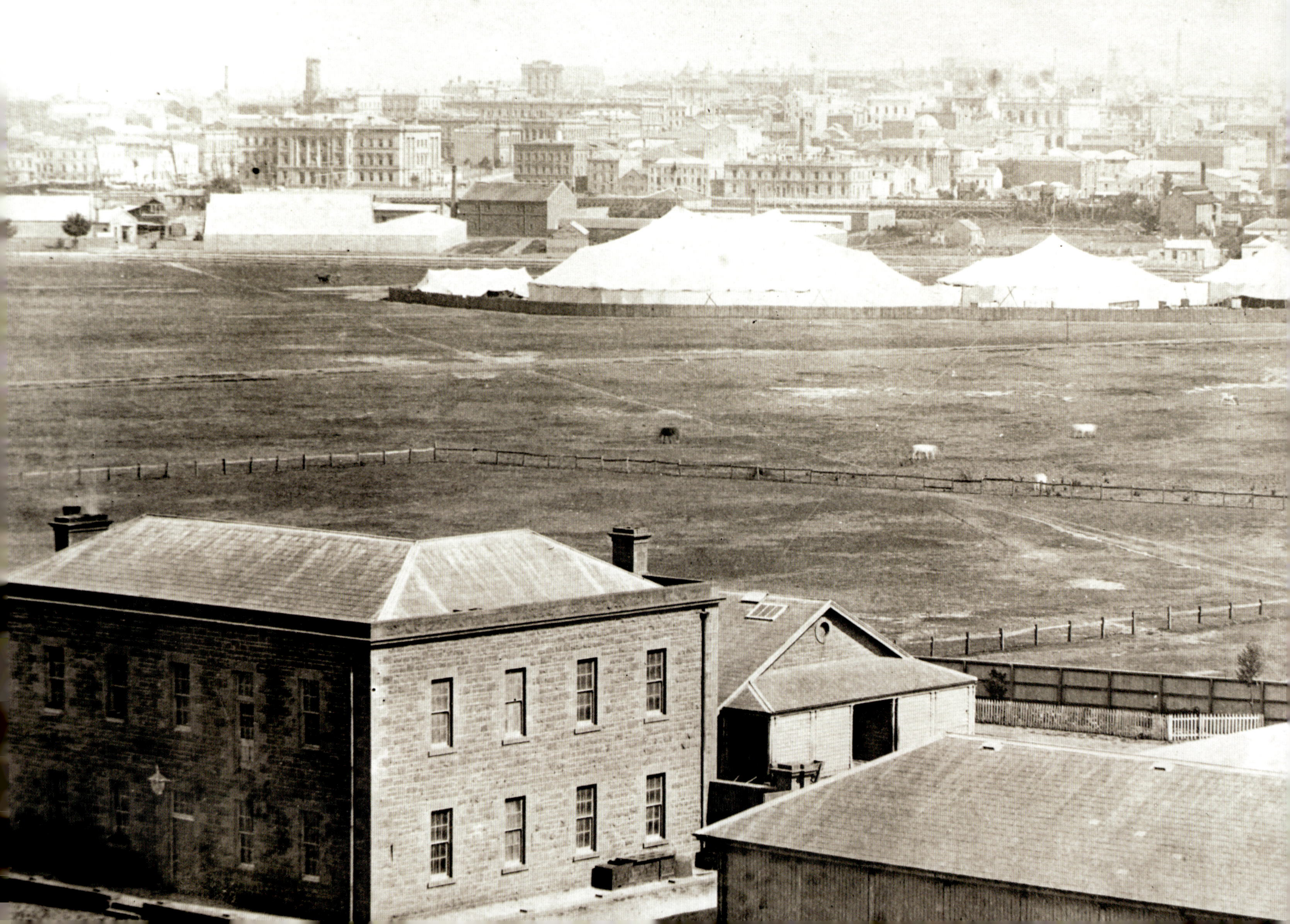

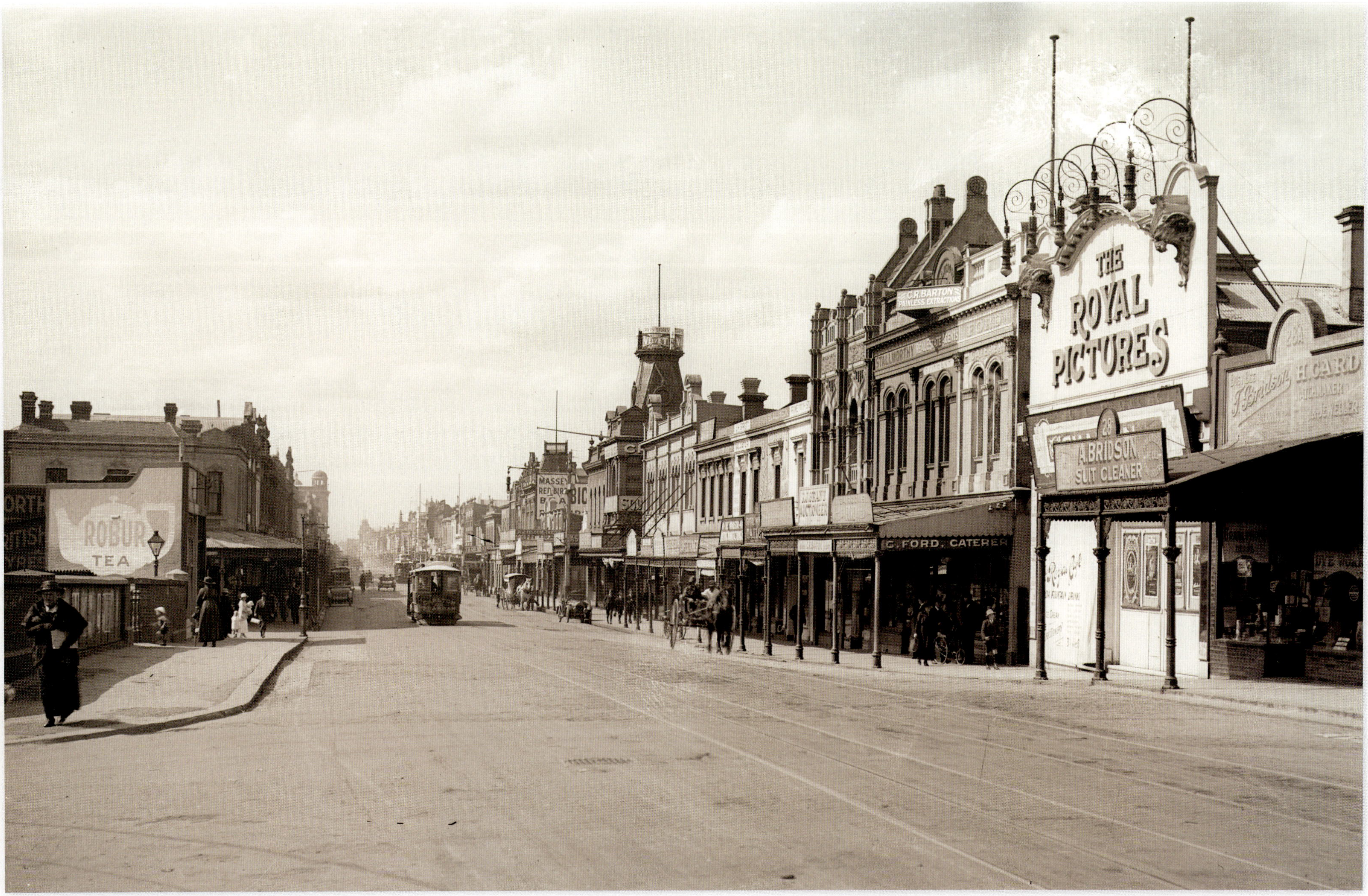

CHAPEL STREET, WINDSOR

c.1920

PHOTOGRAPHER: ROSE STEREOGRAPH CO.

Above is a pretty epic shot of Chapel Street, Windsor, right near Windsor Station. Sadly, the Royal Pictures Building on the right no longer exists (it's now a Paint Spot), but many of the other buildings remain.

Other businesses in the 1920 image include T. Bridson (tailor), A. Bridson (suit cleaner), H. Card (watchmaker and jeweller), C. Ford (caterer), and R.J. Grant (auctioneer).

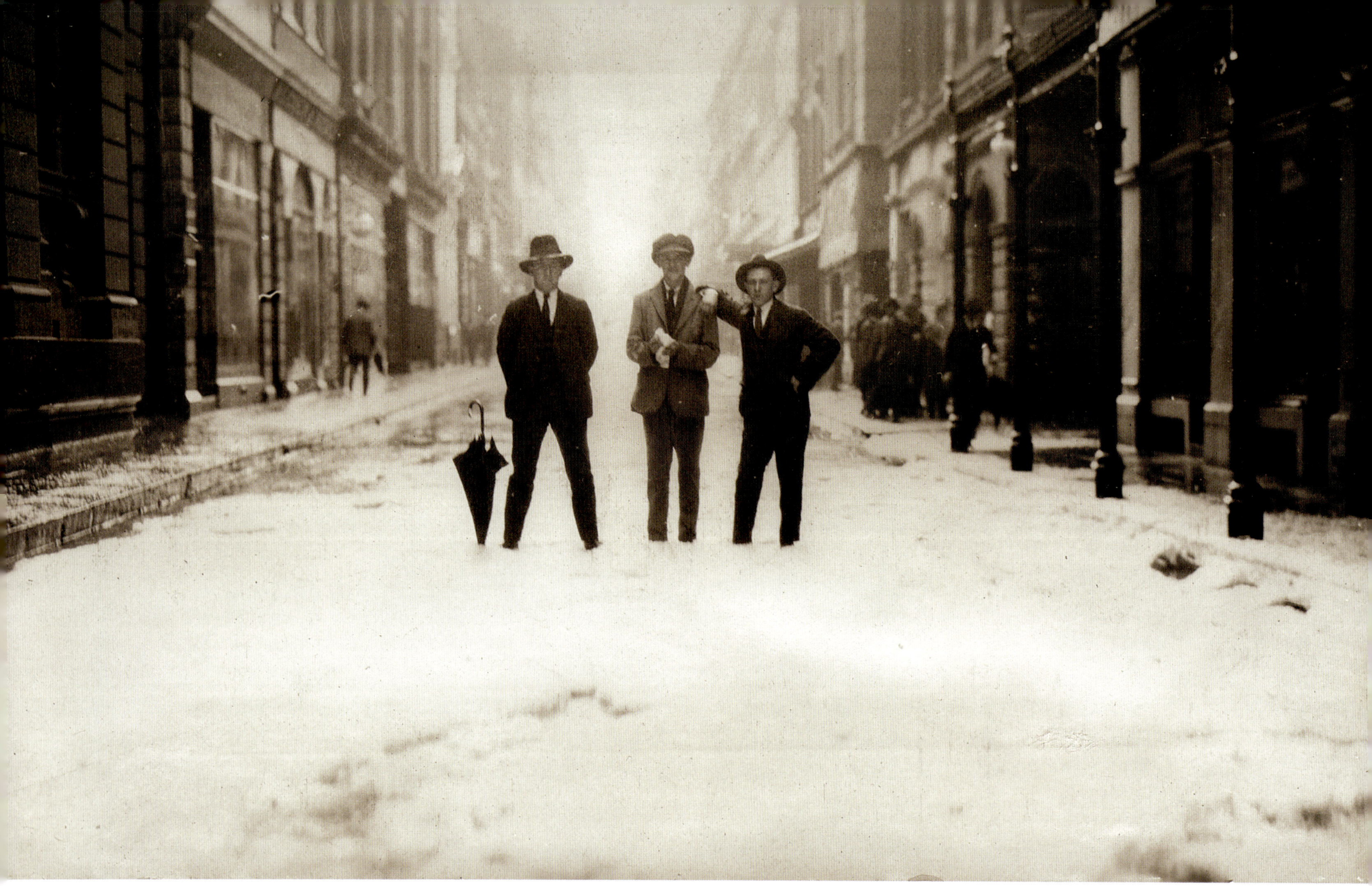

MELBOURNE HAILSTORM

1921

PHOTOGRAPHER: UNKNOWN

Three gentlemen pose in a city laneway after a dramatic hailstorm hit the city on 15 October 1921.

Here are some highlights of what occurred, from an excerpt in *The Australasian*:

'Hailstones as large as marbles beat a deafening tattoo on roofs, shattered skylights and windows, and levelled shrubberies, and stripped trees in public and private gardens.

'A little boy, who sought to rescue his dog from a deep drain in Hawthorn, was overwhelmed by the sudden rush of floodwater and swept into the Yarra.

'Thousands of people were drenched before they found shelter in the streets, which were almost instantly flooded. Bourke and Collins streets were wonderful sights after the storm. They were carpeted in white, and boys began to fight with handfuls of hailstones.

'It was a considerable time before trams and motorcars were able to proceed, and then, for fear of skidding, they had to move slowly.

'Although no estimate could be obtained during the week-end, the damage caused in warehouses in Flinders lane by flooding, it is believed, will amount to several thousands of pounds.'

FLINDERS STREET

c. 1925

PHOTOGRAPHER: SUTCLIFFE PTY LTD

When you think about iconic landmarks and symbols that represent the city of Melbourne, Flinders Street Station and Melbourne trams spring to mind immediately.

This image depicts both, with tramway construction going on at the corner of Flinders and Swanston streets.

What else stands out to you? From the 'Cross Crossings Cautiously' signage on Flinders Street Station, and the iconic Young and Jackson Hotel on the right, to the somewhat familiar bumper-to-bumper traffic, this image is a real feast for the eyes.

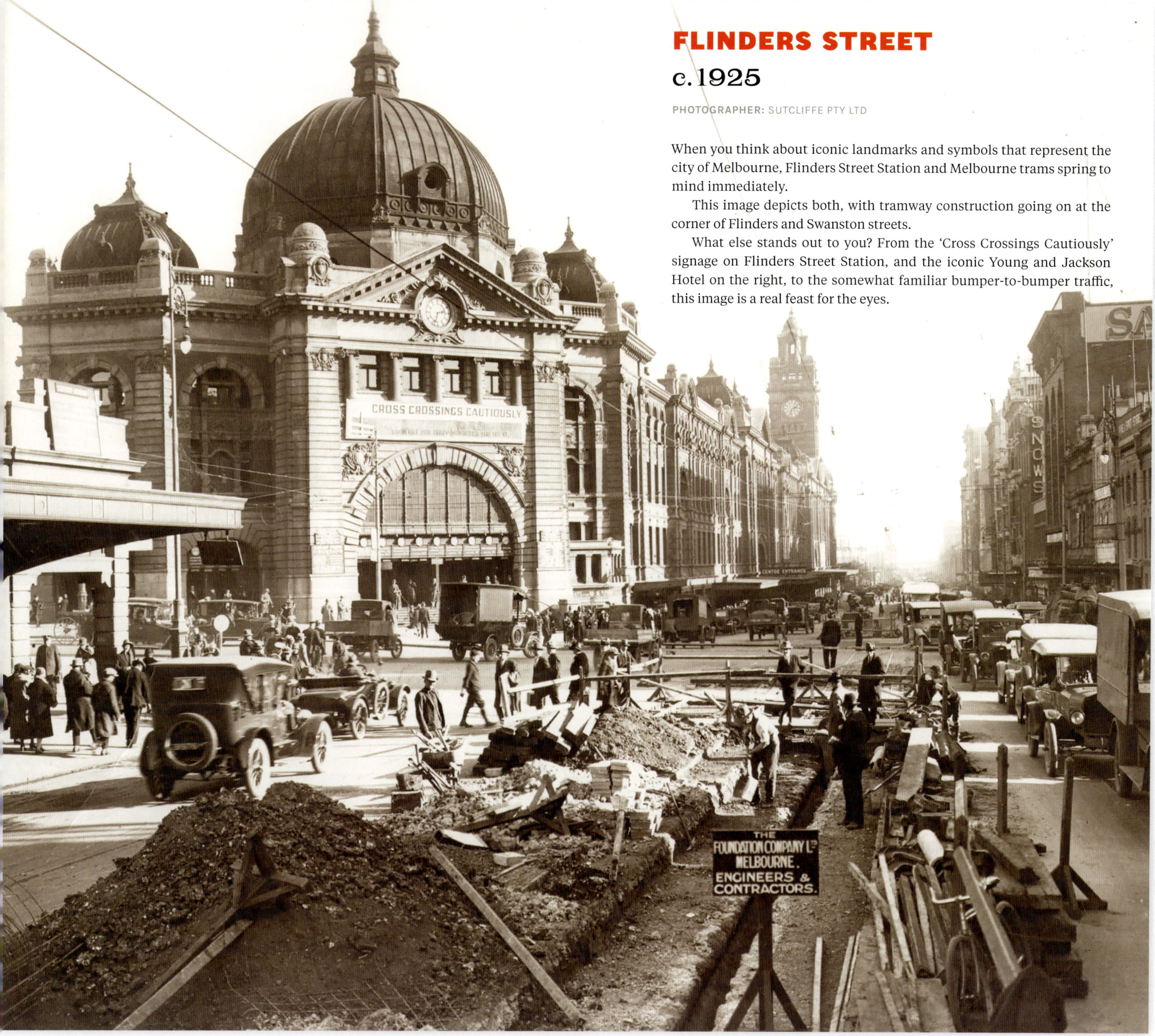

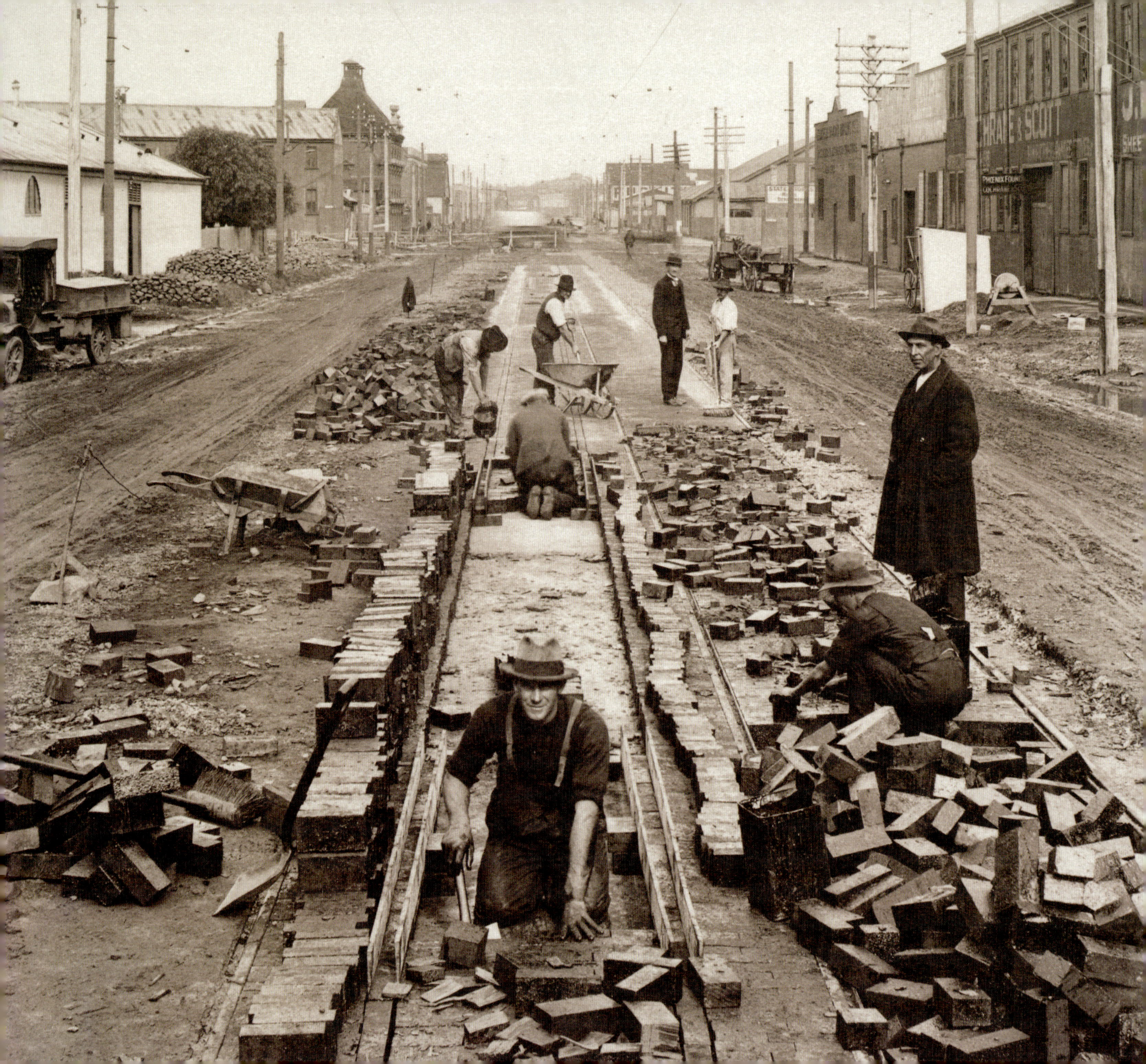
SCOTT

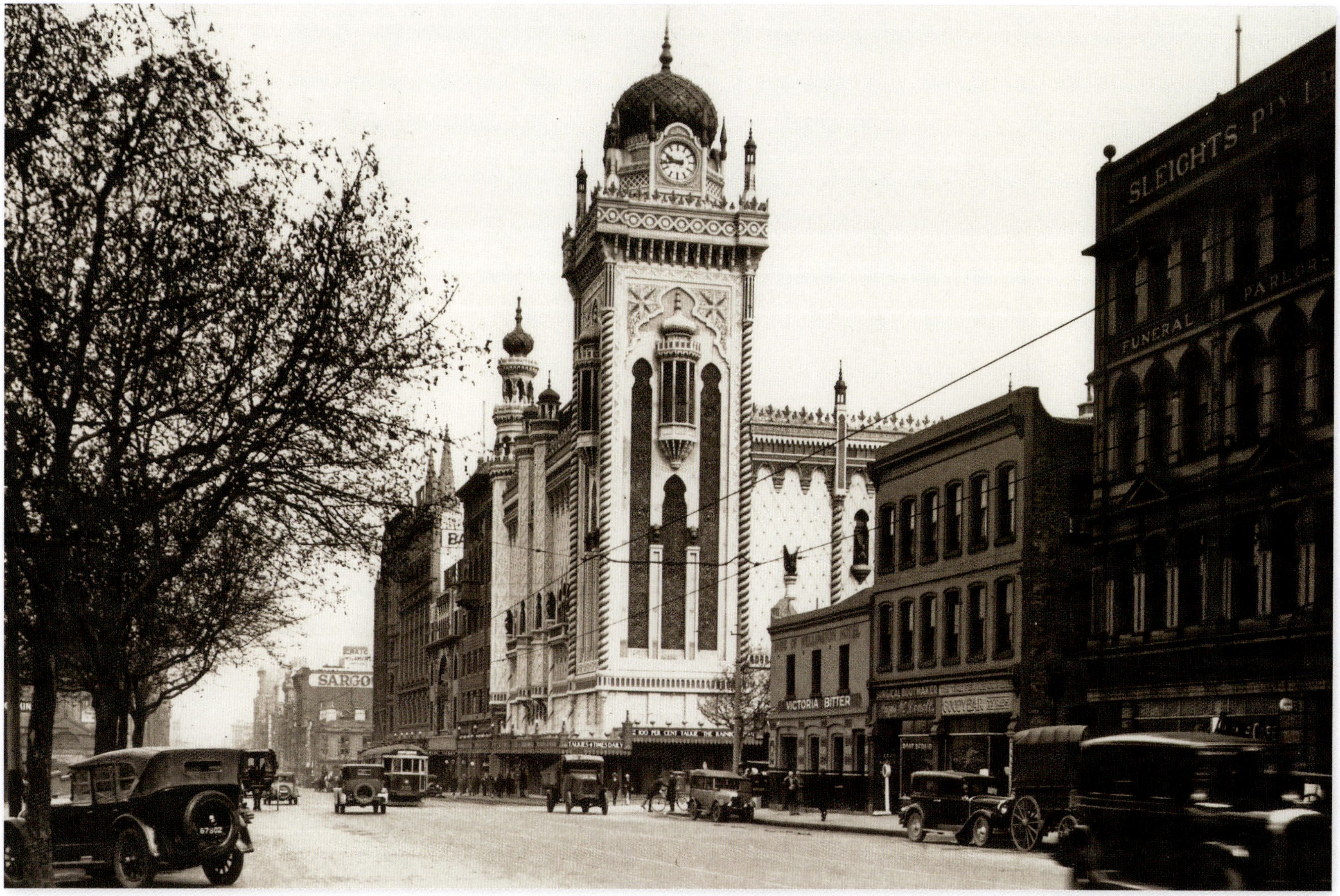

◀ STURT STREET, SOUTH MELBOURNE

1925

PHOTOGRAPHER: UNKNOWN

A smiling chap and his fellow workers lay bricks as they construct tramways in Sturt Street, South Melbourne, on 13 May 1925.

Before European settlement, South Melbourne was largely a flat area with a hill in the centre (where the town hall now stands). The hill was traditionally a social and ceremonial meeting place for the Aboriginal tribes of the area.

In the 1840s, the area became known as Emerald Hill. A decade later, during the gold rush, South Melbourne had become a massive slum, home to tens of thousands of fortune-seekers from around the world, newly arrived in Melbourne and on the hunt for precious metal. The area was called Canvas City because of the abundance of tents.

FLINDERS & RUSSELL STREETS ▲

c. 1929

PHOTOGRAPHER: ROSE STEREOGRAPH CO.

The opulent and instantly recognisable Forum Melbourne (originally the State Theatre) was brand spanking new in this image, having opened that year with the largest seating capacity of any theatre in Australia.

If you zoom in, you can see that the theatre is advertising a '100 per cent talkie', which means it's showing a film with dialogue — something pretty new at a time when films were making the transition from silent movies.

The film showing is *The Rainbow Man*, a 1929 comedy. This was the debut of George 'Gabby' Hayes, who went on to feature in dozens of Hollywood Westerns.

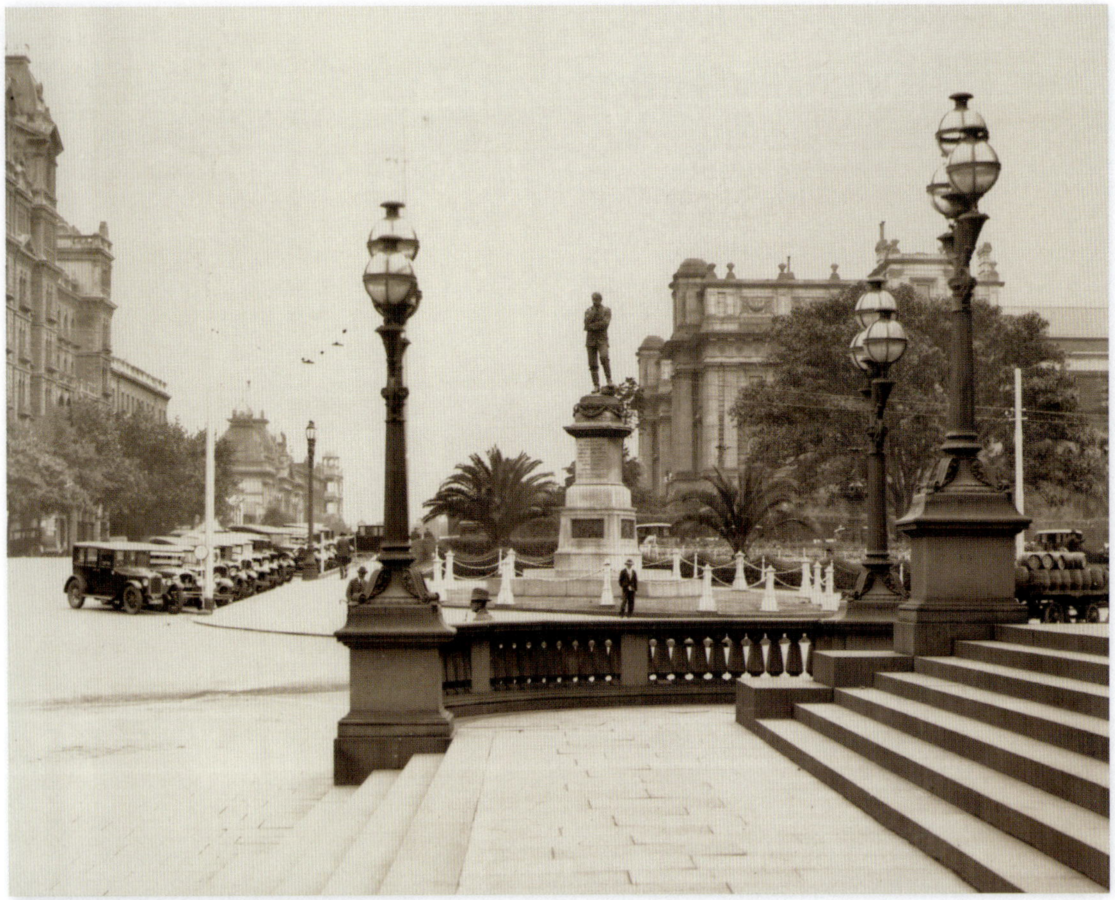

◀ SPRING STREET

c.1930

PHOTOGRAPHER: ALBERT JONES (TOP IMAGE); CYNTHIA PELOSI (BOTTOM IMAGE)

THEN AND NOW: Spring Street from the steps of the Treasury Building.

It is unclear why the eastern-most street on the original Hoddle grid was named Spring Street. Some say it was named after Baron Thomas Spring Rice, the chancellor of the exchequer under Lord Melbourne. Another theory is that it was named after the golden wattle trees that were in full bloom during Richard Bourke's visit to Melbourne.

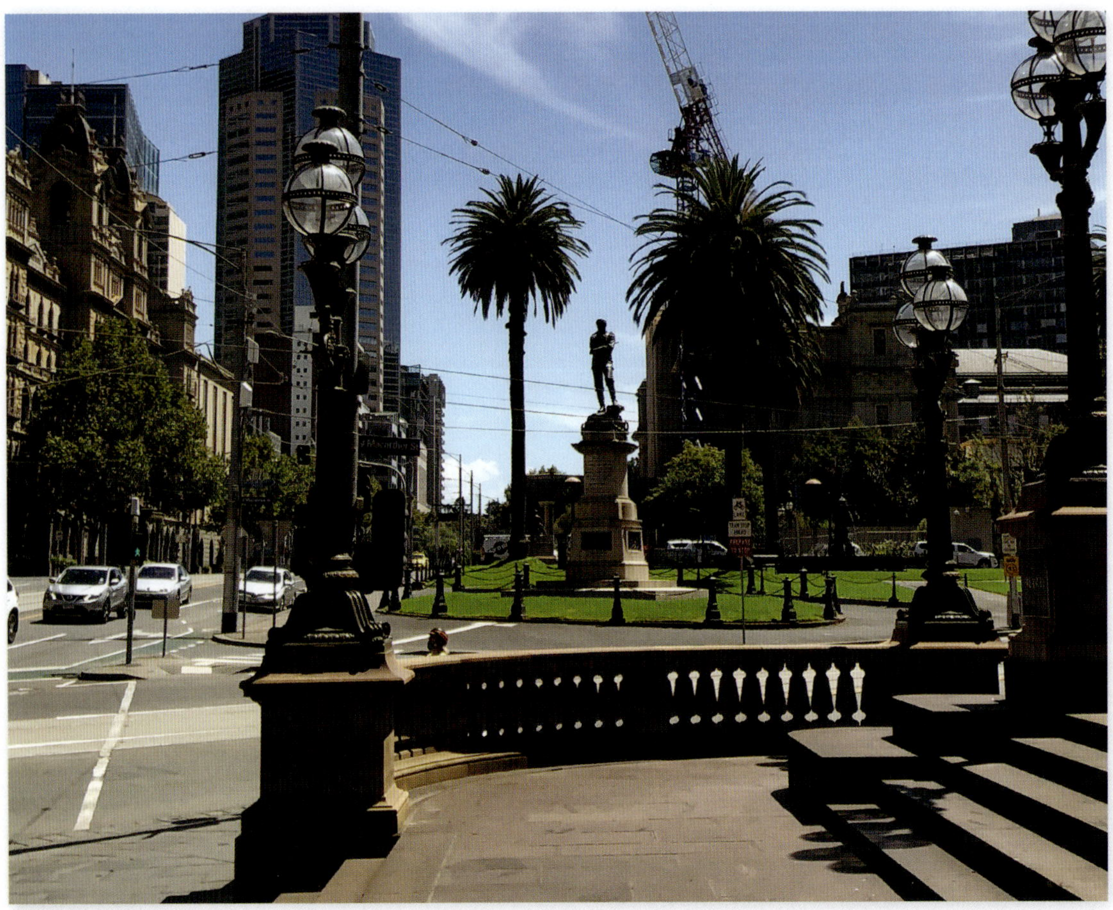

ELIZABETH STREET ▶

c.1930

PHOTOGRAPHER: COMMERCIAL PHOTOGRAPHIC CO.

The bustling Melbourne of the 1930s! That large billboard advertisement gives me major *Great Gatsby* vibes. This isn't New York City, but Melbourne's very own Elizabeth Street.

The advertisement is for Coles & Garrard Opticians, a pioneer in Melbourne's optometry industry, and the largest optometry firm in Melbourne until it was sold to OPSM in 1988. Established in March 1922, it was located at 370–72 Bourke Street. Other branches were opened in country towns from the 1940s onwards, and at Chadstone Shopping Centre in 1960.

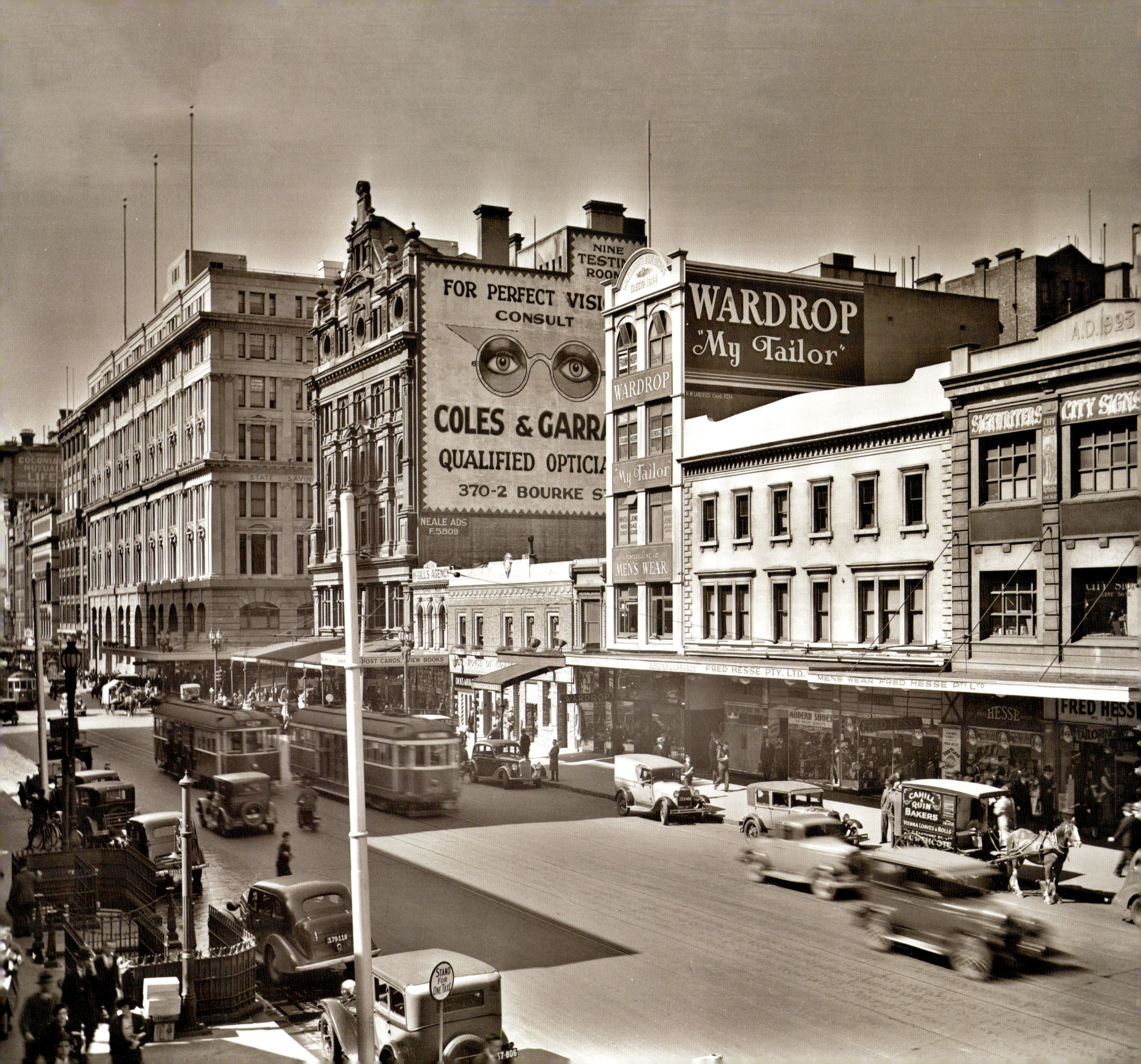

FOR PERFECT VISI
CONSULT
COLES & GARRA
QUALIFIED OPTICIA
370-2 BOURKE S
NEALE ADS
F.5809
NINE
WARDROP
"My Tailor"
WARDROP
My Tailor
Specialist in
MENS WEAR
A.D.1923
SIGNWRITERS
CITY SIGNS
POST CARDS
VIEW BOOKS
FRED HESSE PTY. LTD.
MENS WEAR FRED HESSE PTY LTD
MODERN SHOES
HESSE
FRED HESSE
CAHILL QUIN
BAKERS
VIENNA LOAVES & ROLLS
STAND FOR ONE TAXI

THE AGE OFFICES, COLLINS STREET

1934

PHOTOGRAPHER: THE AGE

En route from Ballarat to the Melbourne Museum, the Aisbett Concord coach is pictured here outside *The Age* newspaper office on Collins Street, on 7 August 1934.

A sign for *The Australian Women's Weekly* can be seen behind the carriage, and another sign on the building reads: 'Advertising Centenary Arts Ball — Wednesday August 15th — 100% fun & frolic — single ticket 10'6 — Palais de Danse — St Kilda.' Melbourne hosted many centenary events in 1934.

Three Melbourne businessmen founded *The Age*: brothers John and Henry Cooke, and Walter Powell. The first edition was published on 17 October 1854.

The Age was published from these offices on Collins Street until 1969, when it moved to 250 Spencer Street. It moved back to Collins Street — this time opposite Southern Cross Station — in 2009, and moved again, to Bourke Street in the Docklands, after it was acquired by Nine Entertainment Co.

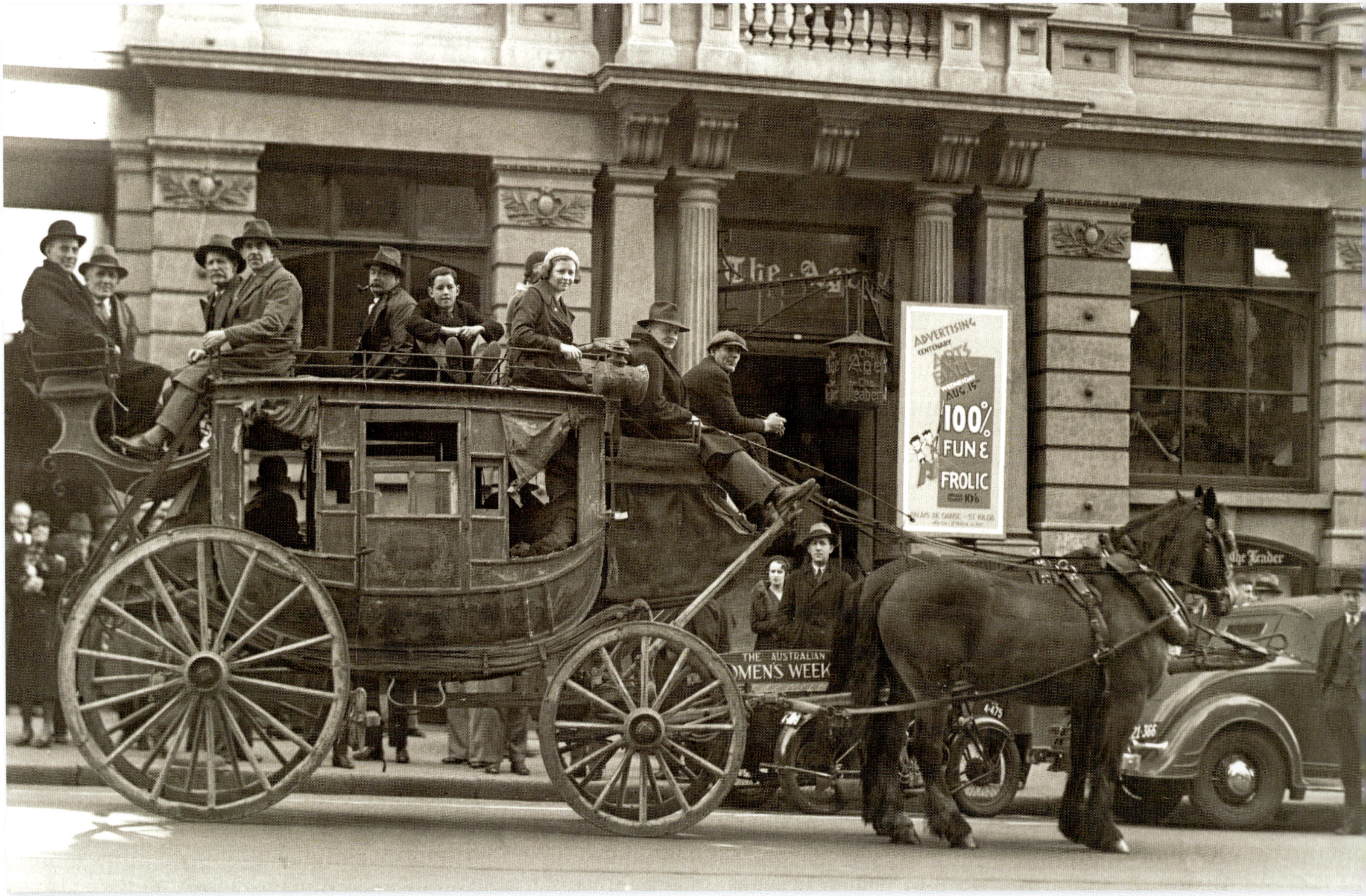

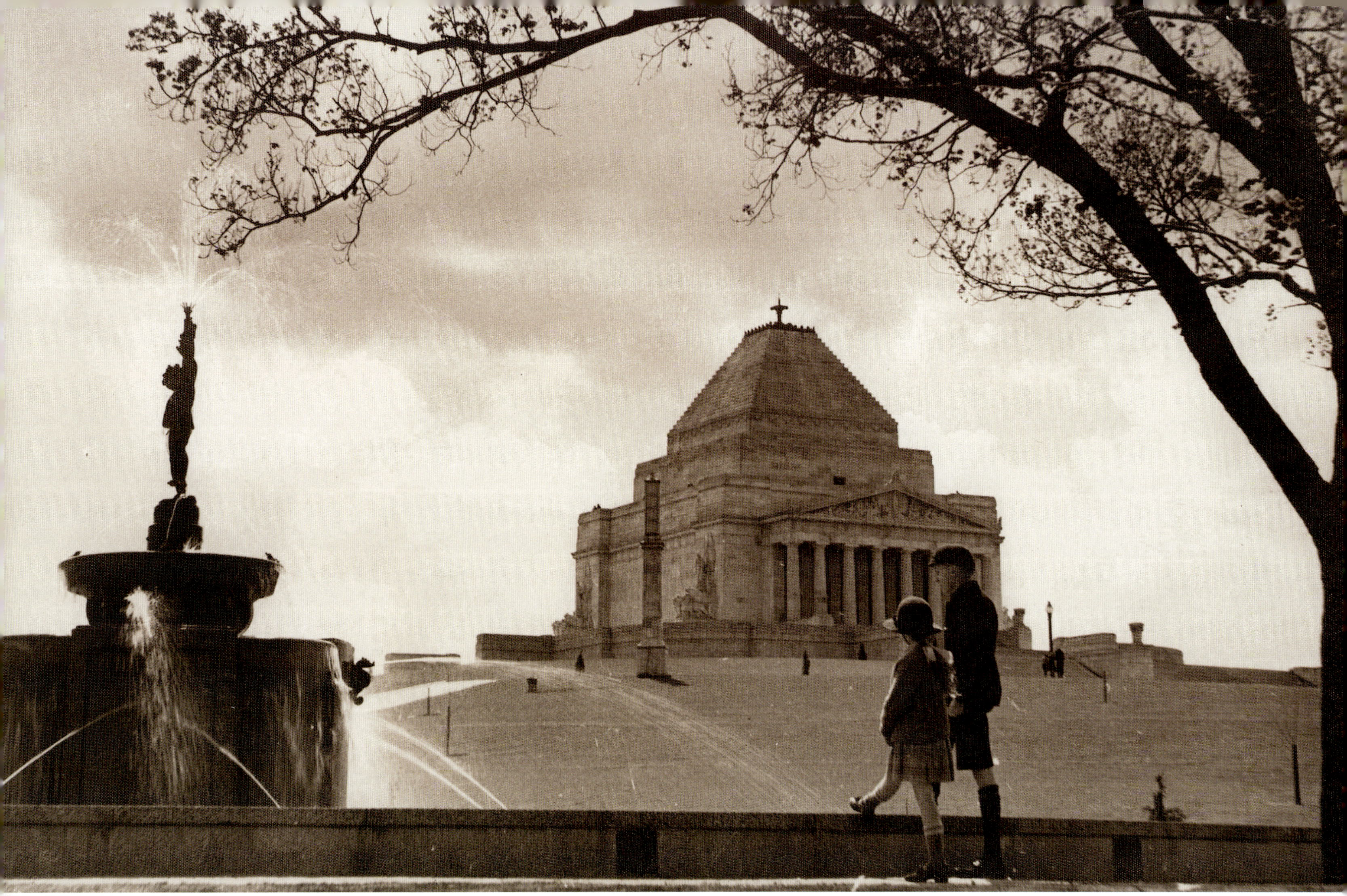

SHRINE OF REMEMBRANCE

c. 1934

PHOTOGRAPHER: ARTHUR W. HEADLAM

Lest We Forget.

A young boy and girl stand before the MacRobertson Fountain, at the corner of Domain and St Kilda roads, looking north towards the Shrine of Remembrance.

The Shrine is the Victorian state memorial to Australians who served in global conflicts throughout our nation's history.

The structure was completed in September 1934, making it very new in this image.

The Shrine was formally dedicated on Remembrance Day, 11 November 1934. Around 300,000 people attended the dedication ceremony, which was substantial given that Melbourne's population was 1 million at the time. According to historian Carl Bridge, it was the 'largest crowd ever to assemble in Australia to that date'.

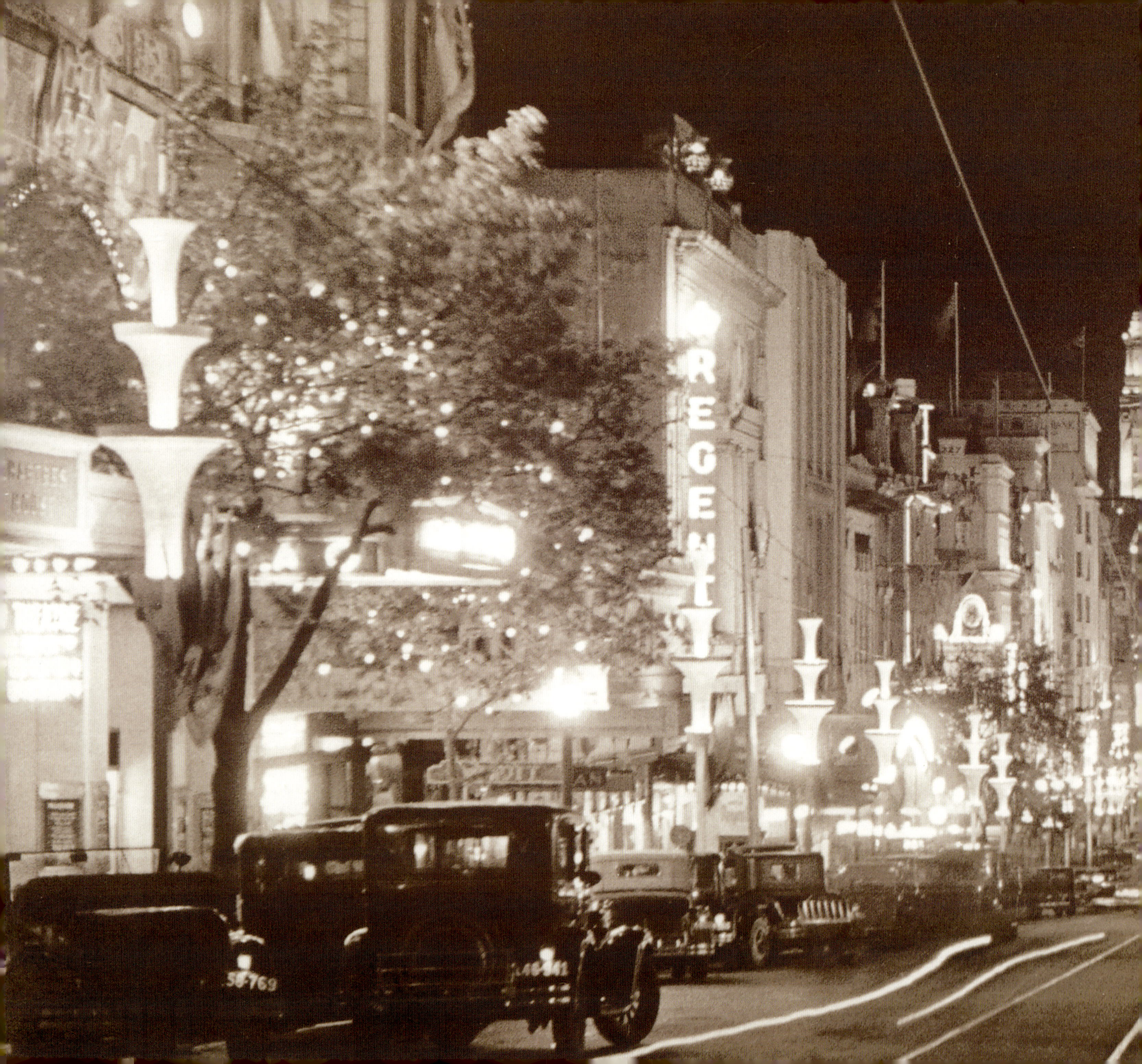
REGE
50-769

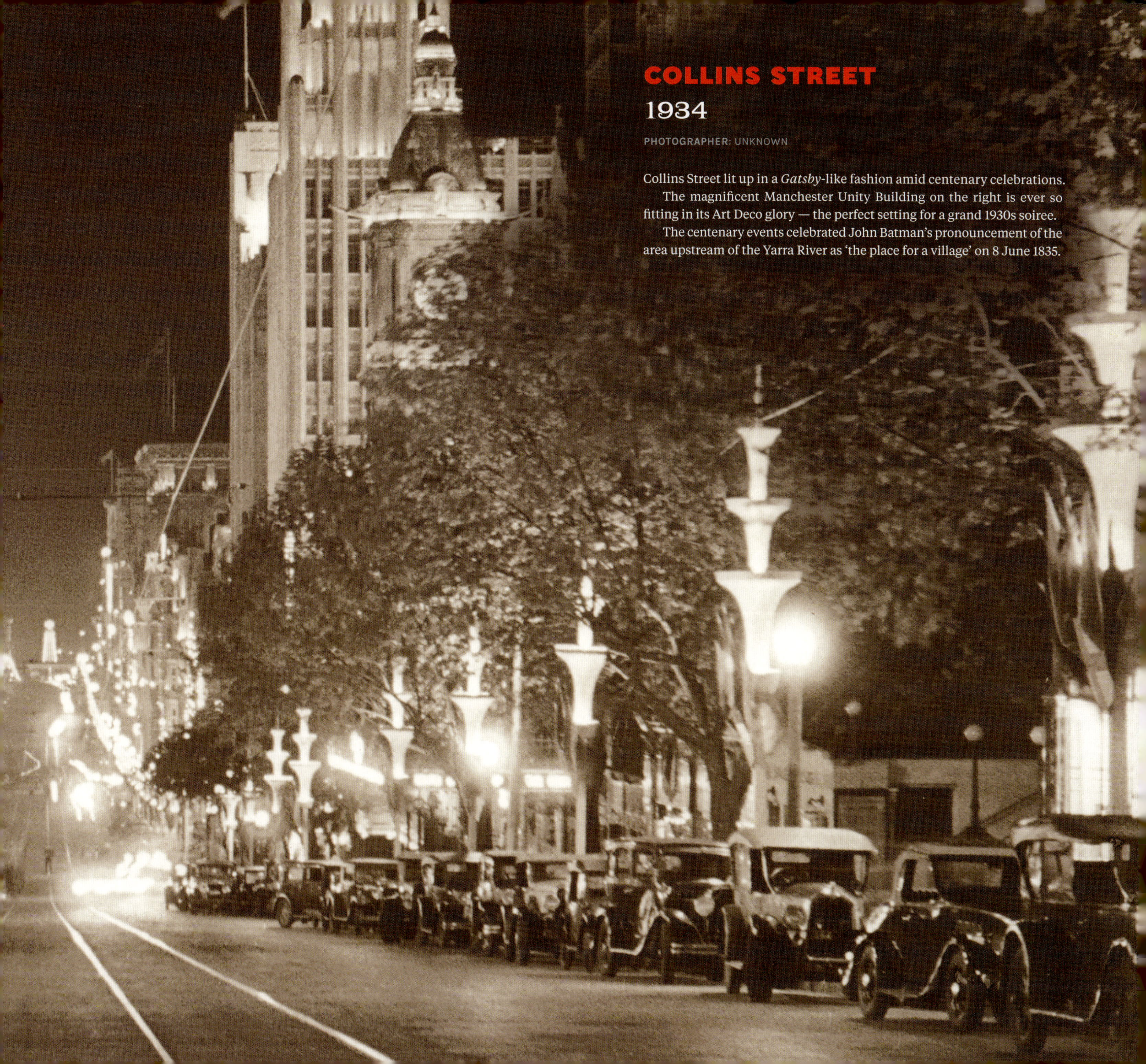

COLLINS STREET

1934

PHOTOGRAPHER: UNKNOWN

Collins Street lit up in a *Gatsby*-like fashion amid centenary celebrations.

The magnificent Manchester Unity Building on the right is ever so fitting in its Art Deco glory — the perfect setting for a grand 1930s soiree.

The centenary events celebrated John Batman's pronouncement of the area upstream of the Yarra River as 'the place for a village' on 8 June 1835.

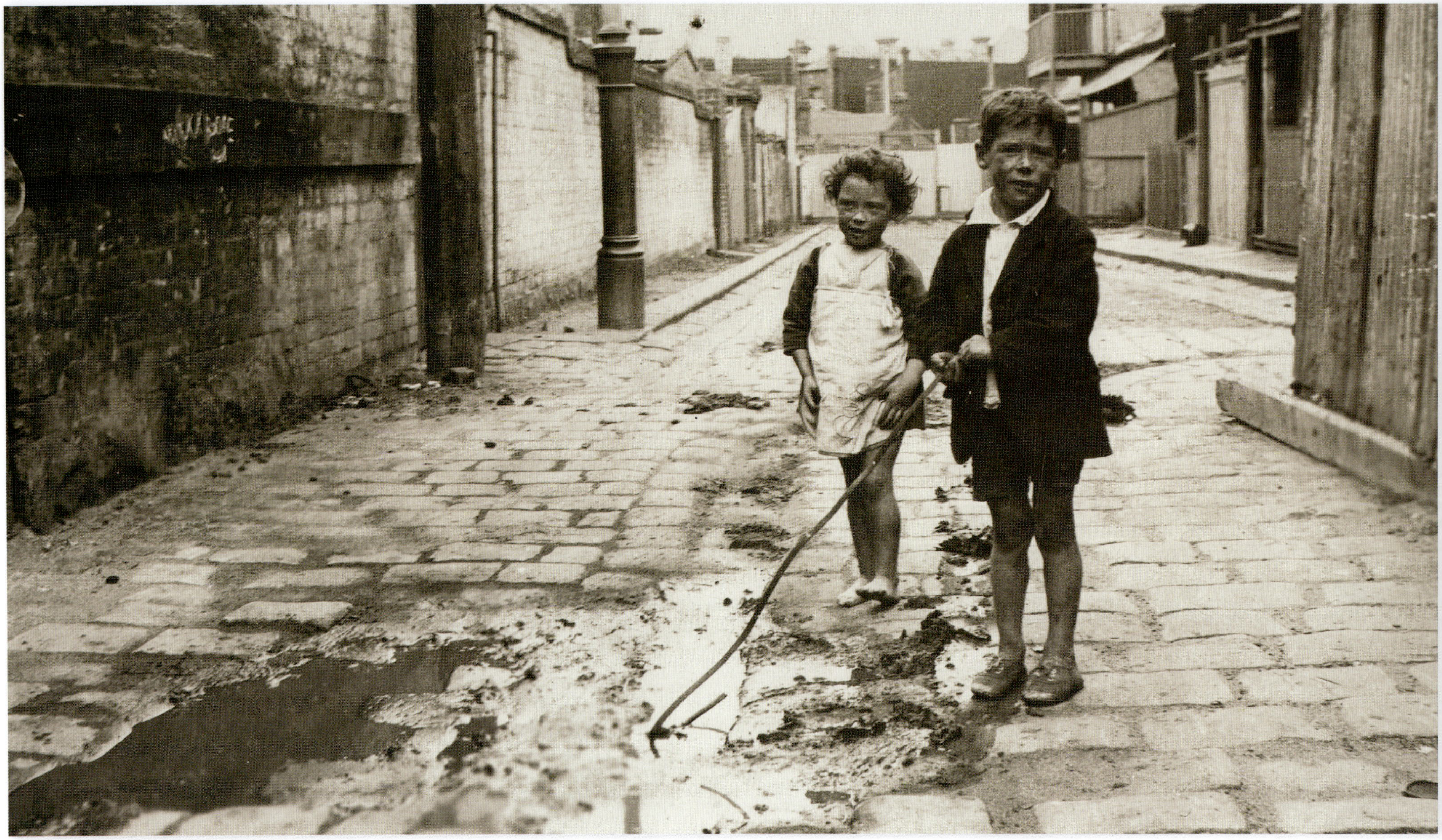

SLUM POCKET, CARLOW PLACE, CARLTON

c. 1935

PHOTOGRAPHER: FREDERICK OSWALD BARNETT

Two young children playing in a bluestone-paved alleyway, in what was considered a slum pocket in Carlow Place (off Rathdowne Street), Carlton. The pool of water in the foreground is drainage from a stable.

There are a series of similar images taken in 1935, by social reformer Frederick Oswald Barnett. In his attempt to expose poor living conditions and remedy them with liveable housing, he went around photographing slum pockets in Carlton, Collingwood, Fitzroy, Richmond, and North Melbourne. The rather high-end, pricey real estate in those areas today are the antitheses of slums.

'The slums are prisons in which many of our young lives are damned from birth, with very little hope of escape,' Mr Barnett wrote in Melbourne's *The Herald* in 1934.

While much of the housing and buildings were demolished, many remain. The next time you pass a chic, renovated property in Carlton or Fitzroy, bear in mind that at one point it may have been a slum house.

FOY & GIBSON DEPARTMENT STORE, BOURKE & SWANSTON STREETS

c.1935

PHOTOGRAPHER: LYLE FOWLER

First established in 1870 by Irish immigrant Mark Foy as a drapery on Smith Street, Collingwood, Foy's became one of Australia's first and largest department stores. This store on the corner of Bourke and Swanston streets was rebuilt with an extension in 1935 for a cost of around £250,000. In today's currency, adjusted for inflation, that translates to just under $25 million.

The store underwent a merger; endured depressions, economic crashes, and industrial movements; became a pioneer of the post–gold rush manufacturing industry; and was one of the country's most iconic retail empires.

In 1955, Cox Brothers bought the company. The Bourke Street store was sold to Woolworths in 1967, and the next year Cox Brothers went into receivership, sealing the fate of Foy's and leaving behind a great legacy.

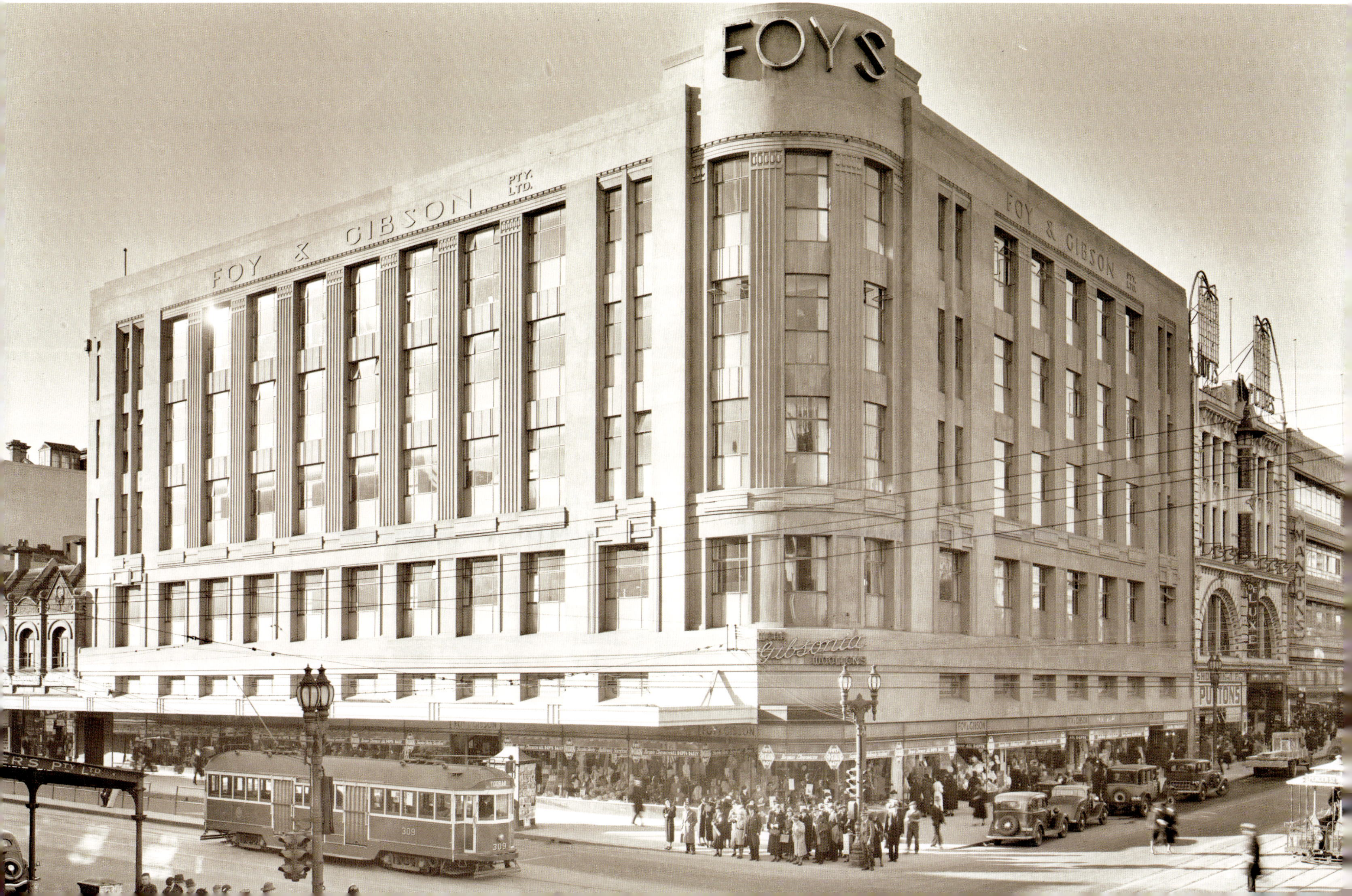

OLD MELBOURNE GAOL

1937

PHOTOGRAPHER: ARGUS (MELBOURNE)

Depicted here is the demolition of part of the old Melbourne Gaol, on 19 April 1937.

Construction began on this former gaol, on Russell Street, in 1839. It operated as a prison between 1842 and 1929, and was used briefly during World War II.

One hundred and thirty-five convicts were executed in this institution, including some of Australia's most notorious criminals, such as Ned Kelly, Frederick Bailey Deeming, and Martha Needle.

Over the years, the gaol was decommissioned bit by bit.

Bluestone grave markers of executed prisoners were used in the 1930s to build a sea wall in Brighton — including that of Martha Needle. (Martha Needle, the 'Black Widow of Richmond', was a notorious serial killer who was hanged in 1894 for the poisoning of her husband, three children, and brother-in-law.)

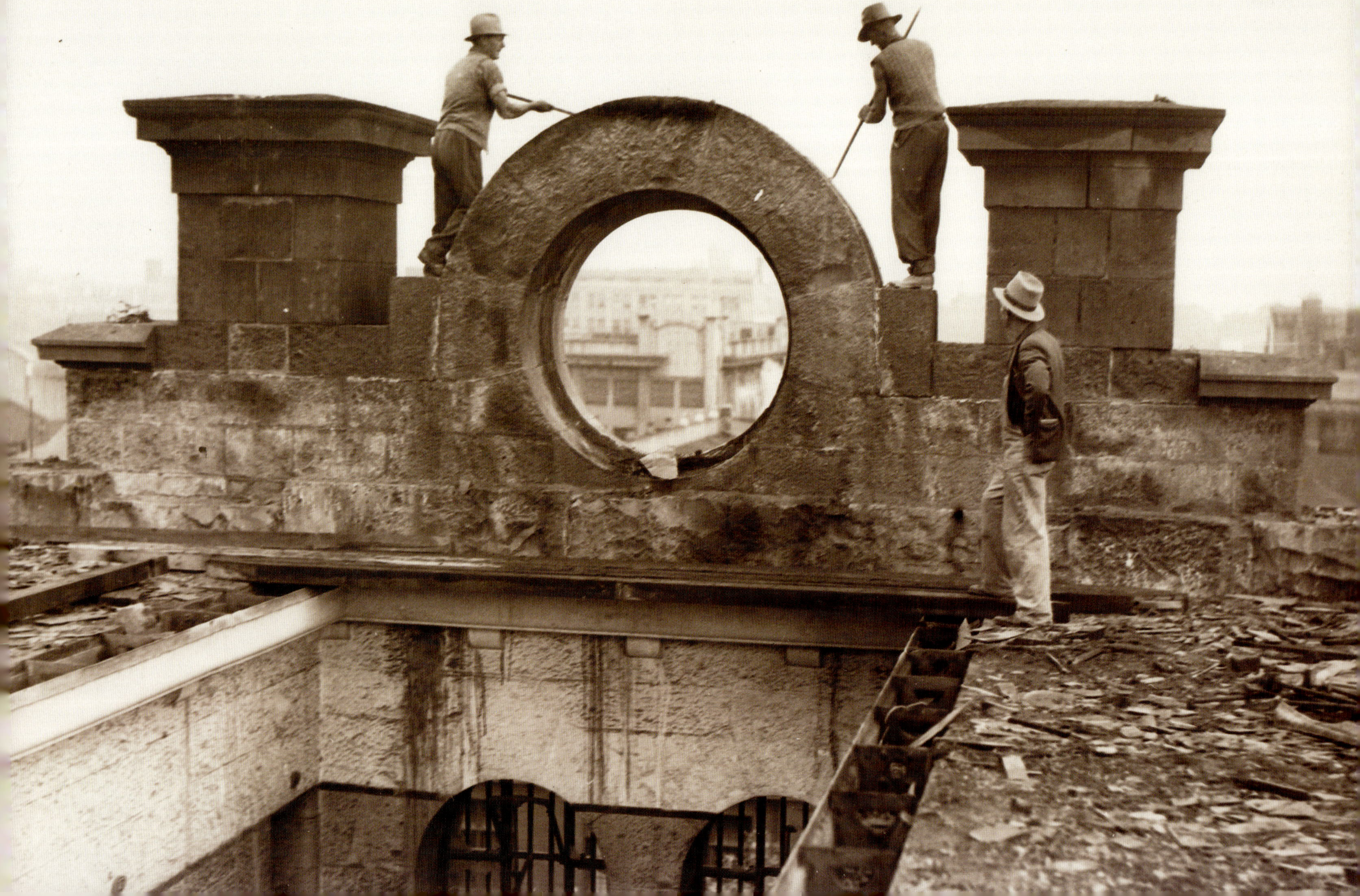

CENTRAL BUSINESS DISTRICT & SOUTH MELBOURNE

c.1938

PHOTOGRAPHER: VICTORIAN RAILWAYS

This fabulous aerial view is from above Russell and Little Collins streets, looking south across the Yarra River to South Melbourne.

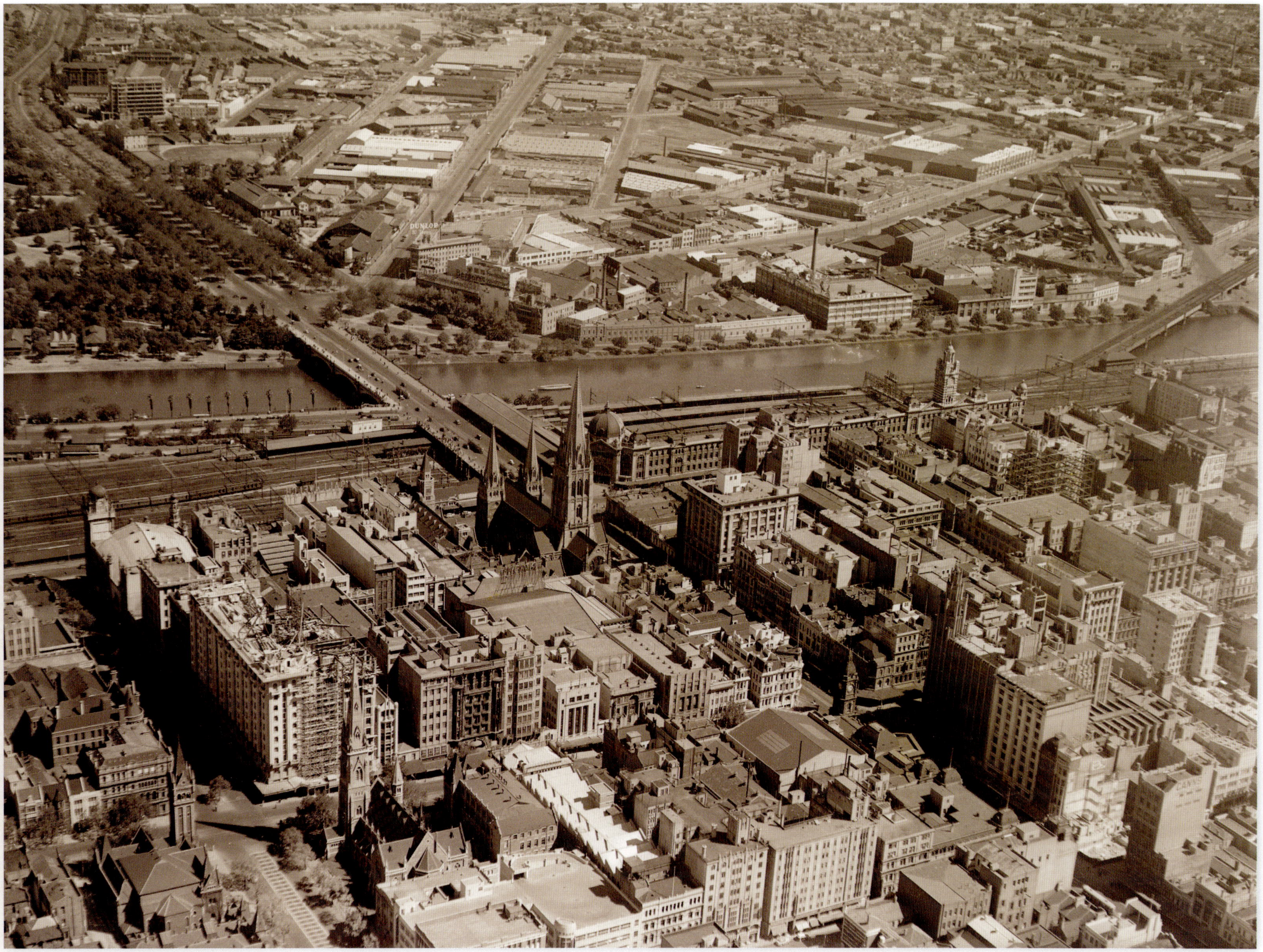

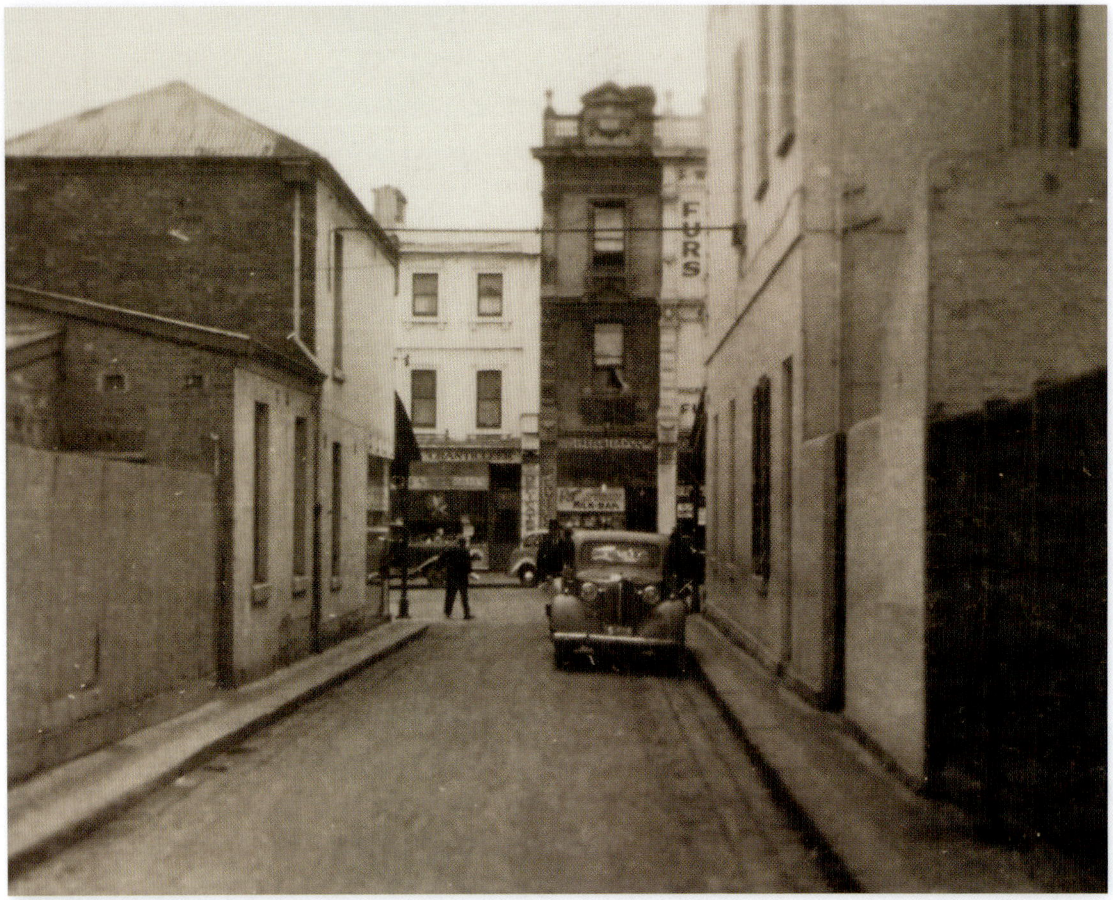

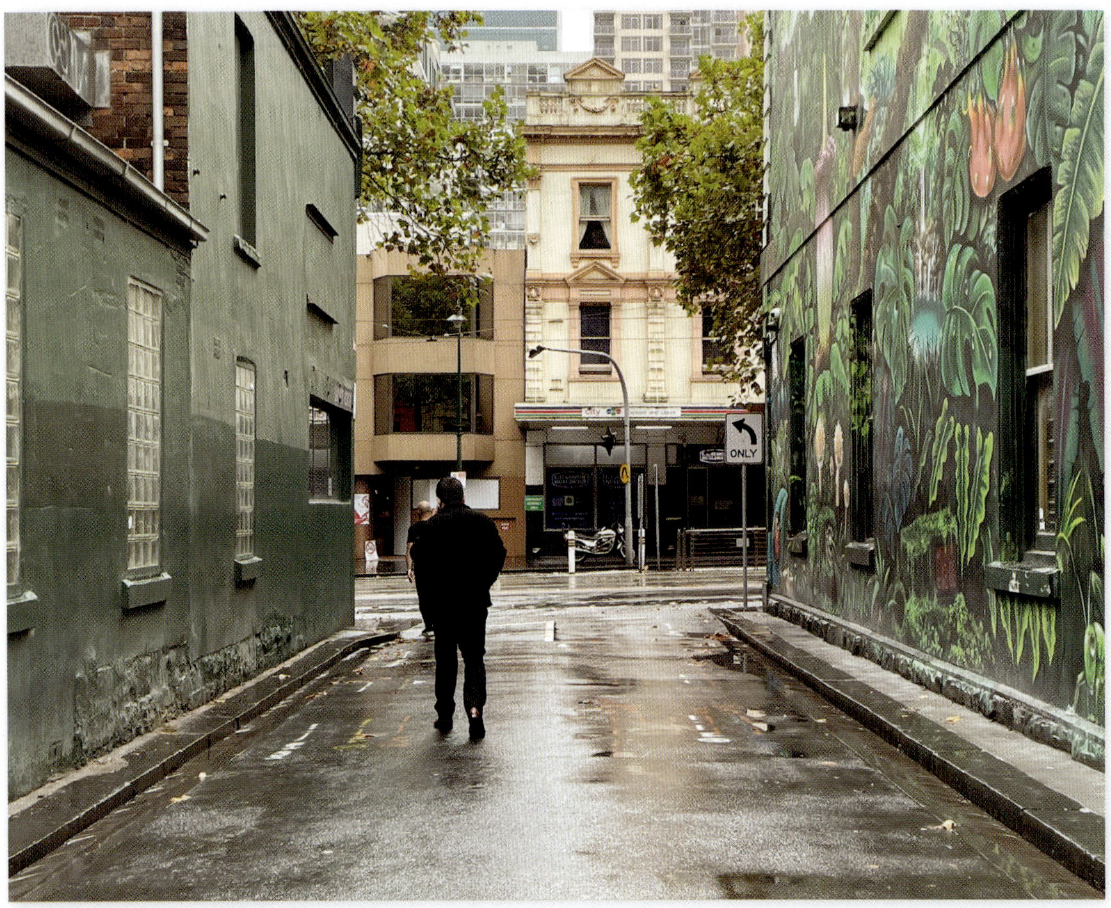

MEYERS PLACE

c.1939

PHOTOGRAPHER: ALBERT TUCKER (TOP IMAGE); CHRIS MACHERAS (BOTTOM IMAGE)

THEN AND NOW: Meyers Place, looking out towards Bourke Street. Like me, you have probably passed this laneway countless times, unaware of its historical value.

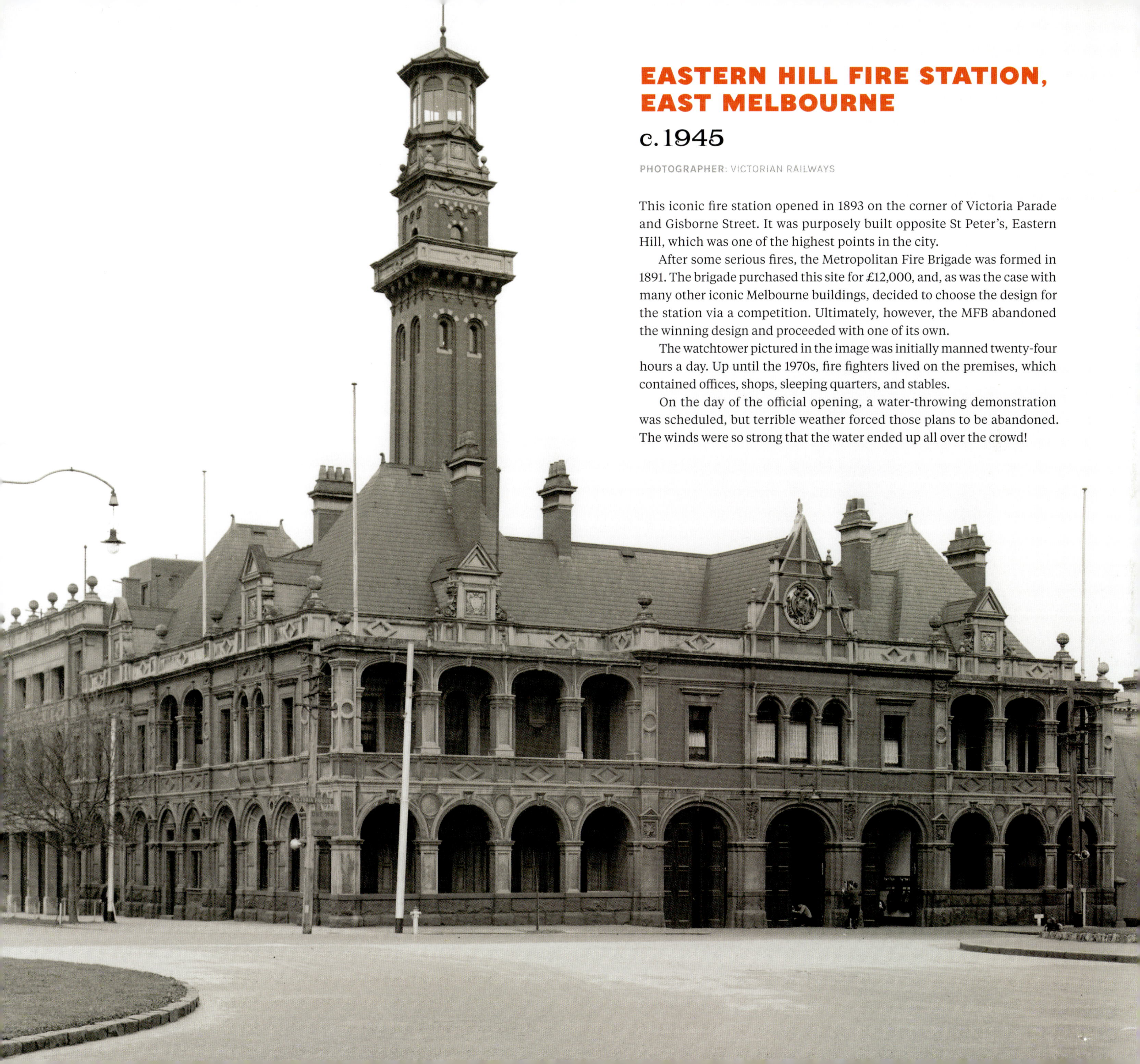

EASTERN HILL FIRE STATION, EAST MELBOURNE

c. 1945

PHOTOGRAPHER: VICTORIAN RAILWAYS

This iconic fire station opened in 1893 on the corner of Victoria Parade and Gisborne Street. It was purposely built opposite St Peter's, Eastern Hill, which was one of the highest points in the city.

After some serious fires, the Metropolitan Fire Brigade was formed in 1891. The brigade purchased this site for £12,000, and, as was the case with many other iconic Melbourne buildings, decided to choose the design for the station via a competition. Ultimately, however, the MFB abandoned the winning design and proceeded with one of its own.

The watchtower pictured in the image was initially manned twenty-four hours a day. Up until the 1970s, fire fighters lived on the premises, which contained offices, shops, sleeping quarters, and stables.

On the day of the official opening, a water-throwing demonstration was scheduled, but terrible weather forced those plans to be abandoned. The winds were so strong that the water ended up all over the crowd!

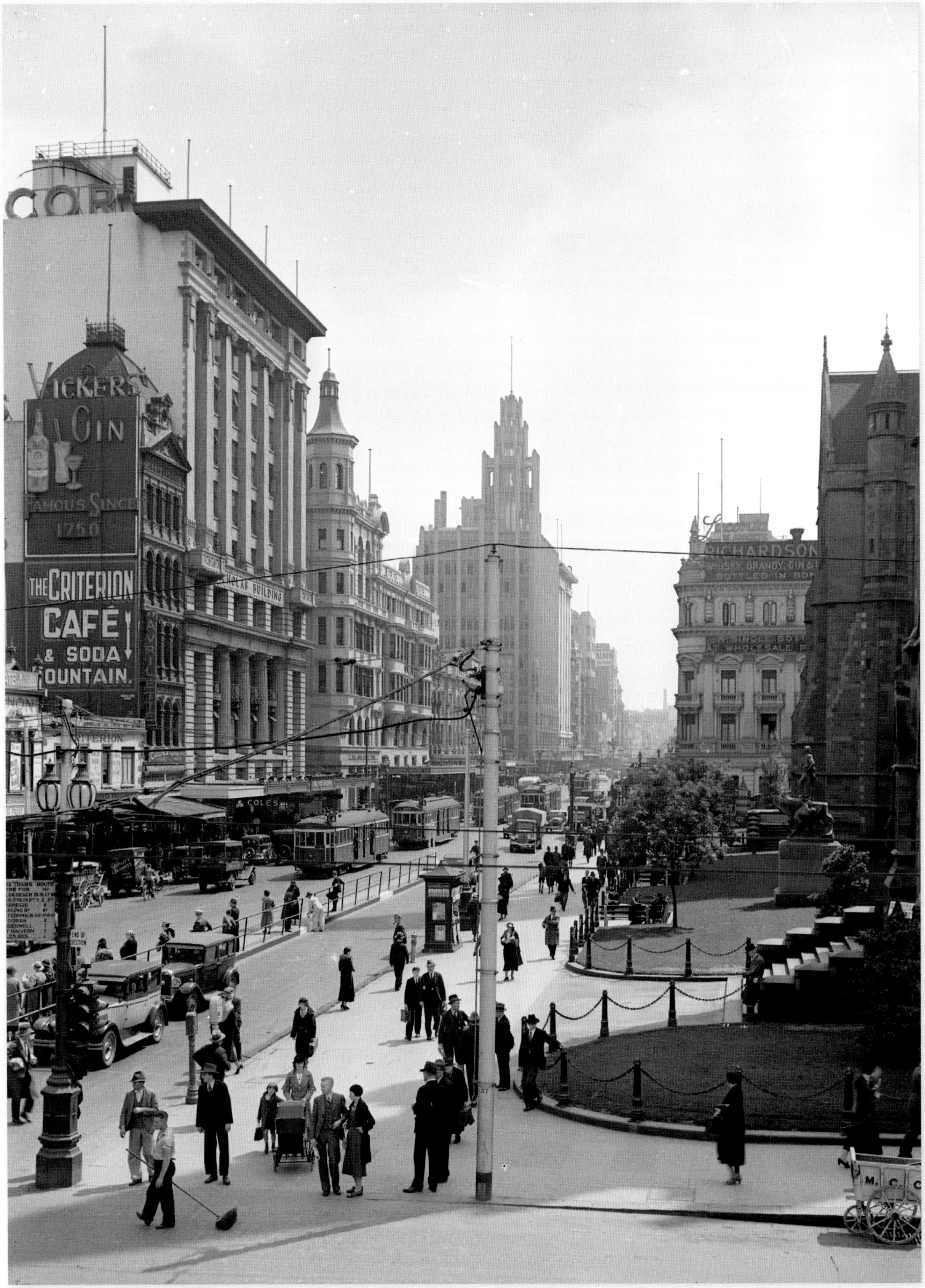
VICKERS
GIN
AMOUS SINCE
1750
THE CRITERION
CAFÉ
& SODA
OUNTAIN.
RICHARDSON
WHISKY BRANDY, GIN &
BOTTLED IN BOND
COLES
M C C

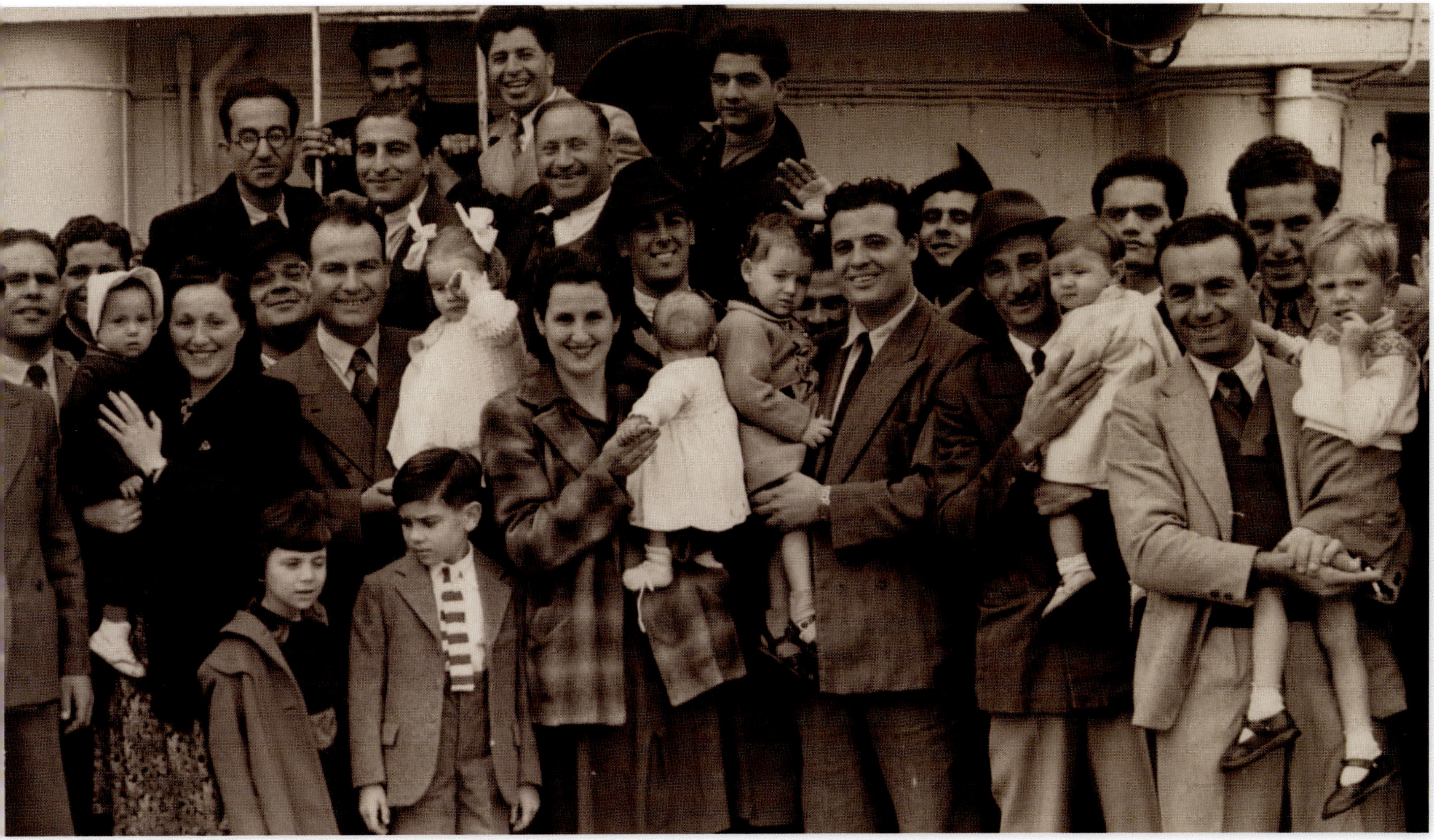

◀ SWANSTON STREET

c. 1945

PHOTOGRAPHER: VICTORIAN RAILWAYS

Melburnians strolling along the streets, on their way to work, to shop, and to see the city.

It was an interesting time in Australia and the world. World War II was finally over, with Germany and Japan surrendering to the Allies in May and August, respectively.

Next to the Nicholas Building (on the corner of Swanston Street and Flinders Lane), you can see the great State Savings Bank of Victoria (at 55 Swanston Street). It was a beautiful building, sadly torn down in the 1970s.

The State Savings Bank of Victoria, established in 1912, used the name State Bank Victoria from 1980. In 1991, following a period of financial disasters, it was merged into the Commonwealth Bank of Australia.

GREEK MIGRANT ARRIVALS ▲

c. 1948

PHOTOGRAPHER: UNKNOWN
SOURCE: AUSTRALIAN NATIONAL MARITIME MUSEUM COLLECTION

Greek migrants with smiles on their faces, ready to dock at Station Pier after enduring the very long journey from Athens.

Between 1945 and 1965, more than two million migrants came to Australia in search of a better life.

The devastating effects of World War II and the Greek Civil War resulted in over 160,000 Greeks migrating to Australia. The vast majority secured work in factories or farms.

As a result of this large wave of migration, Melbourne has the largest Greek-speaking population outside Greece today.

MYER EMPORIUM

c. 1948

PHOTOGRAPHER: LYLE FOWLER

The Myer Emporium interior.

Myer was a household name by 1948, having been listed on the Melbourne Stock Exchange in 1925.

This was not too shabby, considering the empire's very humble beginnings. While Bourke Street is its flagship store, the first Myer was opened in Bendigo in 1900.

It took a decade of growth and success before Myer purchased the business of Wright and Neil, Drapers, on Bourke Street near the GPO, and a new building was completed and opened in 1914.

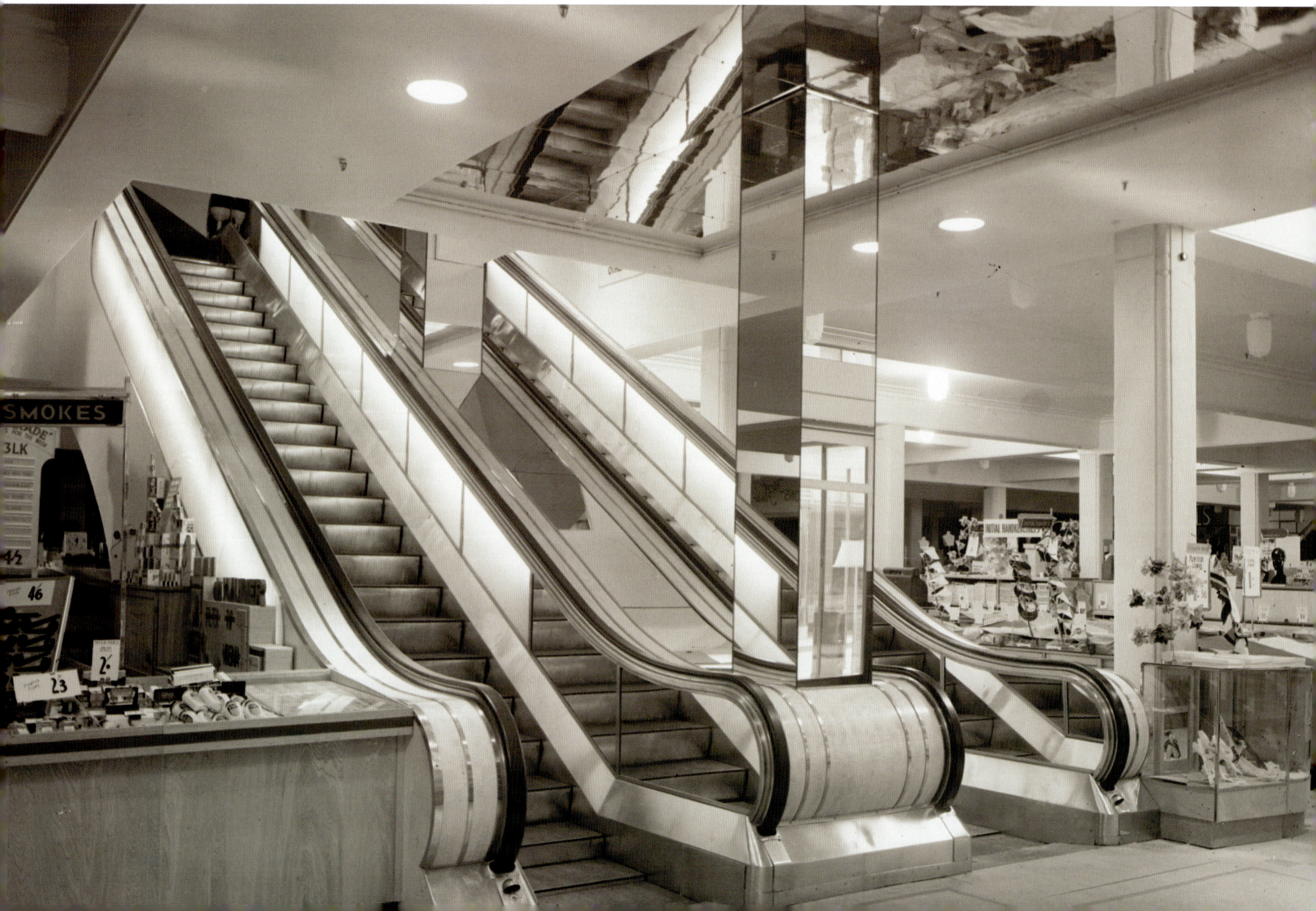

CORNER SHOP, CARDIGAN STREET, CARLTON

c. 1949

PHOTOGRAPHER: FRANK NORMAN HEATH

Here is an elaborately painted double-storey brick terrace at Cardigan Street and Palmerston Place, Carlton.

Featuring large advertisements for well-known products of the day — Robur Tea, Bushells, and Pure Velvet Soap — it also screams, 'We sell everything'!

Although the advertisements have been removed, the building remains.

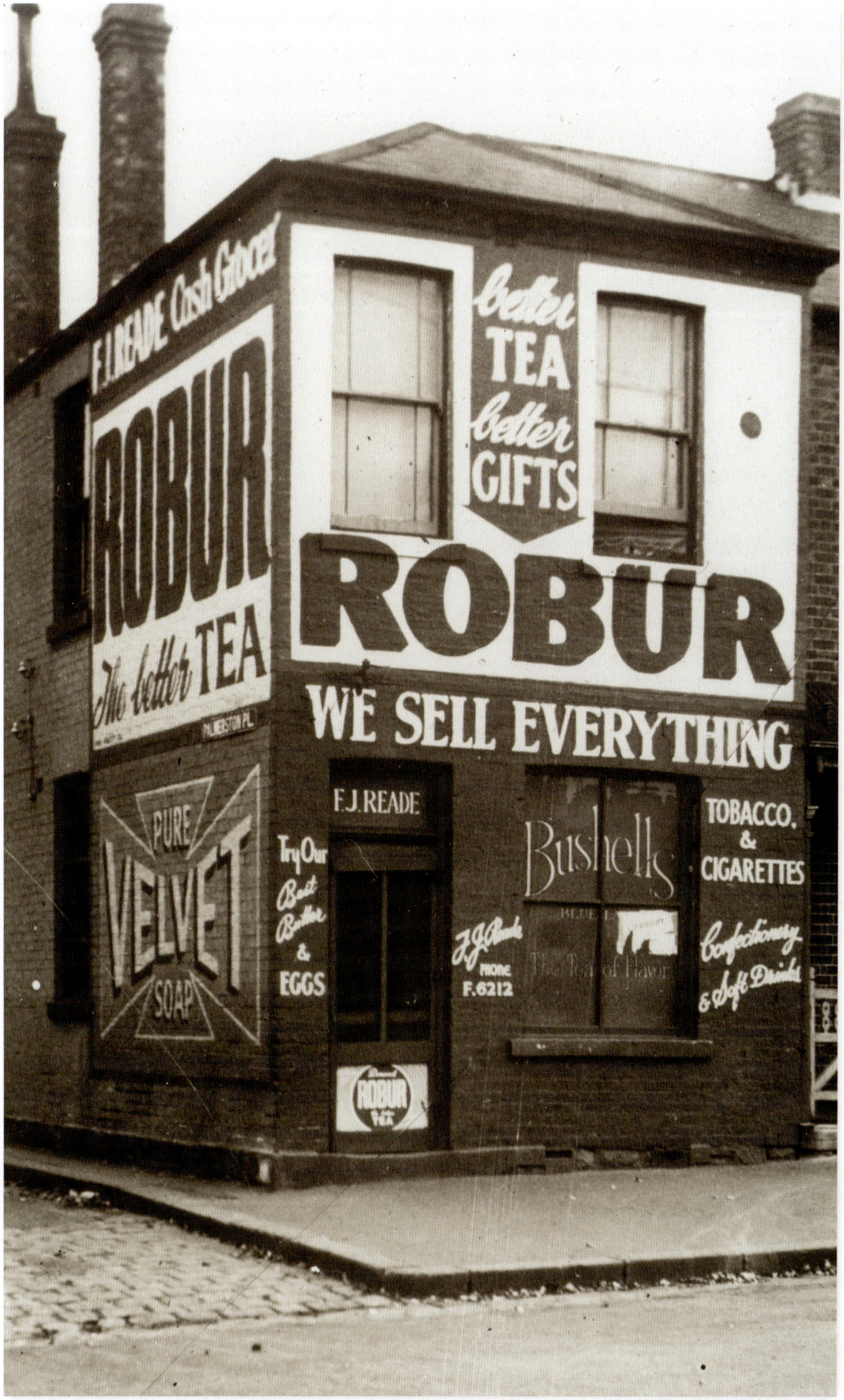

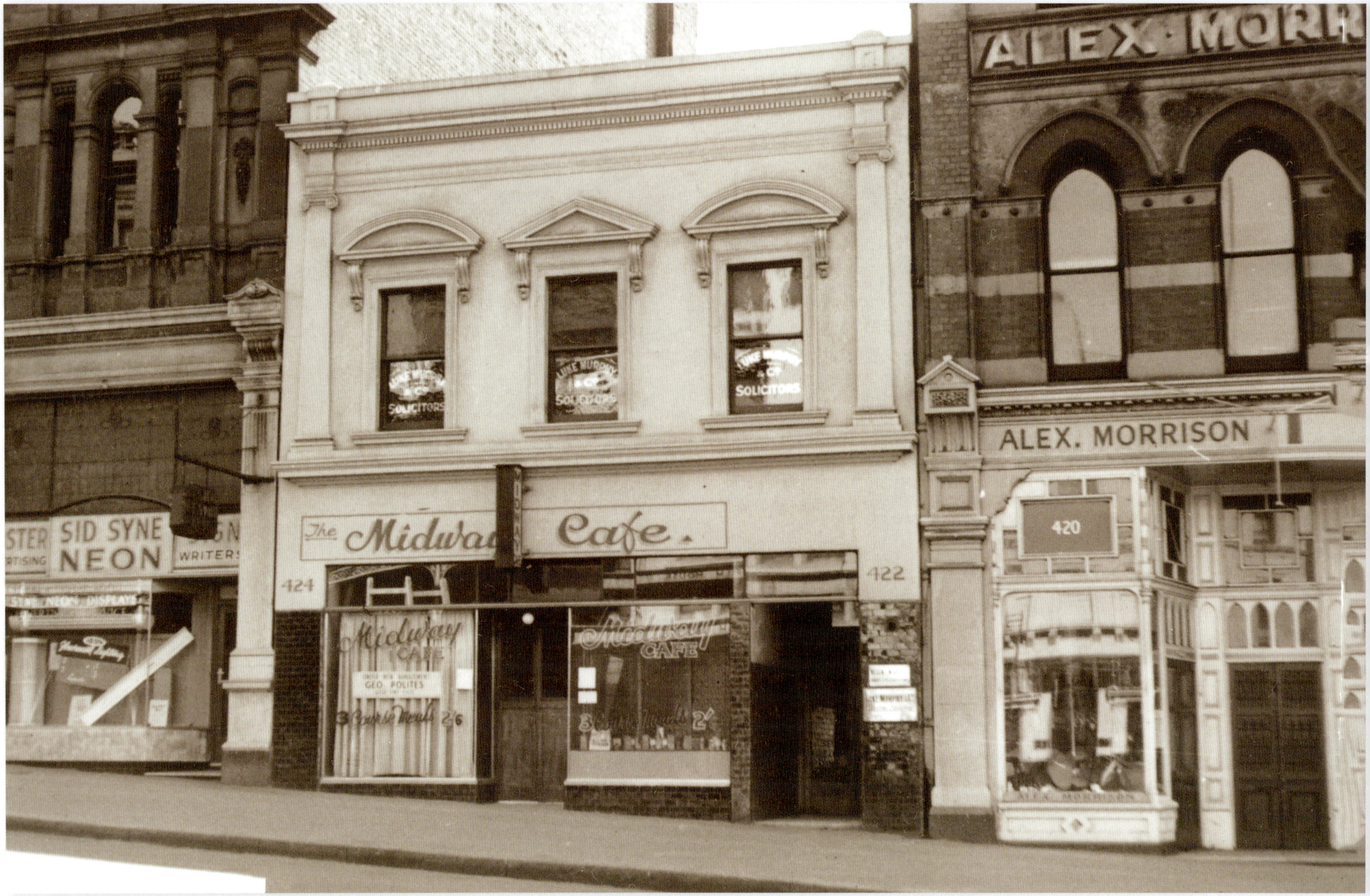

422-24 BOURKE STREET

c. 1949

PHOTOGRAPHER: COLIN CALDWELL

Note the wholesome Midway Cafe on the ground floor, advertised as being under new management by Mr Geo Polites. George Polites went on to form the Confederation of Australian Industry in 1977 (intended to be the employer equivalent of the Australian Council of Trade Unions). He was a representative of employers from the 1950s to the 1980s, and became an industrial-relations veteran.

The upper floor was occupied by Luke Murphy Solicitors; the building remains today, as well as 420 Bourke Street next door.

POLISH MIGRANTS, BONEGILLA

1950

PHOTOGRAPHER: UNKNOWN

Polish migrant Mrs Czeslawa Galaska and a friend, becoming familiar with their surroundings at the Bonegilla Migrant Reception and Training Centre in north-east Victoria.

Melbourne has the largest Polish population in Australia, with the majority arriving around the time of this photo, after World War II, along with millions of other Europeans.

In the late 1940s, the Australian government negotiated a series of migration agreements with countries such as the Netherlands, Italy, Austria, Belgium, West Germany, Greece, Spain, the United States, Switzerland, Denmark, Norway, Sweden, and Finland. From 1947 until 1951, all Bonegilla migrants came from eastern and southern Europe.

It is estimated that over 1.5 million Australians are descended from migrants who spent time at Bonegilla.

The camp's major functions were to process migrants and find them suitable work and housing. English courses were also provided in an attempt to introduce migrants to the 'Australian way of life'. The camp operated for twenty-four years, and in that time it is estimated that around 309,000 migrants went through Bonegilla. It remains the largest and longest-lasting migrant camp in post-war Australia.

Other former residents include Karl Kruszelnicki, Franca Arena, Arvi Parbo, Les Murray, Susan Duncan, and Raimond Gaita.

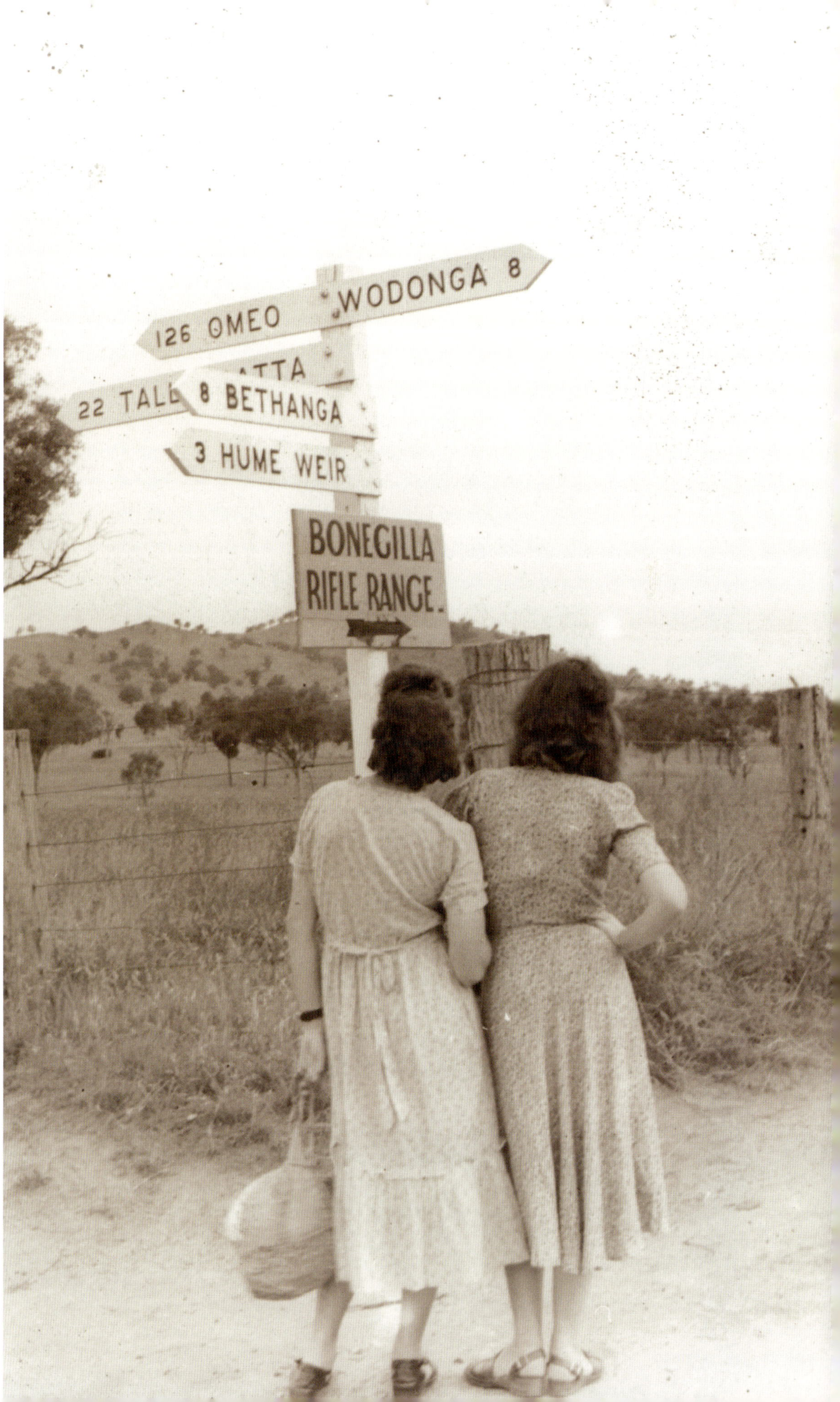

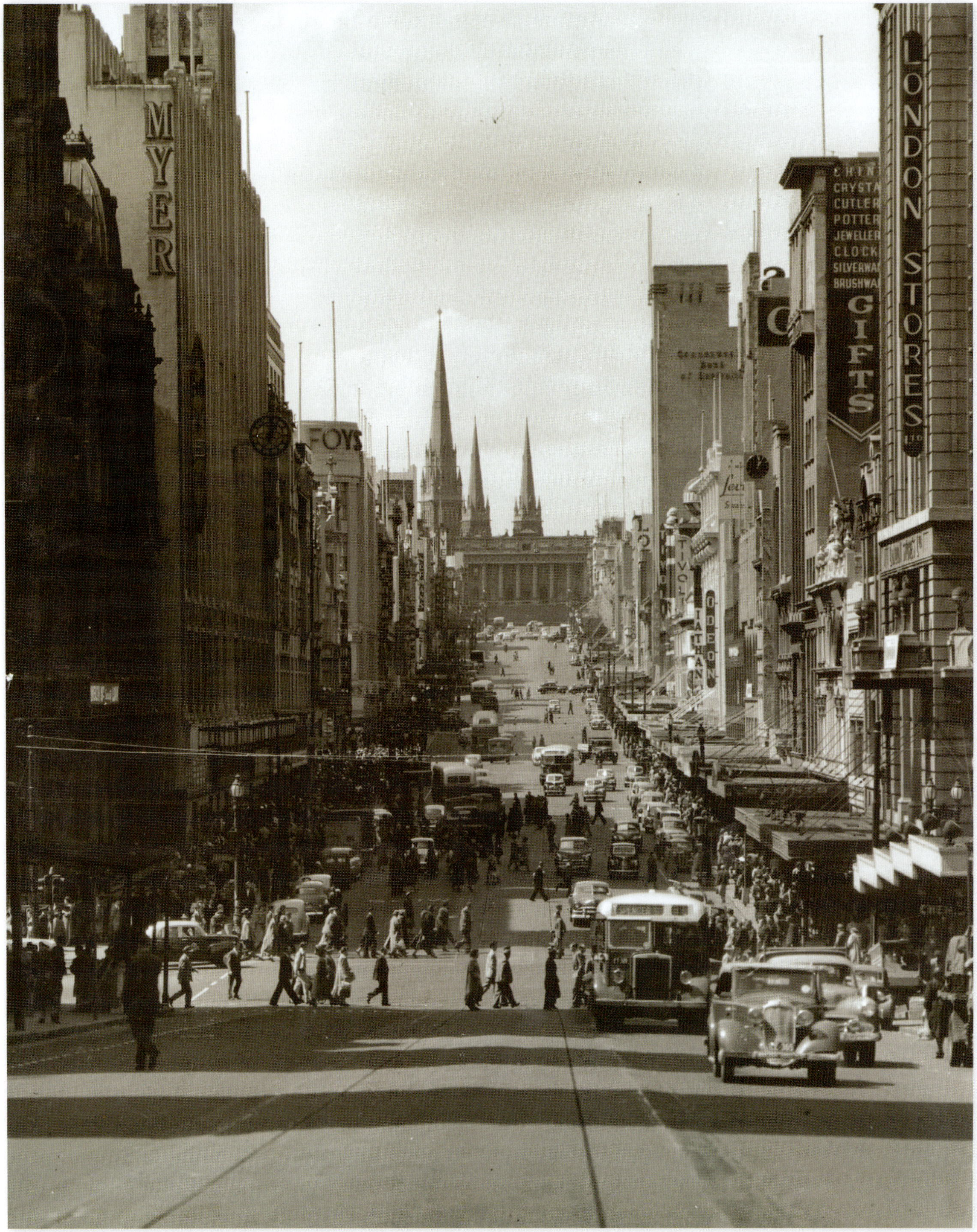
MYER
FOYS
GIFTS
LONDON STORES
ODEON

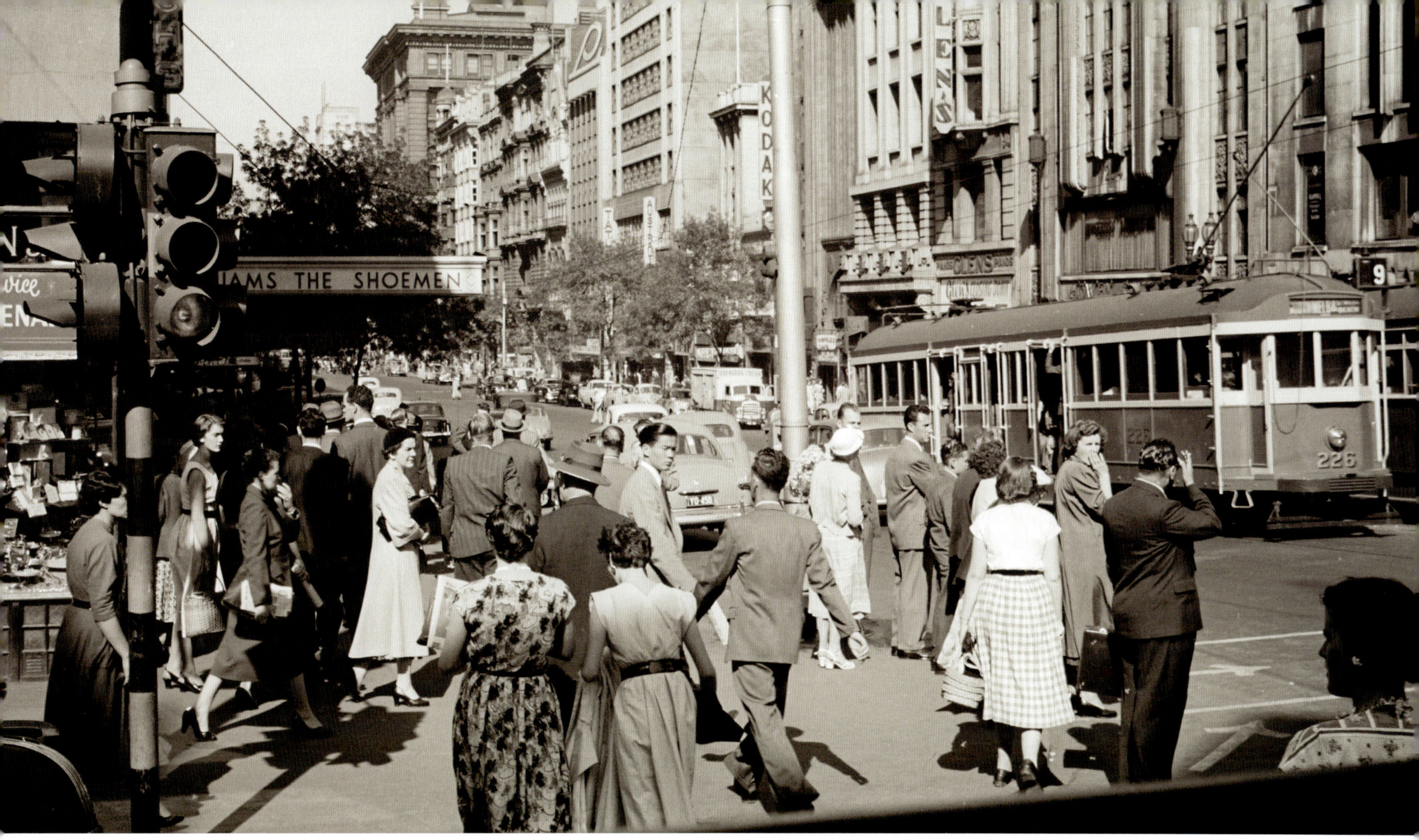

◀ BOURKE STREET

c.1950

PHOTOGRAPHER: NEIL MURRAY, AUSTRALIAN NEWS & INFORMATION BUREAU

Bustling Bourke Street. What an incredible view of Myer, Foy's London Stores, Parliament House, and St Patrick's Cathedral.

This was a politically significant time in Australia: Victoria held a state election; at the federal level, Parliament passed the Communist Party Dissolution Bill, effectively banning the Communist Party of Australia, and the government announced that the country would send troops to the Korean War. The first Australian forces landed in Korea on 17 September.

On the lighter side, Aussies were tuning into the radio and listening to the vocal styles of Perry Como, Nat King Cole, and Bing Crosby.

COLLINS STREET ▲

c.1954

PHOTOGRAPHER: MARK STRIZIC

I love this street scene on Collins Street. Note the No. 9 tram, and the signs for Glen's Pianos (having a closing-down sale), Kodak, and Williams the Shoemen.

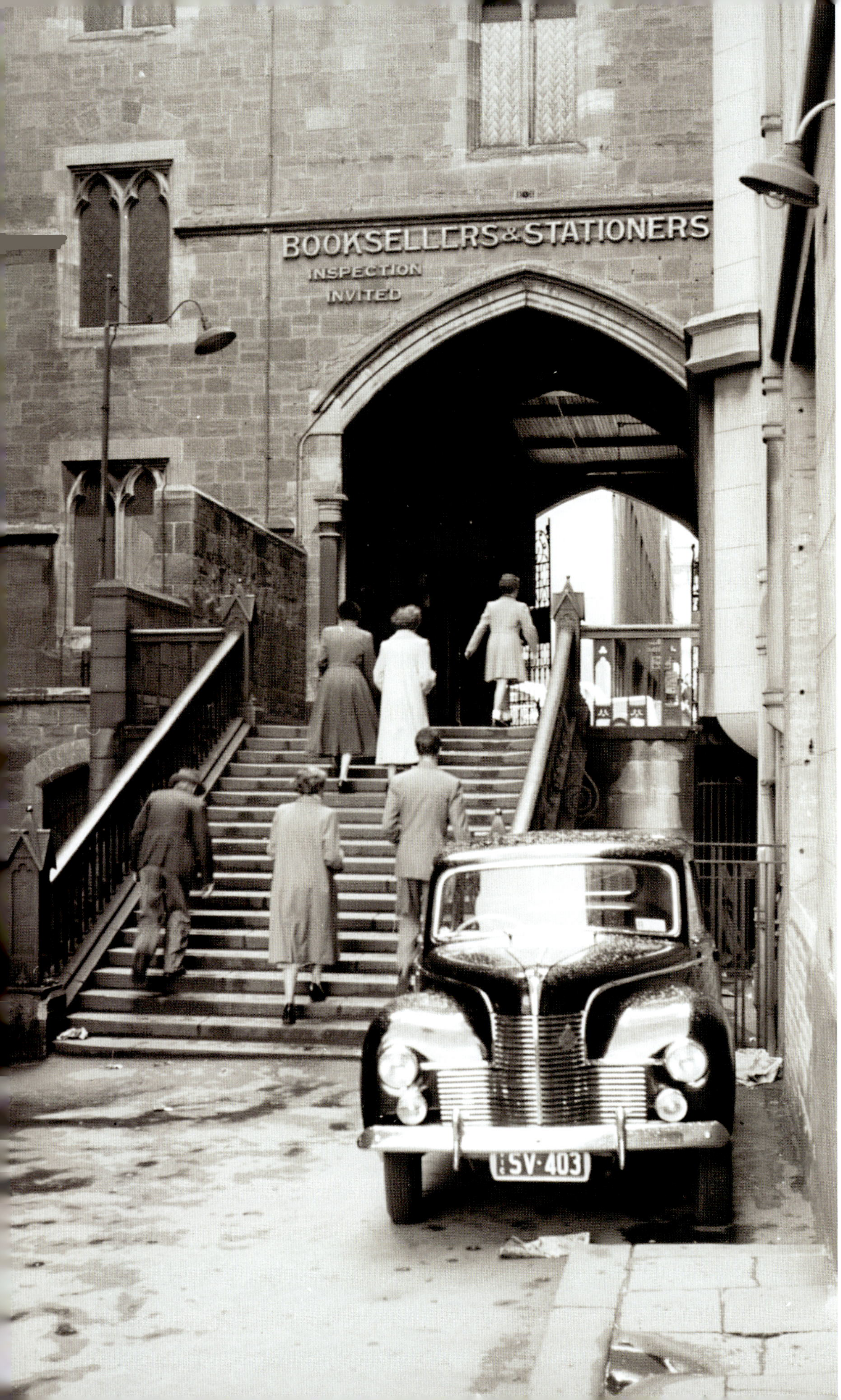

CHAPTER HOUSE LANE

c.1954

PHOTOGRAPHER: MARK STRIZIC (LEFT IMAGE);
CHRIS MACHERAS (BOTTOM IMAGE)

THEN AND NOW: Chapterhouse Lane, beside St Paul's Cathedral. At the top of those stairs is a walkway through to Flinders Lane. Chapter House stands on the site of what was once a corn market in Melbourne's early days. As the city grew, the site was levelled to make way for St Paul's Cathedral, which was built over a period of eleven years, and completed in 1891.

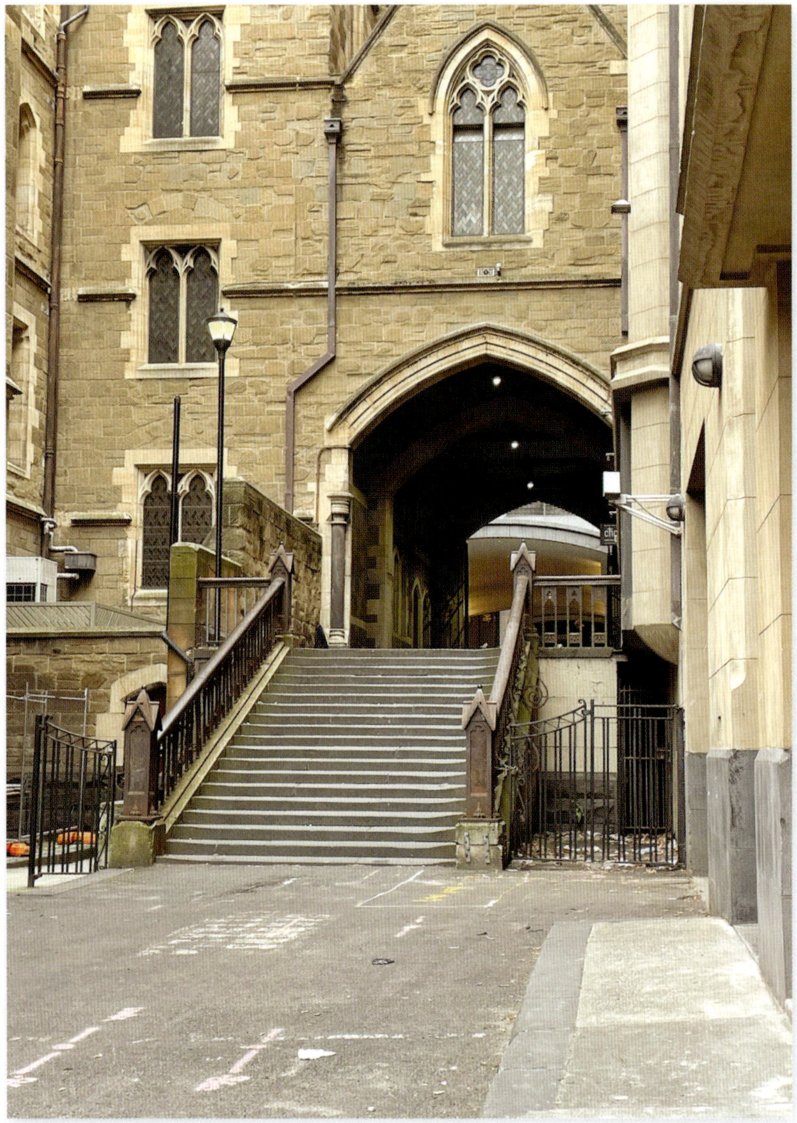

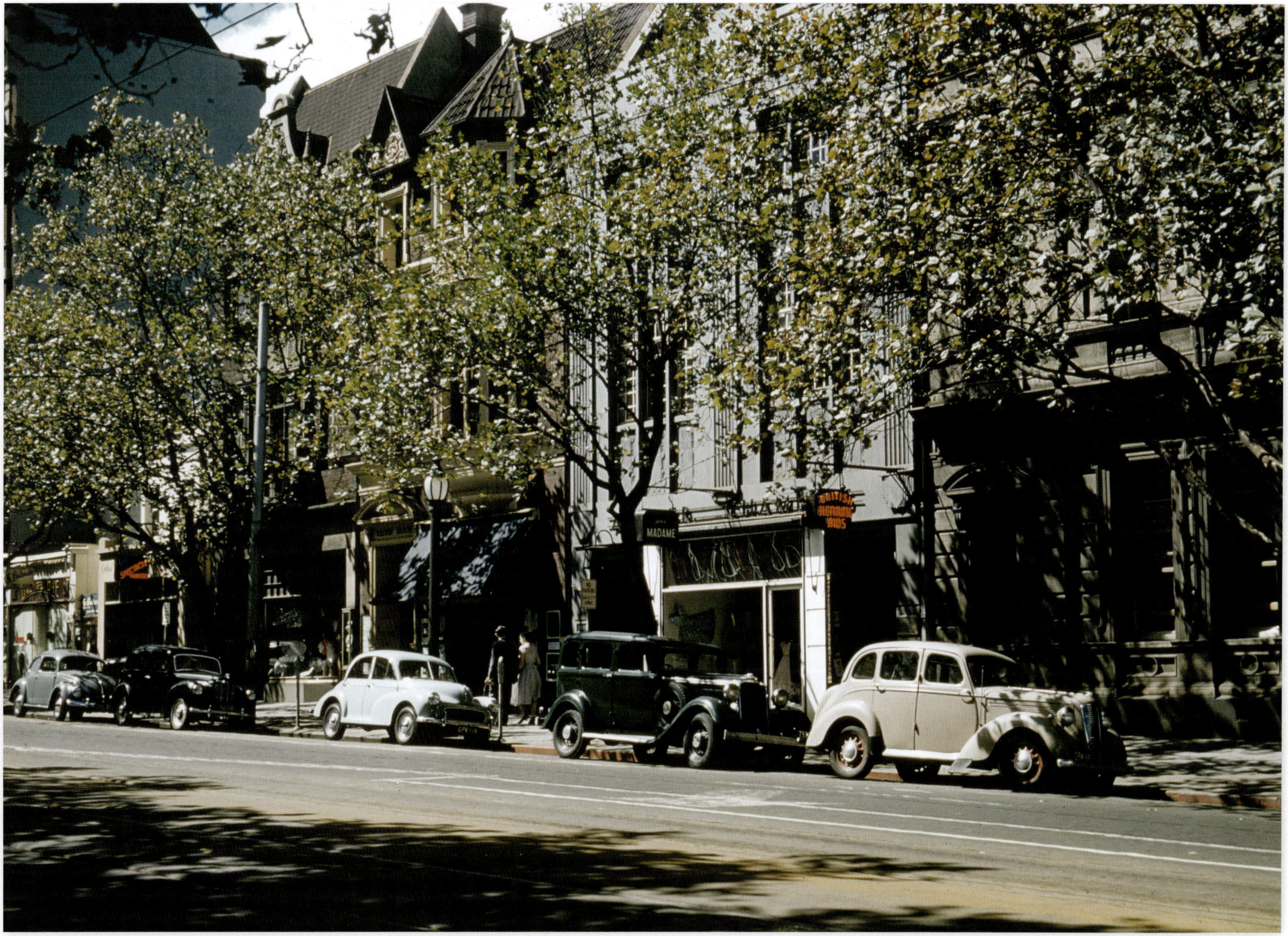

COLLINS STREET

c. 1954

PHOTOGRAPHER: ALLEN KELSO

It was from around this time that the Spring Street end of Collins Street began to be referred to as 'the Paris end'. The designation arose due to the combination of heritage buildings, high-end boutiques, lush tree-lined streets, and the first sidewalk cafes.

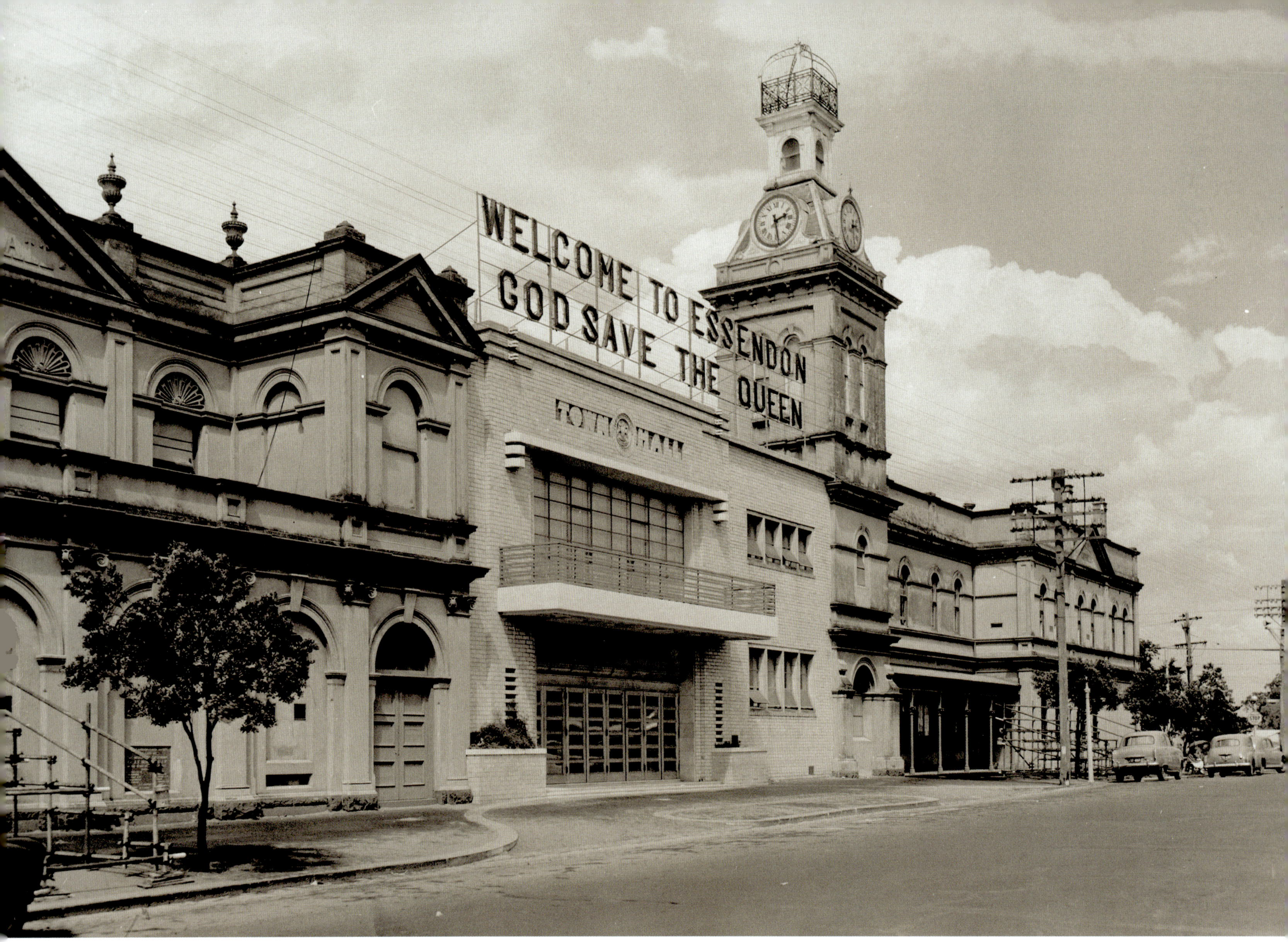

ESSENDON TOWN HALL

c. 1954

PHOTOGRAPHER: VICTORIAN RAILWAYS

Known today as the Clocktower Centre, the previous Essendon Town Hall was built in 1880, and is located in the suburb of Moonee Ponds.

The building was known as the Essendon Mechanics Institute until 1886, when it became the town hall. Over the years it has operated as a civic centre, function centre, community centre, and theatre.

Note the sign: 'Welcome to Essendon. God Save the Queen.'

FLINDERS STREET STATION

1954

PHOTOGRAPHER: UNKNOWN

Flinders Street Station elaborately decorated, crown and all, in anticipation of the royal visit of Queen Elizabeth II.

On 24 February 1954, nearly a million people lined the roads from Essendon Airport to Government House to welcome Her Majesty and the Duke of Edinburgh.

This visit was perhaps the most popular of all royal visits. Aside from being the first tour of a reigning monarch, it was also the first royal tour to Australia in twenty years.

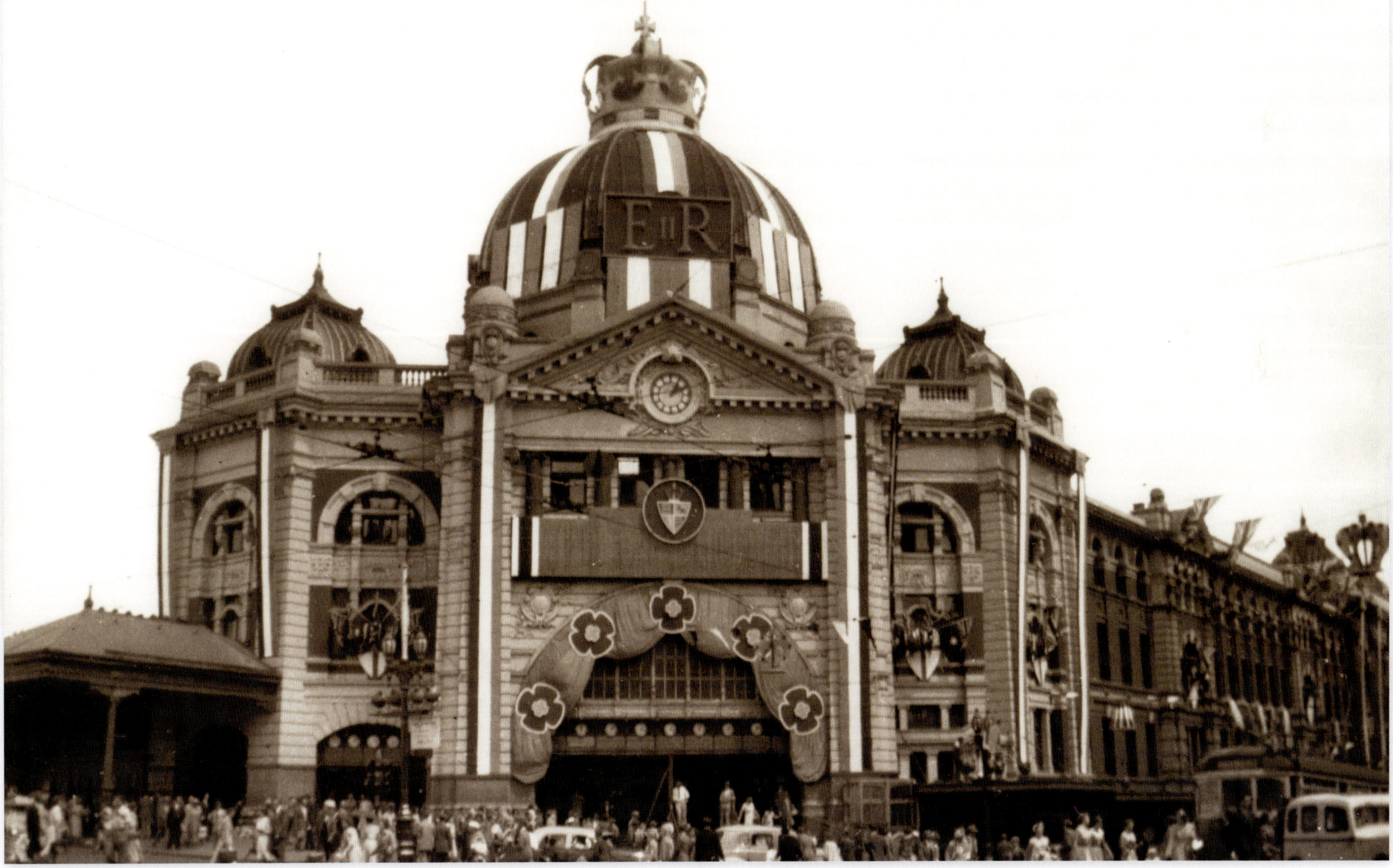

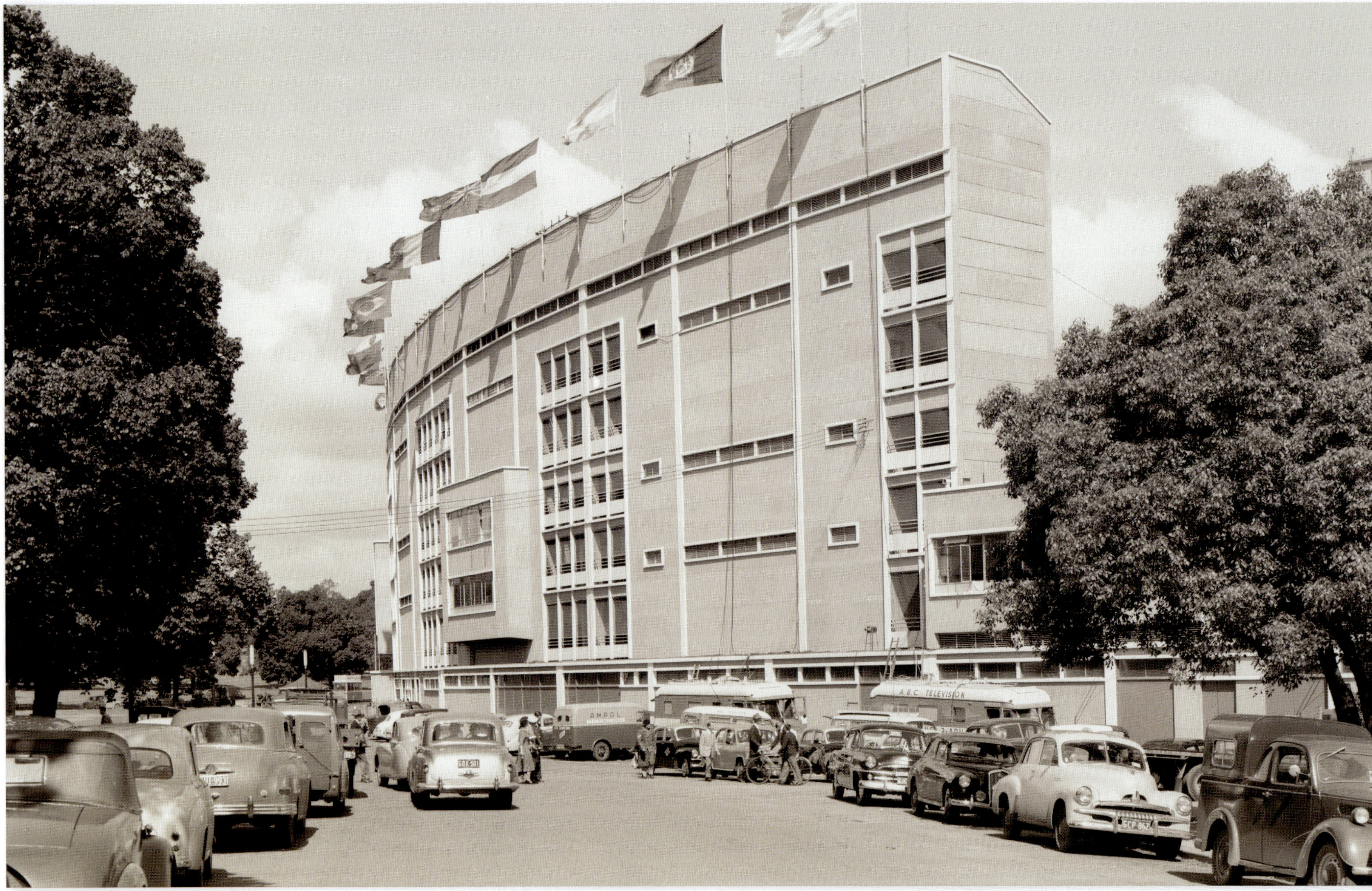

MELBOURNE OLYMPIC GAMES, MCG

1956

PHOTOGRAPHER: LYLE FOWLER

Pictured here is the Melbourne Cricket Ground (MCG) before the staging of the Olympics in 1956.

Melbourne broke some records when it hosted the games. They were the first Olympics to be hosted in the southern hemisphere and Oceania, and the first to be held outside Europe and North America. Melbourne was also the most southerly city to host the games, which is still the case today.

International political tensions — the Suez Canal crisis and the Hungarian Revolution — were high at the time, which resulted in eight nations choosing to boycott the games.

The Olympic flame arrived in Melbourne on 22 November 1956, the day of the opening ceremony. Nineteen-year-old athlete Ron Clarke lit the flame, despite burning his arm, and went on to have a stellar career as a middle- and long-distance runner.

SPRING STREET

c. 1957

PHOTOGRAPHER: COMMERCIAL PHOTOGRAPHIC CO.

An aerial view along Spring Street looking towards South Melbourne.

The image includes the Parliament Gardens, Parliament House, and the Treasury Building on the left.

In the distance you can see the railyards, the Yarra River, and Government House.

The fabulous Windsor Hotel is near the centre of the photograph, and the Princess Theatre is at the lower right.

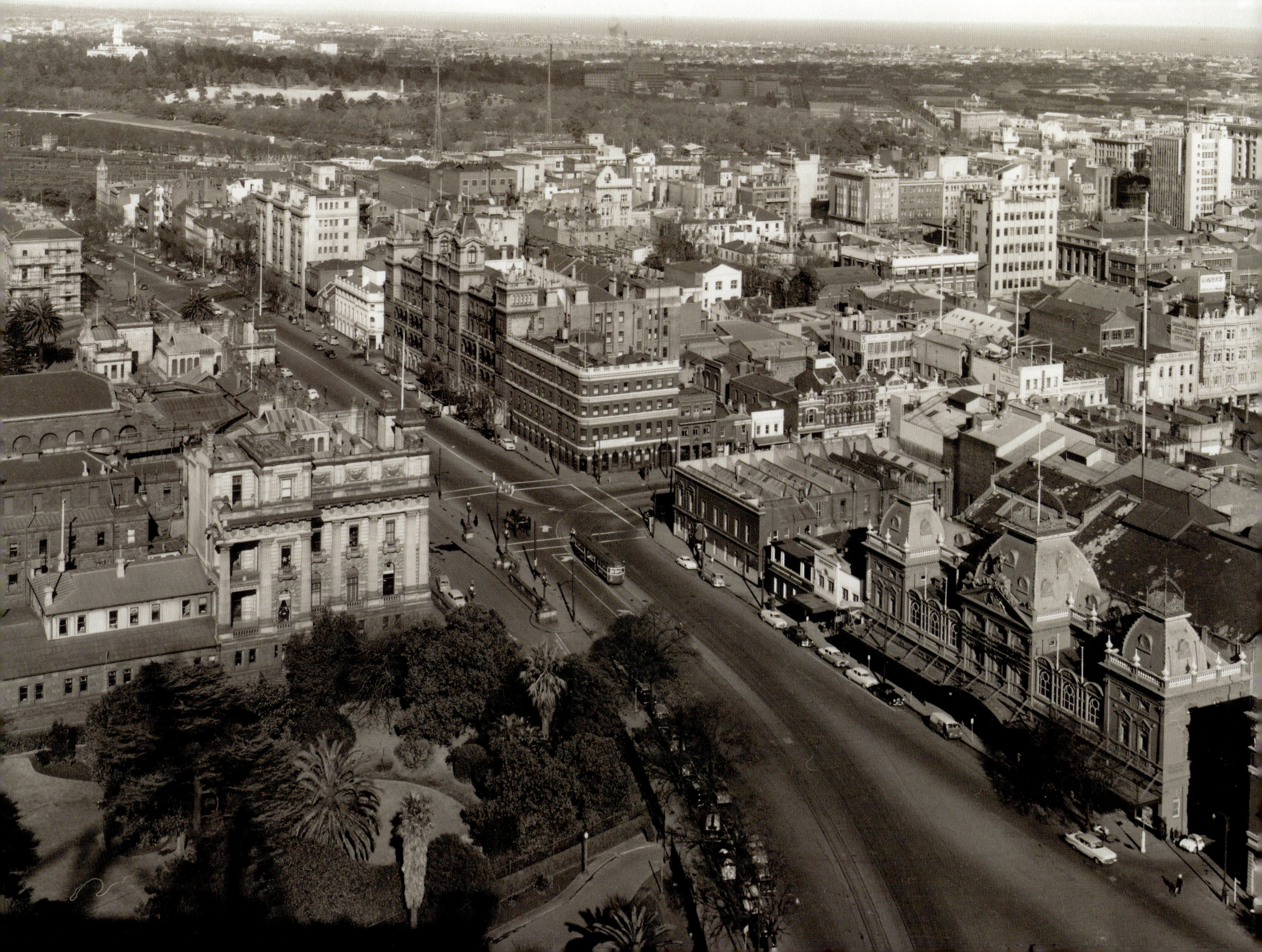

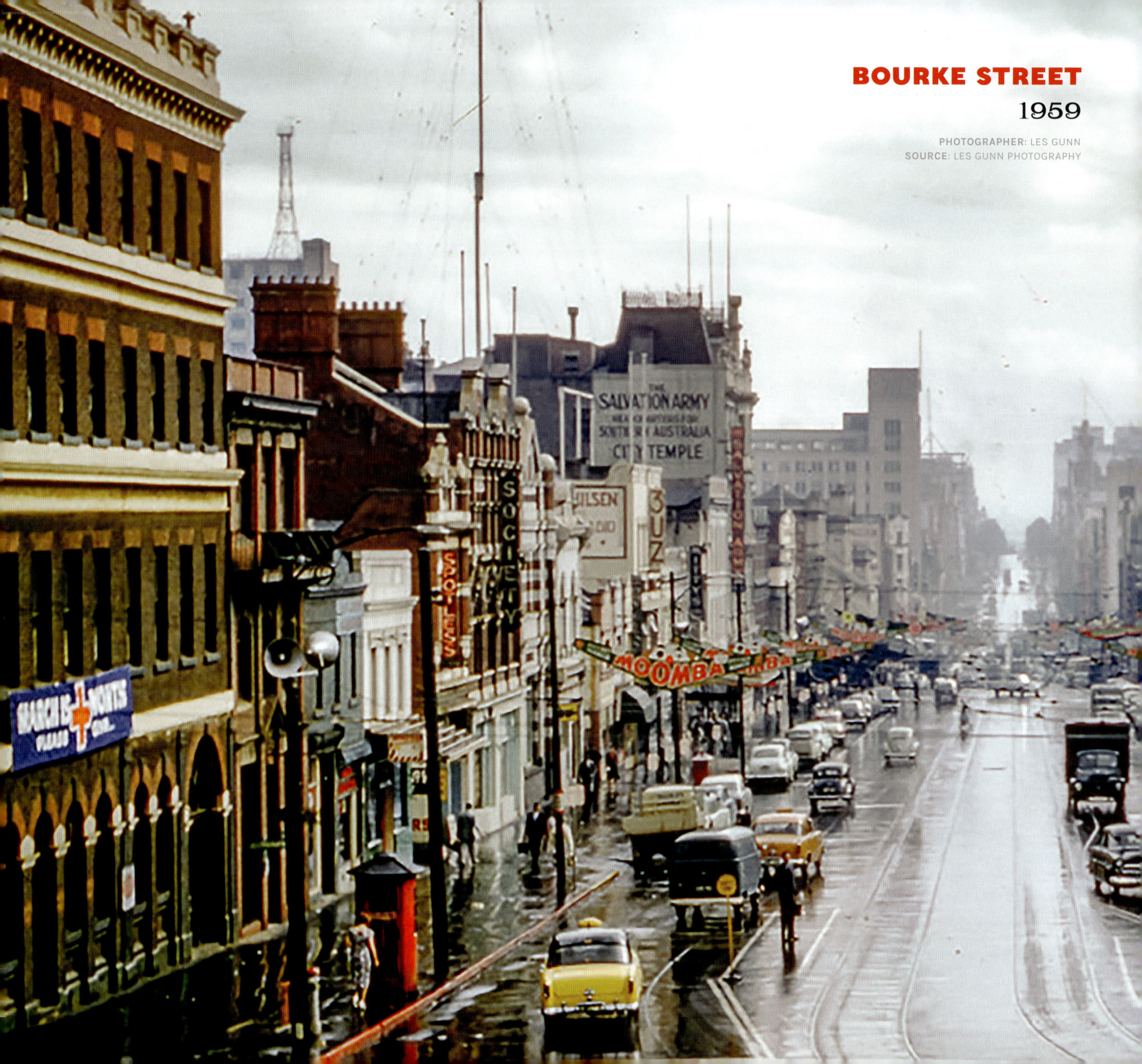

BOURKE STREET

1959

PHOTOGRAPHER: LES GUNN
SOURCE: LES GUNN PHOTOGRAPHY

A vibrant colour image of a rainy day on Bourke Street, taken from the steps of Parliament House in March 1959.

The talented photographer Les Gunn took this shot when he was just thirteen years old, and just hours before the 1959 Moomba Parade.

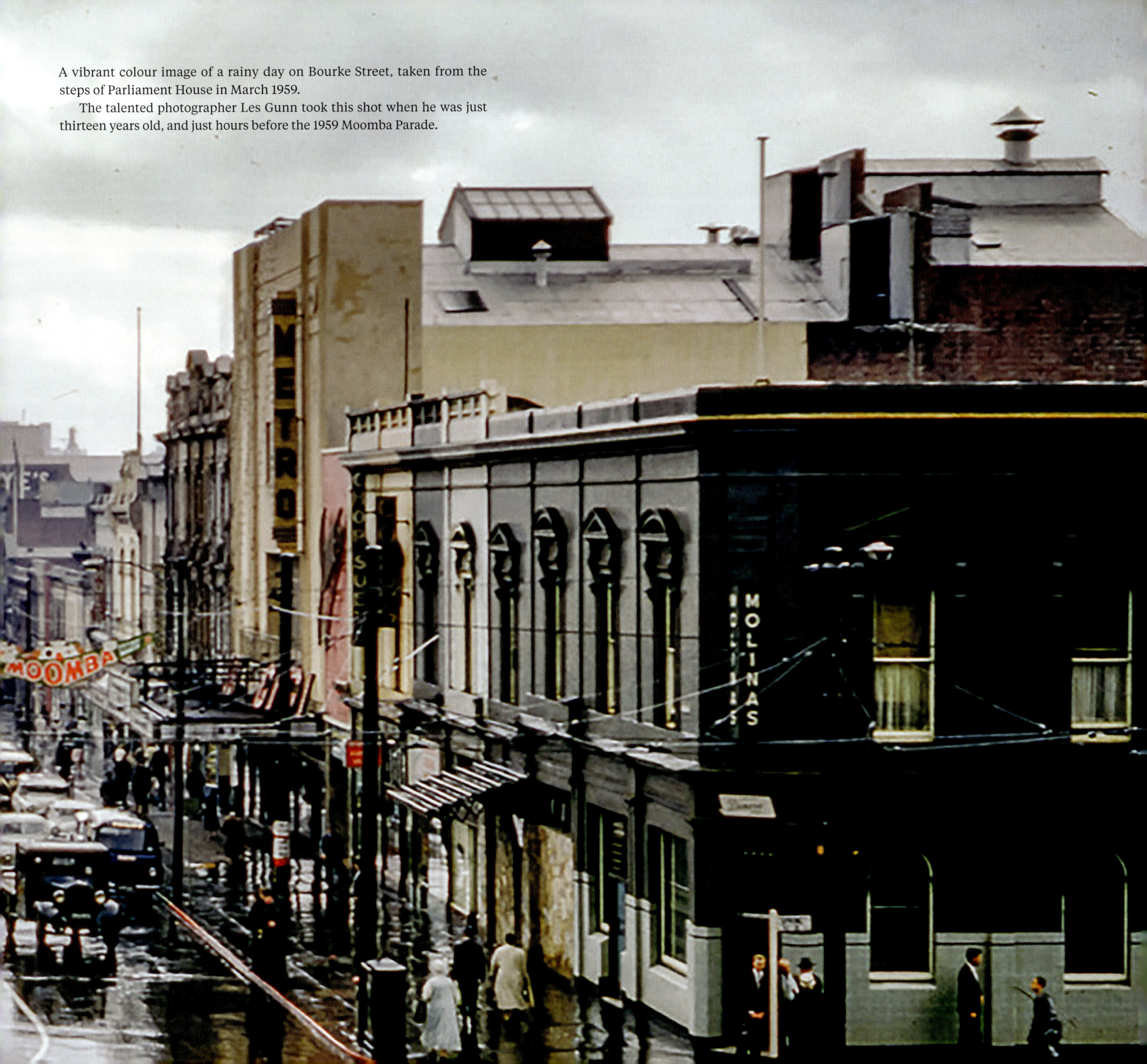

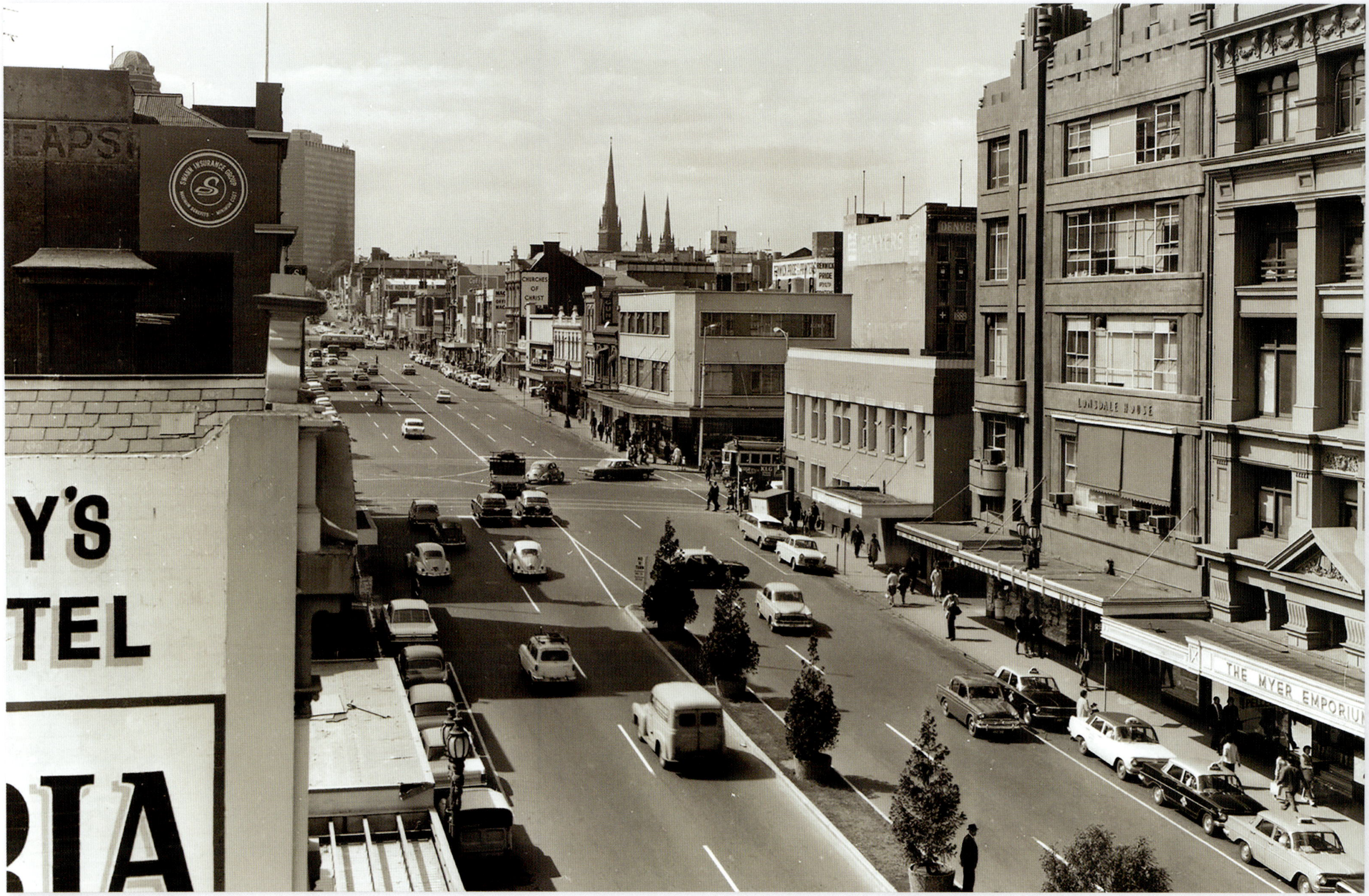

LONSDALE STREET

c. 1960–1970

PHOTOGRAPHER: COMMERCIAL PHOTOGRAPHIC CO.

A fabulous elevated view of Lonsdale Street, looking east past the Swanston Street intersection.

In the distance you can see St Patrick's Cathedral. Closer to the camera, you can see the Myer Emporium on the left, and Lonsdale House, one of Melbourne's landmark Art Deco buildings.

Lonsdale House, on Lonsdale Street near Caledonian Lane, was reconstructed in 1934 from two Victorian-era buildings. Sadly, it was demolished in 2010 to make way for the Emporium shopping centre.

PUCKLE STREET, MOONEE PONDS

c.1966

PHOTOGRAPHER: K.J. HALLA

Buzzing Puckle Street was named after Vicar Edward Puckle, who came to the area in 1858.

To give you an idea of Melbourne's exponential rate of growth: in 1881 Puckle Street had five businesses listed in the suburban directory; a decade later, in 1891, there were fifty; twenty years later, there were almost one hundred.

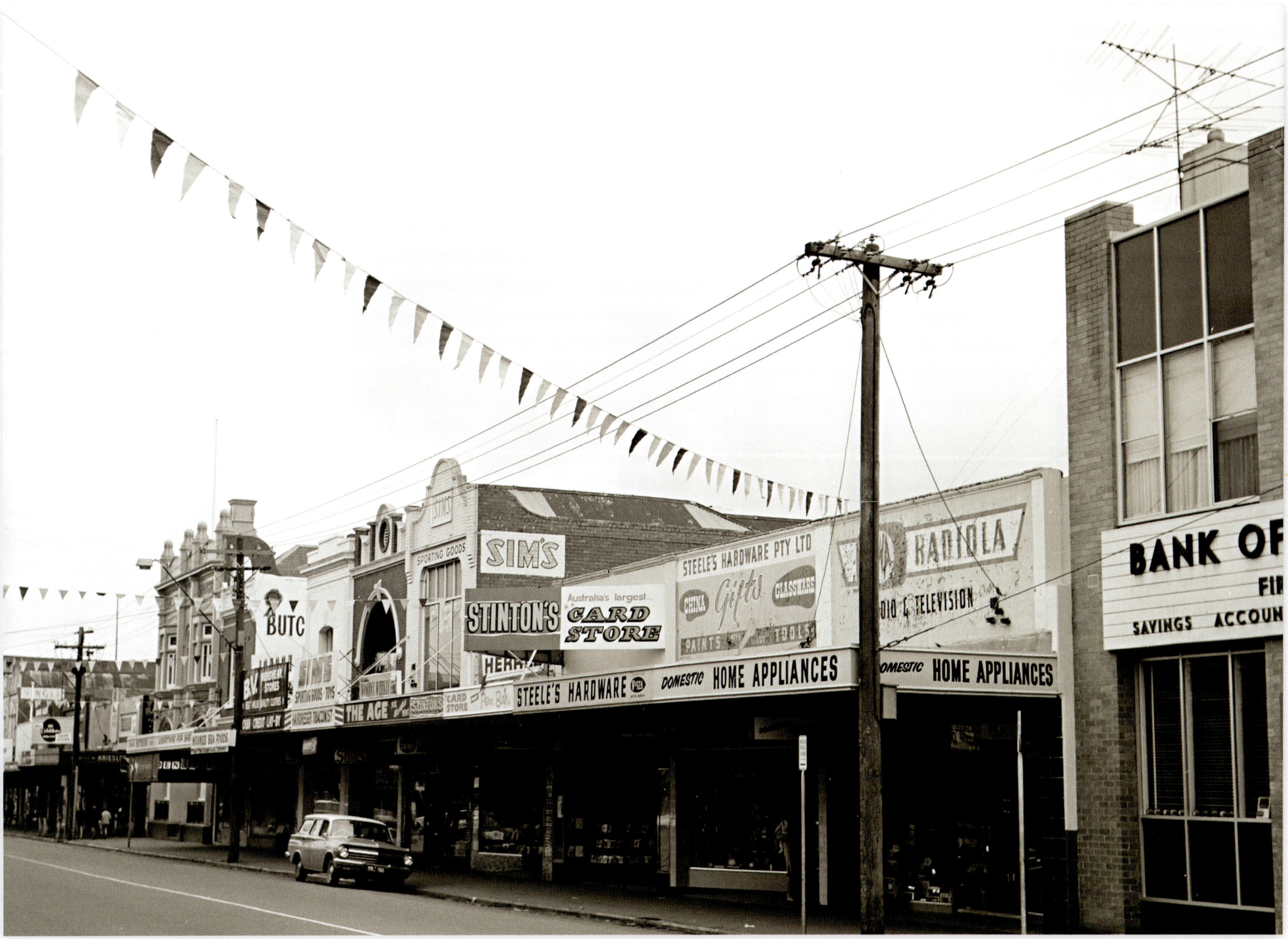

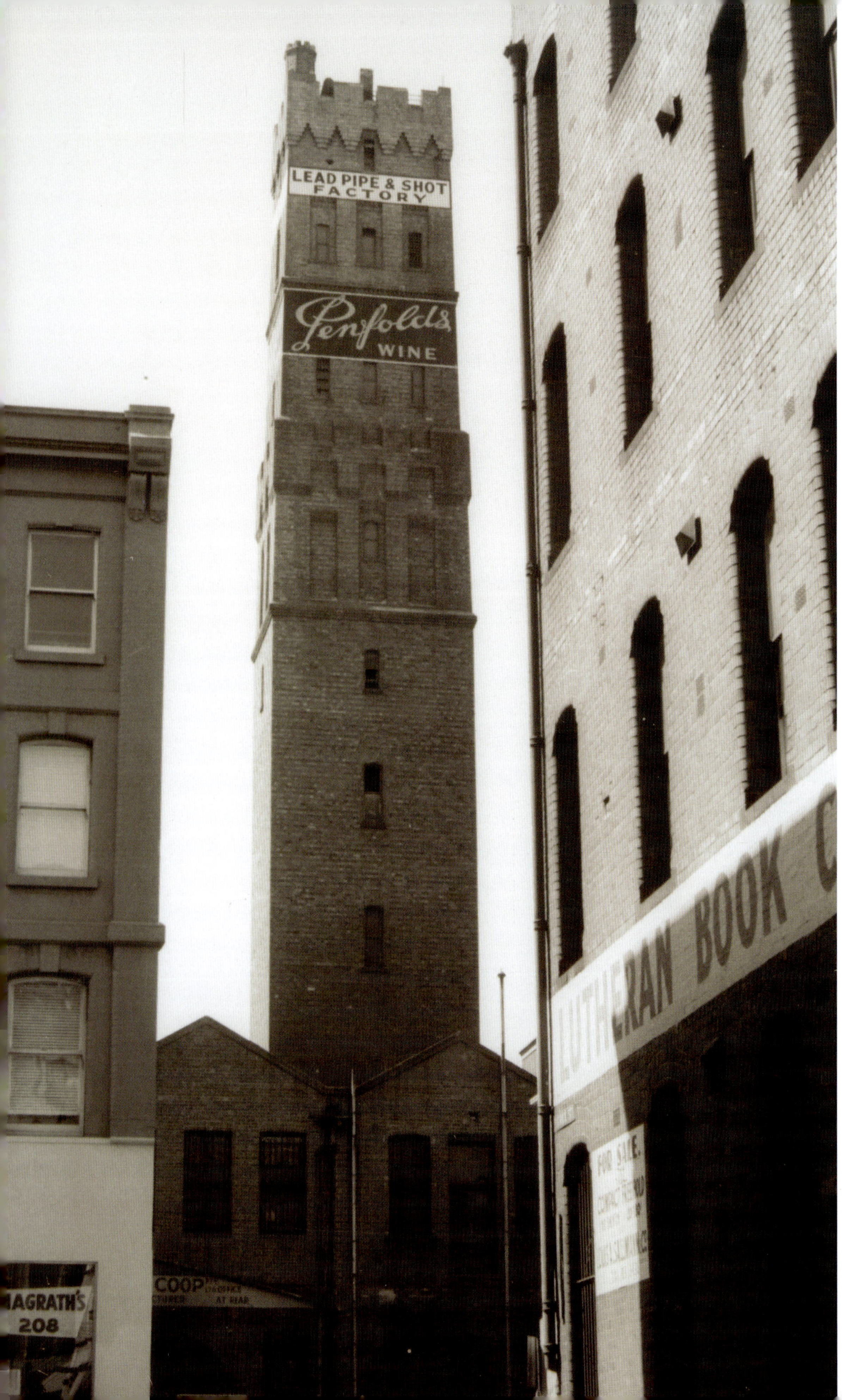

COOP'S SHOT TOWER

c.1964

PHOTOGRAPHER: JOHN T. COLLINS

You can't help but look up every time you walk into Melbourne Central. Coop's Shot Tower has become one of Melbourne's most enduring landmarks, standing 50 metres high since 1889.

Shot is a term for small pellets of lead used for products such as shotgun bullets. Up until around the time this photo was taken, the shot tower produced six tonnes of shot per week. At one point, Coop's was the largest manufacturer of shot in the southern hemisphere. As access to firearms became more restricted, demand for the product decreased. But production was not limited to shot: the company also manufactured items ranging from old-fashioned weights to nails and solder, as well as the stair grips for Melbourne's trams, and all of the lead pipe that was used in the city's first electricity system.

The shot tower was the tallest building in the Central Business District until the mid-1940s. In 1961, however, scientific research showed that the lead-manufacturing process involved the use of arsenic, which could be lethal. As a result, the tower was shut down.

The historic Romanesque building was saved from demolition in 1973, and was incorporated into the Melbourne Central complex in 1991. It's now one of the most photographed landmarks in Melbourne.

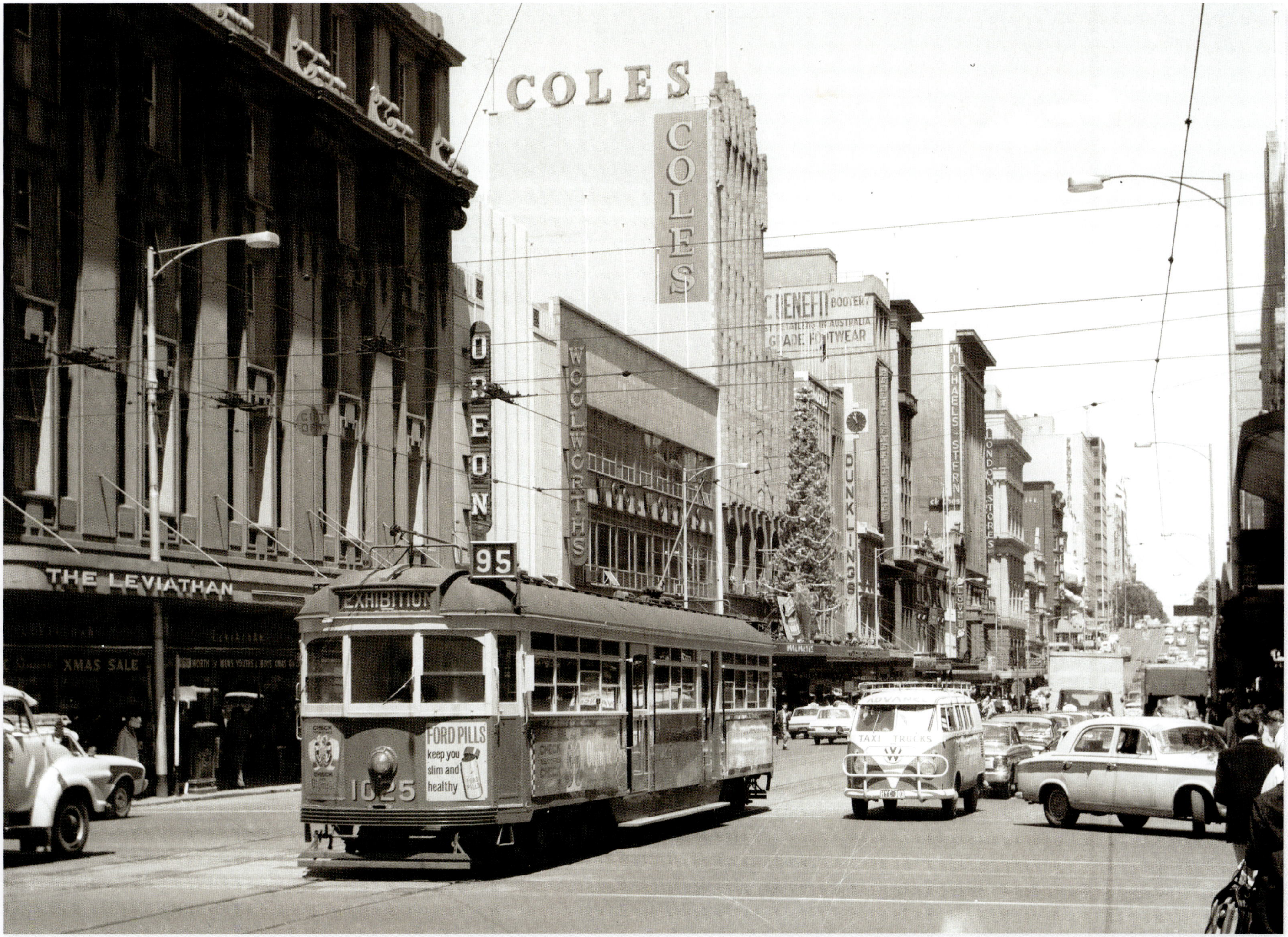

BOURKE STREET

1966

PHOTOGRAPHER: A.E. SMITH

Christmas time on Bourke Street.

This scene features a W-class tram travelling east along Bourke Street with views in the background of the facades of the Leviathan building, the Odeon Theatre, and the Woolworths and Coles stores.

Note the Volkswagen taxi van — very 1960s! And the advertisement on the tram: 'Ford Pills — Keep You Slim and Healthy.' These were a popular laxative marketed as a dieting solution in the 1960s and 1970s.

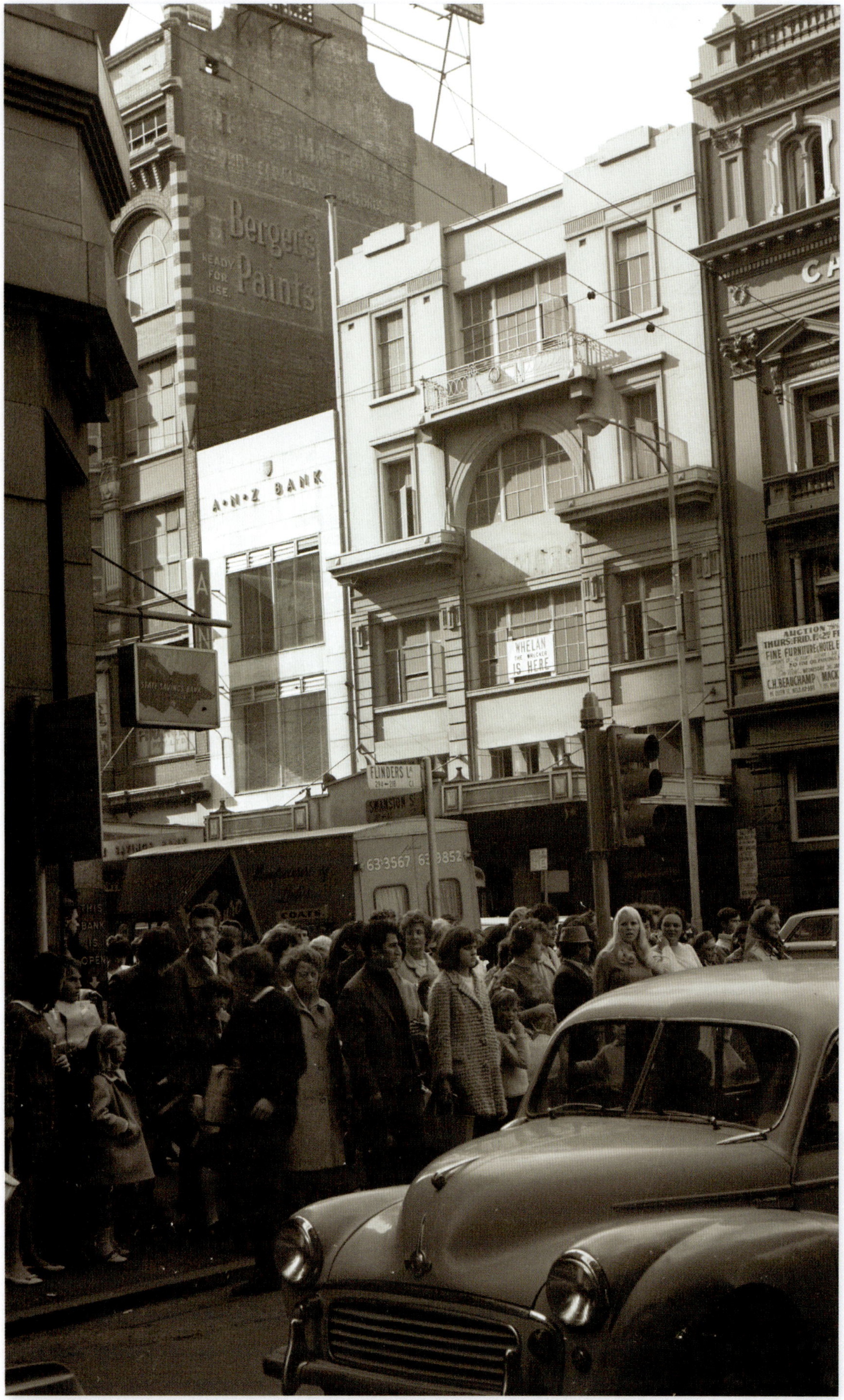

FLINDERS LANE & SWANSTON STREET

c. 1966

PHOTOGRAPHER: K.J. HALLA

Pedestrians wait to cross Flinders Lane. The Cathedral Hotel, which can be seen on the right, was demolished within a few months of this photo being taken. The buildings to the left were also demolished to make way for the new City Square.

If you look closely, there is a sign on the building that reads 'Whelan the Wrecker is here'. Whelan the Wrecker was a demolition company based in Brunswick. During the 1950s and 1960s, the company became synonymous with the demolition of many grand Victorian-era buildings.

Some of the historically significant buildings demolished by Whelan include the Flinders Street Fish Market, Cole's Book Arcade, and the Royal Insurance Building.

Side note: parts of the Royal Insurance Building were saved and used to build the Montsalvat artists' colony in Eltham. If you visit Montsalvat, you'll recognise it instantly.

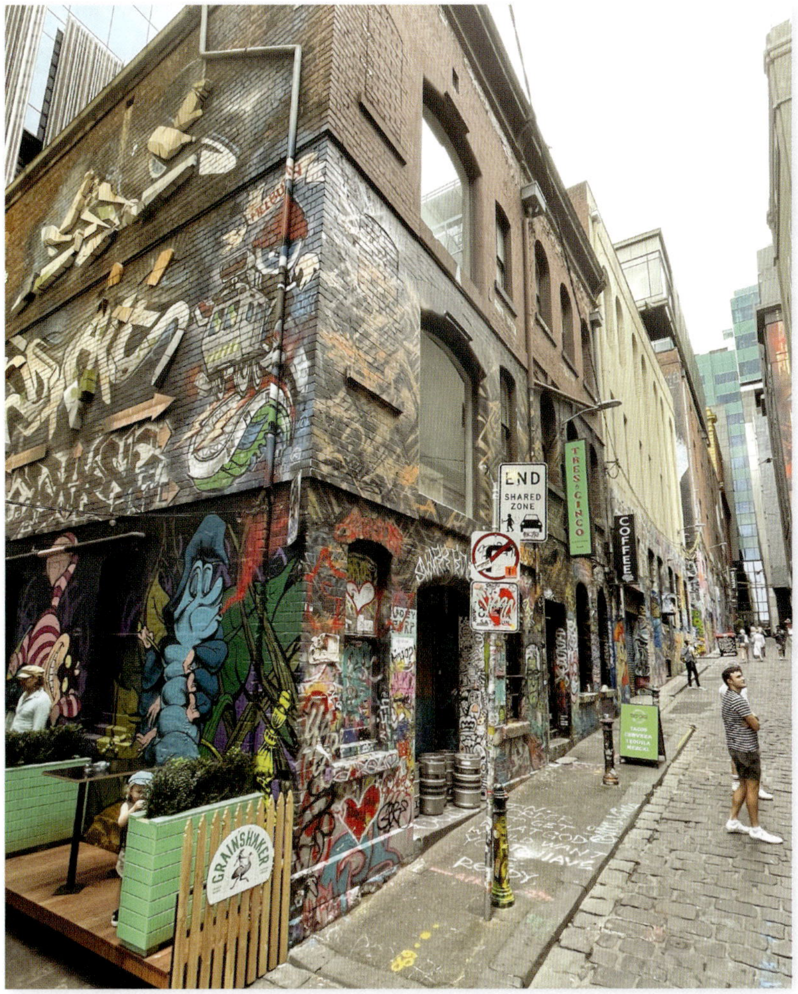

HOSIER LANE

c. 1972

PHOTOGRAPHER: K.J. HALLA (RIGHT IMAGE);
CHRIS MACHERAS (TOP IMAGE)

THEN AND NOW: The blue cobblestone laneway is renowned for its ever-changing murals and artworks, from political pieces to pop-culture references and more.

In 1920, Hosier Lane was located in the clothing-manufacturing district, and included businesses as diverse as an organ manufacturer, a warehouse for a men's clothing company, and a costume manufacturer.

The laneway opened as a street-art gallery in 1998.

In recent times it has been subject to criticism, with some graffiti being regarded more as vandalism than as art.

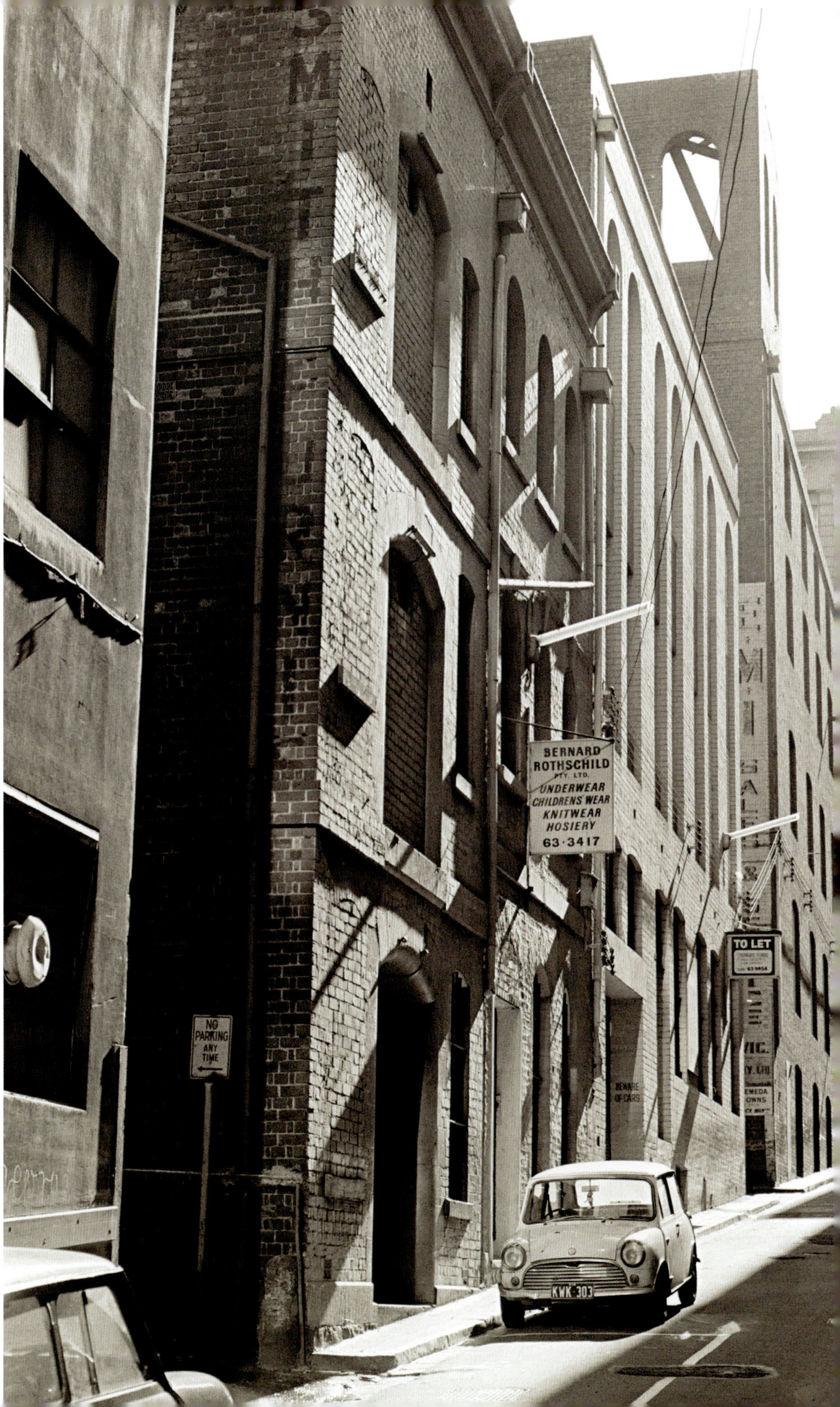

VIEW FROM SHRINE OF REMEMBRANCE

c.1973

PHOTOGRAPHERS: JOHN T. COLLINS (LEFT IMAGE); ALLAN WILKINSON, @A.J.WILKO (RIGHT IMAGE)

THEN AND NOW: A view of the city from the Shrine of Remembrance. The growth of the skyline is fascinating, and so is the extent to which the trees have grown — especially the baby ones on the right.

What a difference between the two images! The tallest building in Melbourne in 1973 was 140 William Street (formerly BHP House), standing at a height of 152 metres. Today, Melbourne's tallest building is Australia 108, at Southbank, which reaches 316.7 metres.

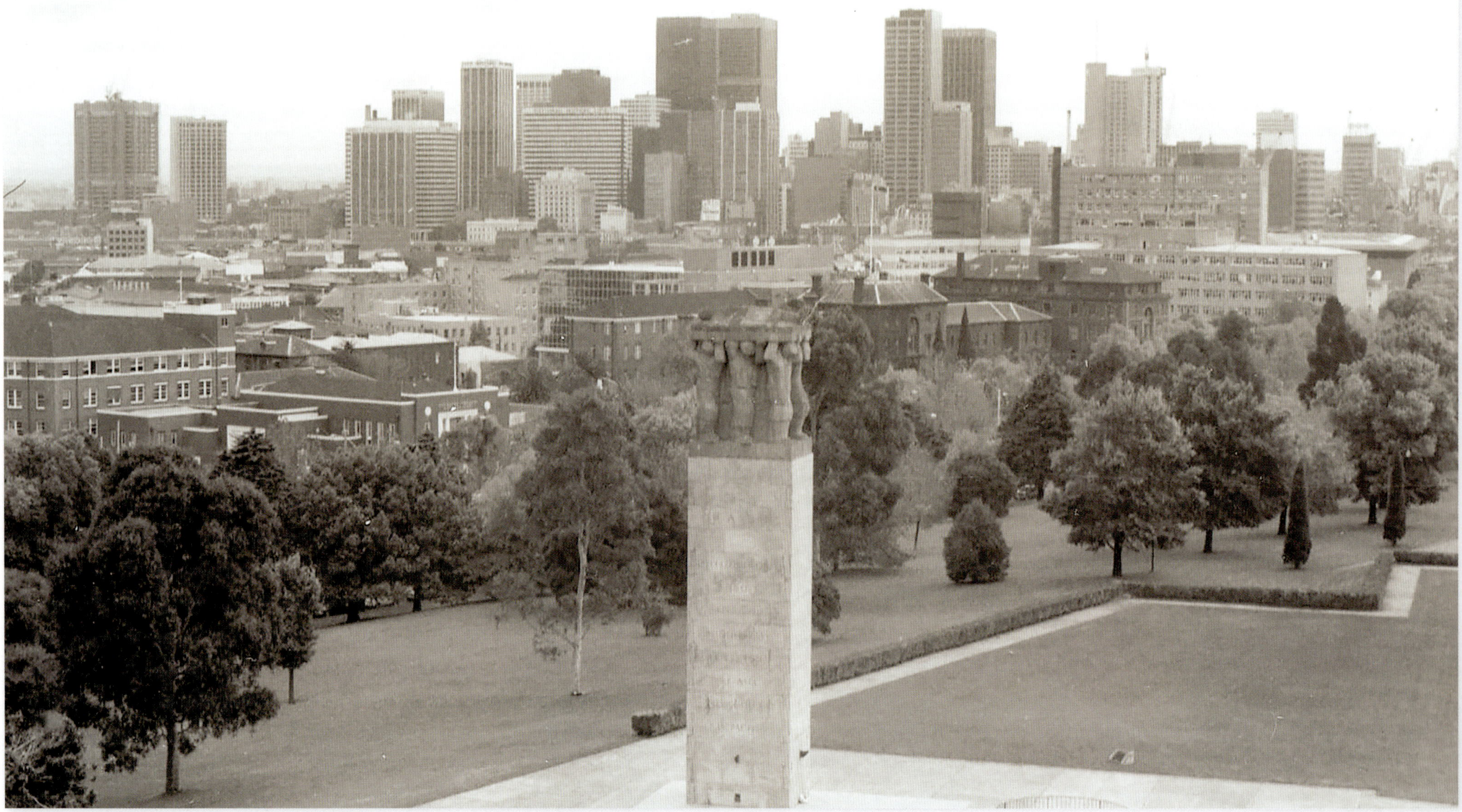

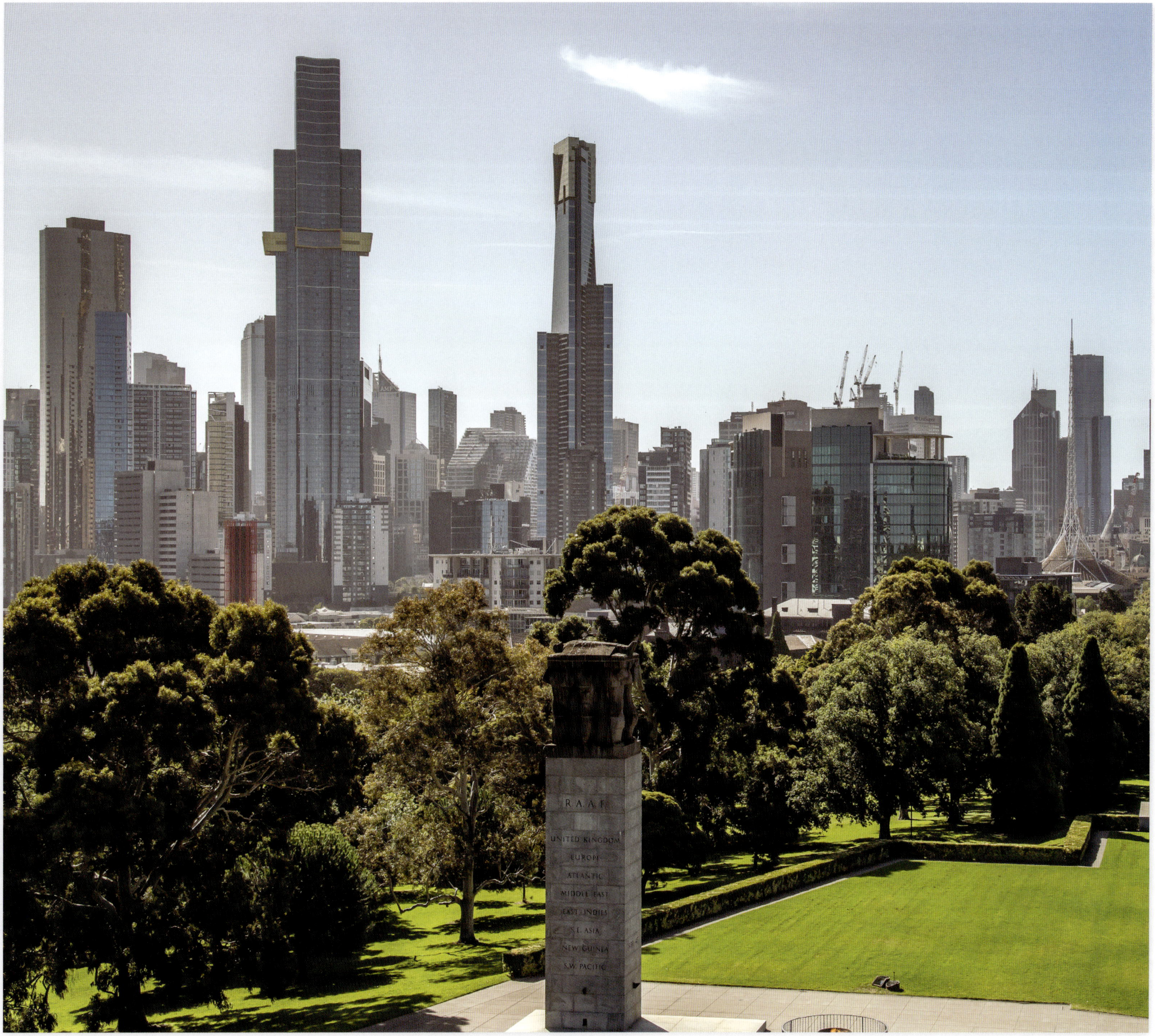
R.A.A.F.
UNITED KINGDOM
EUROPE
ATLANTIC
MIDDLE EAST
EAST INDIES
S.E. ASIA
NEW GUINEA
S.W. PACIFIC

WESTGATE BRIDGE

1978

PHOTOGRAPHER: PHILLIP ROGERS

Many Melburnians today travel across the Westgate Bridge on their daily commute.

On 15 October 1970, only two years after construction began, a 112-metre long, 2,000-tonne section of the bridge collapsed into the muddy terrain fifty meters below. The collapse also caused a gas explosion that was heard up to twenty kilometres away. Thirty-five construction workers were killed and eighteen injured, in what remains Australia's most tragic industrial accident.

Construction resumed two years later and was completed in 1978, when this image was captured.

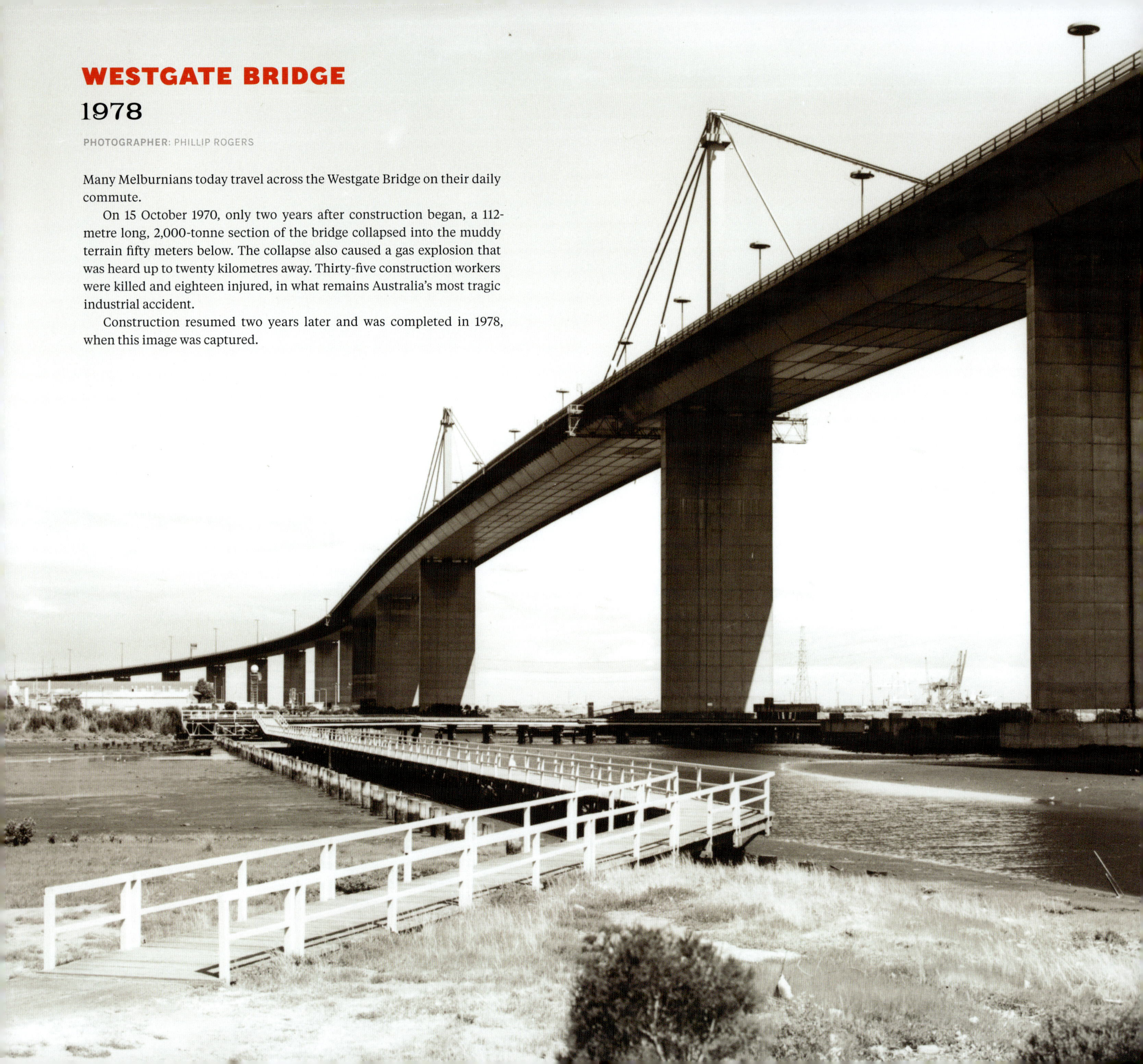

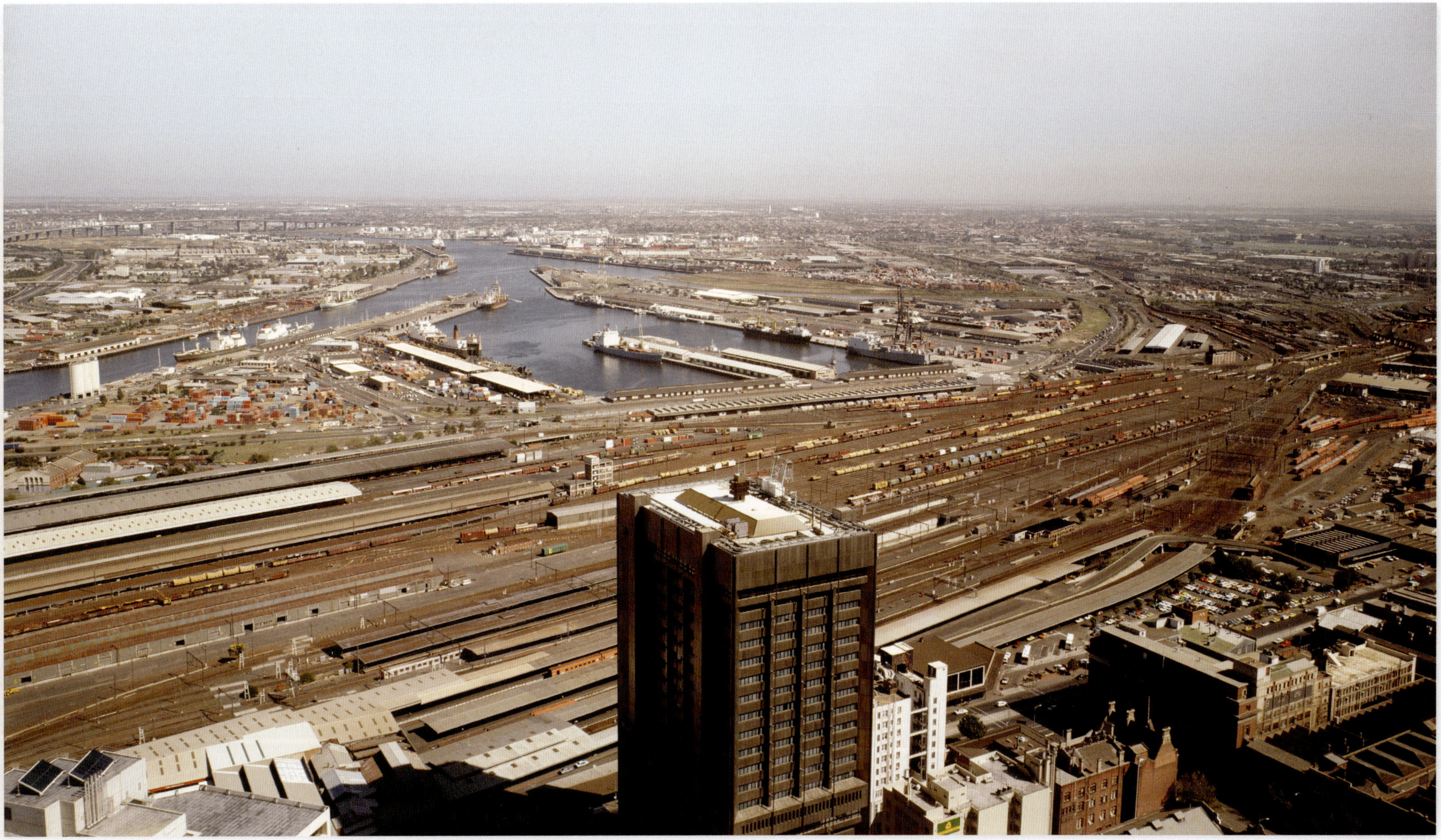

DOCKLANDS

c. 1983

PHOTOGRAPHER: LAURIE THOMAS

What a view across the Spencer Street marshalling yards, towards the Yarra and the west, taken from the Rialto Tower. The area pictured here has been significantly developed since.

Victoria Dock opened in 1892; by 1908, it was handling around 90 per cent of Victoria's imports.

Before that, the area was swamp land, filled with crabs, fish, and leafy vegetation. Behind the swamps, other native Australian animals such as kangaroos ran free. The traditional custodians of the land, the Wurundjeri people, considered it to be sacred, a giver of life and nourishment.

YARRA RIVER & SOUTH MELBOURNE

c.1983

PHOTOGRAPHER: LAURIE THOMAS

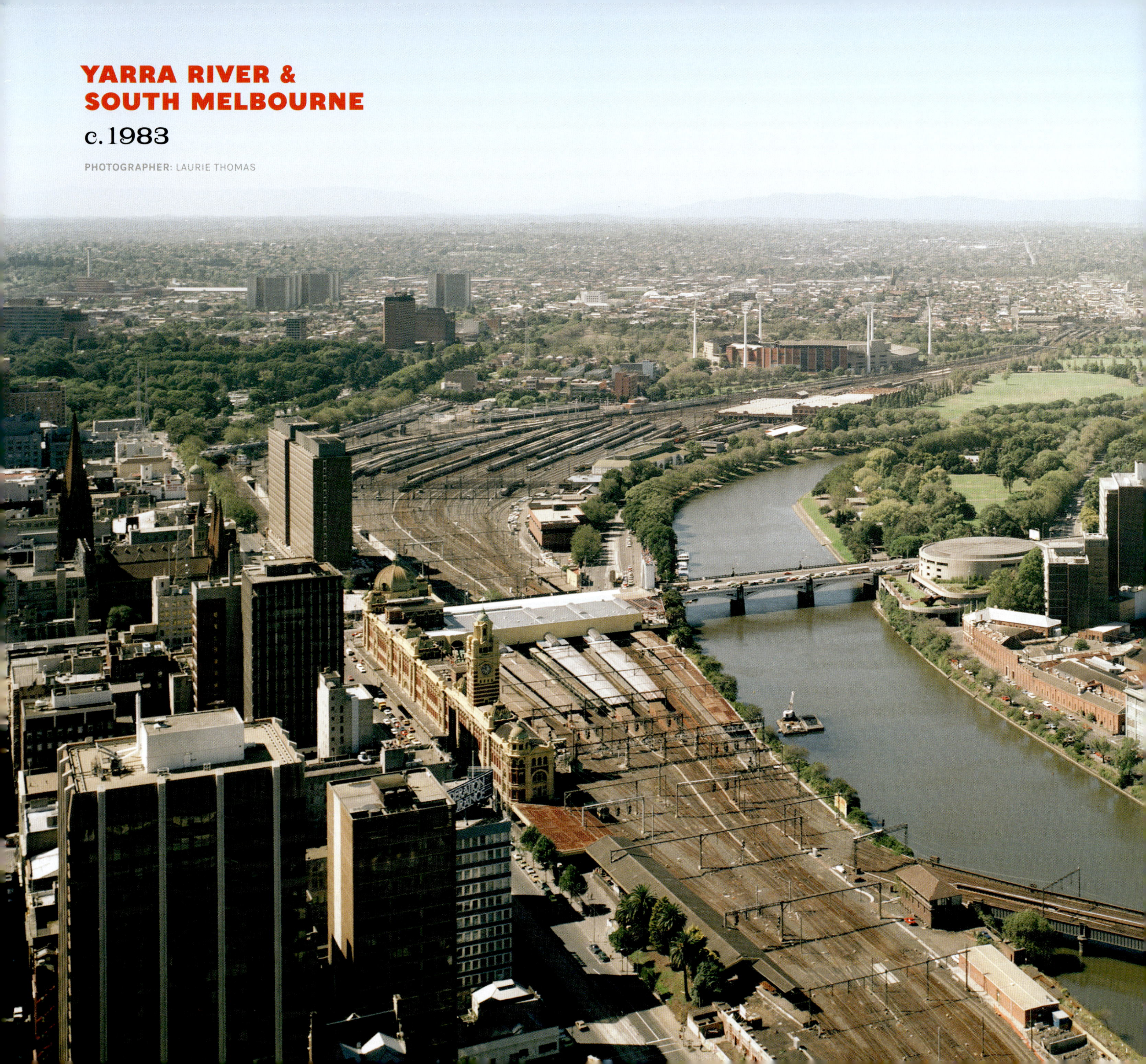

Here is a mesmerising aerial view from the early 1980s, looking south-east over Melbourne.

As you may notice, the area we know today as Southbank looks almost entirely industrial, with factories, warehouses, manufacturers, and a large parking lot. It was first rezoned as an area for redevelopment in 1984.

The residential population of the area has increased almost four-fold in the past twenty years.

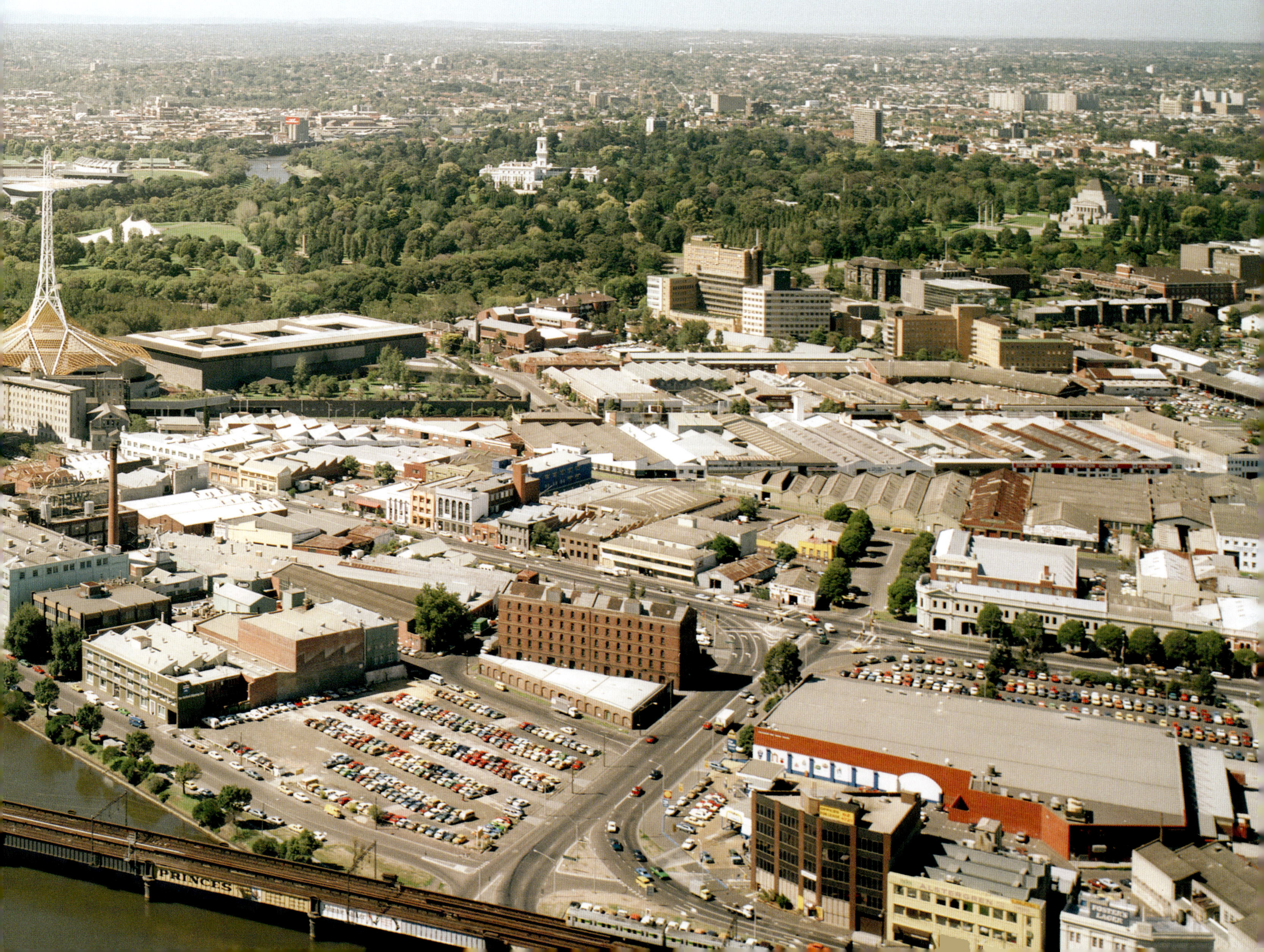

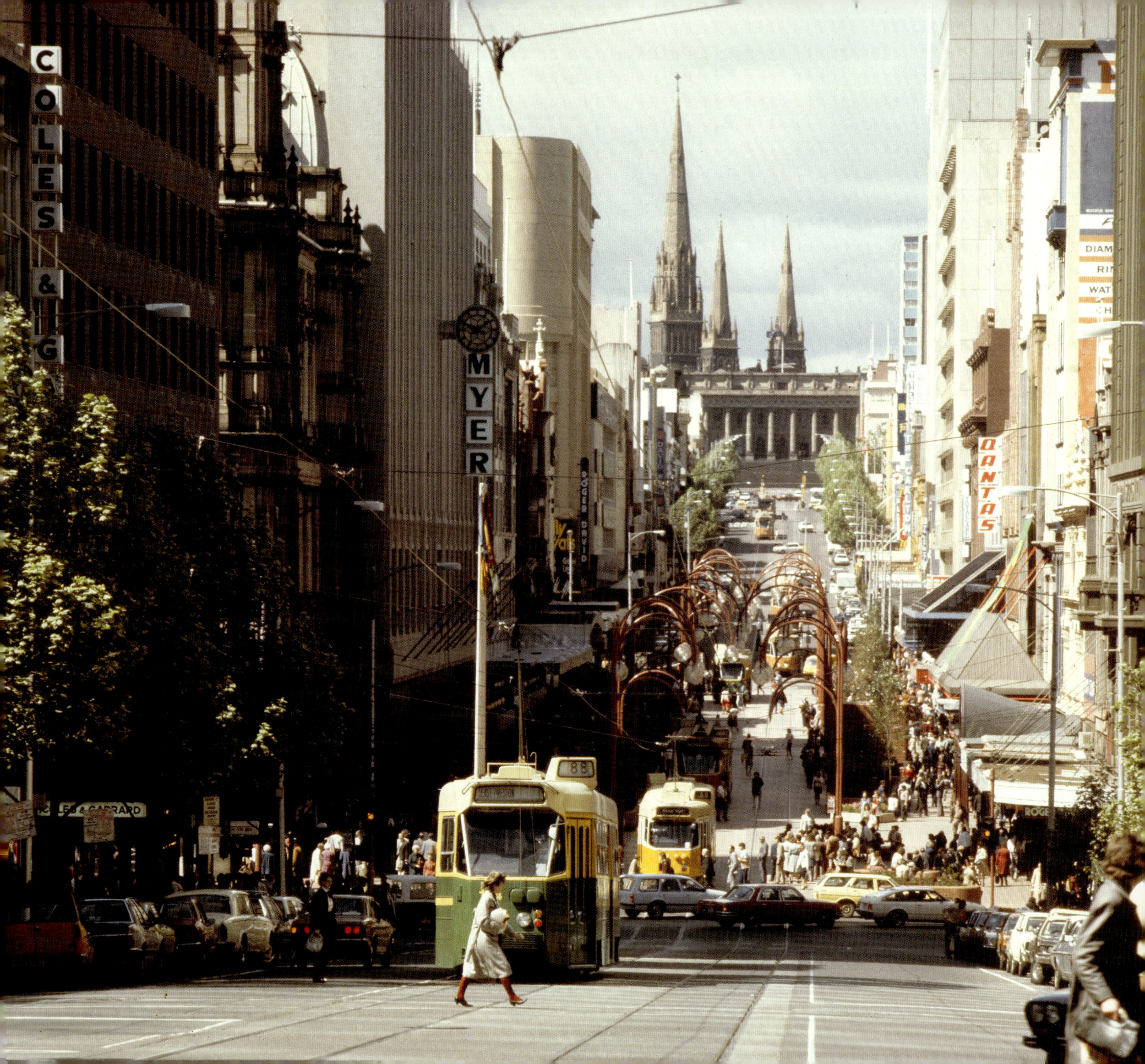
COLES & G
MYER
QANTAS
88

BOURKE STREET MALL

c. 1983

PHOTOGRAPHER: LAURIE THOMAS

I love this elevated view along Bourke Street, showing Parliament House and the spires of St Patrick's Cathedral in the distance.

Bourke Street Mall was officially opened as a pedestrian mall that year. The opening ceremony was officiated by Prince Charles and Diana, Princess of Wales.

There were several significant events in the same year. On 8 February, Melbourne and much of Victoria experienced a phenomenal dust storm, followed just over a week later by the devastating Ash Wednesday bushfires. Later that year, in a 4:3 split decision, the High Court handed down its landmark judgment in the Tasmanian Dam case, allowing the federal government to prevent the building of the Franklin Dam in Tasmania.

GAS & FUEL BUILDINGS

c. 1996

PHOTOGRAPHER: IAN HARRISON HILL

Here is a view of Flinders Street looking east, with St Paul's Cathedral to the left and the MCG in the distance on the right.

The focus of the image, however, is the Princes Gate Towers, otherwise known as the Gas and Fuel Towers. Note the large billboard advertising the 1996 Moomba Festival.

When unveiled in 1966, the towers received a somewhat mixed public reaction. Many Victorians considered them to be rather ugly; some critics deemed them modernist masterpieces.

Demolition plans were announced in 1996 to make way for the development of Federation Square.

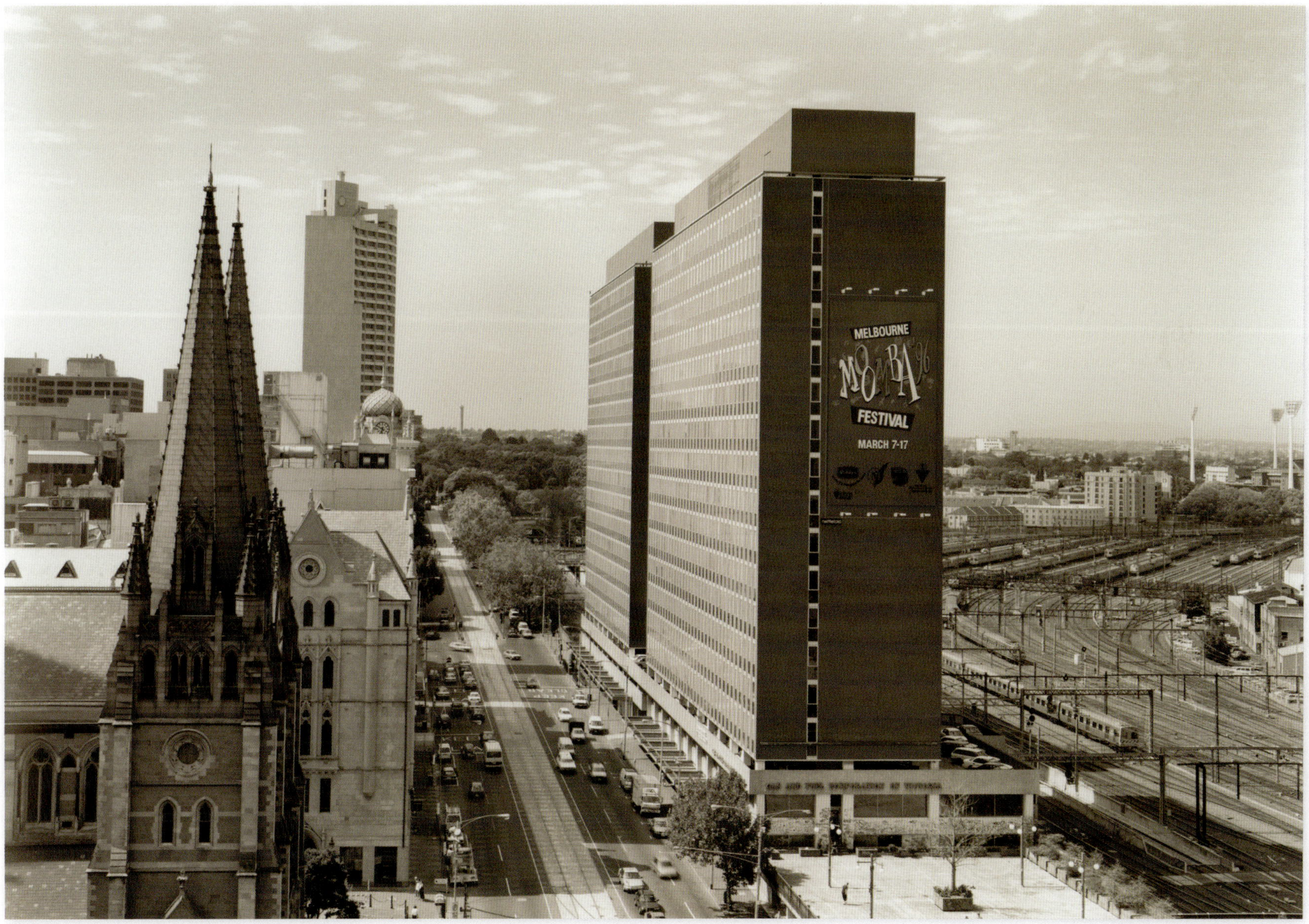

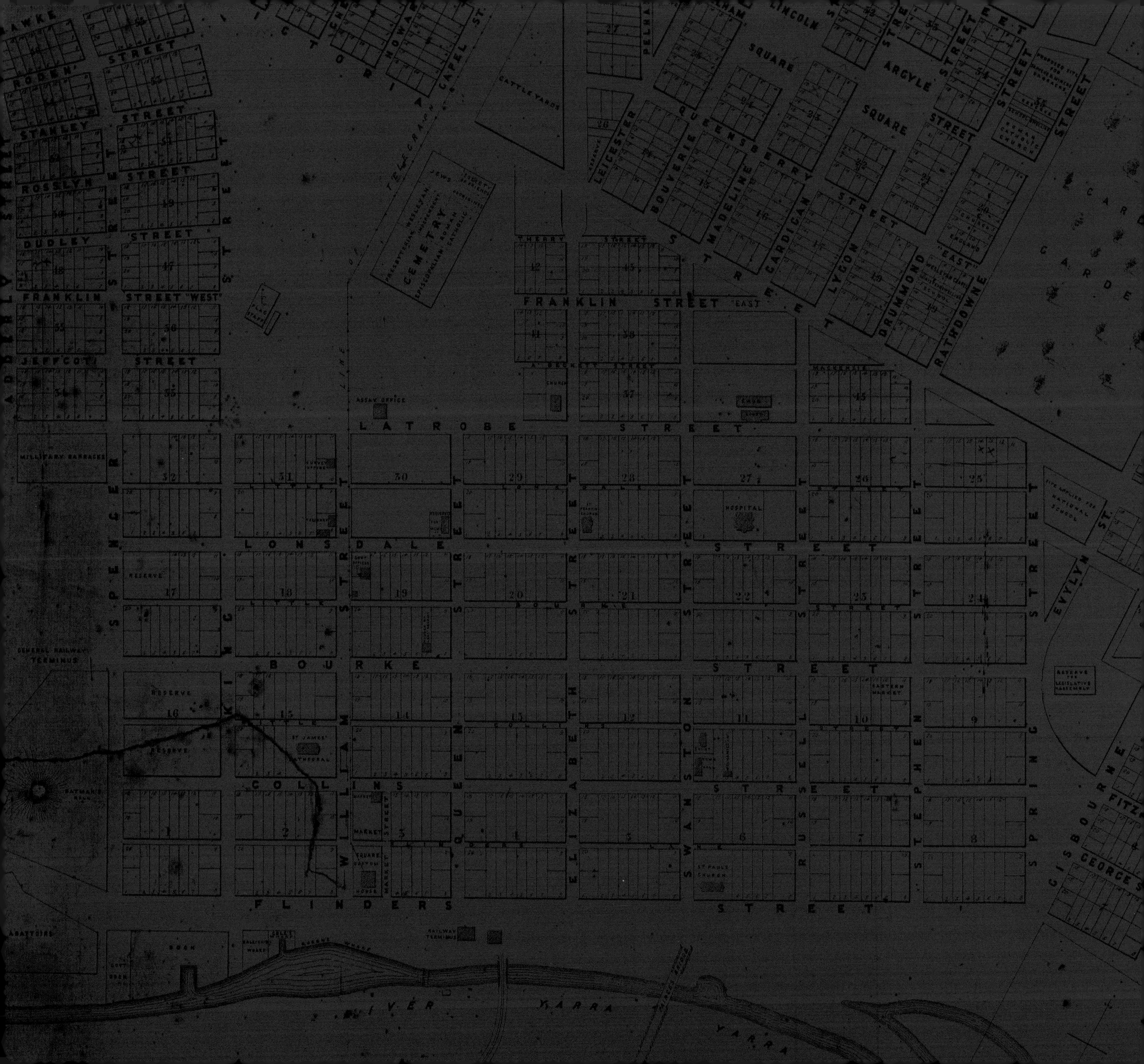

LATROBE STREET
LONSDALE STREET
BOURKE STREET
COLLINS STREET
FLINDERS STREET
SPENCER STREET
KING STREET
WILLIAM STREET
QUEEN STREET
ELIZABETH STREET
SWANSTON STREET
RUSSELL STREET
STEPHEN STREET
SPRING STREET
FRANKLIN STREET "WEST"
FRANKLIN STREET EAST
JEFFCOTT STREET
DUDLEY STREET
ROSSLYN STREET
STANLEY STREET
RODEN STREET
THERRY STREET
A'BECKETT STREET
MILITARY BARRACKS
GENERAL RAILWAY TERMINUS
RESERVE
HOSPITAL
ST JAMES' CATHEDRAL
ST PAULS CHURCH
EASTERN MARKET
ASSAY OFFICE
CEMETERY
CATTLE YARDS
CAPEL ST
QUEENSBERRY STREET
LEICESTER
BOUVERIE
MADELINE
CARDIGAN
LYGON
DRUMMOND
RATHDOWNE
ARGYLE SQUARE
LINCOLN SQUARE
PELHAM
EVYLYN ST.
GISBOURNE
GEORGE S
FITZ
RESERVE FOR LEGISLATIVE ASSEMBLY
SITE APPLIED FOR NATIONAL SCHOOL
MARKET STREET
ABATTOIRS
RAILWAY TERMINUS
RIVER YARRA
YARRA

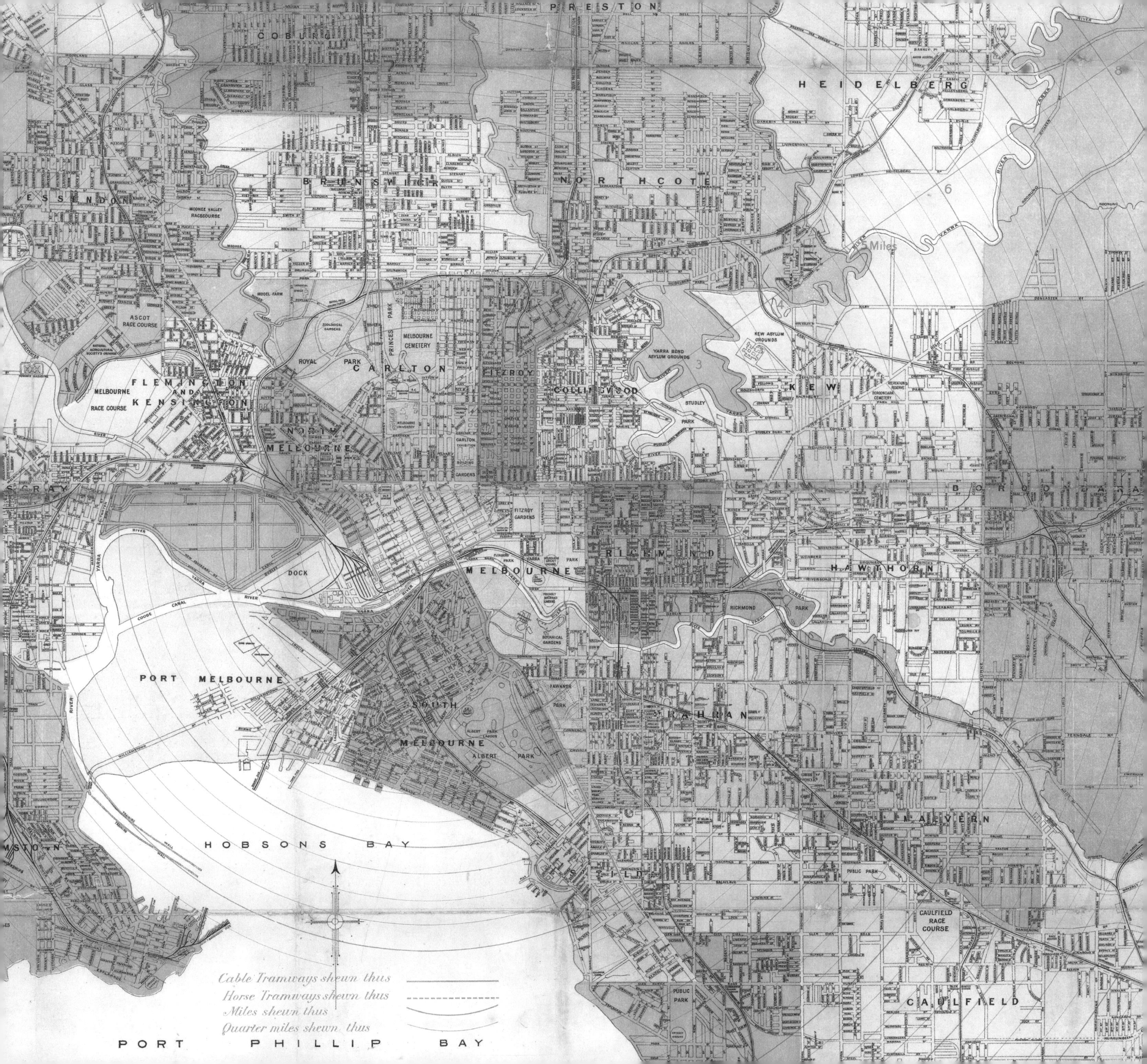
PRESTON
COBURG
HEIDELBERG
BRUNSWICK
NORTHCOTE
ESSENDON
MOONEE VALLEY RACECOURSE
ASCOT RACE COURSE
ZOOLOGICAL GARDENS
PRINCES PARK
MELBOURNE CEMETERY
ROYAL PARK
CARLTON
FITZROY
COLLINGWOOD
YARRA BEND ASYLUM GROUNDS
KEW ASYLUM GROUNDS
KEW
STUDLEY PARK
FLEMINGTON AND KENSINGTON
MELBOURNE RACE COURSE
NORTH MELBOURNE
BOROONDARA
FITZROY GARDENS
RICHMOND
MELBOURNE
DOCK
HAWTHORN
COODE CANAL
YARRA RIVER
RICHMOND PARK
BOTANICAL GARDENS
PORT MELBOURNE
SOUTH MELBOURNE
ALBERT PARK
FAWKNER PARK
PRAHRAN
MALVERN
HOBSONS BAY
ST KILDA
PUBLIC PARK
CAULFIELD RACE COURSE
CAULFIELD
5 Miles
Cable Tramways shewn thus
Horse Tramways shewn thus
Miles shewn thus
Quarter miles shewn thus
PORT PHILLIP BAY

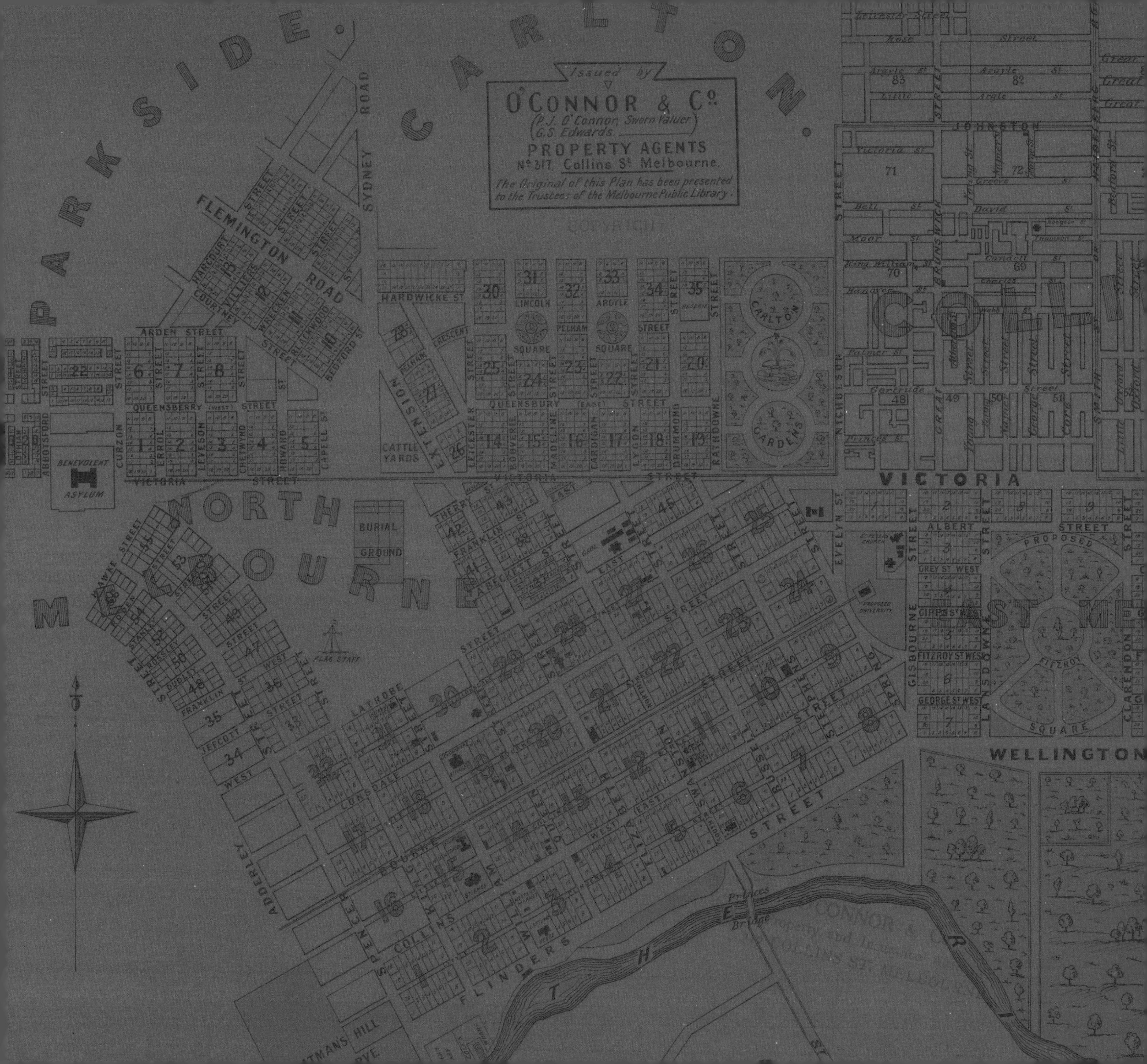

Issued by
O'CONNOR & Co.
(P. J. O'Connor, Sworn Valuer
G. S. Edwards.)
PROPERTY AGENTS
No. 317, Collins St. Melbourne.
The Original of this Plan has been presented to the Trustees of the Melbourne Public Library.
PARKSIDE.
CARLTON.
NORTH MELBOURNE
EAST MELBOURNE
FLEMINGTON ROAD
SYDNEY ROAD
ARDEN STREET
QUEENSBERRY (WEST) STREET
QUEENSBURY (EAST) STREET
VICTORIA STREET
HARDWICKE ST
LINCOLN SQUARE
ARGYLE SQUARE
PELHAM
CARLTON GARDENS
BENEVOLENT ASYLUM
CATTLE YARDS
EXTENSION
BURIAL GROUND
FLAG STAFF
PROPOSED UNIVERSITY
PROPOSED FITZROY SQUARE
ALBERT STREET
GREY ST WEST
GIPPS ST WEST
FITZROY ST WEST
GEORGE ST WEST
GISBOURNE STREET
LANSDOWNE STREET
CLARENDON
WELLINGTON
NICHOLSON STREET
EVELYN ST
BRUNSWICK STREET
SMITH STREET
CURZON STREET
ERROL STREET
LEVESON STREET
CHETWYND
HOWARD ST
CAPELL ST
ABBOTSFORD
LEICESTER STREET
BOUVERIE STREET
MADELINE STREET
CARDIGAN STREET
LYGON STREET
DRUMMOND STREET
RATHDOWNE STREET
LATROBE STREET
LONSDALE STREET
BOURKE STREET
COLLINS STREET
FLINDERS STREET
SPENCER STREET
KING STREET
WILLIAM STREET
QUEEN STREET
ELIZABETH STREET
SWANSTON STREET
RUSSELL STREET
STEPHEN STREET
SPRING STREET
ADDERLEY STREET
FRANKLIN ST
A'BECKETT ST
JEFFCOTT STREET
DUDLEY
ROSSLYN
HAWKE STREET
BATMANS HILL
Princes Bridge
THE RIVER